THE VOYAGE OF THOMAS BEST

TO THE EAST INDIES

1612-1614

THE VOYAGE OF
THOMAS BEST

TO THE EAST INDIES
1612-1614

EDITED BY

WILLIAM FOSTER

GYAN

Published by

GYAN

Gyan Publishing House
5, Ansari Road
Daryaganj, New Delhi-110002
Phone: 011-47034999, 9811692060
E-mail: books@gyanbooks.com

Distribution Network
gyanbooks.com
India, USA, Canada, UK, Australia, France

ISBN : 978-81-212-4201-1 (PB)
First Published, London, 1934

2nd Impression 2020

Printed at: Gyan Press, Delhi.

The Voyage of
Thomas Best to the East Indies
1612-1614

Edited by: William Foster

THE VOYAGE OF THOMAS BEST TO THE EAST INDIES 1612–14

Edited by

SIR WILLIAM FOSTER, C.I.E.

> Nay, looking into other old log-books, I discern, in the Far East too, a notable germination...England herself has a traffic there, a continually increasing traffic...At Surat and elsewhere, certain poor English Factories are rising—in spite of 'the Portugals of Goa'...Shah Abbas, Jehangire, Great Mogul, and fabulous-real Potentates of the uttermost parts of the Earth are dimly disclosed to us; Night's ancient curtain being now drawn aside.
>
> CARLYLE, *Hist. Sketches*, p. 90

LONDON

PRINTED FOR THE HAKLUYT SOCIETY

1934

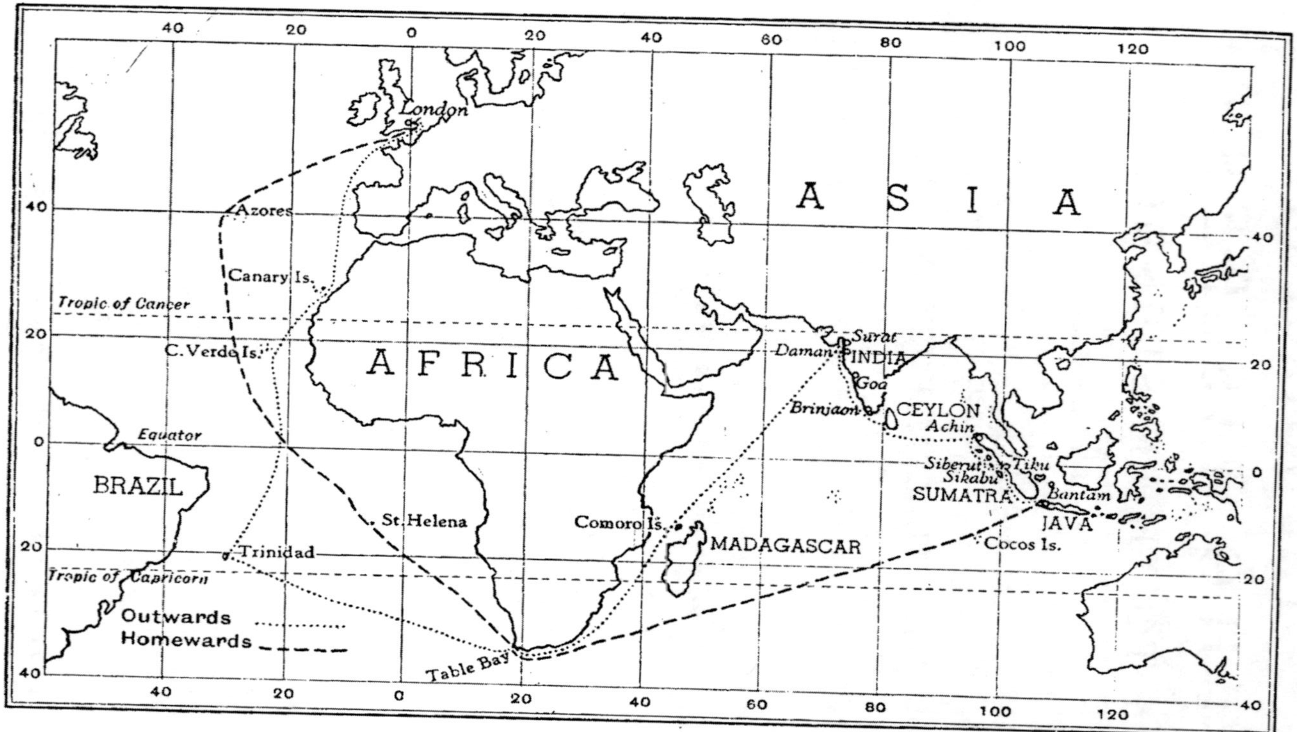

THE VOYAGE OF CAPTAIN BEST

CONTENTS

MAPS

INTRODUCTION

AT a general meeting of the East India Company held after Captain Best's return, the Governor (Sir Thomas Smythe) summed up the achievements of the voyage by saying that Best had 'performed worthie service, both for the honour of this kingdome and English nation and for the setling of a beneficiall trade in Cambaia, for the good of this Company: a service of very greate moment and consequence, in the prosecutinge whereof he had many oppositions, assaults, and sundrie attempts made by the Portugalls, divers fights and encounters; in all which yt pleased God soe to blesse his endevours as that he repeld them, setled a factory on shore, upon good capitulations with the cheefe governours of those parts, authorized from the Emperour, and those articles afterwards confirmd under the seale of the lannd from the Grand Magore himselfe' (*infra*, p. 267). Although this statement deals only with the results obtained in India, it gives a fair account of the outstanding features of the venture, and it explains why the Tenth Voyage has always been considered to have been of special importance in the early history of the East India Company.

To understand the aims of its promoters it is necessary to look back to the commencement of the Company's endeavours to get into touch with the markets of the Indian peninsula. The first two of its ventures (1601–3 and 1604–6) had been directed to the countries of the Malay Archipelago, and had clearly shown that on the one hand there was small outlet for English goods in those parts and that on the other hand Indian calicoes were much in demand, and would be of great service in securing the pepper and spices which formed the chief items of the return cargoes of all vessels employed in the trade. It was obviously advisable, therefore, to open up relations with Indian merchants, either on the Gujarāt coast or (since that was understood to be dominated by the Portuguese) at Aden or the Red Sea ports, to which Indian trading ships freely resorted. Hopes were entertained that these merchants would be eager purchasers of English broadcloth and other manufactured goods; while the acquisition of calicoes for sale or barter farther eastwards would not only yield a double profit but would also obviate the necessity of exporting large quantities of money. When, therefore, the ships of the Third Voyage started, in the spring of 1607, its commander, William Keeling, was instructed to call at Aden and, if possible, at Surat, for the purpose indicated. Contrary winds foiled all attempts to reach Aden; but in August 1608 one of the vessels, the *Hector*, reached Surat and remained there for six weeks before proceeding to Bantam (in Java). Moreover, her captain, William Hawkins, finding that the sanction of the Mughal Emperor was necessary before any permanent trade could be settled, remained behind when his vessel departed, and proceeded to Agra to negotiate an agreement. He was cordially received by the Emperor Jahāngīr, who at first promised readily to grant his requests. But the Portuguese, alarmed at the prospect of English rivalry in a market they had hitherto had to themselves, intrigued ceaselessly against him, and further induced the Gujarāti officials to intervene in their favour. At court the matter—like every question of trade—was looked upon as one of small importance; and all the efforts of Hawkins to obtain a decision were met with evasions and delays.

Meanwhile the East India Company had determined to follow up the enterprise; and as a result the *Ascension*—one of the vessels of the Fourth Voyage (1608)—visited both Aden and Mokha, but only to find that the former was merely a fortress and that at the latter no factory could be established without express authorization from Constantinople. She then made for Surat, but came to grief upon a sandbank in the Gulf of Cambay when nearing her destination (September 1609). This unfortunate occurrence greatly weakened the position of Hawkins; and after further fruitless attempts to obtain from the Emperor a grant of freedom to trade, the Englishman, in November 1611, abandoned the struggle and left Agra. On reaching Cambay, he learnt that four English ships, under Sir Henry Middleton, had arrived at Surat in the preceding September; and with some difficulty he managed to get aboard that fleet in January 1612.

Middleton (Sixth Voyage) had left England in April 1610. In the absence of information as to the success or failure of the ships of the Fourth Voyage, he had been directed to go first to Aden and the Red Sea, and then to call at Surat on his way to Bantam. Carrying out this programme, after a futile visit to Aden he reached Mokha in November, and was encouraged to believe that trade would be permitted; but after a short interval he and all his companions on land were treacherously seized by the governor, and were held in captivity for nearly six months. Then they succeeded in escaping to their ships (May 1611), and Middleton took his revenge by blockading the port until some compensation was made. Resuming his voyage, he anchored off the bar of Surat (at the mouth of the Tāpti) on 26 September 1611. For a time the Portuguese 'frigates' (armed coasting vessels) prevented communication with the shore; but the discovery of a spot a little to the northwards, possessing a pool of deep water ('Swally Hole'), enabled the English vessels to anchor close to the shore and thus to command the landing-place with their guns. Mukarrab Khān, the official in charge of the Gujarāt ports, was not sorry to see the fleet arrive, for he knew that the Emperor was still hankering for the European curiosities promised by Hawkins; but this unscrupulous official was in fact entirely on the side of the Portuguese and, when he had acquired as much of the English merchandise as he thought worth while, he abruptly ordered the factors to depart, refusing absolutely to entertain any idea of future trade. Middleton, full of resentment, set sail in February 1612, leaving behind him letters to be delivered to any fresh comers, narrating his experiences and warning them that the people were treacherous and that no commerce was to be expected. He then proceeded to the Red Sea, where he took his revenge by forcing the Indian vessels he found there to exchange goods with him at his own rates, and further—in the case of Gujarātis—to pay a heavy ransom as the price of release. This done, he departed in August for Sumatra and Java, reaching Bantam in December 1612.

In April 1611 the Company had despatched yet another fleet, under John Saris (Eighth Voyage) with orders to call at Aden,

Mokha, and Surat. It was hoped that Middleton had already settled a trade at the last-named port, and that two at least of the ships would there obtain ladings for England. Failing this, Saris was to go on to Bantam, and from thence attempt to open up trade with Japan. The Red Sea was reached in March 1612; and Saris, who was provided with a passport obtained from Constantinople, found a favourable reception at the hands of a new governor. He conceived great hopes of establishing a permanent trade, but this dream was shattered by the reappearance of Middleton on his mission of vengeance. Much against his will, Saris was forced to take part in the subsequent reprisals on the Indian shipping (receiving a share of the proceeds for his own Voyage) and to join in the blockade of Mokha. Then he sailed for Bantam, having given up all expectations of finding a market at Surat, in view of Middleton's experiences there and of the revenge taken by that commander.

We come now to the voyage which forms the subject of the present volume. And here we are much hampered by the fact that the relevant volume of the Court Minutes—running from January 1610 to December 1613—has long been missing, thus depriving us of our fullest and most authoritative source of information. We know, however, that, following the usual practice, a subscription list was opened for this Tenth Voyage, and that, as a result, the sum of 46,092*l.* was obtained and expended (*Court Minutes*, 1650–54, p. 360)[1]. The two vessels employed were the *Dragon* and the *Hosiander*[2]. The former had been flagship in the first three voyages, but had not been used since her return in the autumn of 1609. In the interim she had been

[1] From the same source we obtain the information that the other two vessels of the fleet—the *James* of the Ninth Voyage and the *Solomon* of the Eleventh—had been fitted out upon capitals respectively of 19,614*l.* and an unnamed amount raised by a levy of 25 per cent. upon the adventurers in the Third Voyage. A return given in *Home Miscellaneous*, vol. XXXIX (I.O.) and printed on p. ix of the *List of Marine Records at the India Office*, gives the total of the subscriptions for the three Voyages at 76,375*l.*, of which 17,675*l.* was sent out in money and 10,000*l.* in goods, while 48,700*l.* was expended on shipping, victuals, etc.

[2] This unusual appellation (which often appears as *Osiander*) was a Graecized form (compounded of ὅσιος and ἀνήρ) of the name of Andreas Heiligmann or Hosemann, a German theologian (1498–1552) whose doctrines found wide acceptance in Protestant countries.

thoroughly repaired, and perhaps enlarged, for her tonnage, which at the time of her purchase was reckoned at 600 tons (*Dawn of British Trade*, p. 263), is given by Sir Dudley Digges in 1615 (*Defence of Trade*, p. 18) as 1060. I suspect, however, that the latter figure is an exaggerated estimate. The *Hosiander* was much smaller, being, according to Digges, of 213 tons. She had been specially built for this voyage (Court Minutes, 15 March 1614). The lading of the two ships consisted chiefly of broadcloth, ivory ('elephant's teeth'), quicksilver, lead, and iron; while a large stock of Spanish rials was provided for the purchase of return cargoes.

In the choice of a commander (or 'General,' as he was usually styled) a notable departure was made. Hitherto a merchant, with some knowledge of navigation, had been employed in that capacity[1]; but on this occasion (doubtless at the instigation of the Governor) preference was given to one who, though with considerable knowledge of merchandizing, was first and foremost a practical seaman. This may have been due to two considerations. In the first place, the loss of the *Ascension* had shown the need for expert navigation in approaching Surat. In the second, there was a great probability that fighting with the Portuguese would prove unavoidable; and this could best be carried through by a man of determination who possessed the entire confidence of the sailors under his command.

Such a one was found in Thomas Best, whose previous career we have now to consider. The notice of him in the *Dictionary of National Biography*, written about fifty years ago by the late Sir John Laughton, gives us small help in this respect; indeed, it tends to mislead us by suggesting that the subject of the notice was probably the son of Captain George Best, the companion of Frobisher in his Arctic voyages (1576–78) and author of an account of those expeditions given in Hakluyt's *Principall Navigations*. There is, however, no evidence (beyond the name) of any connection between the two captains; moreover, George Best is described by Hakluyt as a 'gentleman,' and he is believed

[1] At a Court meeting of 10 March 1614 the Governor, Sir Thomas Smythe, declared that the Company expected a General to be 'partlie a navigatour, partelie a merchannt (to have knowledge to lade a shipp), and partlie a man of fashion and good respect.'

to have been killed in a duel with Oliver St John (afterwards Viscount Grandison), who would not have met on equal terms anyone destitute of pretensions to rank; while all that we know of Thomas Best points to his having risen from a comparatively humble position. This hypothesis must therefore be rejected. It must be confessed, however, that, despite a careful search, we have nothing to put in its place, and Best's parentage remains a mystery. The same statement applies to the date and place of his birth. His residence in Stepney for the greater part of his life naturally suggests that he may have been born there; but this is rendered unlikely by the fact that neither his name, nor that of any member of his family, can be found in the parish registers before 1588, though these registers commence twenty years earlier. As to the date of his birth, Sir John Laughton concluded that it took place about the year 1570. In view of the fact that he was a married man by 1587, I should put it at two or three years earlier, say 1567. This would make his age at death about 72; and we may note that in 1626 he considered himself too old to go again to the East Indies (Court Minutes, 24 November).

Best first went to sea about 1583[1]; and apparently he gradually worked his way up to the position of master. He seems to have married early, for his eldest child was born in 1588. The surname of his first wife (Mary) has not been traced, nor the date and place of the marriage (which is not recorded in the Stepney registers). From at least 1588 to 1602 he was living in Limehouse, which was then part of Stepney; and William Adams, writing in 1611 from Japan (for which country he sailed in 1598), mentions him among the men to whom the writer was known in Limehouse and Ratcliffe (*Letters Received*, vol. I, p. 150).

The London Port Books at the Public Record Office show Best as master of the *Mermaid*, which returned in 1599 from a voyage to Barbary: as arriving from the Levant in the same vessel early in 1602[2]: as lading the *Pearl* for Russia in May 1606 and com-

[1] This appears from his allusion, in a letter of 13 July 1623, to his having then served at sea for forty years (*S.P. Dom.*, vol. CXLVIII, p. 93).

[2] She was at Constantinople in April 1601, when John Sanderson embarked in her for Sidon (Sanderson's *Travels*, pp. 90, 124, etc.). From the same work we learn that, while at the latter port, Best contemplated accompanying Sanderson to Jerusalem, but at the last moment decided not to leave his ship, fearing danger to her from bad weather.

manding her again in the spring of 1609, when she was about to start on a voyage to Tetuan, Algiers, and the Levant. Doubtless it was the reputation he had gained in these voyages, as a careful navigator and capable commander, that recommended him to the notice of Sir Thomas Smythe (who was prominent in the Levant Company) for employment by the East India Company.

For the post of master of the *Dragon* the Company's choice fell upon Edward Hunt; but just before the fleet started he was suddenly dismissed and replaced by Robert Bonner. That Bonner was already engaged in the voyage is suggested by the statement (p. 277) that his wages were thereupon 'mended.' He was a son of Abraham Bonner of Leigh, who had commanded one of the merchant vessels (the *Antelope*) contributed by London to the fleet raised to oppose the Spanish Armada, and whose name occurs frequently in the London Port Books as making voyages to Rochelle, Bordeaux, Hamburg, and the Baltic. He died in 1614[1], probably just after his son's return from the East Indies. Abraham's two sons, Robert and Thomas, had followed their father's profession. Thomas is mentioned in the London Port Books as commanding the *Matthew Bonaventure* in 1608 in a voyage to San Lucar in Spain; and seven years later he went out as a master's mate in Keeling's fleet to the East Indies, was promoted during the voyage to be master of the *Expedition*, and died at Tiku on 20 July 1616. His brother Robert, according to the Port Books, was master of the *Mayflower* in 1606–7 and in 1608 commanded the *Josan* in a voyage to Leghorn; while, as we have seen, he was appointed master of the *Dragon* early in 1612. His services in this capacity earned the warm commendation of Best, and the Company left it to the Governor to give him a suitable gratuity (p. 278). He was re-engaged as master of the *Dragon* in the fleet sent out under Keeling, and returned with him in May 1617. In the following autumn he was appointed to command, not only the *Dragon*, but also the other two ships which were to accompany her to the East. His squadron reached Surat in September 1618; and after detaching the *Lion* for a voyage to the Red Sea, Bonner, in February 1619, passed on to Achin with the *Dragon* and *Expedition*. Leaving

[1] Will in *P.C.C.* (*Lawe* 94). Dated 12 May and proved 2 August 1614.

that port early in July, he proceeded to Tiku, picking up on the way the *Rose*, a small vessel which had been despatched from Bantam to warn him that hostilities with the Dutch had broken out. At Tiku the three ships were joined by the *Bear* from England. Her commander, Thomas Barwick, confidently affirmed that the differences between the Dutch and English Companies had been settled; and, lulled into false security by these assertions, Bonner proceeded to fill the *Dragon* with pepper, to such an extent that she could use but few of her guns. On 1 October six ships appeared in the offing. They displayed no colours, and were taken to be Sir Thomas Dale's fleet from Bantam; and it was only when they opened fire that they were discovered to be Dutch. With such guns as could be cleared for action the *Dragon* put up a stout resistance; but the odds were so overwhelming that, after losing from twenty to thirty men, she was forced to haul down her flag. The other ships had done little, and at once surrendered. Bonner had been mortally wounded in the fight. He was carried on shore, where, after lingering a few days in agony, he expired on 9 October 1619. He was buried on a little island in the roadstead, 'so neere his brother Thomas as could be ghessed' (*Purchas His Pilgrimes*, vol. I, p. 662).

Robert Bonner, who was a bachelor in August 1614 (see p. 278), married prior to setting out on his last voyage. From his will (*P.C.C.* 105 *Soame*), dated 26 February 1618, it appears that his wife was Elizabeth, daughter of John Duling, of Rochester, gentleman. After Bonner's death she became the wife of Robert Salmon the younger (mentioned in a note on p. 263); and her claims on account of her late husband's estate caused the East India Company much annoyance, especially as it was felt that Bonner's imprudence had been largely responsible for the loss of their four ships.

The master of the *Hosiander* during the greater part of Best's voyage was Nathaniel Salmon. His parentage is noted on p. 263. In the London Port Books we find him going to the Elbe in 1605 as master of the *Trinity*, and later voyaging to Italy (1606–8) and to Rochelle (1609), in charge of the *Martha*. He was engaged by the East India Company for the present voyage as master of the *Solomon*; but at the Cape, on the way out, in consequence of dissensions on board the *Hosiander* between the master (Richard Petty) and the chief merchant (Paul Canning), Best decided to transfer Petty to the *Solomon* and to replace him by Salmon. When Best left the *Hosiander* at Bantam, Salmon was still her master; but early in 1615 he was transferred to the *Globe*, homeward bound, and in her he reached London towards the end of August of that year. His services had evidently given satisfaction, for in 1617 he was sent out again, this time in charge of a much larger vessel, the *New Year's Gift*, in the fleet commanded by Martin Pring. Swally was reached in September, and it was not until the following spring that the ships resumed their eastward voyage. The *New Year's Gift* had orders to call at Achin; while Pring himself intended to go straight to Bantam. Three days after the fleet had passed Cape Comorin, Salmon died (10 April 1618), and his body was committed to the deep. The extracts from his journal, published for the first time in the present volume, show him to have been a careful navigator; and the references made to him by other members of the expedition are on the whole favourable to his character.

Having dealt with the previous histories of the General and the two masters, we must now say something of the mercantile element in the fleet. The most prominent of the factors sent out was Thomas Aldworth, who was to assume charge of the factory at Surat. He took passage in the *Dragon*. Of his earlier career we know nothing more than that he was a native of Bristol and had been sheriff of that city (Court Minutes, 12 December 1617 and 20 February 1618). He had a wife and family; and seemingly he was in embarrassed circumstances, for after his death a claim was made against his estate for a debt alleged to have been owing to the king from the time of his shrievalty, and his widow was so poor that the East India Company made a yearly allowance for the education of his children. We conclude that he was a rather elderly merchant, who had failed in business but had sufficient reputation to secure (perhaps with the aid of influential friends) employment in a new field, where he might hope to retrieve his fortunes. It is a fair assumption that he was superior to Best in education and social standing; and this may have been the origin of the latter's antipathy to him, noticed later. That Aldworth was upright, zealous, and capable may be deduced from the little we know of him. For his proceedings after Best's fleet left Surat, the reader may be referred to *Letters Received* and *The Embassy of Sir Thomas Roe*. Here it will suffice to record that his career in India was cut short by death on 4 October 1615.

The merchant next in rank to Aldworth was Paul Canning, who took his passage in the *Hosiander*. From a work by George Pryce, entitled *Memorials of the Canynges Family* (Bristol, 1854), we learn that he was a direct descendant of Thomas Canynge, who was Lord Mayor of London in 1456 and belonged to the celebrated family of Bristol merchants of that name; and further (p. 146) that Paul was the seventh son of Richard Canning, of Foxcote, Warwickshire, and Elizabeth, daughter of Richard Petty, of Ilmington. Another pedigree, to be found at f. 81 of Brit. Mus. *Harleian MS.* 1167 (printed in 1877 by the Harleian Society under the title of *The Visitation of Warwickshire*, 1619), gives Richard Canning only four sons—William (a London merchant), Edward, George, and Richard—and makes Paul the son of George. But this is clearly wrong, for the Court Minutes of the East India Company record that on 21 April 1614 William Canning presented a letter of attorney from his *brother* Paul, and claimed 100*l.* as the first year's salary of the latter. This, by the way, was a good wage, and would only have been given to a merchant of considerable experience.

Canning appears to have been a man of hasty temper. His contentions with two successive masters of the *Hosiander* gave Best much trouble; while before leaving Surat he had a violent quarrel with Aldworth. Kerridge, who was a strong partisan of the latter, accuses Canning of conceit and jealousy, and alleges that he was given to drunkenness (*Letters Received*, vol. I, p. 257, vol II, p. 110). On the other hand, it is evident from Standish's narrative that Canning was generally popular; while his bravery is shown by the fact that, when fighting with the Portuguese was imminent, he insisted upon taking his chance with the sailors in the *Hosiander*, when most of the merchants remained in safety upon shore. His mission to the imperial court, to deliver a letter from King James and the presents provided by the Company, was arranged just before Best left India. Canning did not long survive his arrival in Agra, dying there on 12 May 1613. He was buried (as his cousin Lancelot had been) in the Jesuits' cemetery in that city, after some dispute with the Fathers, who were unwilling to allow that privilege to Protestants.

It is interesting to note that from Paul's brother George descended Viscount Stratford de Redcliffe, the well-known diplomatist, George Canning, the statesman, and Charles John, Earl Canning, Governor-General and Viceroy of India. The fact that an earlier member of the family had represented England at the court of Jahāngīr appears to have escaped the notice of the biographers of the last named.

Thomas Kerridge, who was closely associated with Aldworth in the management of affairs at Surat, was a native of Exeter, but particulars of his early life are wanting. More fortunate than his chief (to whom he was distantly related), he survived a considerable period of service in India, during which he was at the head of the Surat factory from 1615 to 1621, and President from 1625 to 1628. Sir Thomas Roe, who had many disputes with him, thought him impetuous and domineering, but admitted that 'his paynes is very great and his parts not ordinarie' (*Embassy*, p. 467); and it is generally conceded that Kerridge is one of the outstanding figures in the early history of the English connection with India. After his final return to England, he took an active part in the direction of the Company until his death in 1657.

The chaplain of the expedition, the Rev. Patrick Copland, is not conspicuous in the present volume, apart from his notes on the voyage (extracted from a longer account given by him to Purchas) which are here reprinted; but he is so interesting a figure that the reader will probably pardon a rather long account of his remarkable career. That he was diligent in the practice of his profession during the voyage is evident from the frequent mention in Standish's narrative of sermons preached by the reverend gentleman aboard the *Dragon*; and it may be added that throughout his life his piety and zeal made a deep impression on all who came into contact with him. He was born in 1572 at Aberdeen, the son of John Copland, merchant, of that town, and was educated at the local grammar school and Marischal College. After completing his college course, he migrated to England; but we know nothing of his further history until, at the age of forty, he was engaged by the East India Company as chaplain of Best's squadron. He seems to have profited considerably by the voyage, doubtless owing to private trade, for soon after his return he intimated his intention of presenting a sum of money to his old college. After some delay, due to some uncertainty as to the exact purpose to which the gift was to be devoted, in 1617 he made over 2000 Scottish merks (about 110*l.*) towards the maintenance of a professor of divinity. After his return from his second voyage to the East, he augmented his gift by another 2000 merks (July 1622); and later still (February 1628) presented a similar sum, making 6000 merks in all. This benefaction is still in operation at Aberdeen University, and in recognition of his bounty Copland's arms figure in the great window of Mitchell Hall, Marischal College.

An interesting incident recorded in the present volume (p. 156) is the gift to Best and Copland, by a Dutch skipper met off Ceylon, of two 'black boyes' found aboard an Indian vessel which the Dutchman had captured. What became of Copland's boy is not stated; but Best brought home the one given to him[1]. This lad the chaplain taught to read and write English; and the East India Company decided to spend twenty marks (13*l.* 6*s.* 8*d.*) yearly upon his schooling and instruction in religion, in the hope that 'hereafter, beeinge well grounded, hee might upon occasion bee sent into his countrye, where God may bee soe pleased to make him an instrument in convertinge some of his nation' (p. 279). In July 1615 Copland reported that the youth was ready for baptism, and the Company resolved to consult the Archbishop of Canterbury as to the performance of the ceremony. This took place at the church of St Dionis Backchurch, Fenchurch Street, on 22 December 1616, the convert receiving the name of Peter, to which King James is said to have added, with cryptic humour, the surname of Pope. He was the first

[1] Ralph Croft, in his will, left a ruff, some lace bands, and a piece of green taffeta, to 'Bengala'—presumably the Indian youth here mentioned.

of his nation to be admitted to the Church of England. When, in the spring of 1617, Copland embarked again for the East, as chaplain of the fleet commanded by Martin Pring, he took Pope with him and continued his instruction, with the result that the youth was able in 1620 to write letters in Latin to the East India Company and to Captain Pring, which were afterwards printed as an appendix to Copland's *Virginia's God be Thanked.* As nothing further is heard of Pope, it is presumed that he died before the conclusion of the voyage.

Between his two visits to the East Indies, Copland appears to have acted as 'minister of Godis word' at Norton, in Northamptonshire. His second expedition was a long one, for it was the autumn of 1621 before Pring's flagship returned to England. In the interim Copland had had some stirring experiences, including a visit to Japan and a pitched battle (Christmas 1618) between the English and Dutch fleets off Jakatra. In the disputes between the two nations he essayed in vain to play the part of peacemaker, gaining only the ill will of both sides. A sermon he had preached during the crisis was censured as likely to 'disanimate' the English mariners; but on his return he protested that he had been misrepresented, and this explanation seems to have been accepted by the Company. Early in the voyage he took a prominent part in collecting about 200*l.* towards the building of a chapel at Wapping (*English Factories*, 1618–21, p. 25); while on the way back he collected about 70*l.* for the erection of a school in Virginia. This brought him to the notice of the Virginia Company, who made him a grant of land in the colony and invited him to preach, at Bow Church, a thanksgiving sermon on the return of their fleet in the spring of 1622—a discourse which was published under the title of *Virginia's God be Thanked.* In July 1622 Copland was appointed to be the rector of a projected college in the colony and a member of the council there; but before he could embark news came that the settlers had been massacred by the Indians, and the scheme fell to the ground. A suggestion made at the close of 1623 that Copland should go again to the East Indies as a chaplain was not pursued, as Captain Weddell, the commander of the fleet, preferred another candidate.

On the dissolution of the Virginia Company in 1624 the money collected for a school was transferred to the Somers Islands (Bermudas) Company; and later this was augmented by a legacy of 300*l.* from Copland's friend, Nicholas Ferrar. In order to establish the school and carry out his evangelistic schemes, Copland, some time before the beginning of 1633[1], proceeded to the Bermudas, with his wife and daughter, and set busily to work. In January 1635 he wrote: 'I here have buried what in their [the East India Company's] service I got, and I have expended one thousand pounds sterling, and a better peny more then I have got by my ministry in these ilands.' Gradually his views on ecclesiastical government hardened, and in 1644 he and his adherents turned their church into a congregational one, Copland renouncing his orders and taking the post of one of the ruling elders. He is said to have been imprisoned for a time, apparently for his share in this movement. In 1648 he and a large party of sympathizers removed to one of the Bahama Islands, to establish there a colony, named Eleutheria, which should be entirely free of state control. The experiment, however, proved a failure, and three years later most of the settlers, Copland amongst them, returned to the Bermudas. He is supposed to have died there at some date before 1655[2].

And now, having introduced to the reader the principal actors in the story, we return to the voyage itself. The instructions given to the leader by the Company have not survived, but doubtless they were similar in the main to those issued for the Sixth, Seventh, and Eighth Voyages, all of which are printed in *The First Letter Book* (pp. 328, 369, 396). In accordance with the general practice, Best was furnished with a royal commission (dated 6 January 1612) authorizing him (or, in the event of his death, Aldworth) to govern all persons engaged in the voyage, to inflict customary punishments for minor offences, and to use martial law in cases deserving the death penalty, such as murder or mutiny. In addition, he was provided with a special com-

[1] In 1626, according to Mr Henry Wilkinson's *Adventurers of Bermuda* (p. 267).

[2] *Memoir*, by E. D. Neill, New York, 1871; *Fasti Acad. Marisc.* (Aberdeen), vol. I, p. 159; *Scottish Notes and Queries*, vol. III, p. 14, vol. V, p. 1, vol. VII, p. 107, vol. X, p. 4.

mission from King James, empowering him to conclude a treaty of commerce with the Great Mogul 'or any [of] his deputies.' Both of these documents are printed in full in the work already mentioned (pp. 437, 441).

In view of the fact that neither Best nor any of his principal assistants had had any previous experience of a voyage to the East, it had been arranged that the *Dragon* and *Hosiander* should sail in company with two other vessels (the *James* and the *Solomon*) which were bound for Bantam. The master of the *James* was John Davis of Limehouse, who had already voyaged to the East Indies four times, and he was now to act as pilot of the whole fleet as far as the Cape. The four ships left the Downs on 10 February 1612, and got clear of the Channel about a fortnight later. The *Hosiander* having lost company, on 22 March the remaining vessels put into Maio (one of the Cape Verde Islands), which had been agreed upon as a rendezvous in such a case. Here the missing ship rejoined, and the fleet sailed on the 24th, steering in a south-westerly direction to catch the trade winds. On 27 April they sighted the tiny island of Trinidad, which lies about 700 miles east of Brazil; and thereupon they changed their course to south-east. The African coast was seen on 4 June, in stormy weather. The *Hosiander* and the *Solomon* got into Table Bay on the 5th, and were joined by the *Dragon* three days later. The *James*, however, failed to make the roadstead, and continued her voyage for Bantam.

From Standish's journal we learn that the crew of the *Dragon* were suffering so severely from scurvy that they were hardly able to bring their vessel into the Bay. Three weeks' rest, however, with a plentiful supply of fresh meat and vegetables, changed all this; and when the *Dragon* and her consort put once more to sea, their men were mostly 'well reffreshed.' The *Solomon* was left behind, and soon after resumed her voyage for Bantam. Running up the African coast, on the last day of July Best's two vessels sighted the small island of Juan de Nova, in the Mozambique Channel. On the previous day a couple of Portuguese carracks, outward bound, had been overtaken. The English sailors were evidently eager to provoke a conflict, in hopes of booty; and the *Hosiander* actually fired a broadside at one of the strangers, receiving a response in kind, which did no harm. Best, however, was well aware that his commission forbade him to allow any such attack, and so he prudently stood away and the *Hosiander* was forced to follow. A few days later they sighted Mohilla, one of the Comoro Islands, but failed to

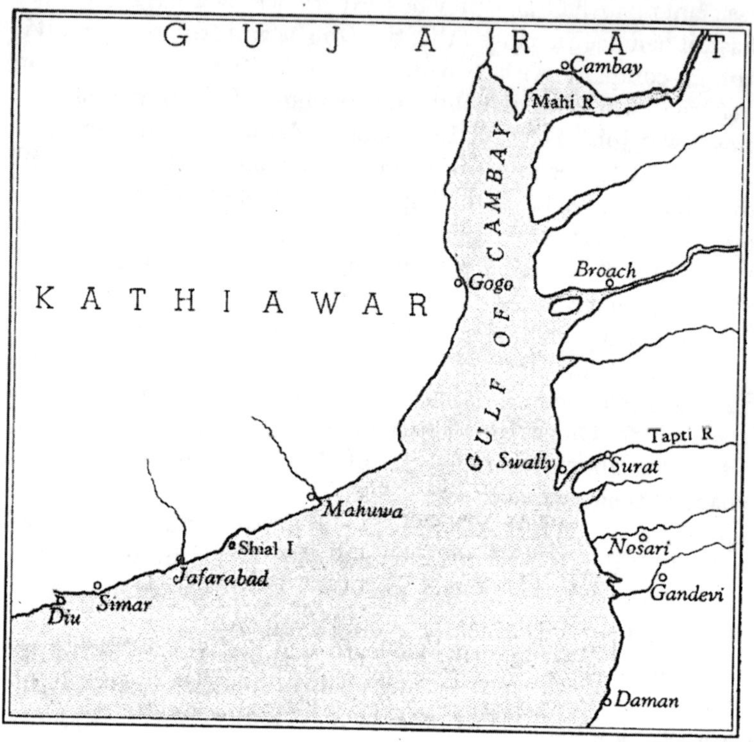

make the harbour and were obliged to continue their voyage. Stretching across the Indian Ocean, at daybreak on 1 September the two ships reached the coast of India near Daman.

Here Best anchored, and despatched the *Hosiander* northwards to the Bar of Surat, to glean intelligence of the state of affairs in that city; but a little later, having procured a couple of Indian pilots, he sailed and overtook his consort on 4 September. Next day arrived a boat from Surat, bringing Jādu (a native broker who had been employed by Hawkins and

Middleton), together with a number of Indians of good standing. Jādu delivered a letter left by Middleton (as already mentioned), warning any new-comer that trade was hopeless. Nevertheless, both the broker and his companions were profuse in their assurances that the English would be welcomed at Surat; and so Best decided to disregard the warning and proceed to the mouth of the river. From thence the Indian visitors, with Kerridge and three other Englishmen, were sent up to the city in a country boat. In a few days Kerridge came back and reported that the party had been warmly received at Surat; and he brought with him a formal assurance, signed by the Governor and the chief magistrate, 'for our quiett and peaceable trade and intercourse with them.' The reasons for this conciliatory attitude are not far to seek. Only seven months earlier Middleton had sailed away, vowing vengeance for the refusal to permit him further trade. Of his reprisals in the Red Sea nothing was yet known; but it may well have been supposed that the new arrivals had come with the same determination to retaliate if commerce were denied. Surat lived by its seaborne trade, and especially by its pilgrim traffic to the Red Sea; and its merchants were painfully aware that their vessels were at the mercy of any well-armed aggressor. They were anxious, therefore, to keep on good terms with the new-comers; and this was all the easier at the moment from the fact that Mukarrab Khān, the opponent of Hawkins and Middleton, was far away and there was no Portuguese agent on the spot to threaten or cajole. Evidently, too, several of the chief merchants were well disposed towards the English and desirous of establishing commerce with them as far as possible.

A council called aboard the *Dragon* on 22 September decided to land a substantial portion of the cargo, and to send a messenger to Agra with a request that the Emperor 'would permitt us trade and to settle a factorye; otherwise to departe his country.' But before anything could be done in the latter respect, two disturbing incidents happened. Some Portuguese small vessels had arrived and had got into the shallow estuary, where the English ships could not follow them. These intercepted a boat in which Paul Canning, Edward Christian (purser of the *Dragon*), and a third Englishman were coming down from Surat, and carried them off captives to Goa. On 24 September a Gujarāti vessel arrived from the Red Sea, followed by another six days later. These brought news of Middleton's depredations; and Best, fearing the effect of this intelligence and anxious also to recover the three men made prisoners by the Portuguese, seized the second vessel and intimated to the Surat authorities that she would be held as a hostage until all the Englishmen on land, together with their goods or the value of the same, were returned to him. This produced a deputation from the city, entreating him to release the ship; but all that he would concede was to allow the passengers and crew to go ashore. On 10 October he took his two ships and the prize to Swally Hole—the roadstead already mentioned—and there awaited developments.

The news from the Red Sea produced at first a serious ebullience of feeling, which threatened the safety of the English factors in Surat. But calmer counsels soon prevailed. The proofs that had been given that the sea-power of the new-comers was as much to be dreaded as that of the Portuguese had convinced the mercantile community that conciliation was the only safe course; while the news from court pointed in the same direction. The Emperor was always eager for European novelties, and had been led to expect that the English would not only furnish abundance of these but would also bring him a handsome present. The intelligence that two ships had reached Surat would naturally revive these expectations, and it seems that Jahāngīr at once despatched orders to the Dīwān at Ahmadābād, who was acting as Viceroy of Gujarāt, to proceed to the port and purchase what he could. Accordingly, on 17 October that functionary (generally styled in the text Governor of Ahmadābād) arrived at Swally, accompanied by the Governor of Surat and a number of the principal merchants. Thereupon Best landed and commenced negotiations.

The Englishman was under the impression that the Dīwān had been given full authority to conclude a formal treaty with him; but though that official was profuse in his assurances that he possessed ample powers, it seems clear that the imperial intentions did not go beyond the present needs. However, no hitch occurred in the negotiations. The Indians were anxious to avoid giving the new-comers any excuse for copying Middleton's methods, and, when Best submitted his demands, these were agreed to without demur. They included permission to settle factories in Surat and other parts of the Mughal dominions, and to keep an agent or ambassador at the capital; customs were to be paid at the usual rate of 3½ per cent.; Englishmen and their goods were to be secured against the Portuguese; and no demand was to be made on the Indian side for compensation on account of Middleton's reprisals. It was also stipulated that an imperial *farmān*, expressly confirming the agreement, should be obtained from court and delivered to Best within forty days. The matter was concluded in so great a hurry that the document embodying the terms was not translated into Persian, but the signatures of the contracting parties were affixed to the English version. Apparently this was taken home by Best (see pp. 254, 259) and has since disappeared. That little importance was attached to the agreement on the side of the Indians was shown by later developments. When at a later date Kerridge, who was acting as the English agent at Agra, appealed to it as binding, he was told that it was of no validity and had been concluded on the authority of the two Governors, both of whom had since died. As a matter of fact, in this, as in more important affairs, the will of the Emperor was the only law; and any *farmān* merely held good until it was contradicted by another.

However, on the surface everything appeared to be satisfactory. Best feasted the Dīwān and showed him the present which was to be despatched to Agra; and on 28 October that official, after buying a quantity of broadcloth, departed for Ahmadābād. Aldworth and other merchants had already proceeded to Surat to establish the factory, and the Gujarāti prize had been restored to its owners. All that was now required was the confirmation by the Emperor of the agreement that had been concluded, and this was confidently expected. So Best had every reason to believe that the chief object of his voyage had been secured, and that a regular commerce in India had been established on a sure footing.

He had yet, however, to reckon with the Portuguese. On

7 November information was received that they were preparing for vigorous action; and three weeks later came letters from Canning and Christian, then captives at Goa[1], warning their countrymen that four powerful galleons, under an experienced commander, Nuno da Cunha, were about to sail for Swally with the proclaimed intention of destroying the English intruders. On 28 November the enemy's fleet appeared in sight; whereupon the *Dragon* and *Hosiander* prepared to meet them. The combats that followed have been described by most writers, following the contemporary English accounts, as a series of astounding victories, won by a very weak force against overwhelming odds. But the narrative of the Portuguese historian Bocarro, translated in the present volume, shows that the disproportion between the contending forces has been much exaggerated. It is true that the four Portuguese vessels were of great size and very heavily manned. Those on board, however, were chiefly soldiers and untrained volunteers, useless except at close quarters, since their chief weapon was the sword; expert gunners were sadly lacking; while a large proportion of the crews consisted of lascars. On the other hand, the English, though few in number, were skilled seamen and trained gunners; every man could handle a musket; their ships were stout and handy and could easily outmanœuvre their opponents; while the national combativeness of the sailors was steeled by the consciousness that defeat would mean the destruction of their vessels and their own immurement in a Portuguese prison. It was the story of the Spanish Armada over again; and the fact that in all the four engagements the English losses were only three men killed and about the same number wounded, while the casualties on the side of their opponents were reckoned by hundreds, shows how handicapped 'the Portugals of Goa' were when it came to naval warfare with a European foe.

The obvious danger was lest the Portuguese, who were overwhelmingly superior in numbers, should succeed in boarding

[1] The Portuguese Viceroy contemptuously ordered the release of the three prisoners. Canning was accordingly put ashore at Surat by the Portuguese frigates; while the other two made their escape at Cambay and rejoined their comrades.

the English ships; and so Best, instead of awaiting attack in the confined space of Swally Hole, surrounded by sandbanks, set sail to meet the enemy. An hour's engagement in the afternoon of the 29th resulted in little beyond a vigorous exchange of shot between the *Dragon* and the Portuguese vice-admiral's ship, wherein the latter was much damaged. Next morning the combat was resumed at dawn, and three of the enemy's vessels were driven on the sands near the Bar of Surat. They got off again when the tide rose; but they were well pounded all day by both the English ships, who approached their targets so closely that every shot told. The Portuguese stood up bravely to their punishment, to which they could make no effective reply; and the loss on their crowded decks was very heavy. On the English side only two men were killed and one was wounded. That night a Portuguese frigate, supposed to have been fitted as a fireship, approached the *Hosiander*, but was driven off or sunk by a few well-directed shots.

Thus far the conflict had gone entirely in favour of the English. However, the risk of being boarded, should their ships come aground, was still great, and Best determined to go further to sea. This was done; but the galleons did not (as was hoped) follow them, and on 3 December the English returned and anchored in sight of the foe. Da Cunha gave no sign of wishing to renew the combat; and Best, finding himself in need of water and other supplies, decided to go over to the coast of Kāthiāwār in search of these. The Portuguese made a show of pursuing him, but soon desisted. On the 6th the English vessels anchored at a spot to the eastwards of Diu; from thence they moved first to Jafarābād and then to Mahuwa, a port which had already been visited by the *Ascension*. At this place they procured water and food. Near Mahuwa a Mughal general, Khwāja Yādgār, was engaged in besieging a fort occupied by a number of alleged pirates[1]; and at his entreaty Best proceeded to the spot with his two ships. The general received his visitors very courteously and urged the English leader to land some artillery for the purpose of reducing the fort; but this Best refused to do, being

[1] Apparently they were intruders from the Malabar Coast. Withington pp. 209, 218) calls them Rājpūts; but this is a mistaken inference.

well aware that Da Cunha, who was recruiting his forces at Daman and Diu, might at any moment reappear. His decision was wise, for on 22 December the Portuguese fleet arrived and anchored that night within shot.

It was perhaps fortunate for Best's reputation, as well as for the safety of his fellow countrymen whom he had left stranded at Surat, that his hand was forced by Da Cunha's determination to make a fresh attempt to crush the intruders. The English commander appears to have been at the time in a state of painful indecision. On board the *Dragon* there was a strong party, including, it would seem (p. 128), the chaplain, who were urging the advisability of abandoning the merchants at Surat to their fate, of cruising for a while on the coast in the hope of capturing some Portuguese merchantmen, and then of resuming the voyage for Sumatra and Java; and Best, keenly aware that the loss of his vessels, either by hostile action or by shipwreck on the treacherous sands of the Gulf of Cambay, would mean absolute ruin, was shaken by their arguments. According to Standish (p. 124), it was by the persuasion of these individuals that Best had gone over to the coast of Kāthiāwār instead of returning at once to Swally; and it was apparently under their influence that he lingered on that coast for three weeks, though all the time Paul Canning was pleading with him to go back to the opposite coast. Still undecided, on 14 December Best took the unusual course of convening the crews of both vessels and putting to them the question whether or not to risk such an attempt. He let it be seen, however, that personally he inclined to the more vigorous course; and the result was a unanimous vote for a return to Swally, even in the face of Portuguese hostility. Thus heartened, Best announced his firm determination to sail thither within a few days; but the opponents of this course were still active (p. 128), and no move had been made when, eight days later, the Portuguese squadron made its appearance and offered battle.

Then at last Best acted, and acted with great resolution and vigour. Putting to sea on the following morning (23 December) he made straight for the enemy, 'steered from one to another, and gave them such banges as maid ther verie sides crack'

(p. 135). The little *Hosiander* was not a whit behind the *Dragon*, and both vessels engaged the Portuguese at such close quarters that not a shot was wasted. A few hours of heavy punishment materially abated the ardour of the enemy, and the English had the satisfaction of seeing their opponents take to their heels. They followed for two or three hours, and then came to an anchor, having, as on the previous occasion, inflicted much damage at very small cost to themselves. Next day, the two ships overtook the Portuguese, and fought with them for four hours, until both sides were weary. A fireball flung aboard Da Cunha's ship set her on fire, and her crew had the greatest difficulty in extinguishing the conflagration.

Best now took stock of his position. He had spent a great quantity of powder and shot, and had no immediate means of replenishing his stores. The enemy had been severely punished, but not disabled, and Da Cunha showed no sign of abandoning his aim. Moreover, he had fortresses at hand from which he could draw fresh supplies of men and munitions; while Best, who had the return voyage to provide for, could hope for no assistance until he reached Bantam, if then. Opinion in the fleet was against wasting any more of their precious ammunition; and Best, agreeing in this, did not attempt to renew the conflict, but made for Swally, anchoring there unmolested on 27 December.

Kerridge and Christian came at once on board to report the state of affairs at Surat. The General inquired eagerly for the promised *farmān*, but was told that it had not yet arrived, though expected daily. The long delay rendered him suspicious; but nothing could be done but to wait a little longer. Meanwhile the water casks were filled, provisions were procured, and a quantity of merchandise was taken on board. As the days passed without any sign of the promised *farmān*, Best concluded that he was being deceived, and consequently resolved to give up all idea of leaving a factory at Surat. He therefore summoned the merchants to wind up their affairs and come aboard with their goods. Here, however, Aldworth's determination to remain proved an insurmountable obstacle. Though there is no direct evidence on the point, we suspect that the relations between the General and the chief merchant had throughout the voyage been correct rather than cordial. Best in his journal seems to avoid mentioning Aldworth; according to Standish (p. 143) he treated him very coldly on at least one occasion; and we know that he wrote from Swally (p. 243), advising the Company to send someone else to take over the control of affairs at Surat. Aldworth, on his part, may have resented being placed under Best, and he appears to have regarded himself as entrusted with the superintendence of mercantile affairs on land. There are signs also of two contending currents of opinion. One suspects that the seamen, and probably some of their officers, would willingly have broken with the Indians and thus have provided an excuse for taking their vessels, as Middleton had done (see p. 289); while the merchants of the expedition were on the contrary eager for a peaceable settlement and the establishment of a lasting trade. Whatever the reasons, Aldworth now refused to quit Surat, whether the *farmān* arrived from Agra or not. This created a difficult situation; but fortunately, on 6 January 1613 the long-expected document arrived. No copy of this is extant, nor is anything known of its contents, beyond the statement that it gave a general approval to the arrangement concluded with the English; but that its terms were vague and non-committal may be inferred from the fact that the local authorities endeavoured to evade the formal presentation of the *farmān* to the General. Best, however, firmly refused to accept it otherwise, and after some hesitation it was delivered with all due ceremony, and with many asseverations that it was a solemn confirmation of the treaty and that any merchants left in the country would be well treated and allowed to start branch factories in any part of the province. Best was able, therefore, to fall in with Aldworth's determination to remain, with several of his colleagues, and further to sanction the despatch of Canning to the court with the present intended for the Emperor.

Preparations for departure had been going on all the time; and these were hastened by rumours that Da Cunha's squadron was again approaching. On 13 January his ships came in sight, but did not venture upon hostile action. Best hurriedly completed his arrangements, without embarking his full complement of goods[1], and on the 17th he put to sea. The galleons followed him until it was certain that he had really quitted the coast. Then they returned, with the intention of driving the English merchants out of Surat; but the report of one of the Portuguese captains, who went up to the city in disguise, was so unfavourable that the plan was given up, and Da Cunha led his ships back to Goa. Though he had failed in his loudly expressed determination to destroy or capture the English intruders, he could at least claim that he had driven them away, though at a heavy loss in killed and wounded; and despite an undercurrent of dissatisfaction, this claim was officially accepted.

Before leaving Swally, Best made arrangements to acquaint his employers with the success he had obtained, by sending a messenger overland with letters. For this purpose he chose his steward, Anthony Starkey, who had already been found useful as an interpreter (p. 111)[2]. Taking with him 100*l.* (*Letters Received*, vol. II, p. 101) and a Musalman servant, Starkey started on 28 January 1613, with the intention of making his way through Sind to Persia (probably via Kandahar) and so reaching Aleppo, from whence it would be easy to get to England. In March the Surat factors received a letter from him, acquainting them that he had arrived at Tatta, though both he and his attendant were in very bad health. After that they heard no more, save for a rumour (repeated below by Copland) that he had been poisoned by two friars[3]. It would seem, however, from an entry in the Court Minutes for 17 January 1614, that he had got at least as far as Aleppo before succumbing. After his death the letters he was carrying fell into the hands of Luiz Pereira Cotta, a Portuguese who was on his way from Persia to Spain with letters from the Bishop of Sirene. In this manner they reached Madrid; and thereupon the Spanish King forwarded translations of them to the Viceroy at Goa in February

[1] There had been a proposal to send the *Hosiander* back to England with a cargo of Indian goods; but the preparations were abandoned upon the first appearance of the Portuguese fleet.

[2] Possibly he was a son of Alderman Thomas Starkey, who was prominent in the trade to Barbary. If Anthony took part in those ventures, he would naturally acquire some knowledge of Arabic.

[3] The same explanation is given in the Court Minutes for 17 January 1615.

1614, accompanied by a demand for information regarding the alleged English successes, and instructions that vigorous measures were to be taken to prevent the intruders from obtaining a footing (*Documentos Remettidos*, vol. III, p. 70). Meanwhile the Surat factors had sent copies home in March 1613, by way of the Red Sea. Withington was to have been the bearer of the packet; but he heard such terrifying reports of the risk to Christians attempting to pass by that route that he finally declined to undertake the venture. A substitute was found, who 'understoode the Arabian tonge and had formerlye ben that way.' According to Withington, this man actually reached Mokha; there, however, he learnt that the Turks, exasperated by Middleton's proceedings, were imprisoning all the Englishmen they could find, and so he sent back the letters by the same ship, which reached the Indian coast in the middle of September (*Early Travels*, p. 202). Copland, however, says (p. 209) that copies of the letters, delivered to a mariner, duly reached the East India Company; and it would seem from p. 240 *n* that they came by way of Aleppo and were received in London in December 1613. These copies are not in the India Office records, and we are dependent, therefore, on the Spanish translations already mentioned, as printed in *Documentos Remettidos*, vol. III, pp. 71–88. It is from them that the versions now given have been prepared.

After quitting the coast of Gujarāt the *Dragon* and *Hosiander* stood down the western side of the Indian peninsula, capturing and plundering a few native vessels suspected of having Portuguese goods on board. Some time was spent at Brinjaon, near Cape Comorin, where a supply of provisions was obtained; and a vain attempt to procure a further quantity was made on the south coast of Ceylon. The southernmost point of that island was passed in the middle of March, and a course was then set for Achin, at the northern end of Sumatra.

No serious attempt had been made to develop trade in that region since Lancaster in 1602 had concluded an agreement with the King of Achin, which promised a free trade with complete exemption from the payment of customs. It is true that in 1609 the *Union* had called at Achin and other Sumatran ports, and had been well received; while in the summer of 1612 not only Middleton's fleet but also the *Thomas* of Saris's fleet had visited Tiku and Priaman, though with scant success. The reason for this neglect of Sumatra appears to have been that for some years the English found Bantam a more convenient centre for the purchase of pepper, as well as a better mart for disposing of their European goods. As time went on, however, the Bantam authorities grew more and more exacting in their dealings with

foreign merchants, with the result that both the English and the Dutch began to consider removing to fresh headquarters at Jakatra or elsewhere, and resorting again to the pepper ports of Sumatra, especially Tiku and Priaman. These places, however, had recently come under the rule of the King of Achin (grandson of the monarch with whom Lancaster had negotiated), and he had adopted a policy tending towards the exclusion of foreign traders from those ports and the concentration of the commerce at Achin, where it would be more immediately under his control. Best had therefore been directed by his employers to call at Achin and conclude a fresh treaty, which should include a renewal of the freedom from customs which had formed a special feature of the previous agreement.

The *Dragon* and *Hosiander* anchored in the roadstead of Achin on 12 April 1613. Five days later Best repaired to the royal palace at Kotaraja (a few miles inland) and delivered to the monarch a letter from King James, accompanied by a suitable present. He was graciously received, and on the following day he commenced his negotiations in a hopeful frame of mind. But 'wee ended without concludinge of anye thinge'; and succeeding attempts to pin down the capricious monarch to a definite and lasting agreement were equally ineffectual. The King was delighted to entertain the new arrival at banquets, animal fights, and other spectacles displaying his riches and power; but he was disinclined to talk business, and was entirely averse from making any concessions in the matter of trade. He evidently wished to induce all foreign ships to come to his capital, where he would deal with them as his inclinations prompted; while Best, on the other hand, was anxious to obtain for his countrymen permission to resort freely to the actual pepper ports, without losing time and incurring expense in visiting the King on each occasion.

The negotiations dragged slowly on. A Dutch factory was already installed at the port, the members of which gave the English a friendly reception, being doubtless glad of intercourse with Europeans; while the tedium of waiting was further relieved by the presence of a couple of Siamese ambassadors, who told Best wondrous stories of the importance of their sovereign and of his earnest desire for commercial relations with England. In the middle of May an awkward contretemps occurred. A Portuguese vessel from Malacca landed on the coast some envoys sent by the Governor of that city to the King. Best, regarding all Portuguese shipping as his lawful prey, sent the *Hosiander* to capture the vessel and bring her into the harbour. The King naturally resented this high-handed action, and threatened to imprison the English merchants ashore. At first Best refused to surrender his prize; but finding little of value aboard, and learning that the King was really angry with him, he made a virtue of necessity and yielded up the vessel. Thereupon the monarch was pacified and, glad to be extricated from an awkward situation, promised the Englishman 'letters of favoure unto Pryaman.'

Thus the days passed until early in July, when Best determined to waste no more time. He could get nothing in the shape

of a treaty, nor would the King listen to any plea for exemption from paying the usual customs duties. All that he would grant was permission for Best's ships to proceed on the present occasion to Tiku and Priaman and purchase pepper there on the current terms. With a letter to this effect, and also a reply and present for his sovereign, the English General sailed on 13 July 1613. He had promised the factors at Surat to return in the autumn and take in any goods provided by them in the interim (p. 255); and, after his return home, he told the Company that, when at Achin, he had no expectation of proceeding to Bantam (p. 264). He had now, however, changed his plans, and on 12 July he wrote to the Surat factors that he hoped to complete his lading at the Sumatran pepper ports, and so 'you cannott expect us to come any more for Suratte this voyadge' (p. 258).

Tiku was reached on 7 August, and two days later Best and his merchants went ashore, only to meet with the customary delays. On the 12th the *Hosiander* was sent to Priaman, to see what pepper could be procured there; and on her return (six days after) she was despatched to Bantam for news. Finding the Tiku officials bent upon standing out for higher prices than he was willing to give, Best sent a boat to Pasaman, a port a little to the northwards, the inhabitants of which willingly agreed to sell their pepper to the English. This brought the Governor of Tiku to a further parley, with the result that an agreement as to prices was at last reached. All hands were now busied in weighing and lading pepper, paid for partly in coin and partly in Indian calicoes; while the need for an early departure from this fever-stricken coast was emphasized by almost daily deaths from sickness.

On 21 October the *Hosiander* returned from Bantam, bringing confirmation of the death of Sir Henry Middleton and the loss of the *Trade's Increase*, together with assurances from the English factors there that an ample supply of pepper awaited Best. Next day the *Darling* also arrived from Bantam, on her way to the Coromandel Coast with a cargo of cloves. According to her captain, John Jourdain, Best at once coveted these goods for his own return cargo; and he urged Jourdain to give up his voyage and go back to Bantam in his company, alleging that it was the wrong season for the Coast. Jourdain sturdily refused to listen to this proposal; and so Best called a court of merchants, which naturally decided in his favour. Accordingly, on 30 October the *Dragon* and *Darling* sailed together for Bantam, leaving the *Hosiander* behind to embark the rest of the pepper.

Bantam was reached on 11 November 1613. At this point Best's journal grows still more concise; while we lose the assistance of Croft's—our other chief authority. However, some welcome light is afforded by *The Journal of John Jourdain* (p. 312), not to mention other scattered sources. From the Court Minutes we learn (see p. 284) that, assisted by Captain Saris, Best induced the King of Bantam to grant permission to build a suitable factory, to secure their goods from all risk of fire. Another service rendered to the Company by him was the steps he took towards the amalgamation of the various factories set up on account of the different Voyages, placing them under one head—to which post he procured the appointment of Jourdain, notwithstanding their former differences. He then bought from the factors of the Sixth Voyage the pepper they had provided for the lost *Trade's Increase*, together with the *Darling's* stock of cloves; and having thus filled the capacious hold of the *Dragon*, in the middle of December 1613 he sailed for England. His instructions from the Company had contemplated that he should proceed to the Moluccas before returning; but having already secured a quantity of spices, he felt justified in ignoring these directions, especially as it had been arranged that the *Hosiander*, when she reached Bantam, should be sent to the Moluccas.

The *Hosiander* did not reach Bantam from Tiku until after the departure of Best. Her intended visit to the Moluccas was abandoned, and it was determined that, as soon as she could be refitted, she should follow the *Dragon* to England. This plan, however, was quickly changed, and two larger ships, the *James* and the *Globe*, were despatched home instead. The *Hosiander's* stock of pepper was transferred to the *Globe*; while the greater portion of her crew was divided between that vessel and the *James*, both being shorthanded. As part of the bargain, Christian, the captain of the *Hosiander*, and Salmon, her master, were allowed to go home as captain and master of the *Globe*. Later in the year the *Hosiander* voyaged to Tiku, arriving there on 26 June and getting back to Bantam on 26 November 1614. In the following February it was decided to send her to Japan, calling at Sukadana (Borneo) and Patani (Malay Peninsula) on her way. She sailed accordingly in April, reached Japan at the end of August, departed again in February 1616, and got back to

Bantam on 22 March[1]. In the following year she sailed to Masulipatam, and in returning called at Achin (August 1617). A letter from Bantam, dated in January 1618, stated that she had got back in safety to that port, but was laid up for want of victuals. Since we hear nothing further of her, we must conclude that by this time she was practically worn out.

Returning to the subject of Best's voyage to England, we may first note that, although he makes no allusion to the fact in his journal, he had on board the *Dragon*, as a passenger, a Scotsman named William Carmichael, who deserves notice as having been the first of his nation to reach the East Indies. Sent as a youth to Portugal in 1579 to learn the language, about two years later he contrived to procure a passage to Goa, where he entered the service of the Portuguese government. After being employed for thirty years at various stations (including, it would seem, Macao), he found his position so unsatisfactory that he absconded at Macassar, hoping that the Dutch would assist him to return to Europe. They, however, suspected him of being a Portuguese spy and kept him under restraint for nearly two years. When at last set free, he made his way to Bantam, and there induced Best to take him to England. Arrived in London, he spent several years in vain attempts to obtain from the Dutch East India Company some compensation for the ill-usage he had sustained at the hands of its servants in the East. He also on three occasions offered his services to the London Company, but without success. At last, in 1626, he was admitted to the Charterhouse, where presumably he spent the remainder of his days[2].

The homeward voyage of the *Dragon* was trying but uneventful. On 1 January 1614 she passed the Keeling (Cocos) Islands, where some three centuries later the German raider *Emden* met her fate in the Great War. Then she settled down to a monotonous south-west course through the Indian Ocean, until on 8 February the south-eastern coast of Africa was descried. Cape Agulhas was passed on the 17th, and three days later the *Dragon* anchored in Table Bay. Here a halt was made

[1] Accounts of this voyage will be found in *Egerton MS.* 2121 (British Museum) and in no. xxiii of the Marine Records at the India Office.

[2] For further details of his career see my article in *The Times of India Annual* for 1934.

until 4 March, and a plentiful supply of fresh meat was obtained. Resuming the voyage, Best reached St Helena on the 24th, and quitted it two days later. The Azores were passed on 19 May, and early in June the English Channel was entered. On the 8th the *Dragon* dropped anchor in the Downs; and a week later she was safe in the Thames, having taken exactly six months on the voyage from Bantam.

Best received a hearty welcome in London. His victory over the Portuguese and the settlement of a factory at Surat were already known; but the details now made available renewed the interest excited by his achievements. The shareholders were gratified to find that the *Dragon* had brought home a cargo which enabled a good dividend to be declared at once[1]; while to the more thoughtful among them the outstanding result of the voyage was the establishment of a hopeful commerce in India. The credit of this, by the way, Best took to himself, without mentioning Aldworth's share in the business—a procedure which drew indignant comments from the latter when he heard of it (*Letters Received*, vol. II, p. 137).

[1] The question of the exact profit made is not free from difficulty; but in the general report prepared in 1654 by the Company's chief accountant (*Court Minutes of the East India Company*, 1650–54, p. 361) it is stated that the 'advance' on the capital was 148 per cent. and this may be accepted as authoritative. The division referred to in the text was 'a double capitall' (*i.e.* 200 per cent.) in pepper, at fixed prices (p. 268). This included the return of the capital, and so only one half represented profit. Moreover, it seems to have been optional for the shareholder to refrain from taking the pepper and to wait for a dividend in money. Such a dividend (of 100 per cent.) was declared a year later (p. 285); and probably another (of a similar amount) was paid during the period (1615–17) for which the Court Minutes are not available. These dividends, of course, would not be due to those shareholders who had exercised their option of taking out their shares in pepper. In September 1615 the arrival of two ships from Bantam, bringing the proceeds of some of the goods left behind by Best, enabled a further division of 25 per cent. in pepper to be sanctioned (p. 286); and finally, at a General Court held on 14 October 1617 it was announced that a dividend of 48 per cent. would be paid to those 'thatt have taken out two capitalls' (p. 294 *n*). This last division was doubtless paid in money, with a proportionate reduction in the case of those members who had already taken out the 25 per cent. in pepper.

A profit of 148 per cent., even after allowing for the fact that it was spread over several years, may seem to the reader very satisfactory. But it was less than had been earned by the Third, Seventh, Eighth, and Ninth Voyages, as the Company did not fail to point out to Best when he was disposed to magnify his success (p. 292).

Besides receiving great attentions from the Company, Best was granted an audience with King James, to whom he delivered the letters and presents he had brought from the King of Achin. Possibly he was not without hopes that on this occasion he would be knighted, like his predecessors, Lancaster and Middleton; but nothing of the kind happened. Remembering his past history, we can well believe that he was rough and unpolished in manners, and it may have been thought that, with all his merits, he was hardly a suitable subject for the accolade.

For a time Best was high in the favour of the 'Committees' (or, as we should say, Directors) of the Company, and was frequently in attendance at their meetings; though it is evident that resentment was growing at the large amount of private trade which he himself had indulged in (notwithstanding his undertaking to the contrary) and had permitted to other members of the expedition. In August 1614 the question was raised of sending him out again in command of a fresh fleet, and the Governor was desired to treat with him on the subject; but it was found that he was unwilling to undertake a new voyage so soon, and the matter dropped. Gradually his relations with the Company grew less cordial. For some time he had been pressing for a gratuity, as a reward for the extraordinary services he conceived he had rendered; but this application was looked upon with disfavour, in view of the fact that the freight upon the goods he had brought home on his own account—in defiance of the Company's regulations and his own bond—was reckoned at 300*l.* or more (p. 282), and that no demand had been made upon him on that account. At last, however, it was decided to give him a 'gratification,' the amount of which was left to the Governor's discretion. Smythe accordingly handed to him a sum of 110*l.*, and with this he seemed at the time to be contented. Nevertheless, after a while Best, irritated by the censures passed upon his private trading, began to grumble at the smallness of the amount and to accuse the Company of ingratitude. On 24 October 1615 he had an interview with the 'Committees' at his own request, and then some plain speaking was indulged in. He was roundly accused of breaking his bond in the matter of private trade, and was further told that 'his service at Suratt was nothinge extraordinary: att Achen costlie and nothinge beneficiall: at Bantam much performed to the prejudice and wronng of the Company: his shipp [the *Hosiander*] lefte behinde: his voyage very poore, and one of the meanest that hath bene made for the Companye...his comission neglected, which directed him to the Moluccas' (p. 292). As for ingratitude, it was he who was the guilty party; and the Governor 'tould him that an ungratefull person is the worst of all others.' Best was cowed by the storm, and protested in reply that he had never intended to wrong the Company and that any fault he had committed was due to ignorance. Thereupon the 'Committees' were pacified and agreed to let 'these things dye'; but all idea of offering him the command of the 1616 fleet was abandoned.

A further break in the series of Court Minutes prevents us from learning the relations that subsisted between Best and the Company from November 1615 to September 1617. Incidental references, however, suggest that in the autumn of 1616 he desired to command the fleet that was being prepared for despatch to India early in 1617, and that he was annoyed when the post was given to Martin Pring instead. In the autumn of 1617 he was still inclined to go once more to the East; and this time the Company seemed more amenable. The reason is probably to be found in the serious situation that had developed. John Jourdain, the capable and energetic Agent at Bantam, had come home in June 1617, and his report had made it evident that the Dutch were taking resolute steps to exclude the English from the Moluccas and the Banda Islands, that is, from the trade in cloves and nutmegs. The 'Committees' were determined not to put up with such an aggression, as they deemed it, and resolved to send out a strong fleet to assert their rights; Jourdain assuring them confidently that the Hollanders 'either dare not or will not sett upon the English,' should this course be followed. A proposal was made that the command of the fleet should be entrusted to Jourdain himself, but this was dropped when it was pointed out that he was 'unexperyenct in maryne causes and for sea fights upon occasion (which is an espetiall thinge to be reguarded).' Other names suggested were those of Sir Richard

Hawkins, Sir Thomas Dale, and Captain William Parker. But the thoughts of the 'Committees' turned persistently towards Best, who was acknowledged on all hands to be a skilled navigator and a doughty fighter, with great influence over his men. Best was more than willing to meet the 'Committees' half-way; and finding them uneasy about the question of private trade, he professed his entire concurrence in the expediency of preventing this and promised for his part 'nott to offend therein.' An agreement was then rapidly concluded and reduced to writing, and Best was duly appointed General of the new fleet.

All went well until the middle of November, when Best, who seems to have been rendered yet more arrogant by the acceptance of his services, began to make a series of captious demands. When the question of remuneration was discussed with him by the Governor and Deputy-Governor, he had stipulated for two suits of apparel for himself and a gold chain for his wife, but these items had been brushed aside as unreasonable, without demur on his part. Now he renewed his demand for these additions, alleging that, although not mentioned in the agreement he had signed, it had been understood that they would nevertheless be granted; and he hinted that, if his wishes were crossed in this respect, he would relinquish all idea of proceeding on the voyage. On the 'Committees' resisting this pretension, he developed another requirement, namely, that he should be left at liberty to return, if he pleased, after a stay of a year or so. The small regard thus shown to his formal agreement, and possibly also a recollection of his previous declaration that he had never intended to observe the terms of the bond he had given before his first voyage, alarmed the 'Committees,' and they decided to require him to enter into a bond for 5000*l.* to keep to the conditions of the new agreement. This he refused to do; and since he still maintained his demands, on 25 November he was dismissed from his post. Sir Thomas Dale was appointed to the command of the fleet; while Jourdain was made Principal Agent at Bantam, with instructions to proceed on arrival to the Moluccas, to direct operations there.

Best appears to have been surprised at this outcome of his obstinacy, and it was reported that he was much dejected at having allowed his pride to 'overcome his reason.' Soon he had cause for alarm as well as annoyance. The 'Committees' could not forgive him for the trouble he had caused them by raising difficulties when the preparations for the voyage were so far advanced; and they resolved to bring his conduct to the notice of the Privy Council, with a view to punishment. He made some clumsy attempts to placate them, sending a present of a bezoar stone, with a letter praising the worth of the Governor and the magnanimity of the Company; and later on another, 'makeinge a darke acknowledgment of an offence and cytinge certaine places out of Solomon to prove that it is the parte of a wise man to passe by an offence.' Nothing, however, would satisfy the majority of the 'Committees' but a personal appearance and absolute submission; and as Best could not bring himself to do this, the petition was presented to the Privy Council in January 1618. Their Lordships thereupon commanded the attendance of the culprit to explain his conduct; and since they had an unpleasant habit of remanding offenders in custody for an indefinite period, Best was thoroughly frightened. On the 27th of the month he appeared before the 'Committees' and humbly begged them not to 'tryumphe over him' but to release him from his trouble. He was told that he must put into writing a complete recantation of all his charges. This, with some prompting, he accomplished to the satisfaction of his accusers; and a promise was then given that the Company would intercede with the Council on his behalf, while he for his part offered to give the 'Committees' the benefit of his advice whenever called upon. Several of the latter then went to the Council chamber and begged that the proceedings against Best might be suspended until a further application were made; and on 28 January 1618 their Lordships agreed to this course (*Acts of the Privy Council*, 1617–19, p. 22).

Relations between Best and the East India Company were finally severed by this episode. The rest of his story must be told more succinctly. He seems to have passed almost immediately into the service of the crown as commander of various vessels of the royal navy. In 1623 he was the central figure in an episode which created no small stir at the time. The Dutch, annoyed at the damage done to their shipping by privateers from Dunkirk, took vigorous measures to clear the North Sea of these pests. One was blockaded at Aberdeen; while another was driven into Leith and destroyed in the harbour itself. This violation of British waters was strongly resented in London. Remonstrances were addressed to the Hague, and Best was ordered to Aberdeen with his own ship (the *Garland*) and another commanded by Edward Christian (the former captain of the *Hosiander*). On arrival he found the Dutch amenable to reason, and they agreed that he should escort the Dunkirker to a Flemish port; taking care, however, to follow themselves to see that she should not escape by the way. Unfortunately, this was exactly what her captain endeavoured to do, relying on the superior swiftness of his vessel. Thereupon she was pursued by the Dutch, who fired a broadside into her and forced her to stop. Best, on overtaking them, was so enraged at the action of the Dutch that he fired at them in his turn. He then anchored with the privateer in the Downs; while the Dutch remained near the South Foreland, watching him. Best chose to regard their proceedings as an insult to the British flag, and, falling unexpectedly on them at night, drove them out of the roads. They quickly returned and demanded satisfaction. Unluckily for him, the authorities at Whitehall were in a more pacific mood, as the result of favourable assurances from Holland. He was accordingly ordered to bring his ship and the privateer into the Thames; and on arrival he was superseded, while the Dunkirker went home with a safe conduct from the Dutch (Gardiner's *History of England*, vol. v, pp. 81–88).

Before long he was re-employed, and in 1627 we find him in command of the *Vanguard*, of Lord Willoughby's fleet. He also took part in the unlucky expedition to Rhè, as captain of the *Repulse* and member of the council of war. Later he sat on various commissions in regard to naval matters, and was also active as a member of the Trinity House, of which in 1633 he was Senior Warden, while in 1634 and 1637 he occupied the post of Master.

He continued to reside, when on shore, at Stepney, where he took an active part in parochial affairs as vestryman or auditor

(Hill and Frere's *Memorials of Stepney Parish*, pp. 45, etc.). His first wife died in July 1624, and from the entry of her burial (on 17 July) in the Stepney registers we learn that Best's dwelling was situated in White Horse Street. When and where he married his second wife has not been ascertained. Her Christian name was Dennis, but of her surname we are ignorant. Best's will mentions his 'brother' John Limbrey of Charmouth; and it also alludes to his wife's 'brother' as a Mr Stock of Colchester; but neither clue leads us to a certain conclusion, since 'brother' in the second case means possibly 'brother-in-law,' as it evidently does in the first.

Best died in August 1639, and was buried at Stepney on the 23rd of that month. No monument appears to have been erected to his memory, and it is not known whether he was interred in the church itself or in the churchyard. His will (*P.C.C.* 148 *Harvey*) was dated 5 August, and was proved 17 September 1639. To his wife Dennis he left 400*l*., besides some plate, etc.; and he ordained that she was to have their dwelling-house for a year rent-free, while for the remainder of the lease she was to pay only half the rent, the other half to be furnished by the estate. The lady, however, quickly provided for herself by marrying (5 October 1640) Solomon Smith, of St Katherine's near the Tower (T. Colyer Fergusson's *Marriage Registers of St Dunstan's, Stepney*, vol. II, p. 7).

Best appears to have had no children by his second wife. Of those by her predecessor the following six are entered in the Stepney registers:

1. Rebecca, baptized 25 August 1588. She appears to have predeceased her father. From a mention in his will of a son-in-law, Trustram Stevenson, it seems probable that this was her husband.

2. Nathaniel, baptized 4 October 1590. In 1607 he took to the sea, like his father, and in March 1614 the East India Company promised to employ him in its next fleet. In the following September Best asked that his son (presumably Nathaniel) should be appointed a factor for Bantam, but this was refused, 'his sonns carriage haveinge beene soe notoriouslie knowne abroad.' A month later Best urged that his son should be engaged

as a master's mate, but was told that 'his evill is soe publiquelie knowne in the cittie' that his employment would cause a scandal. The father made yet another attempt in November 1617 (see p. 299), but this came to nothing. A few years later, however, Nathaniel seems to have been accepted, for in December 1620 he apparently took part in the fights off Jask, when the premature ignition of the fireships was declared to have been the fault of 'General Best's son' (*English Factories*, 1618–21, p. 221 *n*). On 25 July 1622 he was married at Stepney to Anne Hourt (Fergusson, *ut supra*, vol. I, p. 133); their daughter, Marie, is mentioned in Thomas Best's will. In March 1627 Nathaniel was master of the Company's pinnace *Scout*, then bound for the East. This vessel lost company with the rest of the fleet near the Comoro Islands, and was forced into Aden by want of water and provisions; there she was seized by the Governor and her crew were made prisoners. In 1628 the *Exchange* called at Aden on her way back from Mokha to Surat, hoping to recover the pinnace and her men; but she was fired at from the castle and was forced to put to sea. It had, however, been learnt at Mokha that only two of the captives, Nathaniel Best and another, were still living. The President and Council of Surat wrote in April 1630 that a letter had been received in the preceding October from the two survivors, but that all efforts to secure their release had failed. A German, however, who had escaped from Aden, reported that Best might have had his liberty, but would not come away without his vessel; whilst others declared that he had really no wish to leave Aden. The President and Council promised to make further efforts to 'drawe him off by faire or foule meanes,' but we hear nothing more and must presume that he died among the Turks. In 1633 his estate was confiscated by King James, on the ground that he had abandoned his country, changed his religion, and was living in the Turkish dominions. The King then by mistake granted the estate to two different persons, with the result that the second grant had to be cancelled (*Cal. S.P. Dom.*, 1633–34, p. 327, and 1634–35, p. 408; in both cases the name is wrongly given as William Best).

3. Jonathan, baptized 9 July 1592. Presumably he died young, since nothing more is heard of him.

4. Abigail, baptized 25 August 1596. She married (1) John Wallis, ironmonger, on 15 June 1615, and (2) Rowland Jordan of Limehouse, mariner, on 4 May 1624 (Fergusson, *ut supra*, vol. 1, pp. 96, 142). Her son William is mentioned in Best's will; and since two of her daughters-in-law also figure therein, there must have been another son (probably dead by 1639). Abigail was left 50*l.* and 'my picture' (the fate of which is unknown).

5. Josias, baptized 6 December 1598. He was married at Stepney on 29 November 1621 to Martha Salmon of Ratcliffe, the bridegroom being described as a haberdasher, of the parish of St Edmund, Lombard Street (Fergusson, *ut supra*, vol. 1, p. 130). As the sole surviving son he was named in Best's will as executor. His father's shares in five vessels were left to him, as well as the residue of the estate; and it was recorded that the testator had formerly surrendered certain lands and tenements for the benefit of Josias and his wife Martha. The latter was to receive specific legacies, as were also her children, Thomas, Josias, Martha, and Sarah. To the eldest of these, Thomas, were bequeathed 'my Est India sword or semtary [scimitar] and my seale ringe.' We may assume that, after the re-marriage of his step-mother, Josias took up his abode in the house in White Horse Street, for his name appears frequently in the Stepney parish registers as a sidesman and vestryman. His son Thomas (already mentioned) entered the service of the East India Company in January 1645 as purser of the *Lanneret*. Sent to Persia in that vessel, he was there employed as a factor, and remained in the country until his death at Gombroon on 20 October 1651 (*English Factories*, 1651–54, p. 86).

6. Elizabeth, baptized 12 December 1602. She married Henry Dethick, of Poplar, gentleman, on 1 January 1619 (Fergusson, *ut supra*, vol. 1, p. 113), and thus became the daughter-in-law of Sir William Dethick, Garter King of Arms. To her Best bequeathed 50*l.* and his horse; while legacies were also left to her five sons and her daughter Elizabeth. One of the sons, Henry, afterwards became Richmond Herald.

All that now remains to be considered is the material from which the text of the present volume has been drawn. Of this the two principal sections are Best's log of the voyage and a journal begun by the surgeon of the *Hosiander* and continued for a time by the purser of the same vessel. Best's narrative is already known to some extent, owing to the fact that Purchas printed about a third of it (including the most salient passages) in his *Pilgrimes* (vol. I, p. 456). Of the second and more detailed narrative an abstract, with some lengthy extracts, will be found in a previous volume of this Society (*Voyages of Sir James Lancaster*, etc., pp. 228–62), though there the journal is treated as the work of the purser only. To these two accounts have been added (i) some portions (all that survive) of the logs of the masters of the two ships, (ii) extracts from narratives by the chaplain and one of the factors, (iii) a Portuguese account of the sea fights, (iv) a number of letters, and (v) extracts from the Court Minutes of the East India Company.

Best's own narrative is now reproduced at full length from the India Office Marine Records, no. xv. The manuscript is not Best's original log, though it has hitherto been described as such. It is not in his handwriting, but is a 'fair copy,' very neatly and uniformly written. The scribe was evidently a man of education, though, from want of the necessary experience, he seems to have occasionally been mistaken in his interpretation of the original text. In all probability Best, upon his return to London, handed his rough journal[1] to a scrivener to prepare a copy for delivery to the East India Company. The original Best doubtless retained afterwards for his own use, and what became of it is not known. That the copy belonging to the Company was the one used by Purchas is indicated by the fact that, when the reverend gentleman blunders over a word or phrase, this is usually badly written in the extant manuscript. In style the document is dry and succinct; but we cannot be certain that it contains all that Best actually wrote, for it was of course open to him to mark sundry passages for omission in copying.

In point of style and method our second narrative is a welcome contrast to the first, for it is diffuse to the point of redundancy, and is coloured with intimate detail. This journal (no. xvi in the same series), as already mentioned, had a double authorship.

[1] That this was fuller than the formal log seems to be implied in a passage on p. 17.

The title-page indicates that the author of the first portion (about four-fifths of the whole) was Ralph Standish, the surgeon of the *Hosiander*, and this is confirmed by certain references (pp. 117, 123, 145, 162) to his exercise of his profession. Of the personal history of this individual little can be traced. That he belonged to the ancient family of that name is probable[1]; but the only definite information we have about his parentage is derived from the fact that after his death a commission was issued (13 September 1614) to his mother, Anne Bilson (otherwise Standish), and to Ralph Standish, late of the parish of St Saviour, Southwark, to administer his estate, which was inventoried at 28*l*. 12*s*. (*P.C.C.* September 1614, f. 163). From this we infer that his father had died and his mother had married again, probably before he started on his voyage to the East.

Here again we have not the original journal, but a copy[2]. That Standish's portion is not in his own handwriting is shown by the fact that the writing is uniform down to 5 July 1613 (*i.e.* three weeks after his death), though a second hand takes a share in the entries for 30 June and 1 and 2 July. Probably what happened was this. At Standish's death his journal, with the rest of his effects, passed as a matter of routine into the custody of the purser of the *Hosiander*, Ralph Croft[3]. What became of it ultimately is not recorded; but it may have been made over to Standish's representatives at the end of the voyage. Recognizing its interest and knowing that it was only temporarily in his possession, Croft seems to have decided to make a copy for himself; while later on he determined to continue it (hence his substitution on the title-page of his own name for Standish's).

[1] One would like to connect him with an earlier Ralph Standish, who, after graduating at Cambridge and practising as a doctor in London, went to Russia in 1557 and apparently died there shortly after (*Alumni Cantab.*, pt. I, vol. IV, p. 145). This Ralph's will, however (*P.C.C.* 62 *Chaynay*), mentions neither wife nor child.

[2] We may note also that apparently Standish did not put the original into form until after (or just before) leaving Surat, though probably he had already made rough notes for the purpose. This conclusion is drawn from the wording of the title-page and from references in some passages to later events (cf. pp. 103, 105).

[3] Hitherto the name (written 'Crofte') has been read as Crosse; and it appears thus in *Lancaster's Voyages* and the official list of the India Office Marine Records.

The copying was accomplished, and the narrative was continued for about three weeks after Standish's death. Then another hand takes up the task; possibly Croft, busy with other matters, got a friend or an assistant to enter up the journal from his rough notes. This continues until 29 August 1613, when the manuscript comes to an abrupt stop. The *Hosiander* was then on her way from Tiku to Bantam, with Croft on board. That he returned in her to Tiku may be taken for certain; and that at Tiku he was transferred to the *Dragon* is shown by the fact that he died on board the latter vessel, while the *Hosiander* did not quit Tiku until after the *Dragon* had left Bantam on her homeward voyage. As we learn from his will, Croft's new post was that of purser of the *Dragon*. This was a natural promotion, and the reason of it seems to have been that Edward Christian, the former purser, had been made captain of the *Hosiander*. We have here the explanation of the fact that at the reverse of the volume containing the Standish-Croft journal is found an 'acco[unt] of inventoryes in the *Dragon*,' dated 29 October [1613] (*i.e.* the day when that vessel set sail from Tiku); for the keeping of such accounts was one of the duties of a purser. The fact that these accounts appear to be in the same hand as the first portion of the journal is our main reason for assuming that the latter was copied by Croft himself.

Croft died at sea on 23 January 1614, little more than five weeks after the departure of the *Dragon* from Bantam on her homeward voyage. His will, made at Bantam on 14 December 1613, is on record at Somerset House (*P.C.C.* 79 *Lawe*). In this he leaves small gifts to various shipmates, records debts due to other members of the voyage (probably for sums borrowed for private trading) and directs that the residue of the estate should be paid to his father, Christopher Croft, gentleman, living in 'Coram Abba, in Yorkshire.' 'Coram' appears to be Coverham (near Middleham), one of the owners of which, in 1575, was Ralph Croft, who was succeeded by a son Christopher (*Victoria County Histories: Yorkshire, North Riding*, vol. I, p. 220). This Christopher we take to have been the father of our purser, who would thus be the brother of the Christopher Croft who was knighted in 1641 (Burke's *Peerage*, 1931). It may be added that an account of the Yorkshire branch of the Croft family will be found in *The Three Days of Wensleydale*, by W. G. M. Jones Barker (p. 146); but that work affords no direct evidence of the position of Ralph Croft in the family pedigree.

The third journal of our series is represented only by two extracts, copied by some subsequent navigator, for his own guidance, into what is now *Marine Records*, no. xviii (ff. 1 and 15 respectively). Internal evidence shows that the journal was kept on board the *Hosiander*, and either by the master or by one of his mates. In all probability, from the tone of the entries, it was the former; and I have had no hesitation in assuming that we have here portions of the journal of Nathaniel Salmon. The original is no longer extant; but it was consulted by Purchas, who (see p. 208 *n*) made an extract from it (unfortunately not from either of the portions here reproduced). It is mainly concerned with matters of navigation, and in this respect it provides a useful supplement to Best's account of the voyage.

Throughout the volume, in accordance with the practice of the Society, abbreviations in the manuscript have been for the most part extended: capital letters have been reduced to ordinary ones when present-day usage so requires: and the punctuation has been modernized.

The editor has received much assistance in his task from various friends. In most cases such help has been acknowledged in the notes; but here he must record his special indebtedness to Mr W. H. Moreland, C.S.I., C.I.E., and to Dr C. O. Blagden, M.A., D.Lit., both of whom have allowed him to trouble them repeatedly with difficulties which their superior knowledge enabled them to solve for him.

BEST'S SIGNATURE

FULLER TITLES OF WORKS CITED

Acts of the Privy Council of England, 1617–19. London, 1929.

BOCARRO, ANTONIO. *Decada 13 da Historia da India*. Lisbon, 1876.

BOWREY, THOMAS. *A Geographical Account of the Countries round the Bay of Bengal*, 1669–79. Edited by Sir Richard Temple. Hakluyt Society, 1905.

Calendar of the Court Minutes etc. of the East India Company, 1650–54. By E. B. Sainsbury, with introduction and notes by Sir William Foster. Oxford, 1913.

COLENBRANDER, DR H. T. *Jan Pietersz. Coen*. 5 vols. The Hague, 1919.

Dawn of British Trade to the East Indies. Edited by Henry Stevens, with introduction by Sir George Birdwood. London, 1886.

DE JONGE, J. K. J. *De Opkomst van het Nederlandsche Gezag in Oost-Indië*. The Hague, 1865.

DELLA VALLE, PIETRO. *The Travels of, in India*. Edited by Edward Grey. 2 vols. Hakluyt Society, 1891.

[DIGGES, Sir DUDLEY.] *The Defence of Trade*. London, 1615.

Documentos Remettidos da India, vol. III. Lisbon, 1885.

First Letter Book of the East India Company, 1600–19. Edited by Sir George Birdwood. London, 1893.

FLORIS, PETER. *His Voyage to the East Indies in the Globe*, 1611–15. Edited by W. H. Moreland. Hakluyt Society, 1934.

HAKLUYT, RICHARD. *The Principall Navigations*. 12 vols. Glasgow, 1903–5.

HAMILTON, ALEXANDER. *A New Account of the East Indies*. Edited by Sir William Foster. 2 vols. London, 1930.

HERBERT, THOMAS. *Some Yeares Travel*. London, 1638.

John Company. By Sir William Foster. London, 1926.

JOURDAIN, JOHN. *The Journal of*. Edited by Sir William Foster. Hakluyt Society, 1905.

[KAYLLE, ROBERT.] *The Trades Increase*. London, 1615.

LANCASTER, Sir JAMES. *The Voyages of*. Edited by Sir Clements Markham. Hakluyt Society, 1877.

Letters Received by the East India Company from its Servants in the East. 1602–17. 6 vols. London, 1896–1902.

LINSCHOTEN, J. H. VAN. *His Discours of Voyages into the Easte and West Indies*. Translated by W. P[hillip]. London [1598].

— *The Voyages of, to the East Indies*. Edited by A. C. Burnell and P. A. Tiele. 2 vols. Hakluyt Society, 1885.

LOCKYER, CHARLES. *An Account of the Trade in India*. London, 1711.

MACLEOD, N. *De Oost-Indische Compagnie als Zeemogendheid in Azië*. 2 vols. Rijswijk, 1927.

MUNDY, PETER. *The Travels of.* Edited by Sir Richard Temple. 4 vols. Hakluyt Society, 1907–25.

NETSCHER, E. *De Nederlanders in Djohor en Siak.* Batavia, 1870.

PURCHAS, SAMUEL. *Purchas His Pilgrimage.* Fourth edition. London, 1626.

— *Purchas His Pilgrimes.* 4 vols. London, 1625.

PYRARD DE LAVAL, FRANÇOIS. *The Voyage of.* Edited by Sir Albert Gray. 3 vols. Hakluyt Society, 1887–9.

ROE, Sir THOMAS. *The Embassy of, to India.* Edited by Sir William Foster. Second edition. London, 1926.

SANDERSON, JOHN. *The Travels of.* Edited by Sir William Foster. Hakluyt Society, 1931.

SARIS, JOHN. *The Voyage of, to Japan.* Edited by Sir Ernest Satow. Hakluyt Society, 1900.

TERPSTRA, Dr H. *De Opkomst der Westerkwartieren van de Oost-Indische Compagnie.* 's-Gravenhage, 1918.

TIELE, P. A. *De Opkomst van het Nederlandsche Gezag in Oost-Indië.* Second Series, vol. I. 's-Gravenhage, 1886.

Tūzuk-i-Jahāngīrī. Translated by A. Rogers. London, 1909.

WINSTEDT, R. O. *A History of Johore.* Journal of the Malayan Branch of the Royal Asiatic Society. December, 1932.

THE JOURNAL of CAPTAIN THOMAS BEST

A JORNALL of the Tenth Voyage intended to the East India, sett out by the Right Worshipfull Sir Thomas Smith, Knight, the Governour, and the Companie of the Merchauntts trading those partes. In which voyage were ymployed two shippes, viz. the Dragon *and the* Hoseander, *accompanied with the* James *and* Salomon (*but those for other Voyages*[1]); *and in them*[2] *to the number of* 380 *persons or thereabouts. Written by me, Thomas Best, cheiffe comaunder thereof (though thereof most unworthy). Which voyage, with eache particuler thereof, the Lord in mercy prosper, even for Jesus Christes sake. February* 1611 [1612].

IN THE NAME OF GOD, AMEN.

1. The first of February we sett saile from Gravesend, and anckored in Tylbury Hope.

3. I departed Tilbury Hope, and anckored about the east end of the Whiteaker[3].

[1] 'Being counted as three severall Voyages—the *James* the Ninth, the *Dragon* and *Hosiander* the Tenth, and wee in the *Salomon* the Eleventh. The reason was because we were directed to severall parts of the East-India.' (Ralph Wilson, in *Purchas His Pilgrimes*, vol. I, p. 486.)

[2] Evidently this refers to all four vessels. The pamphlet entitled *The Trades Increase* states that Best had 'some hundred and eighty men under him when he went forth.' In his letter of 14 January 1613 (*infra*) Best gives the total of the crews of the *Dragon* and the *Hosiander* as 220. Standish says that on 8 March 1613 the number aboard the latter vessel was 37.

[3] The Whittaker Flat, a sandbank off the coast of Essex, five miles north-east of Foulness.

4. We weighed and came at night into the Downes.

10. We did set saile, with a faire winde.

11. At foure in the morninge were thwart of Beachie. At 10 a clocke anckored east from the Ile of Wight, some 6 legues of[f]. The afternoone, winde at west.

12. We laie of[f] and on of Beachie; the winde at north-west.

13. We put into the Ile of Wight, and anckored on the east parte of Stokes Bay[1].

16. Having invited Captain Towerson[2] aboarde to dynner, and takinge their leave in the afternoone, I havinge in purpose to have given them three peeces, and givinge fire to the first, it brake, and killed Richard Greene and greevously hurt John Jackson and James Boswell.

20. At night John Jackson died; he havinge received his deaths wounde by the peece that brake.

21. We all weighed. I and the *James* came out at St. Helens[3]. The *Salomon* at first bare upp for Hurst. The *Hoseander* plyed for St. Helens, but the leeward tyde came before she could get about; [so she] bare upp for Hurst to come out at the Needles, and came to us about 4 in the afternoone. But the *Salomon* anckored in Yarmouth roade (as Mr. Petty[4] toulde us), for what cause I knowe not. Some 16 or 20 saile of shippes came out at the Needells, and she only stayed behinde. All this night little winde.

22. At 7 in the morninge the winde came at E.N.E., a freshe gale. At 12 we were at the Starte; where I layed it by the lee, called a counsell, and in the time of consultation the *Salomon* came into our companie agayne. Blessed be God. At 6 at night the Start was N.E., some 8 legues of[f].

[1] On the Hampshire coast, to the west of Portsmouth harbour.

[2] Not Gabriel Towerson, of the Company's service, for he was in the East at this time. Probably Capt. William Towerson, of Portsmouth, who is mentioned in the *Cal. S.P. Dom.*, 1623–25 and 1625–26, as holding official positions at that port. See also Standish's reference, below.

[3] I.e. by way of Spithead, afterwards going round the south of the Isle of Wight. The other vessels passed out through the Solent (see John Davis's account of the voyage of the *James* (in *Purchas*, vol. 1, p. 440), and Standish's narrative, below).

[4] Richard Petty was master of the *Hosiander*. At the Cape he was transferred to the *Solomon*. After his return to England he was sent out again as master of the *Concord*, and died at Bantam in the autumn of 1614.

23. From 6 overnight to 12 this day[1] S.W. and S.W. by W.[2]; legues 37.

24. W. by S.; legues 36.

25. S.S.W.; legues 52.

26. S.S.W.; legues 56.

27. S. by W.; legues 25. Then our maine yarde broke, 12 foote from the tye short of it; then shewing to be a humlock tree[3], very drie and even rotten. At this tyme the wether very faire and the sea smooth; which sheweth the badnes of the tree, the want of care in Mr. Burrell and of honestie or skill in Chanlar[4].

28. S. and S. by E.; legues 32. This evening we came into the company of the *Hoseander* againe, and the [night ?] after lost her againe.

29. N. and N. by E.; legues 19.

Marche 1. S.; legues 12. At 9 at night, having fithed[5] our maine yarde and fitted all thinges to him, sett our maine saile againe.

2. S. by W.; legues 30.

3. S. by W. and S.; legues 29.

4. W.S.W.; legues 12.

5. S.W. by W.; legues 24.

6. W.S.W.; legues 24.

7. E.S.E.; legues 27.

8. E. by S.; legues 17.

9. E.S.E.; legues 23.

10. S.S.E.; legues 18.

[1] Being now fairly at sea, Best adopts the usual nautical practice of reckoning from midday to midday. Succeeding entries must accordingly be read as recording what happened between noon on the preceding day and noon on the one actually adduced in the log. This continues until land is again reached.

[2] The direction in which they were steering; the rest of the entry shows the number of leagues run.

[3] The North American hemlock fir or hemlock spruce (*Abies canadensis*).

[4] William Burrell, the great shipbuilder of the day, was entrusted with the building and repairing of the Company's ships. Edward Chandler was probably his foreman. He lived on Wapping Wall, and was a vestryman for Ratcliffe from 1616 onwards. He died in August 1634 (*Memorials of Stepney Parish*, p. 72 *n*).

[5] I.e. fished, or strengthened the yard by tying on to it a piece or pieces of wood.

11. S.S.W.; legues 17.

12. S.S.W.; legues 28.

13. S. by W.; legues 30. The ile Lanserotte[1] was from us S.W., 6 or 7 legues of[f].

14. On the south side of Forteventura[2]. At 8 at night we lost sight of the land.

15. S.W. by S.; legues 20.

16. S.W. by S.; legues 38.

17. S.W. by S.; legues 46. At 12 a clocke we were under the Tropique of Cancer.

18. S.W. by S.; legues 52. This day Robert Brandon died, being the purser his man.

19. S.W. by S.; legues 50[3].

20. S.W. by S.; legues 55.

21. S.W. by S.; legues 20. At a 11 at night we lay of[f] to the eastward, and at 3 in the morning we stood W. by S. At 10 we sawe the land Bonavista, bearinge from us N., distant some 5 or 6 legues of[f].

22. At noone latitude observed, 15° 20′. At 2 in the afternoone faire aboarde Mayo. Note that Bonavista and Mayo[4] lye S.W. by S., distant some 12 legues. Note, the N.N.W. and N. parte of Mayo is all fowle grounde; and due N. from the high humockes there lyeth a greate ledge of rockes, from the land some 5 or 6 myles of[f]; and a myle without the rockes you shall have 20 fathome water. On the W. side of the iland you may borrowe [i.e. approach] in 12 or 15 fathome till you come into the roade; where we anckored about 8 a clocke at night in 24 fathome.

23. At night the *Hoseander* came into the roade unto us.

24. At 10 at night we came from Mayo with all our shippes.

25. At noone Mayo was N.N. West, some 15 legues of[f].

26. S.S.E. ½ S.; legues 33. Latitude observed, 12° 50′. Longitude from Mayo, 1° 34′ east.

27. S.S.E.; legues 36. Longitude from Mayo, 2° 15′ east.

28. S.S.E.; legues 38. Latitude observed, 9° 40′. Here the

[1] Lanzarote, one of the Canary Islands.
[2] Another island of the group, lying south-west of Lanzarote.
[3] 'Anthony Clements died' (marginal note).
[4] Boavista and Maio are two of the Cape Verde Islands.

shippe was halfe a degree before me[1]; which was by some current setting to the southward, or rather to the S.E., as I take it.

29. S.S.E.; legues 28. The sunne neare our zeneth. Longitude from Mayo, 3° 30′ east.

30. S.S.E.; legues 40. Longitude from Mayo, 4° 15′ east.

31. S.E. by S.; legues 22. Longitude from Mayo, 4° 52′ east.

Aprill 1. S.E. by S.; legues 18. Longitude from Mayo, 5° 22′ east.

2. S.E. by S.; legues 14. Latitude observed, 4°. Longitude from Mayo, 5° 46′ east[2].

3. S.E. by S.; legues 18. Longitude from Mayo, 6° 16′ east[3].

4. S.E. by S. ½ S.; legues 27. Latitude observed, 1° 40′. Much raine. Longitude from Mayo, 7° 2′ east.

5. S.; legues 8. Calme, with rayne.

6. S. by E.; legues 12. Calme, with raine. Longitude from Mayo, 7° 7′ east.

7. S.W.; legues 6. Calme, with raine. Longitude from Mayo, 6° 56′ east.

8. S.W.; legues 4. Calme. Longitude from Mayo, 6° 48′ east.

9. S.; legues 7. Calme, with raine. This morninge we sawe two saile, a shippe and her pynnace.

10. S.; legues 9. Note that untill this day we have had northerly and easterly windes (calmes excepted) ever since our comminge from Mayo. This day the winde all westerly.

11. S. by W.; legues 16. Latitude observed, 20′ S. Calme. The equinoctiall our zenith.

12. S.S.W.; legues 16. The winde at E. by S., with raine. Longitude from Mayo, 6° 13′ east.

13. S. ½ W.; legues 18. Raine in the night. Longitude from Mayo, 6° 8′ east.

14. S. by W.; legues 18. The winde at E.S.E., with raine. Longitude from Mayo, 5° 57′ east.

15. S., legues 20. The winde at E., with raine.

[1] Meaning that there was this discrepancy between the ship's position, as determined by observation, and that calculated by dead reckoning.

[2] 'Variation, 3° 40′' (marginal note).

[3] 'Variation, 3° 45′' (marginal note).

16. S. by W.; legues 30. Latitude observed, 6° 10′. Winde at E. by S. Longitude from Mayo, 5° 40′ east.

17. S.S.W. ½ W.; legues 36. Latitude observed, 7° 45 Winde at E. by S. Longitude from Mayo, 4° east[1].

18. S. by W.; legues 36. The winde at E. and E. by S. Longitude from Mayo, 4° 29′ east.

19. S.S.W.; legues 34. Latitude observed, 11° 00′. Winde at E. by S. Longitude from Mayo, 3° 51′ east.

20. S. by W. ½ W.; legues 34. Latitude observed, 12° 40′. Winde at E. Longitude from Mayo, 3° 22′ E.[2]

21. S. by W.; legues 28. Latitude observed, 13° 55′. Winde at east. Longitude from Mayo, 3° 6′ east[3].

22. S. by W.; legues 27. Latitude observed, 15° 14′. The winde E. by S. Longitude from Mayo, 2° 44′ E.[4]

23. S. by W. ½ W.; legues 24. Latitude observed, 16° 27′. Longitude from Mayo, 2° 24′ E. The winde E. by S.[5]

24. S.S.W.; legues 18. Latitude observed, 17° 15′. Longitude from Mayo, 2° 05′ E. The winde E. by S.[6]

25. S.W. by S.; legues 16. Latitude observed, 18° 00′. Longitude from Mayo, 1° 37′ E. The wind E.S.E.[7]

26. S.S.W.; legues 17. Longitude from Mayo, 1° 18′. The winde E.

27. S.; legues 28. Latitude observed, 19° 30′. Longitude from Mayo, 1° 18′ E.[8] The winde E. by N. This day we sawe an iland[9]. The 28 in the morninge came close by it. The latitude of it 20° 30′, and longitude from the meridian of Mayo 1° 50′ east. We did not land upon it, but came within 2 or 3 miles of it. I take it there is hardly anckoringe to be founde. There may be

[1] 'Edward Vincent died' (marginal note).

[2] 'We sawe a saile' (marginal note).

[3] 'Morning variation, 10° 20′; evening variation, 10° 30′' (marginal note).

[4] 'Variation, 11° 13′' (marginal note).

[5] 'Morning variation, 11° 49′; evening variation, 12° 10′' (marginal note).

[6] 'Morning variation, 12° 15′; evening variation, 12° 20′' (marginal note).

[7] 'Morning variation, 12° 39′; evening variation, 12° 45′' (marginal note).

[8] 'Variation, 13° 35′' (marginal note).

[9] 'Sawe the land; Triniodado, as I take it' (marginal note). It was the small island of Trinidad, which lies about 700 miles east of the coast of Brazil. Best is accurate as regards its latitude, but far out in its longitude, which is 29° 50′ west of Greenwich, while Maio is 23° 16′ W. He was correct in thinking that the anchorage was unsafe; while fresh water is an uncertain quantity.

some refreshinge on it. Wood there is, and there may be water, for on the souther parte of it there is a faire plaine plott, and it was very greene. We could not finde grounde, cominge within two or three miles of it. From this iland, E.N.E. some 7 or 8 legues, lyeth another iland[1]; and from the first iland, E. by S. or E.S.E., there lye two or three high white rockes, some 4 or 5 legues of[f]; but we came not neare neyther the second iland nor the rockes[2].

28. S.S.E.; legues 28. Latitude observed, 20° 30′. Longitude from Mayo, 1° 50′ E. The winde N.W.[3]

29. S.S.E. ½ S.; legues 28. Longitude from Mayo, 2° 13′ E. The winde N.W., with raine.

30. S.S.E.; legues 32. Latitude observed, 23° 40′. Longitude from Mayo, 2° 49′ E. The winde N.W.[4]

Maye 1. S.E. by S.; legues 29. Latitude observed, 24° 50′. Longitude from Mayo, 3° 38′ E. The winde west[5].

2. E.S.E.; legues 29. Longitude from Mayo, 4° 58′ E. The winde S.E.[6]

3. S.W.; legues 8. Longitude from Mayo, 4° 39′ E. The winde S.E.

4. S.E. by S.; legues 6. Latitude observed, 25° 26′. Longitude from Mayo, 4° 49′ E. The winde S.W.

[1] The largest of the Martin Vas Rocks, lying to the east of Trinidad.

[2] 'The seven and twentieth of Aprill, we in [the] *Salomon* descried an iland in the south latitude of nineteene degrees, foure and thirty minutes; and it bare from us south-east, one third part southerly, fifteene leagues off. This ile is a place which in my opinion yeeldeth water and fish in great abundance. The sea-fowle were so many that our people in the galleries of our ship might strike them downe, they were so tame. To the eastward of this ile lye two ilands more; the one about the bignesse of the first, the other a great ile. By these iles we found a current, which setteth to the northward.' (Ralph Wilson, in *Purchas*, vol. 1, p. 486.)

'Here we saw an iland, south-east from us fourteene leagues. This iland I saw when I was with Sir Edward Michelborne. This iland is like Corvo [one of the Azores]. The latitude is twenty degrees, thirty minutes; the longitude eleven degrees, thirty minutes west from the Lizard; the variation of the needle foureteene degrees, thirty minutes. This iland riseth ragged. Upon the easter end standeth a little pike, but the iland is round, like Corvo. East-north-east from this iland is another iland or two in sight, seven or eight leagues off.' (Davis's journal, in *Purchas*, vol. 1, p. 440.)

[3] 'Morning variation, 13° 16'' (marginal note).

[4] 'Evening variation, 14° 52'' (marginal note).

[5] 'Evening variation, 15° 27'' (marginal note).

[6] 'Evening variation, 15° 22'' (marginal note).

5. E.; legues 5. Latitude observed, 25° 40′. Longitude from Mayo, 5° 4′ E.[1]

6. S.E. by E.; legues 16. Latitude observed, 26° 20′. Longitude from Mayo, 5° 44′ E. The winde N.E.[2]

7. S.E. by S.; legues 29. Latitude observed, 27° 30′. Longitude from Mayo, 6° 33′ E. The winde N.W.

8. E.S.E. ½ S.; legues 27. Longitude from Mayo, 7° 45′ E. The winde S.W.

9. E.S.E. ½ S.; legues 32. Latitude observed, 28° 30′. Longitude from Mayo, 9° E. The winde S.S.W.

10. E.S.E.; legues 12. Longitude from Mayo, 9° 44′ E. The winde S.S.W.

11. E.; legues 6. Longitude from Mayo, 10° 2′ E. The winde N.N.W., and calme[3].

12. E.S.E.; legues 44. Latitude observed, 30°. Longitude from Mayo, 12° 5′ E. The winde N.W.

13. E.S.E.; legues 32. Latitude observed, 30° 40′. Longitude from Mayo, 13° 34′ E. The winde N.W. and S.S.W., with raine[4].

14. E.S.E.; legues 28. Latitude observed, 31° 10′. Longitude from Mayo, 14° 52′ E. The winde S.W.[5]

15. E.N.E.; legues 13. Longitude from Mayo, 15° 28′ E. The winde S.E.[6]

16. S.W.; legues 18. Latitude observed, 31° 38′. Longitude from Mayo, 14° 50′ E. The winde S.E.

17. S.S.W.; legues 16. Latitude observed, 32° 23′. Longitude from Mayo, 14° 33′ E. The winde E.S.E.[7]

18. S. by W.; legues 8. Latitude observed, 32° 45′. Longitude from Mayo, 14° 24′ E. The winde at E.; calme[8].

19. S.E. by S.; legues 10. Latitude observed, 33° 20′. Longitude from Mayo, 14° 40′ E. The winde N.E.

[1] 'Morning variation, 15° 52'' (marginal note).

[2] 'Morning variation, 16° 04'' (marginal note).

[3] 'William Goodmann died' (marginal note).

[4] 'Evening variation, 14° 55'' (marginal note).

[5] 'Morning variation, 13° 45'' (marginal note).

[6] 'Evening variation, 14° 49′. William Crondall died' (marginal note).

[7] 'Morning variation, 15° 33'' (marginal note).

[8] 'Ralphe Cooke died. Morning variation, 15° 27′.' (Marginal notes.)

20. E. ½ S.; legues 30. Latitude observed, 00° 00'[1]. Longitude from Mayo, 16° 10' E. The winde a[t] N.

21. E. ¼ South; legues 44. Longitude from Mayo, 18° 22' E. The winde N.N.W.

22. E. ¼ S.; legues 52. Longitude from Mayo, 20° 58' E. The winde N.W. This morning at 7 our maine yarde broke againe at the tyes, yet strengthned there with 4 or 5 fiches; the wood a humlocke, so rotten as could not be more—a greate faulte in Mr. Burrell, and not lesse in Edward Chanler.

23. E. ¼ S.; legues 16. Latitude observed, 34° 50'. Longitude from Mayo, 21° 46' E. The winde at W.[2]

24. E. ¼ N.; legues 16. Longitude from Mayo, 22° 30' E. The winde at West[3].

25. E. ½ N.; legues 20. Latitude observed, 34° 36'. Longitude from Mayo, 23° 30' E. The winde at N.W.[4]

26. E. ¼ N.; legues 44. Latitude observed, 34° 20'. Longitude from Mayo, 25° 42' E. The winde at N.W. and W.[5]

27. E. by N.; legues 30. Longitude from Mayo, 27° 11' E. The winde at S.S.E.

28. E.; legues 16. Latitude observed, 34° 10'. Longitude from Mayo, 28° 00' E. The winde at N.N.E.[6]

29. E.; legues 45. Longitude from Mayo, 30° 15' E. The winde at N.W. by N. This day we crost our mayne yarde agayne.

30. E.; legues 52. Latitude observed, 34° 25'. Longitude from Mayo, 32° 50' E. The winde at W.S.W. and S.W.

31. E. ½ N.; legues 55. Latitude observed, 34° 00'. Longitude from Mayo, 35° 35' E. The winde at W.S.W.

June 1. E.; legues 55. Longitude from Mayo, 38° 20'. The winde at W.S.W. At 10 before noone with fowle wether we layed it a trye[7] (winde as before) to the southwarde.. At one after noone sett saile agayne. Tried it (?) S., legues 2½.

2. E.; legues 40. Latitude observed, 34° 15'. Longitude from Mayo, 40° 20' E. The winde W.S.W.

[1] Presumably the observation was a failure.
[2] 'William Mann died' (marginal note).
[3] 'Morning variation, 11° 30'; evening variation, 11° 22'' (marginal note).
[4] 'Morning variation, 11° 15'. Symon Limbre died.' (Marginal notes.)
[5] 'Morning variation, 9° 10'' (marginal note).
[6] 'Morning variation, 7° 50'. John Branson died.' (Marginal notes.)
[7] Lay to, under shortened sail.

3. E.; legues 37. Longitude from Mayo, 42° 10′. The winde at West. From 12 to 6 in the afternoone, 10 legues E.

4. From 6 [on the 3rd] to 6 the 4th in the morninge[1], N.E.; 8 legues. From 6 to 9 in the forenoone E. by N.; legues 5. Then at 9 a clocke sawe the land, some 3 or 4 miles from us, N.N.E. and N.E., but coulde not make it; the weather foule and very thicke, with fogge and raine. At 10 laide it about and stood of[f], the winde at N.N.W. Falling thus with the land, latitude per judgement 33° 45′ or 50′, and longitude from Mayo, in my weake judgement, arethmeticall 43° 00′, but by my accompt or reckoninge upon my platt [i.e. chart], 41° 00′; which later [i.e. latter] per the platt agreeth with Mr. John Davis[2], who writeth the Cape land to be 28 degrees in longitude from the meridian of the Lizard, and the Lyzard to be 13° in longitude to the eastward of Mayo.

The storme continuinge, at night layed it a trye with a maine course [i.e. main-sail]. This night the *James* and we lost the company of the *Hoseander* and *Salomon*.

5. At 8 in the morning Mr. Davis bore up, the winde at W.N.W., and steared S.E. and S.E. by E. some 3 or 4 legues,

[1] Being now in sight of land, the log changes back to the natural day and does not resume the noon-to-noon reckoning until the fleet leaves the Cape.

[2] John Davis of Limehouse, the master of the *James* in the present expedition. He had previously taken part in four voyages to the East, viz. Lancaster's (1601–3), Michelborne's (1604–6), and David Middleton's two voyages in the *Consent* (1607–9) and *Expedition* (1609–11), and was thus the most experienced navigator in the Company's service. From an entry on a later page we learn that the master of the *Hosiander* had for his guidance a copy of one or more of Davis's journals, and doubtless Best was similarly provided. Later, Davis embodied his experiences in the well-known *Ruter* (sailing directions) printed by Purchas in his *Pilgrimes* (vol. I, p. 444); and my conjecture (*Athenaeum*, 4 June 1892) that this document was compiled between August 1615 (when its author returned from the present voyage) and the spring of 1616 (when he started on a fresh expedition) is supported, not only by Purchas's statement that it was based upon the experience of five voyages, but also by the fact that a manuscript copy, practically identical with Purchas's text, is found in I.O. *Marine Records*, no. XVIII, associated with documents of 1616–17 and earlier.

In the *Ruter* Davis says that Table Bay is 28° east of the Lizard, and that Sal (one of the Cape Verde group) is 12° 12′ from the Lizard. Both figures are wrong. Cape Town is 18° 25′ east of Greenwich, and consequently 23° 37′ east of the Lizard; while the Cape Verde Islands are about 18° west of that headland.

and we followed him; with which course put ourselves to leeward of Saldania[1], att one of the clocke havinge made the land, the Table, the Sugarloafe Hill[2], etc.; the Sugarloafe Hill bearing of[f] us N.E. by N., the Table halfe a point more easterly. We then kept our loofe[3], but to[o] late. At 3 laide it of[f] againe. The winde increased at N.W., and proved a greate storme. At 9 Mr. Davis tooke in his foresaile, but we continued both courses all night for the ease of our shippe, for she made very fowle wether the night before, like to roule our mastes overboarde. And so lost also the *James*[4]; ourselves nowe alone.

6. At 4 in the morninge laide it about to the northwarde; the winde at W. by N. At 8 in the morning stood of[f] agayne; being not above 4 legues from the land, seeing both the Cape of Good Hope, the Table, and the Sugarloafe Hill.

7. The winde at S.W. Came and lay of[f] and on of the bay of Saldania.

8. In the morning came into Saldania. Here we founde the *Salomon* and *Hoseander*. Both of them came in the 5th ditto.

11. In the morning Edward Collett died.

18. Thomas Elmes died.

22. This day I called a counsell for reformation of discord and dissention aborde the *Hoseander*, betweene the master and cape marchant (Paul Canninge). In fine [i.e. the end], finding their malice eache to other inveterable, we ordered to remove the master (albeit the greatest faulte was founde in the marchant) and to make him master in the *Salomon*, and the master (Nathaniell Salmon) of the *Salomon* master in the *Hozeander*.

23. This day we removed Mr. Salmon from being master in the *Salomon*, and made him master in the *Hozeander*, and Mr. Petty from the *Hozeander* to be master in the *Salomon*.

[1] Table Bay.

[2] Now known as the Lion's Head. It lies to the north-west of Cape Town, and is one of the spurs of Table Mountain (see the drawing in *The Travels of Peter Mundy*, vol. II, p. 326).

[3] Kept close to the wind.

[4] The *James*, failing to get into Table Bay, went on to St Augustine's Bay, in Madagascar. Sailing again in the middle of July, she called at Priaman in September, and reached Bantam on 23 October 1612. She returned to England in August 1615. (See John Davis's journal in *Purchas His Pilgrimes*, vol. I, p. 440.)

26. The Indian[1] died. I warped of[f] into 8 fathome, and in the afternoone the *Hoseander* came to us. The *Salomon* not stirringe, nor at worke to remove, I went aboarde of her, and founde neyther master nor marchant aboard. I sett both her toppmastes and croste both her yardes, and sent the *Hozeanders* long boate ashore to Mr. Warde[2] and Petty to hasten them away. At night they came aboarde. Having reproved them both for neglect in their busines, [I] comanded Mr. Petty to be readie in the morninge to come of[f] (which he promised) and I would send him helpe.

28. In the morning very timely I sent my pynnace and the *Hozeanders* long boate to towe the *Salomon* of[f]. When the boates came to her, both master and company [were] in bedd. In fine, at 10 or 11 a clocke they weyed and came a little way of[f], and then againe anckored. At 1 afternoone the winde came to the N.N.E., with some rayne. I presently weyed, and the *Hoseander*. Mr. Petty and Mr. Warde aboarde of me; I hastened them away. We were about the point before she sett saile. In fine she did sett saile, but coulde not weather the point. They layed it about, and we came to sea at night. A fresh winde at N. and N.N.W. We bore little saile all night, in hope to have seene her the next morninge, but coulde not. Greate fault in Mr. Petty; but it is his common faulte to dreame and to forslowe tyme.

Thus the 28 came to sea, having stayed in Saldania 21 dayes, and bought for the three shippes 39 beeves [i.e. oxen] and 115 sheepe with a little brasse which we cut out of two or three oulde kettles. The sheepe we bought for smalle peeces of thynne brasse, worthe some peny or three halfpence apeece; the beifes with the brasse cut of[f] kettles, to the valewe of 12*d.* for a beife. It is a place of greate refreshinge; for, besides your beefe and mutton, there is greate plenty of good fishe, and fowle of many sorts, greate store of fatt deare (but we could kill none), very excellent rivers of freshe water, and a helthfull and good aire.

[1] Probably an Asiatic sailor who had been brought to England in one of the earlier voyages and was now returning. It was often found necessary to fill up gaps in the crew by engaging natives, and these were repatriated at the first opportunity.

[2] Robert Ward, the chief merchant of the *Solomon*. He died 28 January 1613, just after the vessel had left Bantam for England.

I landed 80 or 90 sicke men, and lodged them in tents 18 dayes; and they all recovered their healthes (only one that died).

This bay of Saldania is a safe roade. Your small shippes to ride in 5 fathom. With the *Dragon* I roade in 6 fathome. Penguine Iland[1] N.N.W., the west pointe W.N.W., some 2 myle of[f]. The Sugarloafe S.W. by W. The Table S.S.W. The N. land you shall see N. by W. or N. from you.

Outward bounde, be carefull of your lattitude, and feare not to come in with the land in 34° 10′ or 34° 20′. And this lattitude will bring you with a faire headland[2] which lyeth S.W. from the west point of the bay of Saldania some 4 legues; and betweene the headland and the point (which is very lowe land) you shall see the Table and Sugarloafe. This S.W. point and the lowe land of the roade lyeth N.E. and S.W.; and from this S.W. point to the Cape of Good Hope the land lyeth S.S.E., distant some 9 leagues. This S.W. point and the Sugarloafe lye nearest N.E. and S.W. And being here of[f] this land to the southwarde of the bay of Saldania, the Sugarloafe wilbe to the northward of the Table. In going in or out, leave the iland to the northwarde of you, and come not neare him; for there is much fowle grounde by him, especially on the S.W. side of him. Neyther may you borrowe within 3 or 4 mile of the maine, for there is much fowle ground; but keepe as neare as you can the middest betweene the mayne and the island. The lattitude of the bay is 34 degrees[3]; variation some 30 or 40 minutes. Your variation is a sure rule to knowe when you come within some faire distance of the shoare; for if you be 40 legues of[f], you shall have one degree 40′ or neare thereaboutes; and so proportion your distance by your variation, allowing 30 legues to a degree of variation (I meane 30 legues east).

29. At midnight the Cape of Good Hope was N.N.E., of[f] some 4 or 5 legues. Winde at N.N.W. At 12 at noone Cape de Augulias[4] was N.E., distant some 4 or 5 legues. Winde at W. The distance betweene the Cape of Good Hope and Cape de Augulies is some 25 or 26 leagues, and lyeth E.S.E. and W.N.W. A faire boulde coaste, free of danger, faire shouldinge (as they write that have had experience).

[1] Robben Island.

[2] Apparently Duyker Point.

[3] Really 33° 56′ S.

[4] Cape Agulhas

Note that from the 7th of June till the day of our departure from Saldania (it being the 28 of June) we had nothing but faire weather, the sunne very warme, and the aire very sweet and helthfull, etc.

30. E.; legues 44. Latitude observed, 35° 00′, and longitude from the Cape of Good Hope, 3° 25′. The winde at West.

July 1. E.; legues 26. Latitude observed, 34° 56′, and longitude from the Cape of Good Hope, 4° 43′ E. The winde at West; calme.

2. E. by S.; legues 15. Latitude observed, 35°, and longitude from the Cape, 5° 27′. Calme half the 24 howres; the rest the winde at West[1].

3. E.; legues 25. And longitude from the Cape, 6° 42′. Calme half the 24 houres. The winde at W.S.W.

4. N.N.E.; legues 9 upon a right lyne. Latitude observed, 35° 12′; longitude from the Cape, 6° 53′ E. The winde from the S.E. to E.N.E., and partly calme, with some raine. The 3rd day we could not take the sunne. Nowe havinge observed, I finde that theis 2 dayes we have bene in a greate current that hath set us to the southward, S.S.W. or neare thereabouts. Note that we were 100 legues E. from Cape de Augulias before we founde any current, and then founde it stronge.

5. N.; legues 9 upon a right lyne. Latitude, 34° 37′, and longitude from the Cape 6° 53′ E. Winde at E. and calme. Againe out of the current, we being to the northward of it and not above 5 legues from the land. High hummockes here. We sounded, and had 63 fadome, black sand. From Cape de Augulias to this place, in sight of the land (6 or 7 legues of[f]), we sounded at tymes, and had 70, 65, and 60 fadome, blacke, osye [i.e. oozy] grounde. So that on this coaste there is no danger. Keeping your leade, you may be boulde to 60 or 70 fathome, having the winde to hale of[f] agayne; and by your depth you shall knowe when you are shott to the westwarde of the Cape of Good Hope, for presently it will be deepe water and you shall have no grounde[2].

6. E.; legues 7; and longitude from the Cape, 7° 14′ E. Here

[1] 'Morning variation, 4° 15'' (marginal note).
[2] 'Morning variation, 4° 40'' (marginal note).

we lay becalmed, and by the current much hindred and cast to the westward. At this time some 6 legues from the land, a faire, lowe land by the water side and in the countrey very high mountaines and hilles. The winde at West[1].

7. E.; legues 23. Latitude observed, 34° 37′, and longitude from the Cape, 8° 23′ E. The winde at West. From Cape de Augulias to this day we have founde the lande to lye E. ½ N., and from this place it falleth away N.E. by E. and N.E. A very faire, lowe land, and as goodly a coaste as may be seene. This headland, where the land falleth away N.E. or nere thereaboute, and 10 or 12 legues of[f] but 65 fadome, hath in lattitude 34° and is from Cape de Augulias 130 or 140 leagues E. ½ N. And keepinge within 8 and 10 legues of the land we founde ourselves within the current; and being 20 legues of[f], we founde a stronge current[2].

8. S.E.; legues 4. Latitude observed, 34° 47′, and longitude from the Cape, 8° 31′ E. Calme 18 houres, the winde at N.E. Yet we finde smalle current, being of[f] the land 14 or 16 leagues[3].

9. S.E. ½ S.; legues 28. But being here in the current, I finde she hath made her waie S. by E. Latitude observed, 36° 10′, and longitude from the Cape of Good Hope, 8° 46′ E. The winde at N.E. by E., a freshe gale.

10. S.E. by E.; legues 27. Latitude observed, 37° 00′, and longitude from the Cape, 9° 53′ E. Here we still finde a small current, which still casteth us to the southward. The winde at N. by E. and N.N.E., a freshe gale.

11. E.N.E. ½ N.; legues 21. Latitude observed, 36° 36′, and longitude from the Cape, 10° 47′ E. Here we finde ourselves out of the current. The winde at N. and N.N.W., a faire gale. Calme 4 houres before noone[4].

12. E. by N. ½ N.; legues 24. Latitude observed, 36° 15′, and longitude from the Cape, 11° 56′ E. Much winde at N.N.W. and N. by W. Here no current. Note that full five weekes we have had very faire wether: 20 daies in the Bay of Saldania, and

[1] 'Evening variation, 5° 00'' (marginal note).
[2] 'Evening variation, 5° 40'' (marginal note).
[3] 'Evening variation, 5° 50'' (marginal note).
[4] 'Morning variation, 8° 10'' (marginal note).

nowe 14 since we came from thence. We finde ourselves out of the current[1].

13. E.; till 4 in the morning, legues 16. Then did 3 or 4 of our fiches of our maine maste breake. Then layed it by the lee. At 6 filde[2] our shippe againe. At 8 all the fiches breake, only one. Then bore upp before the winde, tooke in the maine saile, tooke downe the maine topmaste on the hatches; which done, kept our loofe with foresaile and missen. From 4 to 12 I allowe 6 legues, S.E. by E. The winde at N. and N. by W., a stiffe gale. And longitude from the Cape of Good Hope, 12° 46′ E.

14. N.E. by E.; legues 17 upon a right lyne. Latitude observed, 35° 50′, and longitude from the Cape, 13° 25′ E. At 2 in the morning the winde came at W.S.W., and after at S.W.[3]

15. N.N.E.; legues 7. Latitude, 35° 30′, and longitude from the Cape, 13° 33′ E. From 12 to 6 the winde at S.W. and southerly; the rest calme. This day I called a counsell to determine whether to keepe our olde maine yarde, or to make a newe of our two maine topmastes. To this meetinge I called both masters, all their mates, the cape merchants, the master carpenters and their mates, the boatson and his mates, the gonner and his mates, the 4 quartermasters and all their mates. All which assembled, after much dispute and many objections, it was concluded for the better to make a newe yarde, and with the oulde to fiche our maine maste; which concluded, was presently in action.

16. N.E. by N. Latitude observed, 35° 00′, and longitude from the Cape of Good Hope, 13° 53′ E. The winde S.S.E. 10 houres; the rest calme.

17. N.E. by N.; legues 38. Latitude observed, 33° 27′, and longitude from the Cape, 14° 56′ E. The winde at S.S.W., a fresh gale.

18. N.E. by N.; legues 40. Latitude observed, 31° 40′, and longitude from the Cape, 16° 02′ E. The winde at S. and S.S.E. Faire weather.

[1] 'Morning variation, 9° 20'' (marginal note).

[2] I.e. braced the yards so that the wind filled the sails and set the ship in motion.

[3] 'Evening variation, 11° 00'' (marginal note).

19. N.N.E. ½ E.; legues 36. Latitude observed, 30° 05′, and longitude from the Cape, 16° 52′ E. The winde at S.E., a faire gale. This morninge Robert Worgins died.

20. N.N.E. ½ E.; legues 42. Latitude observed, 28° 10′, and longitude from the Cape, 17° 49′ E. The winde at S.S.E., a fresh gale, with faire wether.

21. N.N.E.; legues 43. Latitude observed, 26° 6′, and longitude from the Cape, 18° 38′ E. The winde at S.E., a stiffe gale.

22. N. by E.; legues 39. But we are here helpt some 4 or 5 legues with a current which setteth us to the northwarde. Latitude, 24° 15′, and longitude from the Cape, 19° 00′. The winde at S.E., a freshe gale.

23. N.E. by N.; legues 24. Latitude, 23° 15′, and longitude from the Cape, 19° 40′ E. The winde at S.E., calme all the morninge[1].

24. N.E.; legues 3. Latitude 23°, and longitude from the Cape, 20° E. The winde at S.E., calme half this 24 houres[2].

25. N.E. by N.; legues 8. Latitude observed, 22° 36′, and longitude from the Cape, 20° 13′ E. Winde at S.E., but calme, with very faire weather. We finde a little current to the northward, and so have had theis 06 dayes a sokinge [i.e. sucking] current putting us northerly 2 or 3 legues each 24 houres.

26. N.E.; legues 10. Latitude observed, 22° 13′, and longitude from the Cape, 21° 2′ E. Calme and very faire wether. The winde at S. and at E.N.E. This morning in sight of St. Lawrence [i.e. Madagascar][3]. Land bearing from us E.S.E. and S.E. by E. The ester land smoothe, of a faire heigth; the sother parte of it more high, with hills, and from us some 10 leagues. So that, by my judgement, as per my particuler daies wrighting appeareth, this land of St. Lawrence hath in longitude from the Cape of Good Hope neare about 21° 30′ E.

27. N. by E.; legues 16. Latitude observed, 21° 25′, and longitude from the Cape, 21° 12′. The winde at E. and N.E. Faire weather.

28. Upon a right lyne E.; legues 5. Latitude observed, 21° 26′,

[1] 'Evening variation, 13° 40′' (marginal note).
[2] 'Morning variation, 14° 24′' (marginal note).
[3] 'Variation here, 14° 30′' (marginal note).

and longitude from the Cape, 21° 27′. The winde at N.E. and E.N.E. Very faire wether.

29. N. by E.; legues 20. Latitude observed, 20° 28′, and longitude from the Cape, 21° 46′. The winde at S. and S.S.W.

30. This day in the morning we sawe two greate shippes, which in the afternoone came faire by us and saluted us with a peece; which we requited with the like, but spoke not with them[1]. N. by W.; legues 40. Latitude observed, 18° 30′, and longitude from the Cape, 21° 16′. Winde at S. and S.S.W.

31. N.N.W. (26 legues) and N. (8 legues). Latitude observed, 17° 8′, and longitude from the Cape of Good Hope, 20° 47′. The winde at S. Faire wether. At 4 in the afternoone we sawe the iland John de Nova[2], from us E.S.E., distant 4 legues. In bignes (so much as we sawe, and I thinke we sawe all of it), for length some 3 or 4 miles; very lowe, and riseth like rockes. Of[f] the west end of the iland (a mile or two from it) we sawe a breache, but we could not gett grounde with 130 fathome, soundinge with our pynnace or skiffe. The latitude of it is 17° 00′, very certenly observed, and in our judgements well laied in our plattes, both for latitude and longitude. It is a most sure signe of being neare this iland of John de Nova, if you finde or see greate store of fowle. From having the iland N.E. to S.E., we sawe much fowle; some white (their winges topped or pointed only with blacke) and some blacke fowle.

August 1. N.N.E.; legues 30. Latitude observed, 15° 41′; longitude from the Cape, 21° 22′. The winde at S. Very faire wether. This morning we sawe againe the two Spanish [*sic* Portuguese] shippes, as farr astarne as we could see them. We could not but judge that they came to the eastward of John de Nova; for when they were by us we were 28 or 30 legues short of the iland. Then did we steare N. and N. by W., and they steared (as long as we had sight of them) N.N.E., and till it was night we did see them. Not that I woulde incourage any to adventure by

[1] For a fuller account of this incident see Standish's narrative (given below). Best's reticence was doubtless deliberate.

[2] The small island known as Juan de Nova (so named after the Portuguese admiral who discovered it in 1501) lies in the middle of the Mozambique Channel, in lat. 17° 3′ S. and 75 miles west of Madagascar. For an account of it see Professor C. Keller's *Madagascar*, p. 164.

that way, there being as yet no knowledge certeyne of a channell on the east side of it; but very like it is that there is chanell inough, both for bredth and depth; the distance betweene the flattes of St. Lawrence and John de Nova being 20 leagues.

2. N.E. by N. $\frac{1}{4}$ N.; legues 26. Latitude observed, 14° 35′, and longitude from the Cape, 21° 58′. The winde at S. and S.S.E. Very faire wether.

3. N.E. by N. $\frac{1}{4}$ N.; legues 22. Latitude observed, 13° 35′, and longitude from the Cape, 22° 30′. The winde at S.S.E.; partly calme.

Noate that, in comminge this course from John de Nova, we have not mett with any currents; whereby it is evident that the current which runneth to the S.W. very strongly aboard the mayne, from the lattitude of 14° S., doth not runne in the offinge, namely [*illegible*][1] leagues from land.

At 4 in the afternoone we sawe land E.N.E. and N.E. by E., from us some 12 legues of[f], having on the easter parte of it a very faire sugerloafe hill. This ile is called Mal Ilha[2], and is one of the iles of Comora. Also at the same time we sawe the iland Comora, bearing of us N.N.W. and N. by W.; high land[3].

4. At 6 in the morning we were faire aboarde the S.S.E. end of Mal Ilha, and haling in with the land to have founde some place to anchor in, when we were some 8 or 9 mile from the shoare, we sawe the grounde under the shippe, but not lesse then 8 or 10 fathome water. The *Hozeander* being two miles within us, she findinge not lesse then 4 or 5; but her boate was in 3 fathome. Then we sent of[f] both our pynnaces, which kept shoaldinge on a bancke in 8 and 10 and 12 fadom, and being from the bancke halfe a cables length, no grounde in 100 fathome. At the north end of this Mal Ilha there is a faire bigge iland, high land, and may be some 4 or 6 miles about, and from this little iland to the maine land of Mal Ilha may be some 8 or 9 miles, full of rockes, two of them of good height. Nowe the bancke or ledge of rockes (for so it is) lyeth all along the west side of Mal Ilha, and con-

[1] Purchas supplies 'twenty.'

[2] Mohilla, one of the four islands of the Comoro group, the other three being Great Comoro (called by Best 'Comora'), Mayotta, and Johanna. For a description of them see Keller, *op. cit.*, p. 159.

[3] 'Evening variation, 15° 00′' (marginal note).

tinueth untill the little high iland before mentioned beare S.E. of you, and then it endeth. Here I had 16 fathome, faire white sand, fishinge grounde. And thus being at the N. end of this ledge, and the litle iland bearinge S.E., you may steare in with [the] land, keepinge the iland faire aboarde; and within the rockes or broken grounde and Mal Ilha you shall see a bay wherein there is good anckoringe. The Dutche shipping hath bene there, 6 or 8 saile of them together; that yeare they were here, when they assaulted Mozambique[1] (two of my men nowe in my shippe were then in the shippes). Nowe, to the eastward of you, as you come in from the bancke or ledge of rockes, you have likewise a greate shoald, and the offermost end of it lyeth from the litle iland N.E. or N.E. by E., but from the iland at least 5 or 6 miles, and no grownde betweene that we could finde in 40 or 50 fathom. In fine, all the north side of Mal Ilha is very dangerous; but the channell mentioned [is] without danger. For we stood in as farre as the litle iland, but, the winde being faire southerly, we could not leade it in; for I would have anchored in the bay, if I coulde have gott in. For a mile to the westward of the bay is a towne[2], the people good, and greate refreshinge, as beefe, goates, hennes, lemons, coker nuttes (of eyther greate store), and good water. The foresaide fleete of Fleminges in this place recovered the health of 4 or 500 men in 5 weekes. In those parts there is no place of greater refreshinge then this. Nowe the best way to come to this place is to come by the S.E. side of the iland, and not by the N. side (as I came). For if you come on the S.E. side of the iland, then you shall have a southerly winde. When you come at the easte end of the land, keepe the shoare aboarde, and come betweene Mal Ilha and the shoald which lyeth to the eastward of the little ilands [*sic*]; the distance some two or three mile, as I understand.

Thus spent tyme till 2 in the afternoone. Then steard away our course, when we sawe no hope to get into the roade. Our desires greate to have strengthened our maine maste in this place

[1] The reference is to the fleet commanded by Paulus van Caerden, which unsuccessfully attacked Mozambique in the spring of 1607. A visit was then paid to the Comoro Islands, to afford the many sick men in the fleet a chance of recovery (De Jonge's *Opkomst*, pt. III, p. 64).

[2] Apparently Fumbuni.

and to have crossed our newe mayne yarde; but it pleased not God (blessed be His name). All for the best, I doubt not.

This 24 houres our waie N.N.E.; legues 28. Longitude from the Cape of Good Hope, 23° 02′, which is the longitude of the iland Mal Ilha, and the lattitude of it is 12° 30′ (the sother parte of it in 12° 50′)[1]. This iland is well named Mal Ilha[2], for it is the most dangerous of any place that ever I sawe; yet a place of greate refreshinge, and plenty of all thinges, and the people good (as I saied before). This iland is the next to Comora, on the south-east side of Comora, and is distant some 12 or 14 legues.

5. N.N.E.; legues 22. Lattitude observed, 11° 20′, and longitude from the Cape, 23° 27′. The winde at S.

6. N.N.E.; legues 12, but with help of a current I finde she hath made 21 legues. I take it N.N.W.; but I will sett it downe N. So hould the same longitude with the last day (23° 27′). The winde at S. and S.S.W. Calme[3].

7. N.; legues 4, but with helpe of a current I finde she hath made 10 leagues. I take it N.N.W. or N.W., for soe it is thought the current doth here sett, cominge from the N. end of St. Lawrence. The winde at S. and S.S.E., but calme. Longitude as before (23° 27′)[4].

8. N. by E.; legues 16. Longitude from the Cape, 23° 37′. The winde at E.S.E. and S.E., with calme.

9. N.N.E.; legues 26. Lattitude observed, 27° 12′[5]; but I finde the shippe hath had a current, which in theis 2 dayes hath caried her 40 minutes more northerly; which setteth from the north end of St. Lawrence, and setteth us (as I take it) N.W. or

[1] A marginal note gives the variation as 15° 20′. The correct latitude is 12° 20′ S., and the longitude 43° 40′ E. Since the Cape of Good Hope is 18° 30′ E., Best was at least 2° out in his reckoning.

[2] Thomas Herbert, who was there in 1627, says: 'Moella some pronounce it; Molala others; and (worst of all) one Best (thinking the derivation would carry it) Mal-Ilha, or Bad Ile: an incongruity, that from his ill judgement so sweet and usefull a place should be defamed' (*Travels*, ed. 1638, p. 27). The suggested etymology was of course absurd.

[3] 'Varriation 15° 30′' (marginal note).

[4] 'Robert Ackeen broke his arme, fallinge from the foretopmast stay' (marginal note). The name is miscopied; the entry on 30 August shows that it was 'Atkins.'

[5] Obviously wrong (probably a slip on the part of the copyist).

N.N.W. The winde at S.E. I bring the shippe to our lattitude upon the meridian.

10. N.N.E. ½ E.; legues 39. Longitude from the Cape, 24° 32′ E. The winde at S.E. and S.S.E.

11. N.N.E.; legues 44. Lattitude, 3° 30′, and longitude from the Cape, 25° 22′ E. The winde at S.S.E. and S. No helpe of a current.

12. N.E. by N.; legues 46. Latitude observed, 1° 32′, and longitude from the Cape, 26° 37′. The winde at S. and S. by W. No current.

13. N.E. by N.; legues 36. Latitude observed, 7′ S., and longitude from the Cape, 27° 37′ E. The winde at S.S.W. and S.W. This day we crossed the Lyne, with very faire wether; and so we have had it still faire since we came from the lattitude of 37° 30′. Here we finde no current.

14. N.N.E. ½ E.; legues 33. Lattitude observed, 1° 20′, and longitude from the Cape, 28° 22′ E. The winde at S.W. by S. This day we killed 3 dolphins, the first we gott this voyage.

15. N.N.E. ½ E.; legues 20. Latitude observed, 2° 35′, and longitude from the Cape, 29° 04′ E. The winde at S.W. Yesternight and this morninge we sawe two carracks, which I take it were the same we sawe 15 dayes since[1].

16. N.E. ½ N.; legues 36. Lattitude observed, 3° 45′, and longitude from the Cape, 30° 12′. The winde at S.W. Faire weather[2].

17. N.E. ½ N.; legues 20. Lattitude observed, 4° 30′, and longitude from the Cape, 30° 50′ E. The winde at S.W., with faire wether[3].

18. N.E. by N.; legues 25. Lattitude observed, 5° 40′, and longitude from the Cape, 31° 33′ E. The winde at S.W.

19. N.N.E. ¼ E.; legues 32. Latitude observed, 7° 10′, and longitude from the Cape, 32° 17′ E. The winde at S.W.[4]

20. N.N.E., legues 9; and N.E. ½ E., legues 28. Longitude from the Cape, 33° 31′ E. The winde at S.W. and W.S.W. This day the sunne our zeneth[5].

[1] 'Varriation, 16° 30′' (marginal note).
[2] 'Varriation, 16° 55′' (marginal note).
[3] 'Varriation, 17° 20′' (marginal note).
[4] 'Variation, 18° 20′' (marginal note).
[5] 'Variation, 18° 30′' (marginal note).

21. N.E. ½ E.; legues 34. And longitude from the Cape, 34° 50′ E. The winde at W.S.W.[1]

22. N.E. ½ E.; legues 32. And longitude from the Cape, 36° 04′ E. The winde at W.S.W.

23. N.E. ½ E.; legues 39. And longitude from the Cape, 37° 34′ E. The winde at W.S.W.

24. N.E. ½ E.; legues 37. And longitude from the Cape, 39° 00′ E. The winde at W.S.W.

25. N.E. ½ E.; legues 34. Latitude observed, 13° 35′, and longitude from the Cape, 40° 20′ E. Wind at W.S.W.

26. N.E. ½ E.; legues 29. And longitude from the Cape, 41° 27′ E. The winde at W.S.W.

27. N.E. ½ E.; legues 36. And longitude from the Cape, 42° 50′ E. The winde at W.S.W., with gustes and raine, and this day began to blowe hard. And it is the first day of raine and much winde that we have had theis 6 weekes.

28. N.E.; legues 35. And longitude from the Cape, 44° 10′ E. The winde at west, a fresh gale, with gustes and raine this 24 howres. We bated [i.e. reduced] saile; there being no like[li]hood but of fowle weather.

29. N.E. ½ E.; legues 36. Lattitude observed, 18°, and longitude from the Cape, 45° 33′. Winde at west, a faire gale, with some gustes.

30. N.E. by E.; legues 36. Lattitude observed, 19°, and longitude from the Cape, 46° 54′. The winde at west, a faire gale, yet with some small gustes. This day we sawe some snakes swym by the shippes side[2].

31. N.E. by E.; legues 35. And longitude from the Cape, 48° 16′. Winde at west, with some small gustes. This morning at 7 we had grounde at 20 fathome, softe oaze. The same depth and oaze continued with us till 12 a clocke we steared E.N.E. Our way after, 5½ legues per watch. At 2 afternoone we had 16 fathom, it having shoalded in ½ howre some 2 or 3 foote. At 4 afternoone we had 14 fathome, and ½ an houre after but 10 fathom. Then we laied our shipp by the lee and shott a peece for our skiffe; and presently had 15 fathom, having steared from 12

[1] 'Variation, 19° 00'' (marginal note).

[2] 'Variation, 16° 20′. Atkins arme cut of[f].' (Marginal notes.)

to this tyme E.N.E. and made some 7 legues N.E. by E. northerly. The variation 16 degrees from N. to W. From 5 to 2 in the morning we steared E. some 11 legues, and came from the former 10 fathom to 22 fathom, and from 22 it shoalded againe to 14 fathom by 2 a clocke. The *Hozeander*, a mile or 2 aheade, at 2 shott of[f] a peece, finding 12 fathom; for so had I given direction that this night she should not come within 12 fathome, and, finding 12 or lesse, then to shoote of[f] a peece, and come to starrboard tacke; which shee did, and we also, and stood of[f] by the compasse S.W. till 5 in the morning; our depth from 14 to 10.

September 1. At the breakinge of the dawninge[1] we sawe the land, E. from us some 3 or 4 legues of[f]. The land by the waterside full of high trees, but very lowe land. We sawe foure faire high hills, lying each to the N. of other, neare joyninge eache to other[2]; and to the southward of theis 4 hills another hill, but lesse and lower then the other. And to the southward of theis hills, upp in the land, we sawe a very high mountaine[3], rising of a good length; and from the former hills to this mountaine lowe land, full of highe trees. At 7 in the morning we cast about to the northward, and lay N.N.E. and had 9 and 10 fathom. And when the hills were E. and E. by S., then the greate high mountaine was S.E. by E., and then we had 12 and 13 fathom, and Daman E. by N., 3 legues of[f]. Noate that Daman[4] is a faire towne, walled, havinge in it a faire high steeple [i.e. tower], the church whereof is called St. Paulo; also a faire castell and forte[5], both to the northward of St. Paul. The weather faire, it will

[1] As before, a change is made to the natural day on reaching land.

[2] Four hills of fair height—Indaghur, Pyramid Hill, and two others—form a line between Umbargaon and Daman.

[3] Either the high land of Sanjān or the peak of Gambirgarh (2270 feet), further inland.

[4] Daman, about a hundred miles north of Bombay, was then (as now) a Portuguese possession.

[5] The separate fort of San Hieronimo, on the northern side of the river. Herbert (*Travels*, p. 34) describes Daman as 'a lovely towne, lorded by the Portugalls, and conspicuous to passengers. At the north end it has a castle, large, strong, and daring. The materiall is good white, chalky stone; flanckt with ordnance and mounted high to play at advantage. At the south end we perceived a faire church, with white battlements atop; the houses of like stone, strong and beautifull; three other temples affoording joy and pleasure to the heart and eye.'

(both the walls of the towne and castell and the forte) shewe very white. To the southward of St. Paul is a high greate house, shewing like a longe barne, but is a cloyster. To this towne is a faire ryver[1], and they have diverse shippinge, such as this country yeildeth. And W.S.W. and W. of[f], you shall have 13 and 14 fathome, softe oaze. From Daman to Suratt is some 14 legues, and Gandifuy [Gandevi] neare midway betweene Suratt and Daman. The lattitude of Daman is 20° 30′ (for so I made it, observinge 8 or 10 myle west from it), and longitude as per margent[2].

From 7 to 12 a clocke, N. by E., 5 legues. Lattitude observed, 20° 30′. Our depth nowe 10 and 9 and ½ fathome, 3 or 2(?) and ½ legues from land. The former 4 or 5 hills S.E. and S.E. by S.; and a faire high towre (which our 3(?) Indians say is the church of Daman called St. Paul) is E.S.E. from us. And to the north-eastward of this towre some 6 or 8 miles is a faire high land; and the towre bearing S.E. by E., the saide high land did beare E. by S. The winde at W.N.W., we steared alongest the land by our compasse N.E. by N.; for so it lyeth nearest here. Some 3 legues from land, 9½ and 10 fathom, oaze.

From 12 at noone to 3 afternoone, some five leagues N.E. by N.; for we had the tyde of floud, which caried us in a greate pace. Our depth from 9 to 6 fathom. And then anchored at 3 a clocke, in 6 fathom, softe oaze; and at lowe water had 3 fathom ½.

2. At 3 in the morning weyed at high water and stood to the southwarde; and anchored agayne at 7, in 9 fathom at high water and at lowe water had 6 and ½. The church of Daman bearing S.S.E., and we from the land some 7 or 8 miles.

I called a councell, and concluded to send the *Hoseander*

[1] The Damanganga.

[2] 'Daman hath latitude N. 20° 30′, and longitude from the Cape of Good Hope 53° E. When we saw the land, I was short of my reckoninge 80 or 90 legues; which I judge to proceed of some currant from the coast of Melinde seting to the eastward. Neither from the latitude of Socatora to Daman could wee se the sun, to know that variation. But presuminge the shipp hath not overrune me the said 80 or 90 legues, do therfore allowe 3° for the same. So in my best judgment do conclude Daman, as aforsaid, to have longitude 53° E from the Cape Bonis Spei; but if not carried by a currant, then only 50°.' (Marginal insertion in another hand.)

Daman is really 54° 25′ east of the Cape of Good Hope, and its latitude is 20° 25′ N.

away toward Suratt to gett me a pylott and to finde the channell; and also to send Mr. Aldworth in her, with my master[1] and 15 men with armes for her better defence, yf shee mett with the frigetts of the Spaniards[2]. And if she went to the barre of Suratt and there by intelligence understood our factorie setled and all well, the river cleare of men of warre, then Mr. Aldworthe to goe to the towne, with Thomas Kerridge, William Nicholls, Thomas Davis, John Younge[3], and one Indian. At one in the afternoone she sett saile and departed.

3. At 7 in the morning we comaunded 2 boates of the country, by shootinge 4 peeces to them, to come aboarde of us. And they tould us that the towre or church and castell and towne which wee sawe (and nowe did beare of[f] us S.E. by S.) was the towne of Daman. So it hath pleased God, of His greate mercy, to blesse us with a faire passage from England to this place Daman (which is some 14 legues from the barr of Suratt) in 6 moneths and 7 dayes; of which tyme I spent 4[4] dayes at the ile of Mayo and 20 dayes in the bay of Saldania. God make me truly thankfull to Him for it. Out of theis two boats I tooke two men, which undertooke to cary the *Dragon* to the barre of Suratt, with promise that they would not bring me into lesse then 7 fathom water. For their service [they] would not demand ought, but referred themselves to me. I would willingly have had one of their boates to have gone before the shippe, offering them any content; but in no wise they would not. I presented the men every one with a 3*d*. knife; with which they departed, with all content.

4. At 6 in the morning sett saile with the first of an ebb, and checke[5] the tyde; for we lay N. by W., and the ebb setts S.W.

[1] Robert Bonner.

[2] He means 'Portuguese.' Since both nations were at this time under one king, Best does not trouble to discriminate between them.

[3] Kerridge was later to rise to the post of President at Surat. Nichols was purser's mate in the *Dragon*, and was subsequently made a factor. He had previously been a mariner in the *Ascension*, and upon the wreck of that vessel travelled overland from Surat to Masulipatam (see his narrative in *Purchas*, vol. I, p. 232). Davis was the carpenter of the *Hosiander*. Young appears to have gone out as personal attendant on Aldworth, but was afterwards taken into the service of the Company as a merchant.

[4] This does not agree with the statements on p. 4, which make the stay two days only.

[5] Possibly for 'chocke' i.e. 'close up to,' meaning that they took the fullest advantage of the tide.

and by S., and the floud here where we are setts N.E. by N. And so fett [i.e. fetched] of[f] some 10 or 12 miles, not lesse then 6½ and 7 fathom water. And when the northermost [of the ?] hills bare E., then had we 7 fathom; and it bearing E. ½ S., 6 fathom; and it being [*sic*] E. by S. ½ [S.?], 5½ fathom, being then from the land 10 or 12 mile. And the same high hill E. by S. ¼ S., we had 6 fathom, and presently 6½ and 7 fathom. The hill bearing E.S.E., then 8 and 9 fathom. And in this depth came all the way, not lesse then 7½; alwayes oaze, very softe. Stearinge up as the land lay neerest N., at 1 a clock wee sawe the *Hoseander* at an anchor. With her wee steared, N.N.E. and N.E. by N. At 3 anckored a mile without her, in 7½ at high water and 5 at lowe water; wee thinckinge it had bene Suratt, but it was shorte some 10 mile and called Umbra[1]. Here is also a faire river, but for smale vessells.

5. A boate of Suratt came aboarde of us, with Jaddow[2] the broker (which had served Captain Hawkins 3 yeare and Sir Henry Middleton the time of his beinge here), and the Customers brother[3], and 3 or 4 other; all which continued with us till the 7th. And then, at 4 in the afternoone, came to anchor at the barre of Suratt; and presently sent the broker, with all the Indians, Edward Christen, Thomas Kerridge, the steward[4], and Thomas Davis aland in our pinnace to goe to Suratt; but the boate to goe only within the barre, and in the morning to returne. The barre hath lattitude 21° 10′[5]. Here I came to an anchor in 8¼ [fathom] at hy water, and at lowe water 6½, neepe tides; but in the spring tydes it will rise here in the offinge (for so have I founde) 3 fathom and 3½.

8. In the morning our pinnace came aboarde againe. Our

[1] Not shown in modern maps.

[2] Jādu was for many years the chief native agent employed by the English. There are many references to him in Roe's account of his embassy.

[3] The customs of the Gujarāt ports (including Surat) were under the charge of Mukarrab Khān (for whom see p. 63 of *Early Travels*). He, however, was in attendance at court, and meanwhile his brother, who was resident at Surat, was watching over affairs there.

[4] Anthony Starkey, steward of the *Dragon*.

[5] 'Variation, 16° 27′ and lattitude, 21° 10′′ (marginal note). The longitude appears to have been also entered, but is now illegible. Purchas read the doubtful figures as an alternative 'variation,' viz. 16° 20′.

people, from within the barre, gone to Suratt in a boate of the countrey[1].

10. There came a boate aboarde of us, sente to bide us welcome, by some of the cheife.

11. Thomas Keredge came aboarde, and signified of their kinde intreatie and muche welcome to the people, and brought with him from the Justice and Governor of Suratt[2] a certificate under theire seale for our quiett and peaceable trade and intercourse with them; and also a letter of relacion, written by Sir Henry Middleton, which he left with the Mocadam[3] of Suallie. The same day we retourned him [i.e. Kerridge] againe with Hugh Gittuns[4].

12. The Cheife of the Castle[5] sent me a present, vizt. 20 sheepe, 23 hens, 100 lofes of bread, 2 pottes conserves, 2 bottes[6] butter, 20 cheese, a kintall[7] rice, a kintall meale, a basket lemmons, a baskett radishe, a baskett onions, 20 mellons, a baskett plantins, 100 suger canes. In requitall retourned him a faire peece of plate, a faire peece [i.e. gun], a sworde blade, 2 faire knives; and to his servants that came with it, some 34 or 36*s*. in rialls.

13. This day the frigetts of the Spaniards[8] put into the river; of them 16 sayle.

17. John Roche died.

19. The Portingall frigetts went out of the river.

20. The purser [Christian] came aboarde with provision; and the same day retorned agayne.

21. I called all my merchants aboarde, for better satisfaction in trade at Suratt.

[1] 'Mr. Goyte died. Swaine died.' (Marginal notes.) Standish (p. 105) calls the former '*Capttain* Goitt,' and this suggests that he was a man of some military experience, possibly recruited by the Company in view of the likelihood of a fight with the Portuguese.

[2] For his name see Kerridge's letter of 10 October 1615 (below).

[3] Headman (Hind., from Arabic, *mukaddam*).

[4] Gittins was one of the merchants employed in the voyage.

[5] The commandant of the castle was independent of the Governor of Surat.

[6] Butts, or tubs.

[7] The kintal (Arabic *kintār*) was roughly equivalent to 100 lb.

[8] Here again 'Portuguese' is meant. The *fragata* was a small armed coasting vessel, fitted to sail or row, and could thus keep out of the range of the ordnance of the English ships.

22. It was determined by counsell that wee shoulde send a poste to Agra to the Kinge, to signifye of our aryvall and to require his answere certeyne, whether hee would permitt us trade and to settle a factorye; otherwise to departe his country. Also it was determined that wee shoulde land goods, vizt. 20 tons iron, 20 tonnes lead, 20 balls [i.e. bales] cloth, 10 cwt. quicksilver, teethe[1] 50 or 60, one pott vermillion, 1 chest peeces (qt. [i.e. containing] 15). This done, the merchants went on land agayne, to dispeede the poste and to send barks for goods.

24. There came a Guzaratt into the roade from Mocha, who brought letters from Sir Henry Middleton, Captaine Sayres[2], [and] Captaine Sharpie[3], to signifie the honestie of the Mallim[4] and to intreate all the Kings subjects not to molest nor trouble him and to shewe all kindnes to him. The like [letter] myselfe hath given to him.

27. Our merchants sent me 4 peeces tymber. And in the afternoone there came a barke to an anckore by us, laden with tymber, bounde for Cambay. Out of her I tooke 7 peeces, and gave them my note to be paide at the pleasure of the Governor of Suratt[5]. Soe nowe (I thancke God) I am well provided for the fichinge of the mayne maste. This night the Portingall frigetts wente into the river.

29. Before day [they] came out agayne; and the same night followinge wente into the river agayne[6].

30. There came a shippe of Suratt to the barr from Mocha. This morninge I hard of the takeinge of Mr. Canninge, the purser [i.e. Edward Christian], and William Chambers; where-

[1] Elephants' teeth, i.e. ivory tusks.

[2] John Saris, commander of the *Clove* (Eighth Voyage), had joined Middleton in the Red Sea and (as already mentioned) had taken part with him in the reprisals upon Indian shipping.

[3] Alexander Sharpie, General of the Fourth Voyage, after the wreck of his vessel (the *Ascension*) joined Hawkins at Agra. In July 1611 he quitted that city and repaired to Surat, where in October he succeeded in getting on board Middleton's fleet. Sharpie accompanied Middleton to the Red Sea and to Bantam. He died soon afterwards, while on a voyage to Borneo.

[4] Master (Arabic *mu'allim*).

[5] The meaning seems to be that Best gave them an order upon the factors at Surat to pay for the timber at rates to be fixed by the Governor.

[6] 'Mr. Canninge, Edward Cristian, and William Chambers were taken' (marginal note).

uppon I caused the Gazaratt shippe to ancker fast by me, thereby to stay her till I might see and here howe all stood aland. Also a barke of rice wee stayed, being informed that it belonged to the Portingalls of Bassare[1], and from Bassare she came. In fine I tooke out of her 12 or 14 kintalls rice, and gave them 13*d.*[2] for it.

After I had the shippe, I wrott to the cheife aland that they should send me all my men, with the price or valewe of all the goods which I had landed; which performed, I woulde then deliver there shippe, with all there people; and gave tyme to the 5th of October to retorne me answere; by which tyme if they did not, then I woulde dispose of shippe and goods at my pleasure. Some 10 of the cheife men in the shippe I tooke into my shippe; in the shippe there beinge some 400 men, or 450.

October 3. I sent the *Hoseander* to Sually (and sent the Moccadam a present [of] 3 yeardes redd cloth and a peece, for deliveringe to us the relacion of Sir Henry Middleton), partly for water, partly to the steward, who there attended her comminge. This day I received letters from Mr. Canninge and Ned Christian.

4. I landed some 200 men out of the Guzaratt shipp.

6. Medy Joffer[3] came aboarde, accompanied with 4 cheife men and many others. He brought me a greate present, vizt. 20 sheepe and goats, 5 cwt.[4] rice, 2 cwt. meale, lemmons, plantins, sugar canes and onions store. I retorned him for present 5 yards of stammell [i.e. scarlet] cloth, a faire gylt cupp, a peece, a bottle of rose solis[5], and a faire knife; and to the other foure cheife [men] 4 peeces. He came to intreate of trade and release of the shippe which I held. At first he promised much; but in fine, upon denyinge me securitye for my goods and men, we concluded nothinge. At his request I released all the men of the shippe; thereby to honour him and to send him aland with content.

[1] Bassein appears to be meant.

[2] Purchas has '13*d.* a quintall,' but this is probably a misreading, the real meaning being 13 dollars for the lot. Finch (*Letters Received*, vol. 1, p. 31) gives the price of the best rice as one rial of eight (dollar) per kintal.

[3] 'Mede Joffer' (Mīr Jafar) in margin. He was one of the leading merchants of Surat.

[4] 'C.' in the MS.

[5] A cordial flavoured with sundew (*rosa solis*).

10. I left the barr of Suratt and came to the roade of Sualle, and anckored in 8 fathome at hye water. It is from the barr of Suratt some 10 or 12 miles north.

17. The Governor of Amadevar [Ahmadābād][1] came to the waterside.

19. I landed, havinge aboarde of me fower men for pledges.

21. I concluded with the Governors and merchants for tradinge with them and setling a factory in any parte of their countrey. The articles agreed upon and sealed by the Governor of Amadevar, the Governor of Suratt, and 4 principall merchants, and to be confirmed by the Great Magolls seale and firma [i.e. signature], in 40 dayes after the former sealinge, or else to be void.

The articles followeth[2]:

> Inprimis. Articles concluded, determined, and agreed upon with the Governor of Amadevar, by vertue of the Greate Magolls authority given unto him under his seale, in the behalfe of the saide Greate Magoll, and [the] Governor of Suratt, with Thomas Best, cheife commaunder of the *Dragon* and *Hoseander*, in the behalfe of the Kings Majestie of England and the Honorable and Right Worshipfull the Governor and Company of Merchants Tradinge the East Indies, for the settlinge of trade and factorie in the cities of Suratt, Cambaia, Amadevar, Goga, or in any other parte or parts of this countrie within the Greate Magolls dominions; the just and true observacions of the said articles to serve as sure and true pledges of perpetuall amitye and league betweene the saide Greate Magoll, with the Governors aforesaide and their people, and the Honorable and Right Worshipfull the Governour and Company aforesaide and our people; and the breache of the said articles just cause of warrs betweene the said parties irrevocable. Witnessed under our hands and seales the xxith of October anno 1612.

I. Inprimis, that all which concerneth Sir Henry Middleton be remited, acquited, and cleared to us; that they shall never make ceasure, stoppage, nor stay of our goods, wares, and marchandize to

[1] As will appear from subsequent references, he was Shaikh Yūsuf, the Dīwān of Gujarāt, who was acting as Viceroy in the absence of Abdullah Khān (Fīrūzjang), the real occupant of that post.

[2] Other versions will be found in the I.O. *Factory Records, Miscellaneous*, vol. xxv (p. 71), in *S.P. Dom., Jac. I*, vol. LXXV, no. 381 (P.R.O.), in *Purchas His Pilgrimes*, vol. I (p. 458), and (translated into Spanish) in *Documentos Remettidos*, vol. III (p. 87). The two latter versions both contain errors.

satisfie for the wrongs and injuries by the saide Henry Middleton done them.

II. That they shall procure from their kinge, the Greate Magoll, at their proper cost, his graunte and confirmacion of all the articles of agreemente, under the greate seale of his land, and shall deliver the same unto us for our securitie and certainety of perpetuall amitie, commerce, and dealinge with them, within 40 dayes after the sealinge hereof.

III. That it shalbe lawfull for the Kinge of England to keepe and continue his embassador at the courte of the Greate Magoll duringe the tyme of the saide peace and commerce; there to compound and end all such greate and waightie questions as may any waies tend to the breach of the saide peace.

IV. That at all tymes uppon the aryvall of our shippes in [the] rode of Sualley, there shalbe proclamacion in the citie of Suratt, three severall dayes togeather, that it shalbe free for the countree people of all sorts to come downe to the waterside, there to have free trade, dealinge, and commerce with us.

V. That all Englishe comodities shall pay custome (accordinge to the value or price that it beareth at the tyme that it is put into the custome-house) after the rate of 3½ per cento. But the Governor of Amadevar hath graunted unto us to write unto the Greate Magoll to have the halfe per cento abated; the answere whereof wee shall receive, togeather with the Kings firma, within the compasse of forty dayes[1].

VI. That all petty and podlery[2] ware be free of custome, provided that it exceed not in value 10 rialls of 8.

VII. That wee shall have 10 maun[3] for our mamuda[4] caried from the waterside to Suratt, and after the same rate backe agayne. And for carts we are to repaire to the Makadam of Swallie, to send for Suratt; and at Suratt to repaire unto the broker[5] for carts downe againe.

VIII. That if any of our men die in those parts, that then the Kinge nor governor nor underofficer shall make title or challenge to anythinge that to the dead belonged, nor demaund fees nor any kinde of taxes nor customes.

[1] Purchas omits the second half of this article; and certainly the reduction was not made.

[2] Pedlary, i.e. small wares such as pedlars sold.

[3] The maund at Surat was about 28 lb., according to Jourdain.

[4] The *mahmūdi* was a small silver coin, equivalent to about 11*d*. or 12*d*. English.

[5] The Spanish version has 'el corredor [*corretor*, a broker] Jadoe' [i.e. Jādu].

IX. That if all our men die here in theis partes betweene the tymes of the comminge of our shippes, that then, by some office[r] thereto appointed, just and true inventorie, notice, and knowledge be taken of all such monys, goods, jewells, provisions, apparrell, and what else to our nation belongeth; and the same shall safely preserve and keepe and deliver to the Generall, captaine, or merchants of the first shippes that shall after heare aryve; and to receive a discharge from the Generall, captaine, or merchants to whome such goods and moneys shalbe delivered.

X. That they secure our men and goods uppon the land; redeeminge all such, both goods and men, as shall happen to be taken upon the land by the Portingalls, and shall deliver both men and goods againe to us (free of all charges) or the valewe of our goods and men instantly.

XI. That, as in all kingdomes there are some rebells and disobedient subjects, so in our nation there may be some pyratts and searovers which may happen to come into these parts and here may robb and steale; which if any such shall happen, then will not wee, by our trade and factorie here, be liable or answereable for such goods so taken; but will aide them with our best meanes that are so greeved, by justice to our Kinge for redresse and restitution unto them.

XII. That all such provisions of victualls as shalbe spent duringe the tyme that our shippes shall remaine here in the roads of Suratt or Swallie shalbe free of custome; provided it doth not amount unto the mony above 1000 dollers[1].

XIII. That in all questions of wrongs and injuries that shalbe offered to us and to our nation, that wee doe receive from the judges and those that be in authority present and speedye justice, accordinge to the qualitie of our complaints and wrongs done us; and that by delaies wee are not put of[f] and wearied, eyther by tyme or charges.

Finis.

24[2]. I landed the present for the Kinge of Magoll and brought it to the tent of the Governor of Amadevar; who tooke notice of the perticulers, also of our Kings letter to their Kinge, to advertise there Kinge thereof; which done, I retorned the presente to my shippe agayne, according to agreemente with the saide Governor, for I had toulde him that, unlest [*sic*] there Kinge woulde confirme the articles concluded

[1] 'Rials of eight' are meant. The Spanish version has (wrongly) '10,000 reales.'

[2] Purchas reads (quite wrongly) 14 October.

on, and likewise write our Kinge a letter, I woulde not deliver the present nor the Kings letter; for if he refused so to doe, then was he not a freinde but an enemy, and to the enemyes of my King I neither had letter nor present. Also, the same day, (the former finished) I delivered our present to the Governor of Amadevar, and another to his sonne.

24 [*sic*]. Landed 1 cloth[1].

26. Landed 9 clothes.

27. Landed 600 barrs lead.

28. The Governor and his sonne came aboarde my shippe; and the same night departed, leaving his men and mony to finish with me for 2000 covitts[2] of cloth bought of us.

31. Lancelott Canninge[3] was discharged.

November 2. Robert Trulley was discharged.

17. I displaced my boteson and put John Davis into his place.

24[4]. The cafila[5] of frigetts came in sight of us, some 240 saile. I had thought they had come to fight with us; but they were the fleete of merchantmen bounde for Cambaya. And every yeare there cometh the like fleete (all Portingalls) from the south coste[6], Goa, Chaule, etc., to goe to Cambay; and from thence they bringe the greatest parte of the lading which the caricks and gallions carieth for Spayne[7]; by which may appeare the greate trade that the Portingalls hath in theis parts.

[1] Meaning one bale of broadcloth.

[2] Yard (Port. *covado*).

[3] Cousin of Paul Canning, already mentioned. He had come out as a musician—the virginals being his instrument—and was now being discharged for service on shore. Soon afterwards he accompanied his cousin to Agra, together with Robert Trully (see the next entry), who was a cornet-player. Both musicians were allowed to perform before Jahāngīr, who, however, found no pleasure in the virginals; whereupon the unfortunate player (according to Trully) 'dyed with conceiptt' (*O.C.* 110). He was buried in the Roman Catholic cemetery at Agra. Trully was more fortunate, for the emperor was delighted with his cornet and for a time became his patron (though not a liberal one). After a while, becoming discontented with his prospects, Trully stole away to the court of the King of 'Decanne' (Ahmadnagar), and there, turning Muhammadan, he was taken into the royal service with a 'greate allowance' (*Early Travels*, p. 204). After this we hear no more of him.

[4] Purchas gives the wrong date of 14 November.

[5] *Kāfila* was used both for a land-caravan and (as here) for a fleet of merchant vessels.

[6] The Malabar Coast, from Goa southwards (see Linschoten, vol. 1, p. 63).

[7] 'Portugal' is meant (see note on p. 26).

This day Claxson[1] and Johnson[2] ran away and went aboarde the frygetts. I sent 20 clothes to Suratt with the merchants.

27. I received letters from Mr. Canninge and Ned Christian. Both signified of the comminge of 4 gallions to fight with us, and that they were ready rydinge at the barre of Goa the 14th of November. This day I sent 26,000 mamudas and 1500 rialls of 8 to Suratt per the steward and John Cransby. Thomas Poyse died.

29. Mr. Canninge came aboarde. And the Portingall fleete, cominge in sight of us yesterday, drove neere upp with the floode. And at 2 in the afternoone I did sett sayle, and at 4 I was aboute 2 cables lengths from the vise-admirall (fearinge to goe neerer, for wante of depthe), and then began to ploy uppon him, both with greate and smale shott; that by an hower wee had well peperd him with some 56 greate shott. From him wee received one smale shott (sacker or minion[3]) into our mayne mast, and with another he suncke our longe boate. Now night, wee anckored, and saved our boate, but lost many things out of her.

30. As soone as the day gave light, I sett sayle and steered betweene them, bestirringe ourselves with our best endevours, puttinge 3 of the 4 shippes agrounde on the sands tharte of the barre of Suratte. At 9 I anckored. This morninge the *Hoseander* did good service, and came throughe also betweene the shippes and anchored by me. Upon the fludd the 3 shippes on grounde came of[f]. Wee sett saile (they at anchore) and came to them, and

[1] Robert Clarkson, a sailor on the *Dragon*. He had committed some offence and feared punishment (*Letters Received*, vol. 1, p. 304). He soon tired of the company of the Portuguese, and gladly accepted an invitation from Aldworth (sent to him at Daman) to return to English service. He was employed at Surat in curing tobacco (*ibid.*, p. 300); but after a time he followed Trully's example by going to the court of the King of Ahmadnagar and turning Muhammadan. Later still he returned to Surat, professing penitence for his apostasy, and was again employed; only to desert afresh, carrying with him some money entrusted to him to buy goods. He was supposed to have returned to the Deccan court, but his subsequent fate is unknown (*Early Travels*, p. 204).

[2] Johnson also took refuge at Ahmadnagar, where he was given a pension on condition that he turned Muhammadan, 'but within eighte dayes after his circumsizion he dyed' (*ibid.*, p. 204).

[3] The saker threw a 6-lb. ball; while the minion was likewise a small-calibre cannon.

spent upon 3 of them 150 greate shotte, and in the morninge some 50 shotte. And at night, wee givinge the admirall[1] our 4 peeces out of the starne for our farewell, he gave us one of his prowe peeces (either a whole or demi-cullveringe[2]), which came even with the topp of our forecastle, shott throughe our david[3], killed one man, to witt Burrell[4], and shott the arme of[f] another.

This day the *Hoseander* spent wholly uppon one of the shippes which was agrounde, and spente some [*blank*] shoote; and from the enemy received many shotte, which killed the boteson, Richard Barker. Night come, wee birthed ourselves some 6 miles from them and anchored. And at 9 a clocke they sent a frygatt to us; which beeinge neere come, came drivinge right on the halse of the *Hoseander*; and beinge discovered by their good watche, made 2 shotte at him. The first caused him to sett saile. The second went thoroughe his sayles; and so tooke his leave[5]. There purpose doubtlesse to have fired [us], if they had founde us without good watche.

December 1. This day wee roade; they not comminge to us, nor wee to them. They might without danger of the sands have come to us, but wee to them coulde not goe without danger of the sands. This day called a counsell and concluded to goe downe to have a broader channell; hopeinge also that the gallions woulde followe us.

2. Wee went downe some 6 or 7 leagues, but they followed us not.

3. At fludd plyed upp agayne, and anckered faire in sight of them.

4. In the morninge wayed, and wee stood away before them. Litle wind. In the afternoone they gave us over and stood in

[1] The Portuguese flagship.

[2] The shot of a whole culverin weighed from 17 to 20 lb.; that of a demi-culverin about 10 lb.

[3] The 'david' (modern 'davit') was a projection (of wood or iron) from the ship's bow, used in hoisting the anchor.

[4] From a marginal note it appears that his Christian name was William.

[5] 'This frigat was sunke with the shot, as Mr. Salmon (the actor) was author unto me; and eightie of her men were taken up drowned' (note by Purchas, *op. cit.*, who further records that 'Nathaniel Salmon, of Leigh, was master of the *Hosiander*'). See also Copland's narrative, given later.

with the land againe; and at night wee directed our course for Dewe[1].

5. Damam beinge E. from us, we steered to make a west way. And so comminge over wee mett with the first sand, and came over it in 7 fadom; from Damam some 10 or 11 leagues; then 10, 12, 15, 20. And some 4 or 5 leagues from that sand wee mett the other sand and came over it in 6½ and 7 fadom; then 10, 12, 13, 15, 16. At night anckored in 15 fadom.

6. At foure in the morninge wayed and steered W.N.W.; still 13, 14, 15 fadom. And at sunne risinge sawe the land and stood in; still 14 and 15 fadom. At night anckered some 4 or 5 leagues to the eastward of Dewe, in 14 fadom, faire aboard the shore; right within us a faire high rocke; deepe water close abourde him, 10, 12 fadom.

7. In the morninge sent in the *Hoseander* to a faire baye[2], and went aland with our boats and had 2 go[a]tts and 2 hogsheds of water.

8. Wee wayed and plyed to the eastward. Our depth 11, 12, and 10 fadom.

9. Wee came to Madafeldebar[3], and anckored in 8 fadom. It is from D[e]we some 10 or 11 leagues, and lieth nearest east and by north. A faire coaste; no daunger but that you see. Your dep[t]h, if nere D[e]we, 15, 16; when halfe way, 12 fadom; then 10 and 9 (not lesse). It is a faire sandie bay; and on the west side of the bay a river, which goeth farre into the countrye. And this place is some 5 or 6 miles shorte (to the westward) of the iles of Mortie[4].

12. William Perfeit, John Roase, Nathaniell Skynner, and

[1] Diu, a Portuguese possession on the south coast of Kāthiāwār. Of course Best does not mean that it was his intention to visit that port, but merely to go in that direction.

[2] Near Simar (see p. 124).

[3] Muzafarābād, now called Jafarābād, about thirty miles north-east of Diu, on the estuary of the Ranuy.

[4] About seven miles E.N.E. of Jafarābād lies the island of Shial (Salbet), together with an islet (known as Savai-bet) connected with it by a reef which dries at low water. This islet appears to have been known to the Portuguese as I. dos Mortos (see Lavanha's map of Gujarāt, reproduced at p. 108 of vol. I of the Society's edition of *The Book of Duarte Barbosa*). The name may have been derived from a Muhammadan tomb, the dome of which is still conspicuous when the islet is viewed from the sea.

Thomas Clements runne away, beinge sente aland in the longe boate for water. And upon knowledge given mee, I dealt with the Govenor of Madafeldebar to raise a company and to pursue them; agreeinge with him to give him 100 mamodas and a vest, if he brought them to me agayne; which he undertooke, and also performed, and brought them all 4 aboarde of my shippe the 13th.

14. Havinge occasion to call all our men togeather and also the *Hoseanders* company, when I had ended with them (findinge them very resolute and desirous to returne to Sually againe), then they all with one voyce became sutours to me to release and forgive the 4 men which had runne away; which I graunted unto them, and presently freed them of their yrons. Otherwise William Perfeite had surely died, and the other three well whipped.

15. In the morninge departed Madafeldebar to goe to Mova [*sic*], only to discover the bay, because some that were there in the *Ascension* reported it to bee a good place to winter in. At 4 in the afternoone wee anckored in the bay of Moha[1]; havinge founde the coaste and channell very good; depth 10 fadom, no danger but what you see. I sent our pynnace one land, where presently wee had 20 good sheepe, at 3*s*. per sheepe (the best wee have had this voyadge).

16. In the morninge I sent our pynnace aland; where wee founde fewe people, but the ruynes of a greate towne.

17. In the morninge the Captain of the Campe[2] sent to me 4 men, to intreate me to send unto him one of my men, that he might talke with mee. Hereunto I was much urged. In fine sent Mr. Canninge and Mr. Oliver[3]; who by him were kindely intreated, and retourned to me with his letter, and 5 or 6 men, to intreate me to come neare to his campe with my shippes; he

[1] 'Anchored in the baye of Mohar, which is from Maldafeldabar 9 or 10 legues E.N.E.' (marginal note). The place is now called Mahuwa or Mhowa, and lies about 55 miles to the north-east of Diu. For an account of the *Ascension's* visit to this port, see Jourdain, p. 113.

[2] This was Khwāja Yādgār, who, at the head of an expeditionary force from Gujarāt, was besieging a neighbouring fort. He was brother of Abdullah Khān (Fīrūzjang), who was Viceroy of Gujarāt from 1611 to 1616. In the spring of 1613, having presumably brought his campaign to a victorious conclusion, Khwāja Yādgār presented himself at court and was rewarded with the title of Sardār Khān (*Tūzuk-i-Jahāngīrī*, p. 237).

[3] Tobias Oliver, one of the merchants.

lyinge from me some 10 or 12 miles. I called a counsell. It was thought fitt to goe.

19. I sett sayle from Moho.

20. In the morninge I anckored before the campe, in 10 fadom, not a mile from the castell, in a faire sandy bay, some 10 mile from Moho.

21. I landed, and had much conferrence with the Governour of the Campe. He much desired that I woulde land 2 peeces of ordinaunce; makinge many and greate promises of favoure to our nation. But I refused, etc. Hee presented me with a horse and furniture and 2 Agra girdells, and I presented him [with] a veste of stamell [i.e. scarlet cloth], 2 peeces [i.e. guns], 2 bottles aquavitae [i.e. brandy], and a knife.

22. Wee sawe the 4 gallions cominge towarde us; and at 9 at night they anckored within shott of us.

23. In the morninge by sunne [rising] we waighed and beganne with them; and continued fight till 10 or 11. Then they all foure wayed, and stood away before the winde; and so went from us, for they sailed lardge much better then wee. We followed them 2 or 3 howres, and then anckored. This day I spent upon them 133 greate shott and some 700 smale shott. In this fight John Hackwell[1] was kilde with a greate shotte. The 4 shippes anckored from me some 2 leagues.

24. By sonne rysinge I wayed and went to the 4 gallions; and by 8 beganne our fight, and continued it till 12. And this day shott 250 greate shott and 1000 smale shott. By this tyme both sydes weary, wee all stood into the sea and steered away S. by E., the 4 shippes followinge of us. At 2 or 3 aclocke they layed it aboute and anckored. Nowe I beganne to take knowledge of our powder and shott, and founde more then ½ of our shott spent, and of the *Hoseanders*; havinge nowe spente of [on?] the 4 shippes 625 greate shotte and 3000 smale shotte.

Beinge from the land some 4 or 5 leagues, we mett with a sand, whereon there was some 2 or 2½ fadom; and it lyeth from Moho S.S.E. or thereabouts. The end of the saide sand I went

[1] Probably a brother of Thomas Hackwell, master's mate of the *Dragon*, who on his return to England was given (23 December 1614) a gratuity of 5*l*. for having 'bestird himselfe lustelie in the fight against the Portugalls with his muskett.'

over it in 9 fadom, and then were the two high hills which are over Goga nearest north of us. Upon this sand was the *Ascension* cast away. The shoaldinge is somethinge faste. Betweene the land and this sand is 9, 10 fadom. In 9, 8 fadom wee continued stearinge south, with an ebbe. At lowe water anckored in 8 fadom; the tide settinge E.N.E. and W.S.W. by the compasse.

25. At 12 midnight I wayed (winde at N.N.W.) and steered S.S.E.; depth 12, 14 fadom. At 4 steered E.S.E.; at 6 steered east (still 12 fadom, halfe a fadom more or lesse). At 9 wee mett with a bancke, 7 fadom (5 or 6 castes), then presently 10, 12, 14. Then the winde shortened on us. We lay S.E. And aboute 12 wee mett with another bancke, over which wee had 6 fadom at ½ flud; and then sawe the land, Daman, E.S.E., the high land to the southward of Daman S.E. by E. And beinge over this sand, wee had presently 14, 15, 17, 20 fadom. At 2, beinge high water, wee anckored in 17 fadom, faire in sight of land; Damam E.S.E., the highest land to the southward S.E. by S. At 8 at night sett saile [at] ½ the tide, calme; still 15, 16 fadom. Anckored all the ebb.

26. At 9 in the morning sett saile. In the afternoone anckored of[f] the barre of Suratt.

27. In the morning [we] were 3 or 4 mile shorte of Sually; and aboute 12 aclocke anckored in the roade of Sually. In the afternoone Thomas Kerridge and Edward Christen came aboarde.

30. John Michelson died.

January 6 [1613]. The firma[1] came to Sually as a private letter; therefore I refused to receive it, beinge jelious [i.e. suspicious] it was a counterfaite; requiringe the cheife men of Suratt to come downe and deliver it to me, with those rights which to it belonged.

11. The Xabandar[2], his father-in-lawe, Medigoffer, and divers others came to Sually and delivered it to me, with profession of their kings love to our nation.

[1] The Mughal emperor's decisions were usually issued as a *farmān* (commandment). The English were prone to confuse the word with the Italian *firma*, 'a signature' (see p. 31).

[2] A Portuguese form of the Persian *shāhbandar* ('lord of the haven'), the official who controlled the port and saw to the collection of the customs and other dues. His name appears to have been Khwāja Hasan Ali.

12. The Xabandar, the messenger which brought the firma, and many others came aboarde; to whome I gave presents, and at their partinge 7 peeces ordenance[1].

13. Medigoffer came aboarde of me; to whome I gave 2 vests, a case of bottles, and a faire ringe. This afternoone wee sawe the 4 gallions againe.

14. Wee landed all our cloth, 310 teeth, and all our quick-silver. The gallions hath nered us some 3 or 4 miles.

16. I landed Anthony Starkey, to traveile hoame overland.

17. I received all my goods from Suratt. At night sett saile. It fell calme and I anckored. Note that within the land of Cambaia it floweth S.W. and N.E.

18. I sett saile. Came faire by the gallions. They all wayed and followed me some 2 or 3 howres, and then departed, without shootinge a shott of eyther side.

19. Thwarte of Bassine[2] we tooke 3 Mallabares. Had nothinge in them. Wee tooke a boate from one of them.

20. Still we weare faire aboarde [the coast], some 5 leagues of[f], and came longste the shoare; 14, 18, 20 fadom water. At night were faire aboard Chaul[3], seeing both towne and castle.

21. In the afternoone wee weare faire aboarde Dabull[4]. And here [we] were aboarde 3 junckes[5], all of Callicutt, laden with coakers [i.e. coco-nuts].

22. The *Hoseander* in the morning sent her boate unto 2 junckes. At 12 aclock wee were at the rocks which lyeth to the northward of Goa 10 or 11 leagues, and lyeth from the maine 6 or 8 miles; 2 or 3 of the rocks are higher then the hull of any shippe[6]. At 6 were thwarte of Goa; which is easily knowne by the iland which lyeth at the mouth of the river, and upon the iland a castle[7].

From Daman till you come to Goa the shoare is very faire; no

[1] He means a salute of seven guns.

[2] The Portuguese settlement of Bassein, about 30 miles north of Bombay.

[3] In Kolāba District, about 30 miles south of Bombay. Down to 1740 Lower Chaul was held by the Portuguese, and was strongly fortified.

[4] Dābhol, the chief port of the Bījāpur kingdom, in 17° 34′ N. lat.

[5] Country vessels.

[6] Vengurla Rocks, or Burnt Islands. The highest is 135 feet.

[7] Apparently he means the fortified peninsula of Aguada, on the north side of the river mouth.

daunger, and faire shoaldinge, not without 16 or 17 [fadom] nor within 10. Good anchoringe all the coaste. And all this coast from Daman to Goa lieth nearest S. and N.

23. Wee steared longst the land.

24. Wee sawe a fliete of frigatts, some 60 or 80 saile, bounde to the southward. Here, in the lattitude of 13° ¼', the high land by the watersyde left us, and the land began to be very lowe; and faire shoaldinge, 16 and 17 fadom, som 3 or 4 legues of[f]. In the afternoone wee runne into a bay where all the frigatts and 3 or 4 gallies weare, and fetcht out a shippe laden with rice. All the Portingalls fled in their 2 boats, and also their were 2 frigetts aboarde of her; so that all good things they carried away with them.

25. Wee romaged our price [i.e. prize], findinge nothinge but rice and coarse sugar, of which wee stored ourselves; and tooke out both her masts and what firinge wee coulde, and at night suncke her; takeinge out of her all the people, 20 or 25, all Mores.

26. Wee mette with a littell boate of the Maldivar[1], laden with cokers, bound for Canoniere; into which I putt all the people of the prise, only 8 which I kept for labor, one of them a pilott for this coaste. At 12 were thwarte of Canoniere. Lattitude 11°[2].

27. [We] were shotte a litle past Callecutt and were thwarte of Pannayre[3]. At noone, lattitude 10° 30'.

28. In the morning sawe Cochine, which maketh itselfe by the towres and castell, and in lattitude 9° 40' or thereabouts[4]. Note that from Goa to Co[c]hine wee never had above 20 fadom, beinge sometymes 4 or 5 legues from land; and beinge 3, 4, 6 miles of[f], 10, 12 fadom, etc. From lattitude 11° 30' to Cochine very lowe land by the watersyde, but in the country all alonge high land. Noate that shorte of Cochine 4 or 5 leagues you shall see a high land in the country, somewhat like a table, but roundinge alofte; and to the northward of this rounde hill, high longe hills or mountaines. All this day ranne within 6 or 8 mile of the land, in 9, 10, 12 fadom.

[1] The Maldives.
[2] Cannanore is in 11° 52' N. lat. It was then a Portuguese possession.
[3] Probably Ponnani (Pannanee), in lat. 10° 48'.
[4] Really 9° 58'.

29. Calme. Lattitude 8°. Some 6 legues of[f], no grounde in 40 or 50 fadom.

30. Wee anckored in 18 fadom, some 26 legues shorte of the Cape[1], against a little villaidge; and presently 6 or 8 cannoes came aboarde, and brought us all provisions, water, hennes, cokers, etc. The name of this place is Beringar[2]; the kings name Travancar[3].

31. All day the people came to us with hennes, etc.

February 1. The people came with provisions; and the Kinge sent a messenger to mee, to knowe whether I woulde trade with him; which if I woulde, he offred to lade my shippes with peper and synamon.

2. The people came as before unto us.

3. Wee sett our misson maste; the former beinge shott neare asunder in fight.

4. The people still come to us with provisions. At 2 in the afternoone sett saile from Beringar. All night I anckored.

5. In the morning sett saile, beinge faire aboarde Cape Comorine. And here mett with a fresh gaile of winde at E. by N., which splitt our foretopsaile and maine bonnett. Yet a cano with 8 men came aboarde of me 3 or 4 legues from land. In the afternoone came another cano. Here wee were troubled with calmes and greate heate. Many of our men taken sicke; myselfe one of them.

6. Becalmed.

7. Littell winde, at N.W.

8. Came agayne into the roade of Beringam.

11. Our cooke, William Flaile, dyed, and the cooke of the *Hoseander* tooke his place, John [Patteson]. In the roade of Beringam.

13. Wee sett sayle from Beringam. Note that this place gives good refreshing, with plenty of water, and the people harmelesse and not freinds with the Portingall. From this place to the Cape all the poore people that dwell by the watersyde are Christians,

[1] Cape Comorin.

[2] Later Best calls it 'Beringam.' It is Brinjaon (Vilinjam), about seven miles S.S.E. of Trivandrum. Purchas notes that 'our mariners usually call it Bring John.'

[3] A confusion between the king and his kingdom (Travancore).

and have a Portugall frier or preist that dwelleth amongst them[1].

All night anckored 4 or 5 mile from the 2 rocks which lye of[f] the Cape in 18 fadom. The 2 rocks lye five or sixe mile from land.

14. In the morning I sett saile (winde at E.) and plyed to windward. Wee have a littell current to the southward. Note that the coaste of Malebar, even from Daman to Cape Comorine, is free of daunger, and faire shoaldinge on all the coaste from Cochine to the Cape, more neale[2] (16, 18, 20 fadom) faire by the land, and 5 or 6 legues of[f] no grounde after you come within 25 or 30 legues of the Cape. The variation at Daman is 16° 30′; and halfe way to the Cape it is 15° or thereabout, and here at the Cape it is 14°, and hath lattitude N. 7° 30′[3].

In the afternoone ran of[f] open of the Cape, and founde much winde at E.S.E.; which gave me smale hope of goeinge to the eastwarde till the end of the monsoone, which wilbe the fine [i.e. end] of Aprill or thereabouts (as the Indians reporte). So bore up and anckored 4 or 5 legues within the Cape, in 20 fadom, faire by the 2 rocks. Right of[f] from theis two rocks lyeth a sunken rocke, which is very dangerous, and is some 2 miles without the foresaide two rocks. If you come within 20 fadom, you shalbe in danger of them; but safe and free of danger is not to come within 24 or 25 fadom[4].

15. Wee rode still. Winde at E.S.E.

16. Wee rode still. A freshe winde at East.

17. Wee rode still. Litle winde.

18. Wee rode still. Calme.

19. Wee rode still. Winde at S.W.

20. Wee rode still. A sea-turne[5] al day.

[1] At the present day nearly a third of the inhabitants of Travancore are Christians, of whom over a half belong to the Syrian Church.

[2] An old word for 'deep.'

[3] 'Longitude from the Cape of Good Hope 56° 30′' (marginal note). The correct longitude of Cape Comorin is 77° 36′ east of Greenwich, and therefore 59° 6′ east of the Cape of Good Hope.

[4] 'Three rocks on which the sea breaks lie off the south-eastern extreme of Cape Comorin; outside of them foul ground extends to three-quarters of a mile from the shore' (*West Coast of India Pilot*, 1926, p. 88).

[5] A breeze from the sea.

21. Wee rode still. A sea-turne.

22. Wee rode still. Winde at S.E.

23. Wee rode still. Winde at S.E., a freshe gale.

24. In the morning wee waighed (the wind of[f] the land) and stood to the eastward. At 6 at night the Cape Comorine was E. of us, 3 or 4 leagues of[f].

25. In the morning, calme; the Cape N.N.E., some 4 legues of[f]; 24 fadom water. [At] 6 at night the Cape was N.N.W., some 5 or 6 legues of[f]; depth, 22 fadom. From the Cape the land lieth E.N.E. some 4 or 5 legues, then more northerly; all very low land. All this night little winde at N.W. Wee steared S.E. by E.; depth, 24, 26 fadom.

26. In the morninge winde at S.E.; litle winde. Here wee see not the land; but the Cape is N.W. from us, some 12 legues of[f]; depth, 26 fadom. At noone our lattitude was 7° 10′. The Cape from us W.N.W. [N.N.W.?], 10 or 12 legues of[f]; so that the true lattitude of the Cape is neare aboute 7° 30′ or 7° 35′[1]. No ground in 80 fadom. All this night the winde at S.S.W. We steared S.E. by E., some 6 legues.

27. In the morninge calme. Afterward a litle breath, S.S.W. Lattitude observed, 7° N.

28. In the morninge at 6 sawe the land, the iland of Seland [Ceylon], E.S.E., of[f] some 8 or 9 legues. The winde at S. (litle winde). Lattitude observed, 7° N. At 4 we were faire aboarde the land; depth, 13, 15, 16 fadom. At 8 stood of[f] till day. Litle winde at S. Beinge from the land 5 or 6 legues, no grounde in 60 or 70 fathome.

Marche 1. All the morninge becalmed. The afternoone, a sea-turne at N.W. and west. At 6 faire aboard Columbo, whose lattitude is 6° 30′ or neare thereaboute[2]. Depth, 24, 25 fadom, 3 legues off. All night the winde at S. and S.S.E. Wee stood of[f] all night. Here the land lyeth N. and S.; lowe land.

2. Calme all the forenoone. The afternoone, a sea-turne at W.S.W. At 6 Columbo N.N.E., 4 or 5 legues of[f]. The depth, 34 fadom, 6 or 7 mile of[f].

3. The morning, winde at S.S.W. Lattitude 6° 20′. 6 or 7

[1] The correct figure is 8° 05′ N.
[2] The correct figure is 6° 56′ N.

legues of[f], no grounde. All this tyme that wee have bene on this coast of Selon, wee have founde the land to lye S. and N. At 6 at night (lattitude 6°) wee finde the land to lye S.S.E. or S.E. by S., not reckoninge the variation, which is here 12° 30′ west. Winde at S.E. and S.S.E.

4. In the morning, winde at S.E. Lattitude 5° 50′. In the afternoone, calme. All night a freshe winde at E. and E.S.E.

5. All the morning, winde at E.S.E. Lattitude 5° 50′. At noone, within 4 or 5 mile of the land, depth 40 fadom; and a mile farder of[f], no grounde. The Cape Gallo (whose lattitude is 5° 40′[1]) was nowe S.E. from us, some 3 legues of[f]. From Cape de Gallo to the Cape Tenadare[2] the land lyeth nearest E.S.E. and W.N.W., distante some 10 or 12 legues; all faire lowe land. But all this coaste very deepe water. At 2 aclocke the winde come out of the sea, at S.S.E. and at S. Wee ranne in, and had 40, 36, 34 fadom, 3 mile of[f]. The *Hoseander* in 20 fadom, a mile of[f] or more.

6. In the morning, calme. In the afternoone, litle winde (southerly).

7. The morning, winde at E. by N. Calme all the rest.

8. The morning, winde at east. Afternoone, at S.S.E. In the eveninge sawe two shipps, S.E. from us 4 or 5 leagues.

9. The winde at east. This morning wee sawe a shippe, some 3 or 4 legues in the winde of us. At 10 spake with her, shee beinge a shippe of Cochine, come from Bengala laden with rice and taken by the *Greene Lyon* of Holland 2 dayes before; with whome the *Hoseander* spake the same day. At night I anckored. The *Hoseander* some 4 or 5 mile to leeward of me, but shee anckored not. The next morninge wee could not see her.

10. All this day wee rode still, not seeinge the *Hoseander*.

11. At 6 in the morninge sett saile. Stood 2 howres to the southward. Then bare upp to seeke the *Hoseander*. At 9 aclocke sawe her. At 3 were with her. All day litle winde (westerly).

12. Wee stood in with the land, and anckored in 24 fadom.

[1] Point de Galle is 6° 01′ N.

[2] Dondra Head, the southernmost point of Ceylon. Linschoten calls it 'Tanadare' (p. 324 of the work mentioned in a note on p. 48, below); while John Tatton, in his account of the voyage of the *Pearl*, speaks of 'the souther point of Ceylon, called Diundra' (*Purchas His Pilgrimes*, vol. 1, p. 330).

Winde at S.E. and S. I sent my boats on land, 4 legues to the N. of Cape de Gallo; and after some staye a woman came to talke with an Indian that went out of the boate. Shee toulde him that wee shoulde there have no provisions, but saide shee woulde goe and tell the men what wee desired. Afterward 2 men came to my Indian, and toulde him that we shoulde not have any thinge there, for that our nation had some tyme taken a boate of theirs; but it was the Fleminges, and not our nation. The people freindes to the Portugale, and some of them Christians, as our folke thought. Some of them apparrelled after the Portugall fashion; and had a crosse upon the shoare. Greate store of people there was seene. So that hereafter lett no man hope to have any refreshinge upon this parte of Selone, even from Columbo to the Cape de Gallo. You may anckor, all the coaste alongst, within 3 or 4 miles of the land, betweene 30 and 20 fadom; but in some places you have foule grounde.

13. In the morning at 5 sett saile; winde at E.S.E. Afternoone, at S.W. At 6 at night Cape de Gallo was N. of us, some 4 legues of[f]. All night, calme.

14. In the morning at 6 the southermost pointe of Selone (called Tenadare, whose lattitude is 5° 30′[1], and lyeth from Cape Gallo E.S.E., some 10 or 12 legues) bore E.N.E., some 5 legues of[f]. 40, 50 fadom 3 or 4 mile of[f]; but you may rune into 25 and 20 fadom. On all this coaste good anckor[ing]. Here, halfe way betweene Cape de Gallo and Tenadar, wee landed our boate. But the people refused to talke with us, albeit wee sent an Indian neare unto them. At this place the Fleminge purposed to have landed his people he tooke out of the prize; and puttinge one of them on shoare, hee was killed by the people.

15. In the morninge, winde at north-west. Wee bare upp to proceede on our voyage, hopeinge the east monsoone is done. But presently wee sawe a shippe westward of us; to whome wee gave chase, and at 4 aclocke spake with him, beinge the *Greene Lyon*[2] of Amsterdam, whose captaine was Jacob Matheusbus, her master Nicolas Warboutson, and her pylott Nicolas Jacob.

[1] 'Variation, 12° 00′' (marginal note). The correct latitude is 5° 55′.

[2] *Groene Leeuw*. The senior merchant in charge of her was Jacob Mattheuszoon Buijs, and her skipper was Claes Warreboutszoon (Macleod, vol. 1, p. 127).

All the night wee steered E. by S. and east. Winde at N.W. and N.

16. In the morninge, winde at N.N.E. Wee stood to the N.W., in sight of land. At noone the winde came southerly. Wee steared E.N.E. The nighte calme. All day sight of land.

17. In the morninge, winde at N. Wee steared E.N.E. and N.E., faire in sight of the land. Depth, 40 fadom. At 10, the winde at east, wee stood to the land. At 3 laide it aboute, beinge neare to one of the sandes that Linskotte writeth of[1]. It lyeth from the land 2 legues. Wee had 25 fadom when wee stayed. Upon the land, right againste this sande, is a high rocke, like a greate towre. The land lyeth here E.N.E. Winde at E.S.E.

18. Winde at E.N.E. At 4 in the morninge wee stood in. At 8 cast aboute. At night aboarde the land.

19. Winde E.S.E.(?) and S.E. Here the land lyeth E.N.E. The land in the country high, and mountaines; but at watersyde very lowe[2]. The shore full of rockes, even as on the north syde of Cape de Gallo. Here wee finde a little current, that setteth to the west; for we daily leese [i.e. lose], if the winde be easterly.

20. In the morning, winde of[f] the land, and calme. All the afternoone, winde at S., wee steared east. All night, winde at S.S.W., wee steared east.

21. In the morning wee sawe the high land of Seland N.W. from us. Winde at S.S.W. At 12 Cape Gallo was of[f] us, W. by S., distante some 36 legues; and longitude from the Cape of Good Hope, 59° 40′. From 12 to 12, E. by N., legues 15, and longitude from the Cape of Good Hope, 60° 24′.

22. Calme all the afternoone. Litle winde all night, at S.E. Way, some 4 legues N.E., and longitude from the Cape of Good Hope, 60° 33′[3].

23. N.E., 12 legues. Lattitude, 7° N., and longitude from the Cape of Good Hope, 61° 35′. Winde at S.E. Litle winde and calme[4].

[1] Best doubtless carried with him a copy of Linschoten's great work, in the English translation of 1598 (*John Huighen van Linschoten his Discours of Voyages into the Easte and West Indies*). In this the sands referred to in the text are noted on pp. 322 and 324.
[2] 'Lattitude 5° 40′' (marginal note).
[3] 'Variation, 11° 20′' (marginal note).
[4] 'Variation, 11° 00′' (marginal note).

24. S. by W., legues 7; and N.E., legues 4. Longitude from the Cape, 61° 39′. Winde at E.S.E., and calme.

25. S.E. ½ S., legues 16; and longitude from the Cape, 62° 9′. The sunne neare our zenith, that certeynely I knowe not our lattitude, but by the starre 6° 30′.

26. S.E. by E., legues 14; and S.E. by S., legues 3. Lattitude, 06° 00′; and longitude from the Cape of Good Hope, 62° 38′. Winde N.E. and east. Litle winde.

27. S.E. ½ S., legues 11. Longitude from the Cape, 62° 58′. Winde at E.N.E. Litle winde.

28. S.S.E., legues 6; and N., legues 2. Lattitude per the starrs, 4° 50′. The sunne so neare the zenith that wee take her not. Longitude from the Cape, 63° 05′. Winde at east.

29. Calme all day.

30. E. by N., legues 12. Longitude, 63° 40′. Winde at W.S.W.

31. Calme this 24 howres.

April 1. East, legues 8. Longitude from the Cape, 64° 04′. Winde at S.S.E. This morninge, by occasion offred, I measured our mainestay, and found it only 13 ynches; it beinge at hoame measured (before the Governour) 17¾. Were the ropemakers hanged for their so greate abuse, it were just.

2. East, legues 21. Lattitude, 5° N. Longitude from the Cape, 65° 05′. Variation, 10° 00′. Winde at S. and S. by E.

3. East, legues 26. Lattitude, 5° N. Longitude from the Cape, 66° 23′. Winde at S.S.W. and S.W. Here wee finde the shewe of some current, the water riplinge as in a tyde, and is the same that Linskotte writeth of; but which way it setteth, as yet I knowe not.

4. East, legues 28. Longitude from the Cape, 67° 43′ E. The variation wee cannot observe, it beinge thicke and clowdie, both morning and eveninge. Winde at W.S.W.

5. This morninge wee had good store of raine. With a faire gale at west and W.S.W. wee ranne 21 legues east. Longitude from the Cape, 68° 46′ E.

6. This morninge, raine with thunder and lighteninge. Litle winde, westerly. At 6 at night, layd it a trye[1]. At midnight, sett

[1] I.e. kept the vessel with her bows to the wind.

sayle, and ran this 24 howres east, 23 legues. Longitude from the Cape of Good Hope, 69° 54′ east. Winde at west.

7. At 12 the winde came to the north-east in a gust, with raine. This 24 howres, east, legues 13. Lattitude, 05° 10′; and longitude from the Cape, 70° 33′. Variation, 07° 00′. Winde at N. and N.W.

8. East by north, legues 10. Lattitude, 5° 30′; and longitude from the Cape of Good Hope, 71°. The winde at S.W. and E.S.E., with calmes.

9. To 6 in the morninge, E.N.E., legues 8.

10. This morninge at 6 sawe the lande neare about Achine, E. by S. from us, some 7 or 8 legues of[f]. The longitude of it[1] from the Cape of Good Hope is 71° 40′, and from the meridian of Cape de Gallo 14° 00′. Lattitude at noone, 06° 00′. Then were wee faire aboarde Gomespoll[2], west of[f] some 6 or 8 legues. Variation, 6° 40′. Winde at S.S.E. This night a fresh winde at S. Wee lay off and on of the ilands. We lost 2 or 3 leagues.

11. In the morninge, calme. Thomas Gilson died. Lyinge here becalmed, wee founde a greate current sett to the norward. And being within ½ mile of the northermost litle iland, wee coulde not gett grounde in 80 fadom. At the S.E. end of this northermost iland[3] lye 6 or 8 rocks, some of them as high as a shippe under saile. This afternoone the winde came at E.N.E. At 6 at night we were entred within the 2 ilands that lye right of[f] the roade of Achine. This night wee had store of raine and thunder. Betweene these 2 ilands wee spente the night.

12. In the morninge store of raine; the winds vari[a]ble. At 12 came to anchor in the roade of Achine in 12 fadom; but you may ride in 10 or 8 fadom. Your best roade is to the eastward of the castell and rivers mouth. The west land of the maine will beare nearest west of us. The body or middest of those ilands[4]

[1] From a marginal note it appears that the particulars given relate to 'the ilands lying before Achine.'

[2] The island of Pulo Gomes (Kelapa). In the margin the name is spelt 'Gomespola,' showing that Best took it from Linschoten (*op. cit.*, p. 329).

[3] Apparently Pulo Rondo, which has several high rocky islets on its southern side. Best seems to have entered by the Bengal Passage.

[4] Bras, Nasi, etc. See the map on p. xxxv.

which lye of[f] the west pointe (which ilands you must leave on your starboarde syde as you come in) will beare of[f] you W.N.W.; and the northermost greate iland[1] will beare N. and N. by W.; and the rocke to the eastward[2] will beare of[f] you neare N.E.

Comminge out of the sea, if from the westward, come in with the land in 5° lattitude, or 5° 10′; and so shall you fall some 10 legues to the southwarde of the pointe of Achine. The land there lyeth neare N. and S.; and when you come to the pointe of Achine, the land lyeth away E. by N. and E. And here at this pointe you have diverse ilands. You must leave the westermost greate iland[3], and all the litle ones adjoyninge to it, on your starboard side; and the west [*sic*] iland[4] which lyeth E.N.E. from this former, leave on your larboarde syde; and so come in betweene these 2 ilands S.E. and S.E. by E. The distance betweene these two greate ilands is some 10 or 12 mile; and betweene them, as you come in, no danger, nor no ground to be had, though close aboarde either of theis ilands. If the wind shoulde put you to the eastward of this second greate iland, then may you come to the eastwarde of him, betweene him and the maine, free of danger save what you see.

13. I landed the merchants. The Kinge not in towne.

15. The Kinge came, and sente his chope[5] to me for my

[1] Pulo Wai.

[2] The islet of Buru, on which there is now a lighthouse.

[3] Pulo Bras.

[4] Pulo Wai.

[5] The usual term for a licence or passport (Hind. *chhāp*, which really means the seal-impression thereon). Thomas Bowrey, who was at Achin in 1687–88, says: 'The chopp is made of silver, 8 or 10 inches longe, and like to a mace which openeth on the topp, where the signet is enclosed. Before any forraigner can land in this port he must receive this chopp, and then hath he freedom to buy and sell and land his goods at pleasure. The like must be done when he is almost ready to depart the countrey, by the master or commander onely (else it is taken as a most grosse affront)' (*Countries round the Bay of Bengal*, p. 300). Alexander Hamilton, who was there in 1702, gives the following account (vol. II, p. 55): 'On my arrival I took the *chap* at the great river's mouth, according to custom. This *chap* is a piece of silver about 8 ounces weight (made in form of a cross, but the cross part is very short), that we take with both hands and put to our forehead, and declare, to the officer that brings the *chap*, that we come on an honest design to trade; and after that ceremony is over, we go in our boats freely to the town, which stands about four miles up the river; but before we take the *chap*, no boat must go, on penalty of a fine.' Hamilton's description of the *chhāp* suggests that it was

landinge; brought by an euenuche and 6 or 8 more, and also the Zabandar[1]. To them wee gave 120 mam[udis]. Withem [i.e. with them] the same day landed; and 2 howres after my landinge the Kinge sent me a present in victualls, I havinge presently [i.e. immediately] upon my landinge sente the Kinge 2 peeces [i.e. muskets]; for the costome is at landinge to presente the Kinge with some small thinge and he requiteth it by severall dishes of meate.

17. The Kinge havinge sente an ellyphant, with a basen of goulde for the Kings letters[2], I roade to the courte[3], accompanyed with 40 men (all admitted into the Kings presence). And after many complements, the Kinge retourned the letter unto [me?] for to reade it; and so the substance of it was delivered unto him in his owne language. The contence pleased him very well. It [i.e. Yet] skarsly landed, and the day well spent, the Kinge toulde me he would nowe shewe me some of his pleasures, and caused the ellephants to fight before us. And after 6 of them had fought, then he caused 4 bufloes to fight before him; which made a very excellent and feirce fight. There fearcenes such that hardly 60 or 80 men coulde parte them, fast[en]ing roapes to theare hinder legs to drawe them asunder. And after them some 10 or 12 rammes, which likewise made very greate fight; and so continued till it was darke, that wee coulde not see longer. The Kinge presented me with a bankett of the least 400 dishes, with such plenty of hott drincks as might have suffized a druncken armye. Betweene 9 and 10 he gave me leave to departe; sendinge me 2 elliphants to carry me hoame. But I roade not on them, they havinge no keverings[4] on them.

18. I wente to the courte agayne, the Kinge so appointinge; where we began to treate of the articles formerly made by his

originally a representation of the king's dagger, sent as a token that the stranger might be admitted (see p. 54). Lockyer in fact describes it (p. 35) as 'a short dagger in a gold case, like a scepter.'

[1] *Shāhbandar* (see note on p. 40).

[2] The letter Best had brought from his own sovereign. The same ceremony had been observed on the occasion of the delivery of Queen Elizabeth's letter by Capt. Lancaster (*The Voyages of Sir James Lancaster*, p. 76).

[3] Kotaraja, the capital of Achin, lies on a river, about two miles from the port.

[4] Coverings; meaning, probably, howdahs.

grandfather and Sir James Lankaster[1]. And cominge to the matter of havinge all goods both brought in and carried out free of coustome, wee ended without concludinge of any thinge.

19. The imbassadore[2] of Syam came to visitt me, tellinge me of the 3 Englishmen that came to the Kinge of Syam and of there greate enterteynemente and joye of theare Kinge to receive a letter from the King of England; and that it was some 30 moneths since[3]. They also toulde me howe joyefull there Kinge woulde be, if our shippinge came to his coastes; tellinge me what greate quantities of cloth of Portugall (which is English cloth) woulde sell in theare countryes. The coullers most in request stammell and redds, with some other, as yellowes and other pleasinge light coullers, as at Surrat. They also toulde me that there Kinge had made a conquest over the whoale country of Pegu[4], and so is nowe the greatest kinge of this orientall parte, exceptinge the Kinge of Chyna; and hath under him 26 kings, and in the warrs is able to make 6000 elliphants. There coyne all silver; there goulde lesse esteemed then the vallewe thereof. In there country is greate store of peper and raw silke. And saith that the Doutch hath there factoryes (whome they call English) at Patania[5], which is an exellent pourte; the entrance 12, 14 fathome. Likewise Syam is a good pourte[6], and is neerer unto the Kings courte[7] then Patania. Those that do goe to the citty of the Kinge alwayes come to this pourte of Syam, and so from this pourte of Syam to the Kings courte is some 20 dayes jorney by lande. I moved the embassador for his letter to the Kinge (which hee promised me); and also for his letter to the governors of pourts, in favoure of our nation, when wee shoulde come upon those coasts. And lastly, changed coynes with him, givinge

[1] Printed in *The First Letter Book* (p. 69) and in *Letters Received* (vol. I, p. 1).

[2] As we learn later, there were two ambassadors, and the context implies that both were present.

[3] The three representatives mentioned were Lucas Antheunis, Adam Denton, and Thomas Essington. Their arrival at Ayuthia was in August 1612, and the date given in the text is therefore wrong. For details see Floris, pp. 45–47.

[4] This was a gross exaggeration.

[5] Patani, on the eastern side of the Malay peninsula.

[6] The roadstead at the mouth of the Menam is meant.

[7] Ayuthia, the capital of Siam.

of our English coyne and receavinge the Kings coyne of Syam.

20. I wente to the courte, but spake not with the Kinge; whereupon I sente to the Kings deputye and complayned of my dishonnour and of some abuse by the Zabandare offred unto me. He promised that I shoulde have present redress, and that he woulde informe the Kinge thereof; which accordingely hee perfourmed the same day.

21. The Kinge sente two officers unto me to signifye that at all tymes I might repayer unto his courte with free access, and passe all the gates without stopp or attendinge for his creste[1]. And likewise removed the Zabandare; and appointed me the gentleman whome the Kinge sente vice-embassador into Holland[2], to attend me and to accompany me at all tymes to the courte and ellswhere, at my pleasure.

23. I went to visitt the Syam embassador at hoame. Havinge treated of many busines concerninge our enterteynement in his country, [he] did promisse to call a counsell and to wright his letters for me. So tooke leave and departed.

24. I wente unto the courte, and had accesse unto the Kinge; who gave me all contente, and promised the ratefyinge of all the articles formerly agreed upon by his predecessor and Sir James Lankaster. Soe, after divers complements, tooke leave, and [he] sent me hoame, presently after my retourne, an elliphant to attend me and to carry me wheathersoever it pleased me to travill. And this is a signe of the honnour of the honnerablest esteeme that they houlde of the partyes to whom they

[1] The Malay *kris*, or dagger. Evidently the custom was to stay a stranger until the monarch sent his *kris* to him as a passport. Purchas says (*Pilgrimage*, p. 612): 'The King comes little abroad, nor may any goe to him, except he be sent for by an officer with a gilded staffe or dagger. To his palace they passe through seven gates, one after another, guarded with women expert at their weapon, and using both peeces and swords. He hath none other guard for his person.'

[2] When the *Zeelandia* and *Middelburg* visited Achin in 1600–1, they brought away two ambassadors whom the king was sending to Prince Maurice. Both reached Holland in safety; but soon after their arrival the chief envoy, Abdul Samad, died, and was magnificently buried at Middelburg at the cost of the Dutch East India Company. The other, Sri Muhammad, had an interview with Prince Maurice, visited various Dutch cities, and was carried back to Achin in 1604. (*Atchin en sijne Betrekkingen tot Nederland*, by P. J. Veth, p. 71.)

send there elliphants; for none may have an elliphant, nor ride on them, but those whome the Kinge doth honnour[1].

30. Two embassadors of Syam dyned with me; passinge our tyme with many complements and discourses of their country.

May 1. I enterteyned the Doutch broker, Peter.

2. The Kinge invighted me to his founteyne to swime, and [I] was with him; it beinge some 5 or 6 miles from the citty. And sent me 2 elliphants to carry me and my provision. And havinge washed and bathed ourselves in the water, the Kinge presented us with an exceedinge greate bankett, with two much rack[2]; all to be eaten and druncke as wee sett in the water; all his nobles and greate captaynes beinge presente. Our bankett continued from one of the clocke till towards 5, at which tyme the Kinge released me; and halfe an howre after all strangers, and presently after followed himselfe.

4. Christopher Clemance dyed.

6. George Baynes dyed. Both hee and the former dyed of a serfitt, taken by unmeasurable druncken nes.

6 [*sic*]. Nicholas Cavye also dyed.

11. The ymbassador of Syam wente aboarde my shippe. This day also William Day dyed.

13. I gave 2 vests of blewe cloth (3 yards per peece) to the 2 Syam embassadors, and to either of them a faire Mallavar [i.e. Malabar] buckler, and to either of their sonnes a buckler. The same day at night George Feilder dyed.

14. Certeyne Portingalls came into Achin, which came from Mallacca with imbassadge from the Governour to this kinge. The winde shorte, they landed 3 leagues to the eastward of the roade of Achin. This day dyed Leonarde Readwood. I sent the *Hoseander* to seeke the barke which came from Mallacca, makeinge Ned Christian captayne in her.

15. At night I wente aboarde.

17. In the morninge the Portingall boate was brought unto me aboarde the *Dragon*. But before shee came aboarde, the

[1] Bowrey gives (p. 308) an account (with a picture) of a state elephant placed at the disposal of a visitor.

[2] Arrack. 'Their wine, which they call racke. This wine is made of rice, and is as strong as any of our aquavitae; a little will serve to bring one asleepe' (*The Voyages of Sir James Lancaster*, p. 77).

Kinge sente two messingers to me, to desire me to release both shee and that that might be in her; which I refused to do, answearinge that I woulde not release her untill I had seene both the barke and that was in her; but willed them to tell the Kinge that, in honnour of him, whatsoever hee required I woulde doe for him. Afterwards the barke came, and by Edward Christian I was informed there was some 4 or 5 fardles [i.e. bales] in her, and that nothinge was medled withall that was in her. Wherein beinge certifyed, I came aland, and founde my merchants to be at the courte; whoe by and by after came in, informinge me of the Kings greate displeasure for takeinge the Portingall barke in his porte; protestinge by his gods that he woulde make them all presoners, if the barke were not released. The Kinge, havinge intelligence of my comminge aland, presently sent for me. And on the way to the courte, as I was goeinge, I mett a gentleman that came from the Kinge to desire me to release the barke; but toulde him I would first speake with the Kinge. In fyne, [I] came to the courte, and presently was brought before the Kinge; wheare, after much discourse, at the Kings request I gave him the barke and all that was in her; with which hee was much pleased, and gave me an honnorable tytle, viz. Arancaia Pute[1], the significacion of which is the honnorable white; requireinge his nobles to call me by the same name. It is the name that the Kinge doth give to his greatest noblemen, when hee is pleased to grace or honnour any one of them. And further to acknowledge his thanckfullnes to me, soulde me his bengiamin[2] at myne pryce, namely at 25[3] tayle the bahar (it beinge wourth 34 and 35); professinge by generall tearmes his love and much esteeme of me; willinge me to aske and requier whatsoever I woulde of him. I required only his letters of favoure unto Pryaman; which he promised[4]. Of his mangoes which himselfe

[1] *Orang kaya* ('rich man') was the usual honorific of Malay chiefs. The primary meaning of *putih* is 'white'; but the context shows that no allusion was intended to Best's complexion, and a better rendering is 'pure' or 'clear-hearted' (as in Best's letter of 12 July 1613, given later).

[2] Gum benjamin or benzoin, a resin obtained from *Styrax benzoin*. Largely used in India and in Europe for medicinal purposes, as incense, and as a source of benzoic acid.

[3] Purchas has 'twenty'; but the figure in the text is confirmed by Best's letter referred to above.

[4] 'Most willingly promised' (Purchas).

did eate, hee gave me to eate, and likewise to carry hoame; and so [I] tooke leave and departed.

18. In the morninge John Cransbe died. And the same day at night my man Fenn played some reaks [i.e. pranks]; for the which beinge by me trunchend[1], hee drewe his daggor upon me, and afterward his swourde, usinge some presoumtious words. For which his actions he was indighted and founde giltie the 21 dicto, and sewrely had bene arrayned[2] the morninge
21 May. followinge, had not the embassador of Syam come unto me to desire his life; to whome I gave both his life and also the man, and [he] carryed him hoame with him. And presently after I sent to Fenn his cheast, with all things in it; and in his purse there was some 24 or 25 shillings in rialls, which I also sent him.

25. Gowin Brigame dyed.

27. Mallim Gany[3] came to Achein; by whoame I received letters[4] from our merchants at Surratt, and also a coppy of the Kings firma, sent them from Agra, beareinge [date] the 25 day of January and the 7th yeare of the Greate Magoles raigne[5], confirminge all that was past betweene the Governour of Amidavar and I. So nowe there is nothinge wantinge in the domynnions of the Greate Magoll, but sufficiente[6] men to manage the busines.

28. Thomas Kilbe dyed. And the same day [I] delivered from the *Dragon* to the *Hoseander* 800 barrs of leade and 257 eands of iron for ballast.

June 3. The boye Sainte[7] dyed.

6. William Walker dyed.

7[8]. Raphe Standishe, sergion of the *Hoseander*, dyed.

14. Thomas Sargiant dyed.

16. John Yeamons dyed, and Roger Petts.

17. The Dutch Captaine dyed. And the same day came there

[1] Beaten with a truncheon or stick.

[2] Arraigned, i.e. sentenced. This sense is now obsolete.

[3] Apparently *Mu'allim* Ghani had been the captain of the Gujarāti vessel mentioned on p. 29.

[4] Not extant.

[5] 1612–13.

[6] Able (a hit at Aldworth).

[7] The Christian name is given in the margin as James.

[8] An error for '13' (see Croft's journal).

a merchant of the Doutch into Achin from Mercellapatan [Masulipatam], and had bene 8 moneths on his jorney. He toulde us of the death of Captain Hippinge[1], who dyed in Patania, and of Mr. Browne[2], master of the *Globe*, whoe dyed in Mercellapatan, and that they had beene ill dealte with at Mercellapatan, that they left no factory there: that the shippe had bin at Syam and retourned to Patane: and that in Syam and in Patane had setled [a] factory and left the Doutch merchants[3] cheefe in both places, and that the shippe was like to make an ill voyage; and toulde us howe they weare distressed with want of water betweene Bantame and Mercellapatan.

19. Henry Stevens dyed.

20. William Gaskin dyed. And the same day the Kinge zesed [i.e. seized] of a shippe of Surratt and made slaves of all the men, the shippe beinge ritchely laden[4].

24. I received of the Kinge his presente for the Kinge of England, namely, his letter[5], a cresse, a hasega[6], 4 peeces of fyne callyco lane[7], and 8 campher dishes. And also soulde the Kinge 100 barrs[8] of iron, at 5 tayle per barr (monny).

25. John Wilkockes dyed.

26. I landed 1300 ends[9] of iron, which waighed (vz. all the iron) 268 barrs [bahars], Achein waight.

27. I landed 6500 [?] eands, which wayed [*blank*]. George Cox dyed.

28. Peter Tent dyed.

30. George Bence dyed.

3 July. Geffry Thorne dyed, and Thomas Gilbourne. Also the Kings armatha[10] arived, and but 20 dayes from the coaste of

[1] Anthony Hippon, captain of the *Globe*, died at Patani on 9 July 1612.

[2] Robert Browne was not master of the *Globe*, but a merchant who was associated with Floris and Antheunis in the management of the voyage. He died at Masulipatam on 7 September 1611.

[3] Meaning Floris and Antheunis.

[4] See Best's letter (given later).

[5] For this see Copland's narrative (given later).

[6] A lance (now generally spelt 'assegai').

[7] Calico lawn, or muslin.

[8] Bahars (Croft says 168).

[9] Apparently this means 'small bars.'

[10] Armada, or fleet of war vessels (see Copland's account, below). Croft gives the date of its arrival as 28 June.

Joar to Achein. In Joar they tooke the Doutch factory and made a pray of all theare goods, and brought heather prisoners of the Dutch some 20 or 24[1].

5. Arther Poope dyed.

7. I received the Kings letter for Pryaman, and the chopp for my departure.

12. I tooke leave in Achein, and came aboarde.

13. In the morninge sett sayle. And comminge nere the greate westermost iland [i.e. Pulo Bras], open of the nothermost gutt in the same ile wee founde faire shoaldinge, 20 fadom, cleane grounde, sand, a good byrth [i.e. distance] from the lande. This depth, with cleare grownde, contynued almost to the end of the iland; so that on the east syde of this iland there is verry good anckoringe; and on the iland greate store of wood. But beinge neare the greate iland [i.e. Pulo Wai] to the eastward of this, wee coulde gett noe grounde. Betweene theis two greate ilands is your best and saffest course, goeinge in or out to the roade of Achein; likewise to the eastward of the eastermost iland (but that is out of the way).

Noote that from the 12th of Aprill to the midest of June we had much raine (seildome two dayes without raine), with gusts and much winde; from the 15 of June to the 12th July, verry much winde, verry sore stresses, alwayes at S.W., W.S.W., and W.

[1] The Sultan of Johore, Alā-addīn Riāyat Shāh III, had made peace with the Portuguese, and this was resented by the Sultan of Achin, who regarded Malacca as a standing menace to the security of his own kingdom. He accordingly sent an expedition to the capital of Johore, which was at that time Batu Sawar, on the left bank of the Johore River, a little below Kota Tinggi. The Achinese fleet arrived on 7 May 1613 (N.S.) and prepared to attack the city. A Dutch ship, the *Hoop*, was lying in the river, and the Achinese desired her commander to remain neutral, promising in that case to do no harm to the Dutch; but the latter conceived themselves bound by treaty to help the Sultan, and so they sent to his assistance all the men they could spare. Nevertheless, after a stiff resistance, the city was captured, and the Sultan and his brother (Rāja Sabrang) were made prisoners, together with the surviving Dutchmen. The Dutch factory was burnt in the struggle, part of its contents being destroyed and the rest confiscated by the conquerors. The captives were brought to Achin, where an agreement was come to for their release on payment of a ransom. They were duly despatched to Johore; but on the way a Portuguese squadron from Malacca was met, and the Portuguese insisted on taking out the Dutchmen, who were carried to Goa as prisoners. (Colenbrander's *Jan Pietersz. Coen*, vol. 1, pp. 26, 61, 100; Netscher, pp. 8, 29, 30; Winstedt, pp. 32, 33; Floris, pp. 77, 81, 97, 102.)

14. Wee came out betweene the two great ilands. They are distante some 6 or 7 leagues, and the midway betweene them lyeth S.E. and N.W. from the roade of Achein. But noe grounde tell you be within some two myle of the lowe land of Achein, only on the west iland aforesaide. At night the wester iland bare S.E. and by E., of[f] some 7 or 8 leagues, and [at] the poynte of day[1] bore S.S.E. some 12 or 14 leagues of[f].

15. West ½ N., 14 leagues; and longitude from the iles of Achein, W. 40 mynutes. Wynde S. by W.

16. S.S.E., 8 leagues. Longitude from Achein, 32 minutes. Winde S.W., and calmes.

17. South, 15 leagues. Lattitude, 4° 20′. Longitude from Achein, west 31 minutes. Variation, 6° 30′. Winde N.W., and calmes. Thomas Sicklin dyed in the *Hoseander*.

18. S.E. by E., leagues 16. Lattitude, 3° 40′. Longitude from the meridian of Achein, east nyne mynnetts. Winde S.W. Faire weather. Wee finde some small currante to the southwards.

19. S.E. by E., 7 leagues. Longitude from Achein, east 26′. Winde S.S.W. Rayne and calme. In the afternoone wee sawe a small lowe iland, from us some 4 or 5 leagues E.S.E.

20. South, 13 leagues. Lattitude, 2° 40′. Longitude from Achein, 26′. Winde at N. Faire weather.

21. S. by E., 10 leagues. Longitude from Achein, 32′. Winde N.N.W. Calme, and everywheare with raine.

22. S.S.E., leagues 18. Longitude from Achein, east 52′. Winde westerly, and calme, with rayne and gusts.

23. South-east, leagues 14. Lattitude [*blank*]. Longitude from Achein, 1° 22′. Winde att S.W. Calme, with rayne.

24. S.S.E., leagues 4. Lattitude, 25′ north. Longitude from Achein, 1° 28′. Calmes.

25. Calme, with raine.

26. S.E., leagues 20. Lattitude, south 20′. Longitude from Achein, 1° 50′. Winde S.W., with calme and rayne.

27. S.E. ½ E., leagu[e]s 9. Lattitude, south 45′; and longitude from Achein, 2° 14′. Winde north, calme, with rayne. Wee finde a sotherly currante.

28. This morninge wee sawe an iland[2]. The north end of it

[1] At dawn. [2] Siberut, the northernmost of the Mentawi Islands.

bare N. by E., some 3 or 4 leagues of[f], and then wee had 45 fadom, fyne ozie sande. At this tyme wee have made some 15 or 16 legues E.S.E. ½ S. synce yeasterday at noone; so are in south lattitude 1° 10′ or 1° 15′. So the north end of this iland lyeth in 1° 00′, or neare thereabouts. A faire high land, full of trees, lowest at the N. end, and lyeth N.N.W., and is in length some 16 or 18 leagues. Wee came all alonge faire by the land, 2 and 3 mile of[f], and had 30, 25, and 20 fadom; and our boate ½ way betweene the land and the shippe, and had 13 and 14 fadom. All alonge, faire oazey sand. At 8 in the evenninge anckored in 22 fadom; the S.E. poynte of the iland bearinge of[f] us E.S.E. The S.E. end of this iland lyeth in 2°, litle more or lesse, and hath longitude from Achein 3° 14′. There wee founde a good courrante to the southward.

29. At daylight sett saile, and came faire by the litle ilands which lyeth at the S.E. end of this greate iland, and had 24, 25 fadom. Of theis litle ilands there be 5 or 6. As soone as wee weare thwarte of the 2 ilands, wee coulde not gett grownde in 50 fadom. From the S.E. poynte of the greate ile the same iland faleth away E. or thereaboute. And of[f] theis east end lyeth also certeyne ilands. And from the greate iland S.E., 7 or 8 leagues, there lyeth a faire greate iland[1], 8 leagues longe, S.E. and N.W. Nowe betweene the 2 great ilands there lyeth also 2 or 3 smalle ilands, faire aboarde the ends of the greate ilands; and in the midest, betweene the 2 greate ilands, there is goode channell[2] to goe through, broade some 4 or 5 leagues. All this day the winde at N.E. Fowle weather and raine.

30. Lay of[f] and on, betweene the 2 greate ilands. Winde at N. and N.N.E. [In] the afternoone gott into shoalde water of[f] the southermost of the 2 greate ilands, and anckored in 40 fadom grownde. At night calme. The *Hoseander*, 2 or 3 leagues without us, coulde not gett grounde, and soe with the courrante drove to the southeastwarde, that the next mornninge wee coulde see her but out of the topp.

31. Wee sett saile. Litle winde, N.N.E. Wee gatt thorough

[1] Sikabu, or Sipora, the southernmost of the Mentawi group.

[2] The Seaflower Channel, named after H.M. ship of that name, which passed through it in 1806.

betweene the 2 greate ilands, beinge faire aboarde the eastermost, 5 or 6 mile of[f]. Had not lesse then 33, 35, 40 fadom, good anckoringe grounde. Here wee founde a stronge currante, settinge to the eastwarde. And upon all the cost of Sumatra there goeth a good courrante to the S.S.E., as the land lyeth. Robert Acton dyed this afternoone. At night wee anckored, neere midway betweene the two greate ilands, in 50 fadom; the one bearinge S.E., the other N.W., the bodyes of them. Calme at night.

1 August. In the morninge sett saile. Little winde, at E.N.E. We sawe 3 fishinge boats, but they came not to us. The varriation heare, 4° 40′; and lattitude, 1° 45′.

2. Little winde, notherlie. Lattitude, 1° 30′. Nowe the sothermost of the 2 greate ilands S. by E., some 8 leagues of[f]; the westermost of the greate ilands, the body of it west, the nothermost pointe N.W. by W., of[f] some 5 or 6 leagues. No grownde at 80 and 90 fadom. We see [the] maine iland of Sumatra very plaine. The hye land which is to the S. of Priaman some 12 leagues, it beareth of[f] us E.N.E., of[f] some 12 or 13 leagues.

3. In sight of Priaman, 9 or 10 leagues of[f], it bearinge from us N.E. by E., it showinge with 2 greate hie hills, makeinge a faire swampe [i.e. depression] or saddle betweene them both. And sawe also Tecou, the hye land on it; it is not more then ½ so hye as Priaman land, and riseth somethinge flatt. Then sawe also the hie land of Passaman, which lyeth some 7 or 8 leagues to the northward of Tecou, and Tecou[1] middway betweene Parssaman and Priaman; which mountaine[2] is very hie, and riseth like Mungevell or Mount Etnea[3], in Sicilia. This a very hie and goodlie mountaine; and the 2 hye hills of Priaman is also very hie land. Priaman and the body of the greate iland lieth N.E.

[1] This word is badly written in the MS., and Purchas made it into 'even' (which does not give sense). The respective positions of Priaman, Tiku, and Pasaman are shown in the map given in the introduction.

[2] Gunong Ophir, the highest mountain on Sumatra visible from the sea. It is nearly 9500 feet high, cone-shaped, and can be seen 110 miles in clear weather.

[3] Sanderson (p. 37) refers to Etna as 'Mongebella.' Purchas here substitutes 'Monte Gibello' for 'Mungevell,' and omits the next three words.

and S.W., distante some 20 leagues. The winde at N.N.E., wee stand to the westward. At 4 laide it aboute.

4. At noone Priaman E.N.E., 7 leagues of[f]; Tecou N.E., some 8 leagues of[f]. Lattitude, 50′ southerlie. Calme.

5. In the morninge wee sawe 3 or 4 ilands to the eastward of us, and beinge some 6 or 7 miles from them, W.S.W. and S.W. from the northermost, coulde gett no ground. Our lattitude nowe 44′. This day Nathaniel Skynner died.

6. Lattitude, 50′ S. Then was the norther[1] of the 3 ilands of Priaman N.E. ½ E.; the 2 mor E. by E. [*sic*], the S.E. ½ E., distante some 3 or 4 leagues betweene; and the white iland[2], for so it is, all the foote of it very white, with sand round aboute it, and will shewe like breaches. There is noe danger aboute this iland. This iland was E. of us, ½ a leage from us, and lyeth from the 3 ilands of Priaman S.W., some 3½ leagues of[f]. To the southeastward of the white iland you shall see diverse ilands; which I came faire by, but coulde gett no grounde.

Note that the 2 hie mountaines of Priaman lyeth from the 3 ilands of Priaman N.E. by E. and S.W. by W.; and then the 2 hills will make, with a faire swampe or saddle betweene them. The northermost is the hiest, and hath a flatt or plaine upon the toppe of it. The sure course to come for Priaman is to put you in the lattitude of 40 or 45 minutes south, and so come in. Be sure, when you shall come out of the sea, wheather from Acheene, Succatorin, etc., go noe more then 50 minutes south lattitude. So shall you be sure to keepe on the E. side of the greate iland of Nemcame. If more sotherly, you may fall to the westward of this greate iland, and make your way long, as I did, followinge John Davis his writinge[3]; and on the off syde [you] shall finde also a very greate currente to the S. To putt into Priaman you must leave the northermost of the 3 ilands on your

[1] Pulo Anso. The other two are named Tengah and Ujong respectively.

[2] Apparently Pulo Bando, or the coral bank lying four miles to the north-west of it.

[3] In Davis's *Ruter* (as printed in *Purchas*, vol. I, p. 444) he says: 'To the eastward of Priaman there are ilands, in the south latitude of one degree and thirty minutes, which are called the Iles of Nimtam [i.e. the Mentawi group, already mentioned, the 'Nemcame' of the text]. Your course is to goe with these ilands, and come not betweene the maine, but keepe the sea till you see those ilands.'

larboaurde syde, the other 2 on your starboaurde syde, borrowinge in the norther ile, in 4 and 5 fadom; somewhat faire by it, because the channell is narrowe betweene the saide norther ile and the flatt of the river.

Note, as wee steared N.N.W., when the white ile was S.E., 3, 4, and 5 mile of[f], wee mett with shoalde water, 4, 5, 7, 15 fadom well to; and then the iles of Priaman were E. from us some 4 or 5 leagues. Therefore you must be heere very carefull. When the iles of Teco were north of[f] from us, some 2½ leagues of[f], wee had 34, 30 fadom, ozie grounde. Here we anckored all night.

7. In the morninge, the winde at N., wee sett saile. And standing to the westward wee sawe a shoalde, and sente our boate to it, and founde 3 fadom upon it. Then did the 2 hometts [i.e. hummocks] or paps beare of[f] us N. and by W., and Teco Iles N.E. by N., of[f] 4 or 5 miles. Plyinge here of[f] and on, we sawe another shoalde in the offinge, W.S.W. or W. by S. from Teco Iles. Our depth, when wee weare of[f], 32 and 33 fadom (ossie); standinge in, faire shoaldinge, 26, 25, 23. Note that Teco Iles and the hye land of Parssaman beare each from other N. by E. and S. by W.; which course, for any thinge wee sawe, you might come in with the Iles safelie. This day John Pettie dyed.

In the afternoone wee came to Teco, and anckored on the east syde of the 3 ilands, in 7 fadom (the sothermost ile bore W.S.W., the middlemost W.N.W., the northermost north), and ¼ of a mile from the ilands.

On both sydes of theis ilands you have good shoaldinge, and no danger but what you see; but in the offinge full of danger. Manie breaches we saw; but with good lookeinge out they may be avoided by day, for they do all shewe themselves, either by the breach of the sea or the risinge of the sea upon the shoaulds; or if it be very smoothe water, then the collour of the sea will shewe the shoalds. They are all very neall[1] to. This eveninge the *Hoseander* came and anckored by us.

8. This day wee had greate store of raine. I sente Mamote[2] aland.

[1] See note on p. 44.

[2] Evidently the broker they had brought from Achin (see Best's letter of 12 July 1613). Presumably his name was Mahmūd.

9. I landed my merchants; and in the afternone I landed, with the Kings letter.

11. I called a counsell, for sendinge the *Hoseander* for Priaman, with the Kings letter.

12. The *Hoseander* departed. And we went in within the northermost iland and rode in 4 fadom water; and on the barre, comminge in, $3\frac{1}{2}$. Wee rode closse aboarde the iland, and the neere[1] to the ile the more water; and all towarde the maine very faire shoaldinge. Wee ridd in ozey, and so is it all so faire as the depth goeth. The deepest water to goe in or out is on the west syde of the ilands; but wee went in on the east syde of all the ilands.

14. The Governour for the Kinge and Cheife Scrivano[2] came aboord to conferre of price for peper. They stood on 20 rialls per bahar. I offered 14. After much talke they departed, with presents given them. Our pynnace was sente after their landeinge. Much raine this day.

17. The oulde Governour came aboarde and treated of the price of peper, but coulde not agree. I presented him with a peece and a booke[3] of callico; and shott 7 peeces at his departure.

18. The *Hoseander* retourned unto us from Priaman. This day John Davys died.

19. Thomas Biram dyed.

20. I determined the *Hoseanders* goeinge for Bantam, and putt into her 2900 barrs of leade and 51 peeces, and all the tymber of our pynnace which shoulde have beene sett upp[4].

21. The *Hoseander* departed for Bantam. John Onyon died.

24. In the morninge I sente my gundeloe[5] to Parssaman, with William More and Hugh Gittins.

25. There came in a junke of Bantam, the owners Chineses. They confirmed unto me the death of Sir Henry Middleton[6],

[1] An old form of 'nearer.'

[2] Secretary or registrar (Port. *escrivão*, a writer). Later Best calls him the 'Curicoone,' which is the Hindustāni *kārkun*, with the same significance.

[3] Flat roll (hence book-muslin).

[4] A pinnace had been taken out in sections, to be put together at some convenient place (see pp. 114, 182). This was often done in the early voyages.

[5] The Italian *gondola* (now specialized at Venice) was used of a small ship's boat. Later Best calls it a shallop.

[6] On 24 May 1613. For this sad event and the loss of his ship, the *Trade's Increase*, see Jourdain, pp. 301, 302, and Floris, p. 83.

with the losse of most of her men and mainemast, which brake with forcinge her downe to carreene her: and that nowe shee was gone from the iland Panjane[1] to Bantam: that 300 Chineses died in worke on her.

28. My boate and men retourned from Passaman, haveinge bene well intreated; and brought with them the Scrivane of the place to deale with me. With whome I dealt, and went through the 29th for monie at 16 dollars the barr[2] [i.e. bahar of pepper]: for goods, 8 blew bafters (of 3½ mand[3] per baftar) the barr, kanikeens and seilers, 30 the ba[ha]r, kacambar or chirans[4], 45 the ba[ha]r; and tooke the agreemente under his handwritinge. [In the] afternoone hee departed in my shallope, with presents, and peeces [of] ordenaunce given him at partinge[5].

2 September. My shallope retourned from Passaman with good tydings. The same day I retourned her agayne.

5. Thomas Holmes died.

8. My boate came from Passaman, William More in her; tellinge me that the people of Passaman woulde not stand to there agreement, but woulde there way their peper and there receive their callicoes; whereupon I resolved to send goods thither, that so wee might make a beginninge with them. The reason of this their breakeinge with us was that Sir Henry Middleton, the yeare before, had caused them to bringe to the ile of Teccoe good quantityes of peper; which beeinge there, he woulde not give them their price agreed upon[6]; which maketh

[1] Pulo Panjang, a small island at the entrance of Bantam Bay. The ship had been taken there to careen her.

[2] Here, as elsewhere, a dollar means a rial of eight, i.e. from 4*s*. 6*d*. to 5*s*. On p. 68 we are told that about 13 dollars went to the Tiku gold *tael*, though a little later 12 was the usual figure (*Letters Received*, vol. III, pp. 220, 235; vol. IV, p. 71). The Tiku *bahar* was 386 lb. (see Best's letter, below).

[3] This must be the copyist's error for ma[hmūdis]. In the original log the word was probably written 'mā,' with the tail of the 'a' joined to the long mark over that vowel; hence the mistake.

[4] Of these Gujarāti piece-goods, baftas were the common dyed calicoes, sold in the piece; 'kanikeens' were squares or oblongs, cut from baftas, and mostly dyed blue or black; 'seilers' (sealas) were similar pieces, dyed red; 'kacambar' may be the Hind. *kusumbha*, 'safflower,' and this suggests that they were yellow in colour; while 'chirans' were possibly white, with a red stripe (*Letters Received*, vol. IV, p. 70).

[5] Meaning that a salute was fired in his honour.

[6] This charge cannot be substantiated from other records. Downton (in *Purchas*, vol. I, p. 311) says that at Tiku the natives delivered rotten or wet

them nowe thus to deale with us. Eight bailes of goods I put into the shallope, and sente her away the same day, with William More and Tobie Oliver in her, and John Watson to take the charge of the watch there at Passaman, with other 12 men for watch and ward.

13. Dave Leece died. Our boate came from Passaman.

14. John Harmon died, and James Machnew. This day the Governour called me aland, beinge sate with all the cheife. I came to him, and after much talke agreed for the price of peper: monie, 18 dollars the ba[ha]r; last[1], 8 peeces the barr; canikeens, 30 per ba[ha]r; seilars, 35 per ba[ha]r; indentinge [i.e. stipulating] for presents to 16 greate men.

16. George Bucher died.

18. My boate retourned from Passaman, with William More and Hugh Gittins, both sicke. John Chambers died the 15th. This day I tooke in my first peper, viz. 5 ba[ha]rs, and gave 16 presents to 16 greate men.

20. I received 31 ba[ha]rs peper from Passaman, and 11 ba[ha]rs from Teccoe.

22. Hugh Gittins died; and Richard Tapson at Passaman.

23.
25. My gundeloe retourned, and brought 3 sicke men. This day I received from thence some 40 ba[ha]rs, and sente to Oliver 4 bailes goods per one of the country boats. Robert Steward died.

28. At night wee had very foule weather[2], much winde and raine at N.W.; and other 2 stormes wee have had within these 20 dayes, the winde westerly. The stormes continue not 3 or 4 howres.

30. John Feilder died, and William Nealle, and Henry Boswell. This day Henry Long came from Passaman and gave me knowledge of the sicknes of Mr. Oliver; whereupon I sente my shallope to fetch both him and all other men away, and to surcease my factory there.

pepper and put rice or stones in some of the bags; while Jourdain (p. 232) complains bitterly of the trickery and fraud practised. In such circumstances the English may well have refused to give the full price previously agreed upon.

[1] Probably Best wrote 'bafts,' meaning baftas. Purchas failed to make anything of the word, and ingeniously substituted 'lastage' (payment for permission to load a ship), reading 'eight pence' instead of 'eight peeces.'

[2] The change of monsoon usually occurs in the latter part of September.

2 October. I went aland to have wayed 70 or 80 ba[ha]rs of peper, which was brought downe to the Bayleife[1]; where meetinge with the Governour and Curicoone[2] with other officers, they demaunded of me newe coustomes, viz. upon every 3 ba[ha]rs of peper to pay 1 dollour, and for anchoridge[3] 6 tailes (which is 77 dollours): which newe taxes I refused to pay, and they refused to way, and so departed.

3. The Malavour pylott[4] dyed.

4. Robert Hillowe died, and Phillipe Jelley. In the afternoone our shallope came from Passaman, and brought all our goods, parte in her and parte in a boate of the country, but all of it very wett. The shallope suncke upon the barre of Passaman; the contry people very kinde unto them, and tooke greate paynes to helpe them, both to save there boate and goods. John Watson died at Passaman the first of October, and Mr. Olever died the second.

5. I ended with the Governour and people touchinge a newe custome which they demaunded, viz. a riall of eight upon every 3 bahares of peper; of which, after much adoe, I gott dismissed; yet to give a presente to the Governour for the Kinge, and to the other Governour, under the title of ankeredge, 6 taile (which is 77 dollours), I yeilded to pay.

6. I waighed 60 bahars of peper, but coulde not bringe any aboarde (there was so much winde).

7. I brought it all aboarde.

9. I wayed 30 ba[ha]rs, and brought it aboarde.

10. Edward Roads died.

14. William Wilkeson dyed.

17. John Windresse dyed.

18. William More dyed.

21. In the morninge early the *Hoseanders* boate came unto us with Edward Cristen, the shippe at anckore 4 or 5 myle of[f]. They brought me knowledge of the losse of the *Trades Increase*, and of greate store of goods at Bantam; peper at 13 rialls the timbane[5],

[1] This seems to be a perversion of some form of Malay *balai*, a shed or warehouse for the storage of goods (see Lockyer, p. 36, and Jourdain, p. 261).

[2] See note on p. 65.

[3] Anchorage or port dues.

[4] The Malabar pilot taken in January (see p. 42).

[5] Malay *timbang*, 'weight.' At Bantam 'a sacke [of pepper] is called a timbang' (Saris, p. 213).

which is a bahar and a halfe of Teccoe waight. The merchants also from Bantam writinge me the same, and also that they had readye 17,000 baggs of peper, all which, if it pleased me to come thither, I shoulde have, or so much thereof as shoulde seeme good unto me, and [at?] 13 dollours the timban. Out of these and many other consideracions I presently called a counsell, where wee concluded the *Dragon* to goe for Bantam, and the *Hoseander* to stay in the roade of Teccoe upon the sale of Suratt goods; all which goods beinge put aboarde of her, I departed the roade of Teccoe the 30th of October.

In the interim,

22. This day the *Darlinge* came into the roade of Teccoe unto us, bounde for the Coaste of Carrmendell; her captaine Mr. John Jourden, her merchants Christopher Luther [and] Nicholas Bangam[1], the master Thomas Herode. With whome when I had conferred, I called a counsell, and upon divers consideracions changed the purpose of her voyage, and concluded her retourne agayne for Bantam[2].

29. Robert Portman dyed. This day I was under saile, but coulde not gett out. Here in this roade I stayed 11 weeks, and bought 120 or 115 tonnes of peper, and buried of our men 25, all which either dyed or contracted their deaths at Passaman and not at Teccoe. And certeynely, had wee not attempted tradinge at Passaman, they had beene, either all or the greatest parte of them, nowe lyvinge. Therefore I doe wish all our nation never to attempt the sendinge of our men to Passaman; for so contagious is there the ayre, and the water so evell, that [it] is unpossible for a Christian to live.

30. In the afternoone sett sayle. At 6 at night weare thwarte of the offermost of the 3 ilands. All night steered S.S.W.

31. At 6 in the morninge S. and by W. and S. till noone. From 6 to this day [at] 12, wee made some 15 leagues, S. ½ W. Nowe weare from the land some 7 leagues. All this afternoone

[1] For this merchant see note on p. 92.

[2] For Jourdain's account of this incident see his *Journal*, pp. 309–11. He was unwilling to give up his voyage to Masulipatam, and only yielded to Best's insistence and the authority of the council's decision. The *Darling* thereupon accompanied the *Dragon* to Bantam (Jourdain, p. 311).

faire in sight of one of the ilands of Nimtaine. The winde northerly, and calme.

1 November. In the morninge, some 4 or 5 leagues from the maine, we sawe the lowe land, full of trees, and also the second ile of Nimtaine, some 8 or 9 leagues of[f]. This 24 howres wee made some 13 or 14 leagues, S.E. by S. Northerlie, litle winde, and calme. Lattitude, 2° 30′. The currante hath helped us.

2. This 24 howres wee have made 10 or 12 leagues, S.E. by S. Litle winde, northerly. Faire by the lande, 4 or 5 leagues off. A faire coaste, but noe grounde at this distance. Lattitude, 3° 15′. We have still the currente with us.

3. This 24 howres wee made some 16 leagues, S.S.E. The winde everywhere from the land, some 8 or 9 leagues. Lattitude, 4° 0′. We finde still the help of a currant. Here wee stoode in, and at 5 afternone were some 4 or 5 mile from the 2 ilands, in bignes as the ilands of Teccoe, and at both ends of these ilands greate breaches, but likely of a good roade within them for sotherly winds. The shoalding faire, 25, 20, 18 fadom etc. Some 8 or 9 mile S.E. from these 2 ilands there is a faire bigge iland[1], which may be 2 or 3 mile in cirquit, and likely of good roade within it; and wee tooke it to be Celiber[2]. There is here upon the maine of Sumatra a very faire sugerloafe hill[3], which hill and the 2 little ilands beare neerest N.E. and S.W. The coaste faire and boulde.

4. At noone, lattitude 4° 35′. From the maine of Sumatra 4 leagues. Calme, and little winde at W.S.W.

5. Calme this 24 howres; yett wee go to the southward with litle winde and some smale helpe of a currante. From the land 7 or 8 miles. A boulde coaste without danger; noe grounde in 70 fadom. The hye land of Monancabo[4] at 6 at night was N. and by E. from us.

6. In the morninge the former hye land was N. ½ W., and the hye hill which standeth on the south parte of Sumatra was east

[1] Pulo Tikus (Rat Island), about five miles south-west of Benkulen. It is surrounded by a coral reef about two miles in extent.

[2] Sillebar, about seven miles south of Benkulen.

[3] Probably Ujong Kungkaai, a round bluff a little to the south of Sillebar.

[4] Manangkabo, a mountainous district in the interior. Best got the name from Davis.

from us. Lattitude, 5° 50′. Thus wee still go [to] the southwarde with the currente; for these 3 dayes wee have had litle winde. This afternoone wee sawe the smale iland which lyeth in 6° 5′ or thereabouts, shorte of the 3 east and west ilands which Davis writeth of[1]. At night we weare faire by him, some 3 or 4 mile from it. Depth, 90 and 85 fadom. This night raine and thunder, with litle winde.

7. In the morninge, winde at S.E. Wee still finde a sothern currante, which hath caried us this night 5 or 6 leagues to the S.S.E. At 4 in the afternoone wee sawe the middlemost of the 3 Salt Hills or Ilands, from us E.N.E., distante some 12 or 13 leagues. An howre after, wee sawe the sothermost, E. of [us], like distant with the former. Also wee sawe the ilands of Java syde. The winde at S.S.E.

8. In the morninge, faire aboarde the S. iland or Salt Hill, 2 or 3 leagues of[f], W.S.W. from it. The winde shorteninge upon us, wee could not goe to the southward of the south Salt Hill, but bare upp and putt through betweene the south and middle Salte Hills or Ilands, borrowinge with my boate close aboarde the smale ilands which lye on the N.W. and north parte of the greate iland, the shippe halfe a mile of[f]. The boate founde good depth cloase aboarde the shoare, not lesse then 10, 12, 20 fadom, 3 or 4 cables length off; in the shippe not lesse then 23, 25 fadom. Noe danger at all; you shall see all that you neede to feare. The bredth of this channell is 8 or 10 miles[2]. From this channell (keepinge the south ile as nowe I did) your course in with the maine of Java is E.S.E. and E. and by S. 9 or 10 leagues; so shall you go to the southward of the flatt ragged ile[3] which lyeth

[1] Davis (*Purchas*, vol. 1, p. 451) speaks of 'a little island fast by the maine, that lieth in sixe degrees, no minutes, or much thereupon. Heere you shall see a round hill in the countrie east from you, which will be north when you come with the three isles by the point of Sumatra, that lye east one from the other. Then shall you have the Salt Hills east and by south from you...which are three islands that lye south and north one from another.' The 'three isles' may be Saka, Rond, and Sunchal, at the eastern end of Lagundi. The 'Salt Hills' appear to be the islands of Sebuku, Sebesi, and Krakatoa. The last-named is identified with 'the Salt Hill' in *Purchas* (vol. 1, p. 620), and its latitude is that given by Davis for 'the S.E. Salt Hill.'

[2] This shows that Best went through the channel between Sebesi and the Krakatoa group.

[3] Possibly Thwartway Island (Pulo Sangian).

neerest W. by S. from the pointe of Palimbam[1], 4 leagues of[f]. On Java syde there is no danger, but a bould shoare and good shoaldinge to 20, 15, 12 fadom etc. Your depth, comminge over from this channell which I rann through, is 25, 27, 30 fadom.

9. In the morninge, faire aboarde Java; the flatt or raged iland N.N.E., 3 or 4 mile off. Depth, 33 fadom. The pointe of Palimbam E.N.E., some 5 leagues off. Aboute noone (the winde beinge att N. and currente against us) wee anckored, N.W. by W. from the flatt or raged iland, W. from the sothermost of the 2 rocks which lye neare N. and S., and from the sother rocke halfe a mile. Depth, 23 fadom. The pointe of Palimbam N.E. ½ N. The south Salt Hill or iland W.S.W. ½ westerly.

Note that the south Salt Hill and flatt or ragged iland lieth W.S.W. [and] E.N.E., distante some 11 or 12 leagues; so that, comminge to the southward of the sother Salt Hill, east is a good course and will carry you with the maine of Java, and then longst the shoare to the pointe of Palimbam. Here is no danger, neither on the maine nor ilands. Your directest course for the pointe of Palimbam is to goe faire by the flatt or ragged iland and betweene the 2 rocks. You may go within the sother rocke, if the winde be of[f] the land, that then you shalbe neare the land, but depth enough. Note that, runninge here over betweene the flatt ile and the south rocke, wee had 60 fadom, and presently 30; then 20, 23, 25, etc.

At 6 at night wayed, the winde at S. Here, all the tyme wee anchored, wee had a good currante from the N.E.

10. In the morninge, were thwarte of Palimbam poynte. Depth, 40, 45 fadom, 5 or 6 miles of[f] the land; faire by the land, 15, 18, 20 fadom. At 10 anchored in 45 fadom, 5 or 6 mile from Palimbam S.E. At 3 sett saile; and when wee came in faire by the former pointe, it fell calme. The currente stronge, setting to the westward. Came agayne to an anchore at 6; and in bringinge upp our shippe, the cable broake and the anchor lost. Depth, faire aboarde the land, 40, 35, 30 fadom.

11. At 2 in the morninge, sett saile and, with the currant settinge in and boate aheade, gott in, and at 8 or 9 anchored,

[1] St Nicholas Point, the north-western end of Java.

faire aboarde Poolo Pinjam[1], N.N.W. from it 2 or 3 mile. Depth, 20 fadom. At 12 or 1 a clocke, the breese or seatourne came, and carried us in, leavinge Poolo Pinjam of[f] the larbord syde and the 5 ilands[2] on the starbourd syde. And at 4 anchored in the roade of Bantam in 4 fadom ¼ lesse. Blessed be God.

12. I called all the merchants aboarde, and concluded on the price of peper at 13 d[ollers] per ba[ha]r (which is our waitt 600*li.*).

Robert Balderstone died.

13. Davide Hewes died. This day wee tooke in 1000 sacks [of] peper.

16. Thomas Blackman died. I went aland. This day received aboarde 800 bags peper.

17. Received 316 baggs peper. Received baggs 2216 of Priaman peper this day. Received also our Bantam peper, 400 baggs.

18. I wentē unto the Kinge; and laded 1000 baggs peper.

19. I received aboarde 700 sacks peper.

20. I received aboarde 1150 sacks peper

22. I tooke in a 1000 sacks peper.

23. I tooke in a 1000 sacks peper.

24. I tooke in 23,400*li.* cloves.

25. I tooke in 1400 sacks peper.

26. I tooke in 1100 sacks peper.

29. I tooke in 800 sacks peper.

30. I tooke in 500 sacks peper.

1 December. I tooke in 500 sacks peper. This day Richard Nuallo[3] and John Totten departed aboarde the *Darlinge*.

2. I tooke in 150 sacks peper. This [day] here arrived 2 Dutch shipps; one of them from Holland, called the *Newe Seilon*, the other from Siam.

3. I tooke in 320 sacks peper (the last of my peper). In all I have taken in 12,136 sacks. In benjamin, taken in at Acheene and heere, tonns [*blank*]. In silke, rawe and twisted, taken in, tonne [*blank*].

[1] Panjang (see note on p. 66).

[2] There are five small islands on the western side of Bantam Bay.

[3] There seems little doubt that Best wrote 'Nualle' and that the reference is to the Richard Newell whom we find at Sukadana a few months later (*Letters Received*, vol. II, pp. 29, 57).

14. Thomas Pearce and William Larkins wente aboarde the *Darlinge*.

15. In the morninge I sett saile from Bantam, and anchored 2 mile without Pulo Pinjam. Thomas Pattison and William Tuke died. This day the *Darlinge* departed from us for Meslapotan, by the st[r]ayghts of Palimbam[1]. Thomas Whittington died. At midnight wee wayed. At daylight were faire aboarde the pointe of Palimbam.

16. This day greate store of raine. Little winde, but drove out with the currante. In the afternoone the winde at north-east. This day John Whittorne dyed.

17. At 3 in the morninge wee mett with the *Expedicion*[2]. I received from them our letters and tooke leave. Captain Nuport not very well. This morninge wee founde that the currante had drove us backe agayne some 3 leagues.

18. John Giles died, beinge one of the *Trades* company. In the morninge the S. Salt Hill was N.N.E. from us, 9 or 10 leagues. Nowe were wee faire aboarde the westermost of the Java ilands; which is a faire land, and lyeth W.S.W. and E.N.E. some 6 or 7 leagues long. This night much raine. The winde variable. All this day calme. In the eveninge the winde came at S.W., and so all night faire weather.

19. This morninge the S. Salt Hill was E. and by N., 9 or 10 leagues of[f]. Here wee lay becalmed. Litle winde, at S.W.

20. At noone the south Salt Hill was east from us some 16 or 18 leagues of[f], and longitude from the meridian of Bantam, deg[rees] of the greate cirkle 1° 48′. This day John Gray died.

21. From 3 to 12 S.W., 25 leagues. Longitude from the merediam of Bantam, 2° 4½′.

22. This last night at 2 in the morninge with a greate guste at W.N.W. we splitt our foresaile and both topsailes. This 24 howres a stiffe winde from the W.N.W. to the W.S.W., with raine and gusts. Our way S.S.W., 25 leagues. Longitude from the meridian of Bantam, 3° 10′.

[1] The passage between the island of Banca and the coast of Sumatra (district of Palembang).

[2] The *Expedition* (Twelfth Voyage), under Christopher Newport, left Gravesend on 7 January 1613 and reached Bantam on 17 December. She had called at Priaman and Tiku. An account of the voyage, written by Walter Peyton, will be found in *Purchas* (vol. 1, p. 488).

23. The winde at W. and W.S.W., with gusts and raine. Our way south, 24 leagues. Longitude as before. This day Thomas More and John Chock died.

24. The winde at W.S.W. and S.S.W. Our way west, 14 leagues; and longitude from the meridian of Bantam, 3° 50′. Lattitude, 9° 40′. Since our cominge to sea [we] could not see the sunne till this day.

25. The winde at S., and S. and by W. Faire weather. Our way W. and by S., 18 leagues. Lattitude, 10°, and longitude from the meridian of Bantam, 4° 40′.

26. The winde at S. and by W. and S.S.E. Faire weather. Our way W. by S., 17 leagues. Longitude from Bantam, 5° 30′. This day John Smith died.

27. W.S.W., 16 leagues. Longitude from Bantam, 6° 15′. The winde at S. and S.E. Calme, faire weather.

28. W.S.W., 16 leagues. Longitude from Bantam, 6° 58′. Winde at S. and S.S.E. Feaire weather. Lattitude (per judgemente), 10° 50′.

29. W.S.W. ½ S., 26 leagues. Lattitude observed, 11° 25′. Longitude from Bantam, 8° 7′. The variation this morninge, 6 degrees. Winde at S.S.E. Very faire weather.

30. W.S.W., 20 leagues. Longitude from Bantam, 9° 00′. Winde at S. and S.S.E. Faire weather.

31. W.S.W., 26 leagues. Lattitude, 12° 10′; and longitude from Bantam, 10° 10′. Winde at S. Faire weather.

1 January 1613 [1614]. At midnight wee weare faire aboarde Keelinge Iland[1], a lowe flatt iland, it bearinge S.S.E., 3 or 4 mile of[f]. Then our lattitude 12° and 30′; and longitude from Bantam, 10° and 40′ (the neerest of my judgemente). This 24 howres the winde at S. and S.S.W. Faire weather. Our way W. and by S., 26 leagues. Lattitude, 12° 30′; and longitude from Bantam, 11° and 20′.

2. West, 18 leagues. Longitude from Bantam, 12° 14′. Winde at S.S.W. and S.W. Very faire weather.

3. Little winde, at W.S.W., and calme. Our way S.E. by E., 4 leagues. Longitude from Bantam, 12° 5. Variation, 7° 00.

[1] The Keeling or Cocos Islands, lying about 600 miles south-west of Java Head. They were discovered by Captain William Keeling in 1609, and were formally annexed in 1857.

4. Little winde and calme, at W.S.W. and S.S.W. Our way 4 leagues S.W. Lattitude, 12° 00′. Longitude from Bantam, 12° 17′. Varriation, 7° 10′. Here these 3 or 4 dayes wee have had a greate ocean sea that hath cast us to the north; for with the smale gale that wee have had, wee have helde our owne, yet wee finde that wee have lost 30 minits.

5. S.W. by W., 27 leagues. Lattitude, 12° and 33′. Longitude from Bantam, 12° 37′. Varriation this morninge, 7° 20′. The winde at S.S.E. Faire weather.

6. S.W. ½ W., 34 leagues. Lattitude, 13° 45′. Longitude from Bantam, 13° 55′. Variation this morninge, 8° 20′. The winde at S.S.E. and S.E.

7. W.S.W. ½ S., 36 leagues. Lattitude, 14° 30′. Longitude from Bantam, 15° 35′. Variation this morninge, 9° 35′. The winde at S.E. William Westöode dyed.

8. W.S.W., 36 leagues. Longitude from Bantam, 17° 20′. Variation this morninge, 10° 20′. The winde at S.E.

9. W.S.W., 48 leagues. Lattitude, 16° 15′. Longitude from Bantam, 29°[1] 32′. Variation this morninge, 12° 7′. The winde at E.S.E. Still faire weather.

10. W.S.W., 48 leagues. Lattitude, 17° 10′. Longitude from Bantam, 21° 44′. Variation this morninge, 13° 30′. The winde at E.S.E. Faire weather.

11. W.S.W., 48 leagues. Lattitude (per judgemente), 18° 10′. Longitude from Bantam, 24° 8′. Variation in the morninge, 15° 50′. The winde at E.S.E. Faire weather.

12. W.S.W., 46 leagues. Longitude from Bantam, 26° 14′. Variation this morninge, 17° 50′. The winde at S.E. by E. Close weather, but faire.

13. W.S.W., 42 leagues. Longitude from Bantam, 28° 8′. The variation this morninge, 13°[2] 30′. This day the sonne over zenith. The winde at S.S.E. Faire weather. John Tucker, one of the *Trades* men, died.

14. W.S.W., 46 leagues. The nearenesse of the sunne to our zenith is the cause that I write no lattitude. Longitude from Bantam, 30° 15′. This morninge the variation was 21° 20′. The winde at S.E. by S. Feaire weather.

[1] An evident error for 19°.

[2] Probably 18° is meant.

15. W.S.W., 46 leagues. Longitude from Bantam, 32° 22′. This morninge variation, 22° 40′. Winde at S.E. by E. Faire weather. This day James Bevenn[1] died.

16. W.S.W., 40 leagues. Longitude from Bantam, 34° 17′. Variation this morninge, 23° 40′. Winde at E.S.E. Faire weather.

17. W.S.W., 36 leagues. Lattitude, 22° 50′. Longitude from Bantam, 36° 7′. This morninge the variation, 24° 40′. The winde at E. Faire weather.

18. W.S.W., 38 leagues. Lattitude, 23° 40′; and longitude from Bantam, 37° 52′. Variation this morninge, 25° 10′. The winde at E.N.E. Faire weather.

19. W.S.W. ½ S., 40 leagues. Lattitude, 24° 45′. Longitude from Bantam, 39° 40′. Variation this morninge, 25° 10′. The winde at east and by north. Faire weather. This 6 or 8 dayes, the sonne neare the zenith, I coulde not take her certeyne, but nowe perfect. In these dayes I finde the shippe hath overgone me 15′ or 20′.

20. W.S.W., 40 leagues. Lattitude, 25° 35′. Longitude from Bantam, 41° 30′. Variation this morninge, 24° 30′. Winde at E. by N. Faire weather.

21. W.S.W., 36 leagues. Lattitude, 26° 21′. Longitude from Bantam, 43° 5′. Variation this morninge, 23° 30′. Winde at E.N.E. Faire weather.

22. W.S.W., 34 leagues. Lattitude, 27°. Longitude from Bantam, 44° 40′. Variation this morninge, 22° 43′. Winde at E.N.E. Faire weather. Robert Percie died, and Robert Symmons.

23. W.S.W. ½ W., 14 leagues. Longitude from Bantam, 45° 20′. Winde at E.N.E. Calme. Raph Crofts died.

24. W.S.W. ½ W., 16 leagues. Longitude from Bantam, 46° 06′. The winde at north-east and E.N.E. Even calme. Very faire.

25. Calme. Some 5 or 6 leagues, S.W. Longitude from Bantam, 46° 16′.

26. W. and by S. ½ S., 40 leagues. Longitude from Bantam, 48° 4′. The winde at S.S.E.; a freshe gale, with miste, and some smale raine at tymes.

[1] 'Blevenn' in margin.

27. W. and by S. ½ [S.?], 40 leagues. Lattitude, 28° 50′. Longitude from Bantam, 49° 58′. Variation this morninge, 21° 30′. The winde at E. Faire weather.

28. W. by S., 48 leagues. Lattitude, 29° 18′. Longitude from Bantam, 52° 18′. Variation this morninge, 19° 30′. The winde at E. by S., a freshe gale.

29. W. by S., 22 leagues; N.W. by W. and S.S.W., 4 leagues. Lattitude, 29°; and longitude from Bantam, 53° 41′. The winde from S. to W.N.W. Faire weather.

30. W. by S., 32 leagues. Lattitude, 29° 45′; and longitude from Bantam, 55° 16′. Winde at north. Faire weather.

31. W. by S., 28 leagues. Longitude from Bantam, 56° 34′. Winde at S.; a hard gale and a high sea.

1 February. W. by S., southerly, 40 leagues. Longitude from Bantam, 58° 40′. Winde at S.E. Faire weather.

2. W. by S. ½ S., 40 leagues. Lattitude, 31° 5′; and longitude from Bantam, 60° 34′. The winde E.S.E. Faire weather. The variation at night, 13° 50′.

3. W. by S., 35 leagues. Lattitude, 31° 35′. Longitude from Bantam, 61° 16′. This morninge the variation 13° 15′. The winde at E. Faire weather.

4. W.S.W., 36 leagues. Lattitude, 32° 30′. Longitude from Bantam, 63° 56′. Variation this morninge, 12° 30′. Very faire weather. The winde at E.N.E.

5. W. by S. ½ S., 38 leagues. Lattitude, 32° 40′. Longitude from Bantam, 66° 44′. Variation this morninge, 11° 20′. The winde at N.E. Faire weather. At 2 of the clocke this afternoone in a guste the winde came at S.W. and blewe hard.

6. N.W., 15 leagues. Lattitude, 32° 10′. Longitude from Bantam, 67° 14′. Winde at S.W., a freshe gale; but faire weather.

7. W.N.W., 5 leagues. Lattitude, 32° 5′. Longitude from Bantam, 67° 26′. Calme, with little winde at S. and S.S.W. Faire weather.

8. W. by N., 21 leagues. Longitude from Bantam, 68° 27′. The winde at W., with gusts of smale mistinge raine. Nowe at 12 of the clocke wee sawe the land, from us some 6 or 7 leagues of[f]. Our lattitude much aboute 32°, but wee see not the son. The variation aboute 8°, but have not observed. At 2 in the

afternoone wee laide it aboute of[f] the land, then aboute 4 or 5 leagues of[f], bearinge from N. to W. from us. The winde at S.W. by S., with smale raine and mists. Stoode of[f] all this night.

9. In the morninge some 8 or 9 leagues from land. Variation, 7° 00′. Litle winde, at S.S.E. At night the variation 5° and 50′. Here is the currente stronge with us[1]. The winde at east, a freshe gale.

10. Lattitude at noone, 34° 17′; and longitude from Bantam, 74° 3′. The winde at E., a very freshe gale. After 9 or 10 leagues per watch the currente with us very stronge, and hath in these 2 dayes carried us 40 leagues, or rather 50. Nowe at 12 wee are thwarte of 4 high mountaynes, almost equally distante each from other[2]. The westermost of these beareth nowe from us N.W.; the eastermost beareth from us N.E.; the lowe land from us 6 or 7 leagues. Heere the water is also changed, and is of a dead blackish coullour, and faire shoaldinge (50, 60, 70 fadom), as outward I had experience.

11. W. by S., 22 leagues. At midnight the winde came at W. and W.N.W. Stoode off till noone, S.S.W., 8 leagues. Lattitude, 34° 55′, and longitude from Bantam, 75° 10′. The winde at W.N.W. Faire weather. Christopher Luther died.

12. Wee lay of[f] and on, butt gott not that wee coulde perceive. The winde at W. and W.N.W. Faire weather. From the land some 5 or 6 leagues wee had 55 fadom, black sand, full of smale shells, fishinge grounde.

13. The wind at W. and W.N.W. Wee spend the tyme of[f] and on, gettinge a litle. The variation, 3° 10′. Some 5 leagues from land. James Hadlesey died. At night the variation 3° 00′.

14. The winde at W. We have rather loste then gotten. Lattitude, 35°; and longitude from Bantam, 75° 20′. The variation, 3°. Wee lye of[f] and on.

15. The winde at W. and calmes. Very faire weather. Wee gett litle. Some 8 or 10 leagues from land. Lattitude, 34° 40′. Variation this morninge, 3° 00′.

[1] The Agulhas current is strong along this coast.

[2] Possibly this was at Sandy Point, 15 miles north-east of Cape Morgan. Sandy Point has four distinct peaks on it.

16. W. by S., 12 leagues. Longitude from Bantam, 75° 54′. Calme, 4 watches. Faire weather. From the land 8 or 9 leagues. Depth, 60 fadome.

17. At 6 in the morninge Cape de Augulia [i.e. Agulhas] was N.W., some 5 or 6 leagues off. At 12 the saide cape was E. by N., from us 7 or 8 leagues off. Then in lattitude (per observacion) 35° 00′. So the Cape de Augulia hath lattitude 34° 55′, and longitude from Bantam, 77° 20′[1]. Till 6 in the morninge W. by S., leagues 26, and from 6 to 12 W.N.W., 9 leagaues. Our longitude from Bantam, 77° 42′. The winde at easte. Faire weather. The saide cape N.E. by E., 5 or 6 leagues of[f]. 50 fadome, sand and shells. In the afternoone lay becalmed, from Cape de Augulia 10 or 11 leagues west; and from Cape Falso 7 or 8 leagues S.E. by S. of[f]; and from the land thwarte of us 5 leagues. And had 70 fadom, sand and shells. George Burginns died.

18. To 6 in the morninge S.W. by W., 9 leagues. Then laide it a try with a maine coarse. The winde at west and W.N.W. Much winde, with gusts. At 10 at night laide it to the norwarde. Winde at S.W. Faire weather.

19. N.W., 12 leagues. Lattitude, 35° 5′. Longitude from Bantam, 78° 8′. Cape Falso N. by W., some 10 or a 11 leagues of[f]. The winde at S.E. Faire weather, with a freshe gale. From 12 to 5, N.W. by N., 12 leagues. Then had we the Cape of Good Hope north from us some 4 leagues; and [it] hath longitude from Bantam 78° 30′, or neare thereabouts, in my judgemente. At 6 tooke in all our sayles, only our foresaile. At 8 tooke that in also, and huld[2] till 4 in the morninge. The winde at S.E.; a storme.

20. In the morninge, faire aboarde the S.W. pointe. Faire weather. Litle winde at S.S.E. [In] the afternoone anchored in the bay of Saldania[3]. Blessed be God for it. Henry Long, the Indian, died.

[1] Cape Agulhas is in 34° 50′ S., and 20° east longitude. The longitude of Bantam is 106° 8′ E.; so Best was considerably out in his reckoning in this respect.

[2] Drifted with sails furled.

[3] In accordance with custom, an inscription recording Best's visit was carved on the rocks near Table Bay: see *Letters Received*, vol. II, pp. 148, 330, 334, and Edward Dodsworth's MS. journal (I.O. *Marine Records*, no. XIX) under date of 16 June 1614.

1 March. John Spurre died.

4. John Symmes died. This day, at 8 at night, I sett sayle from Saldania; havinge bought heere, with a litle copper (which at 10*d.* per *li.* [i.e. lb.] might be woorth some 3*li.* 10*s.*) bought [*sic*] 194[1] sheepe, 4 beefes, 9 calves. The day of our comminge to sea they brought us more then wee coulde buy or knewe what to doe withall. Wee brought to sea 80 sheepe, 2 beefes, and one calve.

5. At 8 in the morninge the Cape land bare S.E. by E., some 10 leagues of[f]. The winde at N.N.E., with thicke weather and smalle raine. At 10 Connie Iland[2] was E. by W. [*sic*] from us, some 5 leagues of[f]. At 6 afternoone the Cape land was S.E. by E., of[f] 15 or 16 leagues. Faire weather. Winde E.S.E.

6. Till 12 this day, N.W. by W., 20 leagues. Longitude from the meridian of the Cape of Good Hope, 1° 30′. The winde at S. and S.S.W. Faire weather.

7. N.W., 32 leagues. Lattitude, 31° 25′. Longitude from the meridian of the Cape of Good Hope, 2° 38′. The winde at S.E. Faire weather.

8. N.W., 38 leagues. Longitude from the Cape, 4° 00′. Winde at S.E. Faire weather.

9. N.W., 24 leagues. Lattitude, 29° 15′. Longitude from the Cape, 4° 51′. Winde at S.E. Faire weather.

10. N.W., 25 leagues. Lattitude, 28° 20′, and longitude from the Cape, 5° 45′. Winde at S.E. Faire weather. This eveninge the variation 3° 5′ easterly.

11. N.W., 44 leagues. Lattitude, 26° 45′, and longitude from the Cape, 7° 18′. Winde at S.S.E. Wee finde some smale helpe of a currante, 3 or 4 leagues in 24 howres.

12. N.W. ¼ N., 45 leagues. Longitude from the Cape, 8° 48′. Winde at S.E. Close weather.

13. N.W. ¼ N., 38 leagues. Longitude from Cape, 10° 8′. Winde at S.E. Close, faire weather.

[1] Purchas reads 'foure hundred ninetie foure.' In the MS. the first figure looks like a 4 which has been altered to a 1; and certainly the smaller number seems the more probable.

[2] Dassen Island, so called by the Dutch on account of the abundance of dassies, which the English termed conies. It lies 35 miles to the northward of Table Bay.

14. N.W., 28 leagues. Longitude from the Cape, 11° 8′. Winde at S.E. Close, faire weather.

15. N.W., 28 leagues. Longitude from the Cape, 12° 8′. Winde at S.E. Close, faire weather. Our lattitude (per judgemente), 21° 45′. These 4 dayes coulde not take sune nor starrs.

16. N.W. ½ W., 27 leagues. Longitude from the Cape, 13° 10′. Winde at S.E. Close, faire weather.

17. N.W. ½ W., 25 leagues. Longitude from the Cape, 14° 8′. Winde at S.E. Close, faire weather.

18. N.W. ½ W., 18 leagues. Longitude from the Cape, 14° 50′. Winde at S.E. Close, faire weather. Lattitude (per judgemente), 19° 30′.

19. N.W. ½ W., 24 leagues. Longitude from the Cape, 15° 45′. Close, faire weather. Winde at S.E.

20. N.W. ½ W., 26 leagues. Longitude from the Cape, 16° 45′. Winde at S.E. Close, faire weather. Lattitude (per judgemente), 17° 56′. Noe sight cane wee have of the sunne.

21. N.W. ½ W., 28 leagues. Longitude from the Cape, 17° 50′. Winde at S.E. Close, faire weather.

22. N.W. ½ W., till 4 in the morninge, 20 leagues. From 4 to 12, West, 12 leagues. Longitude from the Cape, 19° 12′. Winde at S.E. Wee cannott see the sunne. William Elmes died thi day.

23. W.N.W. ½ N., till 6, 7 leagues. Then West till 12, 24 leagues. Lattitude observed, 16° 35′; and longitude from the Cape, 20° 20′. The winde at S.E. In a 11 dayes wee tooke not the sunne; in which time I had overgone the shippe 20 minutts. I reckonned of some healpe per currante, but finde it not. So, discountinge my surplusse of longitude per rato, my longitude is (as before) 20° 20′. Variation this eveninge, 6° 40′.

24. N.N.W. ½ W., till 9, 10½ leagues. Then West till 6 in the morninge, 12 leagues. Then sawe wee Saintte Helena, from us W.N.W., some 8 or 9 leagues of[f]. Soe I finde the lattitude of it to be 16°[1]. So also wee observed at noone, and [it] hath longitude from the meridian of the Cape of Good Hope, 22°. At

[1] More exactly, 15° 54′ to 16° 1′. The mean longitude is 5° 44′ west of Greenwich, and therefore 24° 14′ west of the Cape.

3 aclocke anchored in the roade, right against the chappell[1]. In comminge for the roade by the east syde of the iland, you must keepe close aboarde the lands [*sic*]. There is noe danger but what you see. [We had] 8 or 10 fadome a shippes length from the shore, and as I came in wee had 30 and 28 fadome very faire by the land. If you shoulde not keepe very close aboarde the land, then shoulde you not hall into the roade to gett grounde, it is so neall too [see p. 44]; and the winde, before you come to the chappell, wilbe right of[f] from the land. Heere is good refreshinge; but it houlds no comparison with the bay of Saldania. For this iland is a meere rocke, consisting only of mountaines, with smalle valleys betweene them, in which the goats and boares do finde pasture. And in theis vallyes is there freshe water, which commeth from springs in the high lands; which freshe water is sildome or never cleare, but thicke as puddell, by reason of the often rayninge, for there is hardly a day in which it rayneth not 4 or 5 tymes[2]. And to fill your water, and boate it, asketh greate laboure; for your boate cannott come to the shoare, so greate is the sooffe [i.e. surf] continually, but all our caske must be halled of[f] to the boate with roapes. And for sicke men here is noe pleasure; no plaines to walke in, but to clime upp the mountaines. Heere are figgs, greate store, and of goats and hoggs[3] as many as you will. With ease you shall kill them, eyther with your peeces or inclosinge them with men and soe to cetch them. But to bringe them to the boate is a laboure beyond measure; for you must cary them 7 or 8 miles over the tops of hye mountaines, then downe into the valleys, then up. You have also heere store of faire partriges and good fishe, which you may cetch on shoare by the rocke sydes. This breefely I have discribed this iland of Stt. Helena. The roade good; your depth, 20, 25, 30 and 40 fadom, all clene grounde.

[1] The Portuguese had built a small chapel in what was consequently termed Chapel Valley. It was afterwards renamed by the English James Valley, and in it they placed their settlement of Jamestown, when they occupied the island in 1659.

[2] 'It raineth there by showers at the least five or sixe times everie day' (Linschoten, *Voyage*, vol. II, p. 256). 'The island is very dry of itself, yet it rains often' (Pyrard, vol. II, pt. II, p. 300). The mean annual rainfall is about 39½ inches.

[3] Early Portuguese visitors left goats and pigs to multiply for the benefit of later comers. A few wild goats are still to be found on the island.

In the chappell[1] I founde a letter, which the gennerall of 2 carricks the laste yeare lefte heere; wherein hee discoursed of his fight with three Flemmish shipps and one Englishe shippe. And beinge bourded[2] by the 3 Flemmish shippes, after 4 or 5 howres fight, the viz-admirall of the Dutch fired [i.e. caught fire] with his owne powder; the Portingalls ascribinge the cause to a shott out of the carricke, which lighted in there powder. At which accident the Dutch, discomfited, the viz-admirall suncke, the rest departed the roade; it seemeth with hast, for they did not attempt to save the men of the shippe on fire, for (as the gennerall writeth) they weare allmost all drowned. Only they saved 4 of them, only (as himselfe writeth) to testifie unto there kinge that the assault was given by the Hollanders and themselves defenders. 3 of the 4 men saved weare Dutch; the other was the pylott of the Englishe shippe; which I take to be Raphe Wilson, pilott of the *Saloman*, for shee kept company with the Dutch and left the company of the *Hector* and *Thomas*[3]. Wee sawe the shippe suncke, for the heade of his mainetopmaste was 2 or 3 foote above the water. I was myselfe by it, and sawe it, with the crostrees and roapes on it. Thus weare the Dutch with much dishonnour repulsed and beaten out of the roade. Theis 2 carricks

[1] It was the custom of the Portuguese and others to leave letters for later comers on the altar in the chapel.

[2] The primary meaning of 'board' was to come close up to.

[3] Best was right in thinking that the *Solomon* was in the company of the Dutch ships, but wrong in supposing that she took part in the fight. The English vessel concerned was the *Pearl*, an interloper commanded by Samuel Castleton. She was at St Helena together with the *Solomon* and four Dutch ships under Jan Dirckszoon Lam, all six vessels being homeward bound. When, on 1 June 1613, her consorts resumed their voyage, the *Pearl* remained behind, to finish watering. A few hours later two Portuguese carracks appeared in sight, making for the roadstead; and thereupon Castleton cut his cable and, leaving half his men and all his watercasks ashore, hastened to overtake the Dutch. Lam, on hearing his story, signalled to his fleet to return to St Helena; but by the next morning only three were in sight, the fourth, together with the *Solomon*, having lost company and resumed the voyage for Europe. The three Dutch ships and the *Pearl* reached the island at noon on the 3rd, and a desperate action ensued. In this the *Pearl* took no part, for Castleton had only 26 men on board and devoted all his energies to recovering as many as possible of those he had left ashore. As described in the text, one of the Dutch ships, the *Witte Leeuw*, was blown up; and thereupon Lam abandoned the attack and put to sea, accompanied by the *Pearl*. That the Englishman captured by the Portuguese belonged to the last-named vessel appears from *Cal. S.P.*, *East Indies*, 1513–1616, no. 657.

in my outward passage I mett withall upon the coast of Stt. Laurence; and so curteous was the admirall that hee saluted me with a peece, which I requited with the like. Shee was the goodliest shippe that ever I sawe; a tire of ordenance beseeminge the wall of a castle. Therefore the Dutch weare ill advised to deale with her.

In my tyme heere I sente my boates to the westwarde, to finde a shorter way to the lemmon trees and to bring downe goats, hogs, etc. with more ease; for from the chappell to the lemon trees is a most wicked way, and even a dayes worke to goe and come. In fine, in seekeinge they founde, some 3 or 4 mile to the southwestward, a faire valley, which leadeth directly up to the lemon trees[1]. It is the greatest and fairest valley from the chapple, and eyther the next or the next save one from the S.W. pointe from the chapple. Heere in this valley there is better water, and more cleare, then at the chapple. The roade all one for grounde and depth. Here of[f] this valley it is much better beinge then at the chapple, both for gettinge of all provisions and for watteringe. It is from the chapple some 3 or 4 miles, and is from the chapple the 4th valley or swampe [see p. 62], and from the pointe to the westward of it the second. So that you cannott misse of it. It is heere much better ridinge then at any other place on the iland. From this place you may go up to the lemon trees and downe agayne in 3 howres. Heere wee gott some 30 hoggs and piggs, and some 1200 or 1400 lemons. In 8 or 10 dayes a man may heere gett 200 hogs and many goats, lyinge on land of purpose to kill them. The variation heere, 7° 30′.

26. At 8 at night I set saile.

27. At 12 aclocke I was from the iland 21 or 22 leagues, N.W. ½ W. The winde at south-east. Longitude from the Cape of Good Hope, 22° 48′.

28. N.W. ½ W., 35 leagues. Lattitude, 14° 10′, and longitude from the Cape of Good Hope, 14°[2] 6′. The winde at S.E. by E. Variation this eveninge, 6° 30′.

29. N.W. ½ W., 28 leagues. Longitude from the Cape, 25° 10′. Winde at S.E. and by E. Variation this morninge, 6° 10′.

[1] Lemon Valley, about two miles to the south-west of James Valley.

[2] An obvious slip for 24°.

30. N.W. ½ W., 28 leagues. Lattitude, 12° 10′; and longitude from the Cape, 26° 18′. Winde S.E. by E. This eveninge, variation, 6° 10′.

31. N.W. ½ W., 18 leagues. Longitude from the Cape, 27° 00′. The winde E.S.E. The varriation this morninge, 6° 10′.

1 April. N.W. ½ W., 29 leagues. Longitude from the Cape, 28° 08′. Winde at E.S.E.

2. N.W. ½ W., 33 leagues. Longitude from the Cape, 29° 25′. Winde at E.S.E. Close weather.

3. N.W. ½ W., 36 leagues. Longitude from the Cape, 30° 48′. Winde, E.S.E. Close weather. Lattitude (per judgement), 8° 50′.

4. N.W. ½ W., 32 leagues. Lattitude, 7° 50′; and longitude from the Cape of Good Hope, 32°. Winde at E.S.E.

5. N.W. ½ W., 31 leagues. Lattitude, 6° 54′; and longitude from the Cape of Good Hope, 33° 12′. The winde S.E. by E. The variation this morninge, 6° 10′.

6. N.W. ½ W., 30 leagues. Lattitude, 6° 00′; and longitude from the Cape, 34° 20′. Windc S.E. by E. The varriation this morninge, 6° 20′.

7. N.W. ½ W., 20 leagues. Longitude from the Cape, 35° 06′. Winde S.E. by E. The varriation this morninge, 6° 15′. This afternoone wee had a guste, with raine, and a fresh winde at north.

8. N.W. ½ W., 18 leagues. Lattitude, 4° 51′; and longitude from the Cape, 35° 47′. Winde N.E.

9. N.W. ½ W., 22 leagues. And longitude from the Cape, 36° 37′. Winde at S.E. by E., with some raine.

10. N.W. ½ W., 27 leagues. Lattitude, 3° 15′; and longitude from the Cape, 37° 40′. Winde at E.S.E., with showres of raine.

11. N.W. ½ W., 34 leagues. Lattitude, 2° 10′; and longitude from the Cape, 38° 58′. Winde at S.E. by E. The varriation this morninge, 6° 10′.

12. N.W., 28 leagues. Lattitude, 1° 9′; and longitude from the Cape, 39° 58′. Winde at S.E. by E. The variation this morninge, 6° 20′.

13. N.W. ½ N., 18 leagues. Lattitude, 30′ south; and longitude from the meridian of the Cape of Good Hope, 40° 33′ of the greate cirkle (and so in all I reckon per the degrees of the

greate cirkle, and not by degrees of the paralele). The winde S.E. by E. Very faire weather. The variation this morninge, 6° 30′.

14. N.W. ½ N., 12 leagues. Lattitude, 4′ south; and longitude from the Cape of Good Hope, 40° 54′. Litle winde, E.S.E. Faire weather. The variation this morninge, 6° 30′[1].

15. N.N.W. ½ W., 16 leagues. Lattitude, 36′ north; and longitude from the Cape, 41° 17′. Winde at S.E. John Isacke died.

16. N.N.W. ½ W., 22½ leagues. Lattitude, 1° 35′ north; and longitude from the Cape, 41° 49′. Winde at east, with some fewe gusts of raine.

17. N.W. ½ N., 22 leagues. Lattitude (per judgemente), 2° 27′; and longitude from the Cape, 42° 30′. The winde at east and N.N.E., with raine.

18. N.W. by N., 21 leagues. Lattitude (per judgemente), 3° 20′; and longitude from the Cape, 43° 5′. Winde at N.E., with gusts of raine.

19. N.W. by N., 24 leagues. Lattitude, 4° 20′; and longitude from the Cape, 43° 45′. Winde at N.E., with gusts of raine.

20. N.W. ½ N., 25 leagues. Longitude from the Cape, 44° 32′. The winde at N.E., with much raine.

21. N.W. ½ N., 26 leagues. Lattitude, 6° 05′. Longitude from the Cape, 45° 22′. Winde at N.E. Faire weather.

22. N.W. by N., 31 leagues. Lattitude, 7° 22′; and longitude from the Cape, 46° 15′. Winde at N.E. Faire weather. The varriation this morninge, 5° 40′ (in circa).

23. N.W. by N., 36 leagues. Lattitude, 8° 54′; and longitude from the Cape, 47° 15′. Winde at N.E. The varriation this morninge, 5° 30′. Faire weather.

24. N.W. by N., 33 leagues. Lattitude, 10° 17′; and longitude from the Cape, 48° 10′. The winde N.E.

25. N.N.W. ½ W., 35 leagues. Lattitude, 11° 44′; and longitude from the Cape, 49° 00′. Winde at N.E. Faire weather.

26. N.N.W. ½ N., 37½ leagues. Lattitude, 13° 30′; and longitude from the Cape, 49° 31′. Winde at E.N.E., a fresh gale. Varriation, 5° 15′.

27. N. by W., 38 leagues. Lattitude, 15° 23′; and longitude from the Cape, 49° 57′. Winde at E.N.E., a freshe gale.

[1] 'We crost the Lyne' (marginal note).

28. N. by W., 38 leagues. Lattitude (per judgemente), 17° 13′; and longitude from the Cape, 50° 15′. The winde at E.N.E., a fresh gale. Heere the sunne is in our zenith.

29. N.N.W. ½ N., 38 leagues. Lattitude (per judgement), 19° 2′; and longitude from the Cape, 50° 47′. The winde at E.N.E., a freshe gale. This day wee came into the Sea Sergasso (as Linskotte writeth it[1]) or of rocke weede.

30. N.N.W. ½ N., 39 leagues. Lattitude (per judgemente), 20° 54′; and longitude from the Cape, 51° 20′. Winde at E.N.E. Much raine.

1 May. N. by W., 32 leagues. Lattitude, 22° 30′; and longitude from the Cape, 51° 38′. The winde at E.N.E. Faire weather.

2. North, 40 leagues. But the shippe hath not made above 35 or 36 of her owne motion; the rest with helpe of a currante. Lattitude, 24° 30′; and longitude from the Cape, 51° 38′. The winde at E. and E.S.E.

3. North, 30 leagues. Longitude from the Cape, 51° 38′. The winde at S. Faire weather. The varriation this morninge, 3° 30′ (litle more or less).

4. North, 3 or 4 leagues. Calme.

5. North, 10 leagues. Longitude from the Cape, 51° 38′. Winde at E.S.E. Varriation, 3° 30′.

6. North, 36 leagues; but the shippe is before me 3 or 4 leagues, which is by some currente. Lattitude observed, 28° 40′; and longitude from the Cape of Good Hope, 51° 38′. The winde nowe freshe at E.S.E.

7. North, 27 leagues. Lattitude, 30° 3′; and longitude from the Cape, 51° 38′. The winde at E.S.E. The variation this eveninge, 3° 30′ east.

8. North, 16 leagues. Lattitude, 30° 52′. Longitude from the Cape, 51° 38′. Winde at S.S.E. Variation this eveninge, 3° 20′.

9. North ¼ E., 23 leagues. Lattitude, 32° 00′; and longitude from the Cape of Good Hope, 51° 35′. The winde S.S.W. Variation this morninge, 3° 10′.

10. N. by E. ¼ E., 24 leagues. Lattitude, 33° 10′; and longitude from the Cape, 51° 17′. The winde S.S.W. Variation this eveninge, 2° 50′.

[1] See Linschoten's *Discours*, p. 176.

11. N.N.E. ½ E., 28 leagues. Longitude from the Cape, 50° 38′. Winde at S.W. The varriation this eveninge, 2°.

12. N.E. ½ E., 32 leagues. Longitude from the Cape, 49° 24′. The winde at N. and N.N.E., a freshe winde.

13. E. ½ N., 24 leagues. Lattitude, 35° 20′; and longitude from the Cape, 48° 14′. The winde at N.N.E. Variation this eveninge, 2° 00′.

14. N.W., 5 leagues. Lattitude, 35° 30′. Longitude from the Cape, 48° 25′. Calme. The varriation this morninge, 2° 00′.

15. N.N.E., 22 leagues. Lattitude, 36° 31′; and longitude from the Cape, 48° 00′. The winde S.S.W.

16. N.E. by N., 22 leagues. Longitude from the Cape, 47° 25′. Calme, with much raine. William Hackwell died.

17. N.E. by N., 23 leagues. Lattitude, 38° 22′; and longitude from the Cape, 46° 47′. The winde all westerly, with gusts of raine.

18. E.N.E., 30 leagues. Longitude from the Cape, 45° 24′. The winde at S.W. Foule weather, with much raine. Coulde weather.

19. N.E. by E., 28 leagues. Longitude from the Cape of Good Hope, 44° 14′. This is our way and longitude at 6 in the morninge. Nowe is Flowers and Corve[1] faire by us; the ile Corve S.E. from us, 3 leagues off, Flowers S. by E., 6 or 7 leagues off; and lattitude, 40° 10′. Thus fallinge with these ilands, wee finde that the N.W. streame or currante from the Line hath put us more westerly then our judgemente, by some 40 or 50 leagues; and so shall all men finde that saile the same way. For from 6 or 8 degrees to the southward of the Line to 25 or 30 to the northward, you shall ever finde a streame or currante to the northward, which I take to sett N.W. or neare thereaboute. Thus hath the Lord blessed us with a faire and shorte passage; for this day fyve moneths wee weare in the Straights of Sunda, 8 or 9 leagues from the South Salt Hill, and from Stt. Helena I have bene only 53 dayes.

At 12 at noone the ile Corve was off us S.W., distante 10 leagues. Lattitude nowe observed, 40° 20′; and longitude from the Cape of Good Hope, 43° 45′. The winde at S.W., a freshe gale, with raine and foule weather at night.

[1] Flores is the westernmost of the Azores group; Corvo lies a little to the north of Flores.

20. N.E., 20 leagues [and] ½; 5 leagues N.W.; and 10 leagues E. Longitude from the Cape of Good Hope, 42° 28′. Very foule weather. The winde sotherly, easterly, and nowe at north. A storme of winde, in with [*read* which] our foretopsaile blewe away, the mainetopsaile spritt [*read* splitt], and both maine bonnett and fore bonnett; and nowe [we] trye under a maine course.

21. From 12 to 6 in the morninge wee tryed with our maine coarse, S.E., 9 leagues. From 6 to 12, N.E., 3 leagues. Longitude from the Cape, 42° and 3′. Litle winde, at north-west. Close weather.

22. N.E., 17 leagues. Longitude from the Cape, 41° 27′. The winde at S.S.E. and S.S.W., with raine and foule weather.

23. N.E. ½ E., 54 leagues. Longitude from the Cape, 39° 24′. The winde at W.S.W., a freshe gale; but at night at S.W., a storme. Wee steered only with a forecourse all night.

24. E.N.E. ½ northerly, 40 leagues. Longitude from the Cape, 37° 39′. Winde at S.W. and S.S.E.

25. E.N.E. ½ northerly, 32 leagues. Lattitude, 44° 50′; and longitude from the Cape of Good Hope, 36° 15′. The winde W.S.W. Faire weather.

26. E.N.E. ½ east, 32 leagues. Longitude from the Cape, 34° 44′. The winde at S. and S.W. Close weather.

27. E.N.E. ½ E., 18 leagues. Longitude from the Cape, 33° 53′. Winde N.E. Close weather. This eveninge the variation much aboute 6° 30′.

28. E.N.E., 18 leagues. Longitude from the Cape, 33° 2′. Winde at N.E. and S.W. This eveninge wee spoke with a smale Frenchman of Rochell, which came from the Newe Founde Land with fish.

29. N.E. ½ E., 34 leagues. Lattitude, 46° 45′; and longitude from the Cape, 31° 44′. The winde at W.N.W. Faire weather.

30. 25 leagues, E.N.E. northerly. Longitude from the Cape of Good Hope, 30° 37′. Winde at N. and calme. Close weather. The variation much aboute 7°. Wee cannott see the sunne risinge nor settinge. This day Henry Long died.

31. N.E. ½ E., 7 leagues. Lattitude, 47° 30′; and longitude from the Cape, 30° 22′. Calme. Litle winde, at south. Variation this eveninge, 8° 00′. William Hoyden died.

1 June. N.E., 14 leagues. Lattitude, 48° 00′; and longitude from the Cape of Good Hope, 29° 52′. Calme, and litle winde, at S.W. Variation, 8°.

2. N.E., 3 leagues, and E. ½ S., 14 leagues. Lattitude, 48° 00′; and longitude from the Cape of Good Hope, 29° 05′. Litle winde, at N.N.E.

3. N.E. by N., 20 leagues. Lattitude, 48° 55′; and longitude from the Cape of Good Hope, 28° 32′. The winde at S.W. Heere wee sounded, and had 78 fadom, white sand (2 or 3 hawkes[1] teeth); right Ushant soundinge, it beinge east-southerly from us some 16 or 18 leagues. Note that yesternight wee sounded at 7 of the clocke, and coulde not have grounde with a 150 fadom, soundinge right upp and with our pynnace (both then and also nowe). From the former soundinge we rann N.E. by N. 11 or 12 leagues; then sounded at 7 of the clocke, and had 62 or 63 fadom, fine pepery sand. Our lattitude at this tyme, 49° 30′.

4. From this last soundinge wee rann N.E., 15 leagues. Then at 5 in the morninge wee sounded, and had 52 fadom, faire brandy[2] sand, fisheinge grownde. And at 9 of the clocke this morninge wee sawe the Lyzard north from us, some 4 or 5 leagues of[f]. And nowe longitude from the Cape of Good Hope, 27° 20′, and two degrees carried by the currente. So that the difference of longitude betweene the Cape of Good Hope and the Lyzard is 29° 20′, or very neere thereabouts[3]. Note that this day three moneths at night I did sett saile in the roade of Saldania. The Lord of heaven and earth be blessed and praysed for ever. Yet notwithstandinge our shorte passage, havinge bene from Stt. Hellena but 2 moneths and 9 dayes, the one halfe or more of our company are laide upp of the scurbute [i.e. scurvy], and two dead of it. Yet plenty of all victualls, viz. breade, wine, beefe, rice, oyle, venigar, sugar; and all these even without allowance. Note that all our men that are sicke have taken there sickenes since wee fell with Flowers and Corve; for since that

[1] As Mr W. L. Sclater has suggested, this may be the copyist's misreading of 'sharkes teeth.'

[2] Possibly this is some form of 'brinded,' meaning tawny or streaked (brindled).

[3] The Cape is 18° 30′ east of Greenwich, and the Lizard 5° 12′ west, making a total of 23° 42′. So Best was very far out in his reckoning.

tyme wee have had it very coulde, especially in two greate stormes that wee have had, thone with the winde at N. and N.N.E., the other with the winde at S.W. From the Cape to the ilands [of] Flowers and Corve I had not one man sicke. The varriation, 4 or 5 leagues of[f] the Starte, is 9° 30′, litle more or lesse.

5. At 9 of the clocke in the morninge wee weare thwarte of Portland. At 6 in the afternoone, thwarte of the Ile of Weight. The variation, 9° 30′.

6. In the morning, thwarte of Bechis [Beachy Head]. Litle winde and calme. At night a little to the eastward of the Nesse [Dungeness]. Heere the winde tooke us easterly; and [we] anchored at night.

7. In the morninge I sente my letters away by Nicholas Bangham[1], putting him into a cetch of Rochester, to be landed at Dover.

8. In the morninge came into the Downes. For it blessed be the name of God for ever. Our just [i.e. exact] tyme from Bantam to the Downes is 5 moneths and 22 dayes.

15. Came into the river of Thames; it beinge the day 6 moneths since wee came from Bantam. Blessed be God.

[1] Bangham had a remarkable career. Going out in the *Hector* (1607) as a carpenter, he was left at Surat as an assistant in the factory. In 1610 he joined Captain Hawkins at Agra, and remained there with him for some time. After his return to Surat, he embarked in the fleet of Sir Henry Middleton, and voyaged with him to the Red Sea and thence to Bantam. There he was appointed by Middleton as an assistant to Jourdain in the latter's voyage to the Moluccas in the *Darling*; and he was subsequently with Jourdain in the *Darling's* voyage for Masulipatam, which (as we have seen) was interrupted by Best at Tiku. On the vessel's return to Bantam, Bangham took passage in the *Dragon* for England. He was well received by the Company and was given a gratuity of 100*l.* for his past services, was re-engaged as a factor, and was sent out in the *Lion* with Sir Thomas Roe. He was made head of the factory at Burhānpur, and remained there until the spring of 1618, when he sailed for England in the *Bull*. He went out again in 1621 and resumed his post at Burhānpur. On the dissolution of that factory he proceeded to Surat, and early in 1623 was sent to Ahmadābād to supervise the investment there. Ill-health obliged him to return to England in the *Dolphin* in 1624; and after that we lose sight of him. In a letter to the Company Roe praised Bangham as 'your best linguist,' and said that, 'though he bee not a bredd merchant, he hath a good head, learns aptly, and is of a judgement not rash nor peremptorye.'

THE STANDISH-CROFT JOURNAL

A JOURNALL of the Tenth East Indea Vaige, maid by the Worrshipfull Mr. Thomas Best, Generall of the Dragon *and* Hossiander, *haveinge parted with the* James *and* Sallomon *at the Cape de Bona Essperannca: our feight maid with the Portingailles at Surat for trade there: and the rest of our procceedinges, as per the sequell will more att large appeare.*

ANNO DOMINE 1611 [1612].

Written by me, Raphe Standige, chirurgeon, being sick of an ague[1].

EMANUELL[2].

3 Februarie. By the grace of God we sett saille from Gravsseend, and we ankered in Tilberey Hopp.

4 Februarie. We sailled from Tilberey, and ankered in the Downnes.

9 Februarie. Our Generall came abord of hus [i.e. the *Hosiander*] in the Downns to muster our men; butt we wantted towe [which] was rune aw[a]y with ther emprest money[3].

10 Februarie. We sett saille furth of the Downnes.

11 Februarie. We ankered about 3 leagues short St Ellens Point.

13 Februarie. We ankered in Porchmouth Roode.

16 Februarie. Captyne Towerson and divers other merchantts of Porchmouth came abord the *Dragon* to see our Generall and to taike ther leaves of him, for that he was bound of so longe a vaige. Att ther departure the Generall comaunded the gonner to give them for ther farwell thre peecc[es] of ordinance. The

[1] Subsequently all the words after 'Raphe' were crossed out, and 'Crofte, pursser' substituted.

[2] This pious invocation is repeated at the head of each page down to the middle of March 1613.

[3] The imprest money, or advance of wages, given upon engagement.

gonner gave fire to a seycker [i.e. saker], which, being overcharged, brok in peecces and killd one man right out, laymed another, which afterwards dyed, and hurtt another.

22 Februarie. We sett saille from Porchmouth. The *Dragon* and the *James* went aboutt St. Ellens Pointt, and we and the *Sallomon* went furth att the Needles.

23 Februarie. Being as hie as the Startt, a councell was calld abord the ammerall concerning the *Sallomon*, who was behind at anker of[f] a Yarmouth in the Wight, becausse she feared that the tyd was to[o] much spentt to come furth when we came furth att the Needles. And being in councell concerning this bussines, the *Sallomon* came upp in sight, of which they were all very glad. And being comed upp with us, the wynd being faire, we all stood our coursse to sea; and lost the sight of the Start about 12 of the clocke.

27 Februarie. This day, by the extremittie of wether, we lost sight and company of the *Dragon*, *James*, and *Sallomon*, being upon the coast of Spayne.

29 Februarie. We spentt our bouspreett in verey fowlle wether, being betwixt the Illandes and the coast of Spayne.

16 March. We had sight of the Illands[1], videcc. St. Francisco, Lancerott, Canares, Pick, and Tynriffe.

23. This day, being 23 March, we had sight of the ile of Maio; where we found the rest of our shippes we had lost att sea. Upon ther discoverey we were nott a litle glad, and so likewisse was our Generall, who, haveing bene ashoare that day to huntt goatts, descried our ship, and presentlie repaiered abord of hus, being comed into the rood.

25 March. We put to sea, with all the rest of the fleett. Our Generall the night before, being abord of us, had ended some contraversses which in his absence had bene abord of us, and chiefflie betwixt our cape merchantt and our master[2]. Our Generall att his departure left us articles in writtinge under his

[1] The Canaries. In repeating what he was told as to their names, Standish made several mistakes. By 'St. Francisco' is probably meant Fuerteventura, 'Lancerott' is of course Lanzarote, 'Canares' Grand Canary, and 'Tynriffe' Tenerife. By 'Pick' he means the celebrated 'Peak' (Pico de Tey), which, however, is on the last-named island.

[2] Canning and Petty.

hand, which he comaunded should be published evrie monnth att the maynemast, in the heareinge of all the company; the copie of which articles heeareafter appeareth[1]:

To thend that Allmightie God may have glorie, the Kinge honor, our merchants profitablie served, and our vaiges soberlie governed, I, Thomas Best, chieff captaine and comaunder of the *Dragon*, *James*, and *Sallomon*, and *Hossiander*, do establish and ordeyne thes lawes and ordinances followinge; straitlie chargeinge and comaundinge both captaines, merchannts, and masters, with all other officers and marriners, saillers, or other persons whatsoever imploied in this vaige, to observe and keepe the said lawes and ordinances, so far as doth concerne him or eyther of them, upon the penaltie herein comprissed, from the daie of the publicacion hereoff.

1. Imprimis. That everie morneinge and eveneing yow, the chief comander or master, assemble together your men or company to heare divyne service; and that care be taken that your praiers and the Word of God be read in all sobernes, as in the presence of God; that He may have glorie and yourselves comfortt, with encreasse of knowledge. And that no man absentt himselfe from thes your publick praiers and excerssies of religion, neyther willinglie nor neicligentlie; nor that no man causse any disturbance, nor lewdlie demeane himselfe, in this your devyne service, upon paine of punishement.

2. Ittem. That yow, the chieff comaunder or master, suffer nott the name of our great and glorious God to be dishonored amoungst yow by blasepheming, sweareinge, cursseinge, or by any other idle takeing of our God in vayne, upon dew punishement, videz. for the first oath sworne, or for the first tyme cursseing or baneinge [i.e. uttering imprecations], to recceve thre blowes from the master with the bole of his wissle[2]; for the second tyme, either sweereinge or cursseinge, to receve six blowes, as aforessaid; for the third tyme, nyne blowes; and for the fourth tyme, to stand 24 houres in the bilbowes withoutt eyther meatt or drink; and so for everie tyme hearafter.

3. Ittem. Thatt muttuall love and concorde be preserved amoungst yow. That no man offer abusse to other, in word or deed. That therfore all drunkennes, all mallice, envie, hatred, backbittinge, and slanderinge be avoided, upon paine of severe punishmentt. That love, kindnesse, humillittie, and humanittie be enttertayned of all and of each man to other. And that no man darr or presume, from wronges

[1] These orders have been printed on p. 228 of *The Voyages of Sir James Lancaster*, but with several minor errors.

[2] The master wore a silver chain round his neck, with a whistle attached. Presumably he would hold the chain in his hand and strike the offender with the whistle.

receved, to revenge his owne causse, upon payne of such punishmentt as to that partie belongeth which first comitted the offence; butt that everie partie so wronged shall repaire to the captayne or master for justice; with whom if yow fynd nott sattisfaccion in justice, that then, oporttunittie and tyme servinge, that then they repaire to me, the Generall or chieff comaunder, from whom he shall have justice, according to the qualitie of the offence.

4. Ittem. That no man, of whatt condicon or place soever, shall darre to challeng into the field or upon the shoare dureing the tyme of this our vaige any of these our men imploied in thes our shippes; nor any person or persons shall darr to acceptt any such challenge; nor no man to accompanye any thatt goes into the field; under paine of 40 strippes upon the bare back, and to stand in the bilbowes att the discrettion of the Generall. Neyther that no man feight nor strike any maliccciouslie of thes our men upon this vaig imploied, in shippboard or on shoare, upon payne of severe punishment.

5. Ittem. Whoesoever shall conspire to maik away his governer by treason, mallice, or otherwisse in any of the shippes, or shalbe a muttiner or facttious fellow to taik partt with any man against his comaunder or governer, or shall have knowledge of such conspiraccies or malitiousse purposse and do nott spedily maik known and discover the same, shall suffer death for the same.

6. Ittem. Everie officer in thes shippes, both att sea and att land, shall do ther best endevoures to reforme all thes disorders, and shall maik known and aprehend all mallefaccters, that they may recceve dew punishment. And that no man lift upp his hand with weappon or otherwisse violentlie to resist any officers, upon payne of grevousse punishement, or to suffer death for yt, if the causse so require.

7. Ittem. Whosoever shall break open or pick any chist or trunke or cabin, to taik any thing therehence, or shall pick any mans pocckett or other place to steall from him, shalbe, for the first tyme, grevouslie punished, and for the second tyme, suffer death.

8. Ittem. That no play att dice, cards, nor tables [i.e. backgammon] be suffred in your shippes, for money nor otherwisse, upon payne of severe punishement.

9. Ittem. Thatt no man lodge out of the shipp wherein he is shipped, or detayne himself aboard any other shipp, for the wholle night, without leave of his captayne, under payne of punishment.

10. Ittem. That no man shoott of[f] any peecce, greatt or small, after the setting of the watch (becausse yt is an alarme to the rest of the shippes), under payne to be punished.

11. Ittem. That greatt and especciall care be taiken for the relieff and cumfortt of all sick men. That they be kept cleanne and refreshed

and cumforted with all good provissions; and that the chirurgions extend ther best endeavours and labors towards ther cure and cumfortts. And if yt should happen, notwithstanding, that any should die, that then good care be taken that a trew inventorie be maid of all the goods, moneys, apparrell, and provission belonging unto the parttie decceassed; and for all aparell and provissions nott fitt to be keeptt to the end of the vaige, that yt be sould att the maynemast, and that therin such order be taken as is provided in the 12th article of our comission; and the purser to have, for regestring of it, 12*ds*. per ll. [i.e. pound].

12. Ittem. That in all placces where we shall staie to relyve, refresh, and cumfortt our men or ourselves, eyther by fresh watter or vittualls, that everie man carie himselfe with sobriettie and meeknesse towards the people of the counttrey, that justlie of our partts no offence be geven. And that no man presume to wander or stragle from his company withoutt leave, butt that he confyne himselffe within his lymitts and boundes, upon payne of punishmentt; for by this indescrettion and liberttie taken many have lost ther lyves, our forcces and strength in our shippes therby weakined, and our mayne vaiges often indangered.

13. Ittem. For so much as the preservacion, care, and good husbandrie of our vittualls is the conservacion of our vaige and of all our lyves, that therfore yow, the officcers, extend your best cares and [end]eavoures to the preservation of all our vittualles; that so all abusses may be preventted, and our vittualles prolonged for the relieff of our countynuall neeccessitties; that so, accordinge to the larg proporcions from the Worshipfull Company recceved, ther may be no wantt.

14. Ittem. That all bartterings and bargaynes, buyinge and sellinge betwene man and man, be regestred and enttered in the purssers booke for that purposse provided, therby to avoid all perloyneinge and steallinge; and that all such bargaynes and bartters that shalbe maid without such regestringe shalbe void, and the offenders to undergoe dew punishment. And the pursser for his service to receive 12*ds*. per ll.

15. Ittem. Thatt esspecciall care be had by yow, the boattson [and] your towe mattes, to see the shipp be keept cleane swept and washed in all corners, as oft as occassion shalbe offered; and to see such portts left open in hott counttres as we may convenienttlie beare outt for the better aireinge of our shipp and health of our men. And that ther be no eatting and drinking under the uppermost decck, excceptt upon neccessity yow be constrayned thereuntto, eyther by rayne or fowlle wether. And this to be performed by yow all, as yow will answeer yt.

16. Ittem. That no man presume to go downe into the hould att any tyme, upon any occassion, without accquayntting of the master, upon payne of severe punishment.

17. Ittem. Whosoever shalbe found absentt from his watch, eyther att sea or in any roode or herber wher we shall come, or, being att watch, bee found asleeppe, shall be severlie punished.

Ittem. That yow, the cooke with your matte, be careffull yow have your vittualls well seasoned, both flesh and fishe, and that yt be provided in dewe tyme, vidz. dynner to be reedie at 10 of the cloke att the furthest, and supper by five acloccke. And likewisse that yow have a specciall care to keepp your steepptubs[1] sweett and cleane, together with the furnacce, kettles, potts, and platters, or any other thinge which shalbe used, eyther about the dressinge or servinge out of the companies vittualles, for yt is a principall thing to be regarded for the preservacion of our healthes. Faille you nott heereof, as yow will answeer yt, by sitting in the bilbowes 24 houres with bread and watter.

Lastlie. The God of all peace so order and guide us that we maie countinewe in all piettie and love each towardes the other, accordinge to place and callinge; that the end of this our vaige maie be with more glorie to Gode and better reformacion of our synfull lives then the begininge thereoff; and that by our example other men maie be encouraged and stirred upe to like laudable enterprisses, in which God, [who] is the giver of all good successe, graunt us prosperittie, in peace to go furth and in saiffty to retourne, to the great glorie of God, honor to the Kinge, comodittie to the comonwealth, gayne to the merchants, creditt and reputacion to us the acctters.

Thes articles above written was by our Generall published att the ile of Maio, and after delivered to our master, to be published evrie monnth att the mainemast, in the heareing of the company. This night, being 25th March, we put to sea.

9 Aprill. By the observaccion of our masters mattes, we were under the Equanoctiall Lyne; where we found yt extreme hott, much rayne (which stank of brimston), and great lightninges of fire.

28 Aprill. We discovered an illeland in the sea, being a rocck that yiellded nothing butt greatt store of fowlle, as greatt as a raven, that came and satt in the bootts [i.e. boats] and upon our mens shoulders; butt they weere so rance [i.e. rank] as we could

[1] A steep-tub was a large vessel in which the salted provisions were soaked preparatory to cooking.

nott eatt them. This illand was unknowne to Mr. Daves[1] or to any of our marieners, for by them yt was never seene before. They named yt S. Trenidade.

4 Maie. We being aboutt 200 leagues shortt of the Cape Bona Essperannca, the Generall sentt us abord of our shipp 2 marriners that had both bene in the Endis before, for feare that in fowlle wether we should loosse the company of the *Dragon* and the other shippes. Thes 2 mariners knew the land, esspeciallie one of them, whose name was Walter Stacie[2], better then our master or his mattes, for that none of them had ever bene in the counttrey before.

8 Maie. Died furth of our shipp an ould Indean, called Candell, which came over into England in the *Expedecion* with Captain Dave[d] Midletton[3].

30 Maie. This daie we had extreame fowlle wether, being by the observacion of our masters mattes aboutt 100 leagues or therupon from the Cape de Bona Essperannca; where we found extreame cold, as sometymes in England.

First June, being Whitt Sunday. We had verie fowlle wether, which had contynued with us 4 or 5 daies. And being at eveninge praier under our half deck, we shiped such a sea as overthrew some of our men and weett many of them to the skinn, allthough yt came butt in att the grattinge.

4 June. We had sight of the land of Cape de Bona Essperannca; all our fleett in company. And the storme still connttynue[n]g, the wether being hazie and foggie, and drawing towards night, we brought our tacks aboard and stod yt of[f] to the sea. This night, by extremittie of wether, we were separatted; for we lost the sight of the *Dragon* and the *James*, and kept company with the *Sallomon*, for that she did nott overbeare us, for we were verie hardlie able to maynetteyne a ccople [i.e. couple] of coursses.

[1] A misstatement; see note on p. 7.

[2] The Court Minutes of 10 February 1615 record that Walter Stacey, who had made three voyages to the East, was appointed a master's mate at 50*s.* a month. Reference to his further service will be found in *Letters Received*, vol. VI, pp. 59–62. In 1618 he was made a prisoner by the Dutch in the Bandas, and the following year was sent to Holland in a Dutch ship.

[3] The Fifth Voyage, 1609–10. Middleton did not go near India, and so the 'Indean' was probably a native of some other Eastern country.

5 June. We and the *Sallomon* in the morneing stod in with the land, and sawe both the Seuger Loaffe and the Table, and was nerer the land then we maid accountt we weere. We steered in with the herber of Salldania E. by S., the *Sallomon* beinge asteerne about a league, she following us. Penguin Illand did beare of[f] us N.E. by E. as we steered into the rod of Salldania, wheere we came to anker aboutt 9 of the cloke in the morning, in 7 fadam watter (God be thanked) in good saiftie.

6 and 7th of this instantt. The *Sallomons* company and we had bene ashoare, butt could nott trad with the salvashes [i.e. savages], for that they would nott sell ther sheepp and oxen for iron, butt for brasse. So they gave us eyther shipp a lamme for a presentt. And thus we contented ourselves to taike the pleassure of the shoare; where we had exccellentt good watter and many good and sweett herbbes, wheerof we maid salletts [i.e. salads]. Heere was grasse [in] aboundannce, and heerbes which gave unto us many sweett and pleasant smells. This land of Cape de Bona Essperannca is within the region and goverment of Prester John[1]; the connttrey being firttille ground and pleasántt, and a connttrey verie temperatt; butt the people bruitt and savadg, withoutt religion, without languag, without lawes or goverment, without manners or humanittie, and last of all withoutt apparell, for they go naked, save onelie a ppeec[e] of a sheepes skyn to cover ther members, that [in] my opinion yt is greatt pittie that such creattures as they bee should enjoy so sweett a connttrey. Ther persons are preporcionable; butt ther faces like an appe or babownne, with flatt nosses; and ther heads and faces both beastlie and fillthye to behould, for want of cleanlienesse. They were aboutt ther neeccks the intralls of sheepp, and doth eatte the pudinges [i.e. entrails] skines with raw sewett [i.e. fat] and rawe blod; and divers other thinges they eatt, which is most beastlie to behold.

8 June. The *Dragon* came into the herber of Salldania; which when we see, we were nott a little glad. She had endured towe daies of extreme fowle wether att sea, and had lost the *James*, thinking that she had gott aboutt the Cape and stood for St.

[1] By this time the legendary Prester John had been located in Abyssinia, but the vaguest notions still prevailed as to the extent of his territory.

Augustyne[1]. The *Dragon* had many of hir men sick and layme of the skurvy, to the number of 90 or 100 men. She had hardlie as many sound men as was able to bring hir into the herber.

10 June. The Generall caussed a tent to be builded with as much expedicion as might be possible, and brought ashoare all his sick men, both of skurvy and other desseasses. And the steward brought brasse ashoare to barter with the salvashes for vittuall. Both oxen and sheepp they sould him. For a peecc[e] of ould brasse, a foott broad, we had an oxe which in England, being fatt, would yield 6*ll.* stterlinge; and for a pece of brasse, a finger longe and so much broad, we had a sheeppe, greatt of bone butt verie thin of flesh, shaped like a gre[y]hound, save onelie the eares longe. The oxen is nott much unlike our English oxen, butt that they are more shortt of haire. Of thes we bought greatt store, and likewisse of sheppe, to reffreshe our men. And with fresh salletts, fresh aire, fresh watter many of our men recovered ther healthes agayne and became stronge.

17 June. Rychard Ryding, one of our boattsons mattes, died; haveing lyen a long tyme sick of a consumption. His corppes was buried ashoare att the Cape.

18 June. This day we sentt in the *Dragons* skiffe 6 of our men to go with ther men to Penquin Illand, which illand was distantt from our shippes aboutt 1½ league, to see ther for fresh vittuall, as sheepp and suchlike; for thither our Englishmen have in tymes past caried sheepp from the mayne and have putt them upon that illand. For if they be never so leane, in a monnth or six weeks tyme they wilbe verie fatt ther; for yt is a shortt, sweetter grasse then the mayne. Butt our men found no sheepp ther butt onelie towe, of which they could butt catch one; and that was worth 4 of the other sheepp in the meane, that had as much meatt upon the taille as of one of the quartters. Upon this illand be many sealles, [which] comes out of the sea, and aboundance of greatt snakes lying upon the ground against the sune. Allso a number of fowlles called penquins, from whence the illand hath yt[s] name. Thes fowlles cannott flie. They are as bigge as a raven, butt of divers collers, both black and whitt,

[1] St. Augustine's Bay, on the south-west coast of Madagascar, in lat. 23° 26'.

parttie collered. Of thes you may lood a shippe, and taik them upp with your hands; butt they stink so strong of fish, and doth smell so rance [rank], that our people could nott eatt them. Our boatt brought of them; butt yt was more to see them then to eatt them.

23 June. Our Generall, by reason of some unkyndnes that was betwixt our cape merchantt and our master, he apoyntted our master for the *Sallomon*, and Mr. Sallmon he apoyntted master of our shipp, with exchange of 3 or 4 saillers, and a masters matte, Mr. Bullerd.

Haveinge staid att the Cape the space of thre weeks, and all the sick men well recovered, the tentts was pulld downne, and everie man comaunded aboard the ships, upon payne of punishementt. Aboard the *Dragon* we recceved the sacrament, after the heareing of a sermon. In the sermon tyme we see a whalle in feight with a swordfish and a thresher[1]. The whalle did so roare that he did much intteruptt the preacher in his sermon, that most of his audience did more regard the whalle and the fishes then they did his instructions[2].

23 June. In this land of Prester John ther was seene by our men lyons and monkeyes, babownns a multi[tu]d, with divers other strange beastes, as antilops, and many other deformed [i.e. unshapely] creattures, verie strange to be sene.

29[3] June. The *Dragon* and we put to sea agayne, with most of our men well reffreshed. We lost att the Cape furth of all our thre shippes 5 men, with one that was drownned furth of the *Sallomon*. The *Sallomon* was reedy to come to sea; yett she did nott come forth with us.

10 July. We had a theft comitted in our shipp. Search was maid by our masters mattes, butt nothing att this tyme was found; but afterwards the partie was taiken in a fresh accion, and verie well whipped att the capstan.

13 July. We strayned our foremast, haveing verie fowlle

[1] It is doubtful whether either the swordfish or the thresher shark attacks whales; and possibly the assailant in this case was really a 'killer' (*Orca gladiator*).

[2] The following passage has been struck out here: 'My ague still conntynueth, with an impostume breaking furth in my arme.'

[3] 28, according to Best.

wether. Yett our carpenters fished yt and wulld[1] yt and maid yt verie stronge agayne; being aboutt 180 leagues to the southward of the Cape[2]. Aboutt which tyme the *Dragon* sprunge hir manemast; whereupon one of hir carpenters tooke such a conseitt that he was sudenlie stricken with death, and maid a most misserable and deseparatt end; which might have beene an example to many of our wicked people we had of our vaige.

30 July. Being by estimacion of[f] the illand of St. Lawrance [Madagascar] (which is aboutt 500 leagues from the Cape), we meett with towe carroccks of 15 or 16 hunderd tonne of burden; which we did think was comed from Lisburne. The vice-admerall bore upp with us, and we, feareing the wurst, shott att hir, and she att us, butt wether in jeast or earnest, we cannott tell. Butt we shott att hir in all aboutt 17 greatt shott, and we had from hir aboutt 12; but she never strok us nor harmed us, allthough I do think they did ther best endevour to have strok us. Butt I am certtayne that, by the captaynes reportt att Goa (after we were aryved in the Endies) to Mr. Caneinge and Edward Christian, being prisoners then, that we had killd them thre men. The *Dragon* was prepared to feight, butt she needed nott, save onelie a saluttinge peecce or tow, and she as much to hir agayne. Our Generall sttered away his coursse, for that yt was contrarie to comission to medle with them, in respeccte of peacce we have with ther kinge. Our companye was all verie willing to feight yt out with them, if our Generall would have consented therto. And thus we partted. She stood after hir ammerall, and we after ours[3].

03 August. We had sight of divers illands.

04 August. We stood in with an illand called Mollellea, and steered in with the herber. Butt we saw so many breaches att the going in, both ahead and to lewards, that our Generall would

[1] To 'woold' was to wind rope or chain round a broken yard or mast, in order to strengthen it where repaired.

[2] He means that they were that distance from the Cape in the direction of Bantam.

[3] The two Portuguese vessels were commanded by Jeronimo de Almeida and Christovam de Sequeira d'Alvarenga, and had left Lisbon for Goa in the preceding March. The account given by Bocarro (p. 10) agrees generally with that in the text, but says that only one Portuguese was killed.

nott venture in with the *Dragon*, but put to sea agayne, with as much saille as we could maike.

14 August. We crossed the Equanoctiall[1] to the southward of the Cape, with a verie faire wynd and the wether more temperatt then yt was when we crossed the Lyne to the norwards of the Cape. This Lyne was aboutt 200 leagues from Soccotora.

31 August. The Generall came abord our shipp, and tould our master he had sounded the night before and found from 40 to 15 fadam watter. This morning the sea was changed whitt from greene and withall verie mudy; which was a greatt sigene [sign] we should be neere the land. Allso manye snakes came swymeing by our shipps side; which is a certteyne signe the land is neere.

Heer (God be thanked) I began to recover my health agayne.

As by English, Porttingailles, and other nations yt is observed, this day att noone we were by observacion in 20 degrees and 20 mynuttes, but no sight of land. This night we stood intto shoare with an eassie saille, hoping that in the morneinge we should see the land and coast of Indies, for by all our marriners reccknínges we could nott be farr of[f].

September first. We had sight of the hie land. To the westward of Daman we sawe a saille, butt could nott descrie [i.e. examine closely] hir. This night we ankered in sixe or 7 fadam watter.

02 Septtember. Mr. Alldsworth, the cape merchantt of the *Dragon*, and Mr. Carridge [Kerridge], with about 20 souldiers[2] more, came abord the *Hossiander*. We weid and stood for the barr of Suratt. This night we ankered of[f] a Gundvee [Gandevi], in 7 fadam watter.

03 Septtember. We had sight of many frigotts saylling alongst the coast. We steered to the barr N.N.W., be [by?] a low land with many pallmetto ttres to be seene as you saille allongst this coast.

04 Septtember. We had sight of the *Dragon* comeinge after us, for that they had taken outt of a frigott 2 pillotts to carie her to the barr of Suratt. This day we mayned our pinis with ½ a dossen small shott and wentt abord a frigott and gott a pillott; butt left a pawne for him, which was one of our carpentters, whose name

[1] Best says they crossed the Line on 13 August.
[2] He means armed sailors (see Best's narrative, p. 26).

was William Finsh. Butt this man we never see moore, as per the sequell will appeare.

05 Septtember. Came abord of us from Suratt one Jadoa, a brooker, accompanied with 6 or 7 Moores, and spok verie good Porttingaille; who brought unto our Generall a leter which Sir Henrie Midletton att his departting from Suratt had left with him. The effecctt therof was no trad ther to be expecctted, nor to trust the conntrey people, and that Mr. Hakins and his wiffe was gone for England[1], William Finsh[2] and all the merchantts disperssed.

06 Septtember. This broker and his frends wentt from us with the Generall, and went abord the *Dragon*; wher the Generall did more conferr with them concerning the hope of trad. The broker did seame to encourage him and to perswad him he might have trad, allthough Sir Henries letter did advisse him to the contrarie.

07 Septtember. We ankered aboutt a league of[f] the barr of Suratt. This night the Generall sentt his skiff ashoare with the broker and his frends and 4 of our English, to go to Suratt to buy vittualle and provission; the broker promisseing to asist them in anything wherin he could, and withall to see ther saiff rettourne.

08 Septtember. Yt pleassed God of His merccie to call Capttain Goitt.

09 Septtember. Came a frigott from Suratt abord the *Dragon* with fresh vittualle, and brought a lletter from our people att Suratt, the effecctt wherof was they had recceved verie kind enttertaynementt by the Governer and chiefe of Suratt, and that they had furthered them to buy all kynd of provissions the place would afford, as bread, ricce, onions, sewger, butter, cheesse, lemons, and other fruitt; of which the Generall sentt us our preporcion, according to the number of our people.

11 Septtember. A frigott came abord the *Dragon*, laden with

[1] Hawkins and his Indian wife left Agra in November 1611, reached Cambay in safety, and in January 1612 embarked in Sir Henry Middleton's fleet. At Bantam they changed into the *Thomas*, homeward bound.

[2] Finch (the factor, not the carpenter already mentioned) started from Lahore with certain other Englishmen, to journey home overland. He died, with most of the party, at Bagdad.

ricce and other provissions, of which we had a share; and likewisse of garvanncces[1] we had a partt.

12 Septtember. Our master sentt his long boatt to help to toow a frigott abord the *Dragon*, loaden with tymber bought att Suratt. Butt our boatt fell so farr to lewards that a Mallabar frigott riding close by the shoare weid and came and tooke hir. We lett slipp both our cables, and shott 2 shott att hir. The boatt was releassed and no harme, save our men a litle pilliged and the losse of a muskett.

13 September. Many gallantts and chieff of Suratt came abord the *Dragon*[2]. The Governer of the Castle, being chieff, brought our Generall a presentt, vidz. aboutt 15 sheepp, 200 kinttalls of ricce, 20 hens, spicced cakes, and soft bread, with divers other dayntties. Of this presentt we recceved partt. Our Generall did requitt the Governer with a faire peecce of platt [i.e. silver]. Our Generall beinge encouraged by thes cavelleroes[3] for trad, sentt Mr. Alldsworth and Mr. Caneing (both the cape merchantts) ashoare with thes gentlemen, and divers others of our English for ther attendantts and asistantts in bussines.

14[4] Septtember. Being Sunday, our merchanntts weere going abord the *Dragon* to heare a sermon. And after the boatt was putt of[f] from the shipp, we espied a fleett of frigotts comeing from southward. Our master retorned abord agayne, and caussed the master gonner to putt furth his ordinance and to pryme them. Our feightes[5] were likewisse fitted, we thinking they would have fought with us. When they came within shott, our gonner maid 2 shott att them; the *Dragon* first haveing geven them tow shott. We and the *Dragon* shott so long that the poore frigotts was glad to rune away within the barr, and ther ankered. We gave them furth of both shippes aboutt 20 greatt shott; they being in all 16 saille.

15 September. Mr. Bonner, with 12 souldiers, came abord of us by the Generalls order, to wey and stand neerer the barr.

[1] An old form of 'calavance,' a term for certain varieties of pulse.

[2] Best dates this visit 12 September, and gives a more reliable list of the presents.

[3] Portuguese *cavalheiro*, a gentleman.

[4] An error for 13.

[5] Screens hung round a ship, to conceal and protect the crew, especially from boarders.

Butt fynding shoald watter, we ankered att the barrs foott, in 4 fadam watter[1].

16 Septtember. Both our boatts, att low watter upon the barr, filld fresh watter.

17 Septtember. Both our botts wentt a fishing, butt catched nothinge.

18 Septtember. Our Generall came abord, and called all our men, to see if any discontent weer amongst them. Butt none would speake att that tyme, allthough before they had murmered and said the *Dragon* had more fresh vittualles then they for ther preporcion. And becausse the frigotts was in the river and stoppt the passag of our vittuall from Suratt, therfore the Generall gave our master order to maik reedy his ship to go to a place called Sualley, where Sir Henrie Midletton long tyme rood with his shippes and furnished himselff both with watter and vittuall, for thatt within a day or towe [we] should goe thitther with our shipp. Watter Staccie apoynetted for the *Dragon*. We shott att a cconntrey boatt, which escaped verie narowlie of beinge sunke. She strok saille, and our master, with our pinis, wentt abord hir and took a pillott to carie us into the rood of Sualley. This day a Portting[all] frigott came within shott of us. Our gonner maid or 8 or 9 shott att hir, butt never came neere hir; they with drawen swords florishing upon the poup or sterne, nott careing for us 2 pins, butt stoad to the barr in a bravado.

19. We weid, and came of[f] and ankered by the *Dragon*, in 8 fadam watter.

20 Septtember. This day our master, merchantts, and most of our company went abord the *Dragon* to heare a sermon and to receve the saccramentt (those that was prepared for yt). Being abord, ther came a boatt from Suratt with 2 of our English and provission of vittualle, of which, after sermon, we had a share. They brought a letter to our Generall from the Greate Magole[2], sealled up in cloth of gould; and allso reportted much of ther kind enttertaynementt by the Guzuratts, [and] how kindlie they had offered them trad. Att our departing abord, we took with us

[1] The bar at the mouth of the Tapti was so shallow that even the *Hosiander* could not cross it; but of course it presented no difficulty to the light Portuguese vessels.

[2] An obvious error. The letter may have been from the Governor of Surat.

our share of provission. They brought newes the frigotts was gone to the northwards, or otherwisse we should have had no vittualle nor passage.

21 Septtember. More souldiers came abord from the *Dragon*, and withall order to wey and stand to the barr, for thatt the Generall meantt thatt we should goe into the river. This day came Mr. Alldsworth, Mr. Caneing, and all the merchannts abord, upon the recceitt of the Generalls letter; wither likewisse our master and merchantts repaired, for the dettermining and concluding of further trad[1]. Att last yt was agreed and concluded by a courtt to send goods ashoare and to rettorne to Zurat agayne, and ther to taike a housse and remayne till furder order or as occasions would permitt.

22 Septtember. Wentt ashoare Mr. Alldsworth, Mr. Caneinge, [Mr.] Caride [Kerridge], and all the rest of the merchannts, with ther attendantts and servantts, and a cook for dreseinge of ther vittualls. Likewisse order was taken for conveyannce of goods ashoare. Our master gave Mr. Caneing, att his goeing ashoare, a casse of bottles full of shippes wyne.

23 Septtember. 2 barks was sentt from Suratt abord the *Dragon* to load goods, vidz. cloth, lead, iron, quicksillver, and suchlike comoditties; from our shipp 1 pott vermillion. Thes 2 barks was loaden this night, and 2 English sent in the barks.

24 Septtember. A Guzuratt shipp came into the rood from the Read Sea, who had spoken ther with Sir Henrie Midletton and Capttayne Saires, and brought ther passe under ther hands. The capttayne of this shipp did certifie our Generall that Sir Henrie Midletton had diswaided Capttayne Sairs for comeing to Zuratt, and that his shipp and the *Thomas* was gone for Java, and the *Hecter* for the Mallaccos; and that Sir Henrie with his fleett was dettermyned to goe for Priaman and Bantam, and that the *Pepercorne* was gone 5 monnthes before for the Mulluccus[2]

[1] From Best's narrative it appears that this consultation was held on the 22nd.

[2] These statements were not altogether correct. The *Thomas* and the *Hector* had been sent to Priaman and Tiku; and Middleton, with the *Trade's Increase* and the *Peppercorn*, followed them to Sumatra in the middle of August 1612. Standish appears to have confused the *Peppercorn* with the *Darling*, which Middleton had dispatched on 19 May to Tiku and Bantam.

Our Generall gave the captayne many thanks for his newes; and att his departture gave 3 peecces.

25 Septtember. The capttayne of [the] Guzuratt shipp came abord of our shipp to see hir; wher we maid him the best entter-taynementt we could, for that his caridge and curttesey deserved yt. He wisht that we might establish a faccttorie (as afterwards we did), [and] tould us of Sir Henrie, how he had taiken many Porttingailles. After some discoursse he seamed to haisten away. We gave him a gun for his farwell. This day we had some provissions of fresh vittualle from the *Dragon*.

26 Septtember. Our boatts wentt both within the river to fill fresh watter. This day our master came from Suratt, and brought newes that Sir Henrie Midleton had taken some Gurzuratts in the Read Sea.

27 Septtember. Being Saboth day, we repaired abord the *Dragon* to sermon.

28 Septtember. The Generall came abord our shipp, and ducktt one of our men att the foreyardarme, upon the com-playntt of one of our masters mattes that he would nott obey his comaund. He [the General] had a peecc [of] ordinance.

29 Septtember. This day we see the Porttingailles frigotts, which came from furth of the offin[g] and had spoken with another Guzuratt ship which was comed from [the] Read Sea, and rood of[f] into the sea. They came within shott of us, and we maid a dossen shott att them, butt never strok any. Yett they rune and rowed away from us.

30 Septtember. In the morneinge our Generall had newes from Suratt, by a frigott sent purpcsselie by the Englishmen, thatt thre of our people or merchantts was taken by the Porttin-gailles in a connttrey boatt comeinge abord the *Dragon*, by verttue of a lletter they had recceved from the Generall to come abord in all haist—Mr. Paull Caneing, Edward Christian (pursser of the *Dragon*), and William Chamers (a musition); upon which newes our Generall caussed us to wey and to fettch upp the Guzurat shipp upon the *Dragons* broadside. Which we did, and tooke the captayne and 10 or 12 of the chieffest mer-chants and caried [them] abord the *Dragon*. Wherupon our General wrott a lletter to the Governer and chieff of Suratt that,

if they would permitt our English to transportt ther goods abord agayne and themsellves in saiftie, then ther shipp should be relleassed, or otherwisse he would keep the shipp and goods. She had in hir above 300 people, passengers and saillers.

First Occttober. Our Generall came abord, and chid our gonner for makeing so many bad shott att the frigotts without doing them any harme. The Generall tould our master thatt he had hard bad newes of our carpentter, William Finsh, that was left for a pawnne of[f] a Gundeve for our pillott; howe that the people had killd [him] the same day they ttook the pillott from them; butt how yt was, the Lord knowes, for we never see him more.

2 Occtober. Both our boatts wentt within the river to fill watter.

3 Occttober. Mr. Bonner came abord of us, and we weid and stood for the rood of Sualley. Our Generall had a lletter from Suratt, writt by Mr. Alldsworth, that for 4,000 dollers Mr. Caneinge and the pursser (with the other) might bee releassed. Mr. Bonner brought from the General a present to give the Moccodom of Sualley.

4 Occttober. We ankered in the rood of Sualley, in fyve fadom watter, above an English mille from shoare. The master sent our longboatt ashoare with 2 English, 2 Indians, that, if yt weere so that the stteward of the *Dragon* [Starkey] were nott there, then one of our English to go tto Suratt yt [*sic* ? and] maik yt known that our shipp was comed to Sualley; and the other to go to the Governer and inttreatt his favour for watter, and to tell him we had a presentt unto him from our Generall, and how our Generall had geven him many thanks for his kyndnesse shewd to Sir Henrie Midletton. Our [men] rettourned from Sualley, butt found nott the steward there. He had bene ther thre daies, butt was gone to Suratt. So one of our English went to Suratt. The other rettourned abord, and tould us we weere nott in the right roodstead. We weyed and stood further in; butt could nott fynd the roodstead withoutt a pillott.

5 Occttober. Haveinge a pillott, we found the right roadstead, closse by the shoare in 8 fadom watter, beinge the same placce wher Sir Henrie was.

05 [? 6] Occttober. [The] stteward came downe from Suratt, becausse of his language, to provid fresh watter. For thatt yt was an English mille from shoare, the people brought yt downne to the seasid in potts and filld the cask[1] ther, to the quanttittie of 7 tonnes; with other provissions, both for the *Dragon* and for us, as sheepp, sopp, candles[2], conserves, grene ginger, and suchlike.

7 Occttober. We weyed, and stood for the barr of Suratt to the *Dragon*; wher we delivered hir such provissions as we had. We understood that divers of the chieff of Suratt had beene abord the *Dragon* to conffer with our Generall, and offered greatt kindnesses, and large offers for the establishing of a faccttorie; butt nottwithstanding the Generall would nott releasse ther shipp; wherupon they went away in greatt disconttentt, and reffussed the Generalls presentt.

08 Occttober. We wentt to Sualley agayne, to sett tow of our merchaunts ashoare. The Porttingals, being in our way with ther frigotts, weyed and rune away. We stood after them awhille, butt they roowed from us. Haveing sett the merchantts ashoare, they rettourned us abord 2 sheepp and other fresh vittualles. Afterwards [we] came to the *Dragon*. The Generall sentt abord for all his men we had of his for souldiers.

09 Occttober. The capttayne of the Guzuratt came to see our shipp, and caried our master abord his sheepp; wher he maid greatt enttertaynementt, and so retourned abord the *Dragon* agayne. The Generall gave him whatt libertie he would desire.

10 Occttober. [The] *Dragon*, we, and the Guzuratt shipp wentt all to Sualley. Our shipp ankered closse by the shoare, within the barr; butt the *Dragon* and the other shipp, withoutt. [Our] boatt went ashoare with both purssers, to buy fresh vittuall, and this night rettourned agayne.

11 Occttober. We had from Sualley sheepp, goatts milk, and other fresh provissions, both for the *Dragon* and for us.

12 Occttober. Our Generall went ashoare, with 80 men in armes to attend him, butt went nott up to Sualley, becausse yt was thought the Governer of Suratt would have comed. So we

[1] This was then the regular plural.

[2] Candles, both wax and tallow, were made in India from an early date; while a crude soap was largely manufactured for the use of washermen and dyers.

spent all this day ashoare, and att night maid a gallantt shew before the counttrey people; performed by himselff [i.e. the General]. Haveing devided his men into tow partts, we had a skrimidg [i.e. skirmish] or tow (Mr. Bonner being the other capttayne); which was verie gallanttlie performed. And so, night drawing on, we repayred abord.

13 Occttober. Our Generall likewisse wentt ashoare, in manner as afforessaid, and pittched 2 tentts, one for himselff and his attendantts, and another for his souldiers, for that the wether was verie hott. This day we did spend in marching upp and downne. Att night the Generall came abord of our shipp to lie (wher he laid till he had perfecctted his bussines with the Governer and the chief of Suratt), and 40 of his souldiers.

14 Occttober. Our Generall wentt nott ashoare, butt sentt the souldiers to keepp wattch. This day yt was such an exttreame gust that yt blew downne both our tentts over our heads. The Guzuratt capttayne staid ashoare this night, and took chark [charge ?] of the tentts after they were sett upp agayne.

15. This day the Generall wentt [a]shoare, with the capttayne of the Guzuratte shipp, thinking to have meett the Governer ashoare, butt did nott, and so rettourned abord the *Hossiander* with his souldiers.

16. [He] wentt nott ashoare, butt remayned [aboard] the *Hossiander*.

17. Came our merchantts from Suratt to Sualley, haveing maid saill of most of our comoditties. The broker came with them, for to maik prisses of rettorne. The Governer of Amedevar everie day to be expeccted att Sualley, with the chief of Suratt, for the establishing of a faccttorie.

18. Being Saboath day, we had a sermon by Mr. Coupland, [the] Generall being redy after dynner to go ashoare and meett the Governers. The text was 9 Proverbs of Sallomon. This day came abord one of the chieffest merchantts in Suratt, called Medejopher [Mīr Jafar]. [He] would have had our Generall ashoare, but he reffussed to go withoutt a pledge. The preacher att afternone conntynued in his former text.

19 Occttober. Came to Sualley the Governer of Amedevar, the Governer of Suratt, and all the chieff in generall. Att the

seaside they had ther tentts redie pittched to recceve them. They sentt abord thre of ther chiefest men, to remayne abord for pledges till the General rettourned. For ther wellcome we gave them 9 peecces, the *Dragon* 5 peecces. Our Generall wentt ashoare, where the Governers and all the rest did verie curtteousslie enttertayne him and recceve him att the watterside; from thence did conductt him to the Governers tentt, wher they did pley [i.e. plead] for the conclusion of peace or factorie. Our Generall had attending upon him 100 souldiers in armes, with our trumpetts and drumes, besides a dossen privatt attendantts which was connttynnallie by him. This day they had agreed of many articles, butt no full conclussion; tyme would nott permitt. Our Generall had presentted him by one of the cavelleroes a gallantt horsse, with all furnitture apertteyneing thertto. Our Generall, haveing taken leave of the Governers and the chieff, repaired to his horsse and rood downne to the watterside, accompanyed with his souldiers, took boott, and came abord our shipp.

20 Occttober. Our Generall repaired ashoare (after the pledges was comed abord) with 40 men, and att the watterside was recceved by the Indians, who conductted him to the Governers tentt, wher the day before they had conferred upon the establishinge of a faccttorie att Suratt. This day[1] they did absolutlie agre upon all such artticles as was by our [Generall ?] desired. Copies of the articles was taken of both sides, and likewisse the copies of ther authoritties from ther Kinges [*sic*] was taken. Likewisse the Governer of Amedevar promissed our Generall that the King would firme to that he had done, and that within the space of 40 daies he should expecctt the Kings firma; for that he meantt the next daie to dispatch away a post for the courtt for the accomplishing of this bussines. And so for this day they partted. Upon the agrementt of this peace, the Guzuratt shipp was discharged and delivered up to the capttayne, without any damage or losse of the least thing they had in ther shippes [*sic*].

21 Occttober. Our Generall went ashoare [and] did conferr with the Governer of Amedevar and the rest of the cavelleroes.

[1] Best says that the agreement was made on 21 October.

An Indian came and plaid upon a strang instrewmentt before our Generall. Afterwards our musittions plaid before the Governer off Amedevar and all the rest of the chieff; which muzick they did verie highlie comend. Our Generall caussed a paire of virginalls[1] to be brought ashoare, and upon them one of our musitions[2] plaid; which musick did please them the best of all. Our Generall left thes virginalls with the Governer of Amedevar, and tould him he would present them unto the Kinge, and he likewisse that plaid upon them; and in the meane tyme, so long as he staid ther, he should have both the man and the virginalls att his servicce.

22 Occttober. Our Generall wentt abord the ***Dragon,*** with the Governer [of Surat?] and many more of the chief, to see his shipp. Where they were riallie entterttayned, and after retourned ashoare agayne. The Governer [of Ahmadābād?] was expecctted, butt came nott; thes was the pledges, who att ther partting had 3 peecces.

23 Occttober. Our master comaunded our men to go ashoare and sett up a tentt for the souldiers, and likewisse to pitch the Generalls tentt. Yt was thought he would have builded the pinis[3] heere, butt yt was deffered. Our Generall had presented unto him 2 antilopes by one of the chieff.

24 Occttober. Our Generall caried the Kinges present ashoare to shew yt to the Governer, and afterwards sent yt abord agayne; and withall tould the Governer that, as soone as he had recceved the Kinges firma, he would send up the present with one of his merchantts, and likewisse the Kinges letter. This day our Generall did present the Governer of Amedevar and his sonne with eyther of them a rich presentt. The Governer bought of our Generall this daie 2000 covads of broadcloth att 20 ma[hmūdis] the covade, to paie him ½ money, ½ comodittie, eyther in callicoes or any other comodittie the counttrey would presenttlie yield. This day our Generall did presentt Medejopher (a merchant and one of the chieff of Zuratt) with a rich gift.

25 Occttober. Being Saaboth day, we had a sermon abord of

[1] The ancestor of the spinet, and thus of the modern piano; but it was in a box or case, not set upon legs. Roe took out a specimen as a present to the emperor, 'which gave him good content' (*Embassy*, p. 98).

[2] Lancelot Canning (see p. 34). [3] See note on p. 65.

us. Becausse the General lay abord, the preacher came to us. Text, 9 Pro[verbs], 5, 6, 7 versses. The Governer sent our Generall a presentt of vittualle, reedy dressed by his ownne cooks.

26 Occttober. Our Generall wentt ashoare, to see cloth delivered. [He] desired the Governer to haisten the bussines, for that they weere tedious in meassureinge. One of the Governers men and one of our English did shott for a waiger, both for farnesse and neerest a mark; but the English gott the creditt. His name is John Harisson, master cooper of the *Dragon*.

27 Occttober. Our Generall wentt ashoare to hasten the bussines, both for delivery of cloth and receitt of money. [He] did recreatt himselff with his horsse, by rydinge 2 or thre milles intto the counttrey. Repaired abord agayne.

28 Occttober. The Governer off Amedevar and many of the chieff went abord the *Dragon*, by long entreatie of our Generall; where they [had] verie riall enttertaynementt, and did much admire to se such a shipp. The Governer wrott a lletter for his sonne to come abord, and wrott him that who had nott sene that shipe had nott seene the world. The *Dragon* gave them for ther wellcome 9 peecces, and att ther farwell 17 peecces. After, they came abord off our shipe. And att that tyme we had a man in the bilbowes for theifft he had divers tymes comitted. The Governer sse him in prisson [and] demaunded the causse of his beinge ther. Our Generall tould him that he was there for theift, and that his offence was sso heynous that within towe dais he meantt to hange him. Being setting in our greatt cabin, the Governer dessired our Generall to send for him, and would nott ceasse till our Generall had grantted his pardon; which he did, and pressinttlie sett him at liberttie. The Governer did much rejo[i]ce he had saved a mans liffe. At ther deperture our shipe shott 9 peecces. This daie one of the *Dragons* men leapt overbord furth off our shipe and would have drowned himselffe, for feare of punishment for beinge drunk. Our skiff saved him.

29 Occtober. The Governer wentt away. Left his servantes to receve cloth and paye money.

30 Occtober. Our Generall wentt ashoare to recreatt himselffe. [He] took horsse and rood into the fieldes.

31 Occ[t]ober. Our Generall staid abord.

First November. Being Saboath daíe, we all repaired abord the *Dragon* to heare a sermon, for that the Generall was removed from us to his ownne shipe.

2, 3, 4 Occttober [November]. The Generall staid abord his ownne shipe [and] came not ashoare.

05 November. The Generall had one off his men rune away to Zuratt. [He] countterfeitted his masters hand to the merchants for 30 doll[ars]. The steward was sentt post after him, and took him beffore he had receved the 30 doll[ars]. He had long punishmentt in the bilbowes.

06 November. The pursser took the examinacion off Captain Hermon[1] and others againest the offender.

07 November. A Moore brought newes to Captayne Hermon (who staid ashoare conntinuallie with 50 souldiers) that the Porttingailles was shorttlie to come to feight with us with 2 shipes and 2 gallies and 20 frigotts. This newes was presentlie brought to our Generall; whereupon he comaunded Capttayne Hermon abord with all his souldiers and both the tentes; [and] sentt his horsses to Sually.

8 November. Being Saboath daie, we repaired to the sermon.

9 November. Both the masters sounded the barr; but they found nott watter enowgh for the *Dragon* to go over.

10 November. Our Generall sent ffor our boattsson and others of our men, which he duckt for swimeinge ashoare of the Saboath daie and drinkinge drunk with houres [i.e. whores]. The boattsson lost his place, and Ricchard Barker [was] maid boattson, and Perfey taiken into the *Dragon*. This daie the Generall punished many of his ownne men for dicce and cardes.

11 November. Boatsson Barker took his place and had the stores surrendred up to him by the pursser.

12 November. The Generall came abord of us and sse the choice off some cloth maid by the Indians. Affterwardes [he]

[1] Presumably the 'John Harmon' whose death at Tiku on 14 September 1613 is recorded at p. 67 and in *Letters Received*, vol. IV (p. 22). From the title given to him it is inferred that he had had some military experience and had for this reason been engaged to train and lead the sailors in the events of attacks by the Portuguese. We have already (p. 28) surmised that 'Capttain Goitt' had been sent out for the same purpose.

went ashoare, devided the souldiors, and we had a skrimidge. The countrey people lefft ther wares and shopes to come and looke att us. Some brok ther swordes; some cutt ther fingers; some hurtt in one place, some in another; but no great harme. Capttayne Hermon with his souldiers staid ashoare this night and sett up ther tenttes againe.

13 November. Certaine Indians came abord to buy cloth, and paid ther money, accordinge to the quantitie of cloth they bought.

14 November. The Generall staid abord this daie.

15 November. We repaired abord [the] *Dragon* to sermon, beinge Saboath daye.

16 November. [The] Generall abord all daie.

17 November. An exchange off boattsson abord the *Dragon*. A letter receved from Goa from Mr. Caneinge and the pursser.

18. Receved some provissions off vittuall abord.

19 November. This morneinge earlie our Generall went ashoare, took horss [and] his company waggins, and rood 4 or 5 milles into the countrey, with his trumpetts ssoundinge. In the woodes he had the company off many counttrey people; which afterwardes accompanied him to Sualley, and ther did pressent him with many small pressentts. This daie, by the Generalls order, Captayne Hermon with his souldirs began to maik a fortt ashoare.

20 November. [The] master off the *Dragon*, his matte, and divers others, dined abord our shipe. [The] Generall sentt for 10 off his men we had abord off us.

21 November. The merchantts att Suratt sentt our masters boy back againe to the shipes. They found him amongst the Moores, with Moores aparell. The causse was the steallinge off a sillver cupe of the cape merchants [i.e. Canning]. His master tyed his handes to the shipe side, and whiptt him till blood came. I dessired the master to whipe him well, and I would taik some paines with him to heall him; which I did, and would do as much agayne, iff he might have another whippinge. But I am afraid whiping will nott maik him good, allthough I wish yt otherwisse, for his frendes causse. The merchantts came all from

Suratt in generall. Mr. Aldsworth brought the Generall a fatt doe. This night came from Suratt 16 balls of callicoes.

22 November. We repaired abord the *Dragon* to sermon; where we had hott veneson to dynner.

23 November. This daie the goods was shipped in the *Dragon*. The merchanntts with the Generall in councell for furder bussines.

24. Thies daie the merchantts wentt all to Suratt, haveinge concluded by a courtt to send home the *Hossiander* for England. The Generall wentt ashoare with the merchantts, and did accompany them 3 or 4 mille of ther waie to Suratt. Afterwards the Generall went abord, with the captayne of the Guzuratt shipp, who brought him a present of goatts and came to buy some cloth.

25 November. The Generall comaunded Captayne Hermon to pull downne his tentts and repaire abord with his souldiers, for that there was in [sight?] 100 frigotts standing towardes our shipes. We both off us maid redy our shipes to preventt the wurst. Albeitt, they did nott medle with us at this tyme. They countrey people that keept shopes ashoare conveyed ther goodes to Sualley. Yett this night Captayne Hermon was apointed ashoare againe with his souldiers. The frigotts was gone for Cambaia. Of this newes the counttrey people were nott a litle glad, becausse they might more securelie keepe ther goodes ashore. This daie came from Zuratt with the Sabendor a captaine to procure the Generalls passe for the Read Sea, for that [if] he should channce to meett with any English shipes, the passe might certiffie them we had concluded peace and established a factorie at Suratt. The Generall verie willingelie graunt[ed] yt him; for which the captane retourned him many thankes, and sso partted.

26 November. Yt pleassed God off His mercie to taik awaie Thomas Pois, one off our quarttermasters, by longe contynuance of a flix [i.e. dysentery]. His bodie [was] buried at shipesydde in Sualley roode. The *Dragons* baiker came abord, to teach our steward to baik sofft bread.

27 November. This daie the Generall had letters from our merchantts at Suratt, and allsso a letter from Mr. Caneinge and the pursser from Goa, dated the 11th of this instant, wherin

they did certiffie the Generall of 4 gallions and 25 saille off frigotts, verie well apointted with men and munittion, was put to sea to come for Suratt and taik our shipes, our goodes and moneys, and to maik slaves off us. Upon which newes the Generall comaunded Captaine Hermon abord with his tentts and souldiers, and likwisse sent post for his master gonner and all his men he had geven leave to go to Suratt. [He] comaunded our master to come off with his shipe and ride by him in the offen, to maike readie our feights [see p. 106 *n.*], and to beatt downe all our cabins and fitt the shipe for feight, for that the Porttingall had vowed to taik us, and receved the sacramentt upon ytt, [and] had promissed cloth to many of ther frendes, as iff we had bene allreadie taken. They promissed the pursser both money and cloth, and that they would sett Mr. Caneinge and him abord the *Dragon*, for they meant to have all our men ther slaves and our shipes ther prisses. The captaine of one off the carrackes we meett att sea tould Mr. Caneinge that we had killd him thre men, but Nuno de Guno should requit that blood.

28 November. We [had] newes from Suratt the Porttingells had delivered Mr. Caneinge into the English housse, off which newes many weere glad. This daie we had sight off the enemye about the barr of Suratt, being 4 gallions and 25 frigotts.

29 November. In the morneinge, being Saboath, Mr. Alldsworth, Mr. Caneing, and all the rest of the merchauntts were comed to the watterside; where Mr. Caneinge did take leave of Mr. Aldsworth and came abord; haveing verie importtunattlie perswaided John Jooson[1] to repaire abord, with others of our yong merchauntts, which refussed and found many delayes, or elles durst nott. Everie man was reedy with great spiritt and courage to encountter the enemïe. The names of our merchantts which remained ashoare are thes: Mr. Thomas Alldsworth (cape merchantt), Thomas Carridge (his seconnde), William Mooree, Hewgh Gettinges, William Beedulph, John Joosson, Nicolas Withington, John Yonge. Mr. Caneinge did first repaire abord

[1] Probably the 'John Johnson, a voluntary of the Tenth Voyage, who came out with Paul Canning in the *Osiander*,' of *Letters Received*, vol. II, p. 123. He was left by Best at Bantam, and was afterwards employed as a factor at Patani and Ayuthia, dying at the latter place on 12 August 1617.

the *Dragon*, where he did relatt unto the Generall so much as he knew was prettended by the Porttingaille against us: how they meantt to taike both our shippes, money, and goods; which before they came from Goa they had vowed and recceved the sacrament upon yt, and then yt must needs be performed: how they had in ther shippes, some 200, some 150 men; ther frigotts, 50 or 60 souldiers, besides saillers; which number the Lord knowes was far unequall with us, they being aboutt 2000 men, we little more then 200 in both our shippes. Butt the Lord, I hop, will feight for us; in whom is our trust in the daie of battaille. Ther ammerall [had] 36 peecces, cullverin and deme-canon, the rest 20 (some more, some lesse); all brasse ordinance. And further, they Porttingailles die verielie think, when wee see ther forcces, that we would nott feight butt yield, in hope of favour. Furder, Mr. Caneing did certiffie our Generall how Edward Cristian, the pursser, by the meanes of one Chambers, who went away from Sir Henrie Midletton heere att Sualley and wentt to the Porttingailles, who afterwards repented (as yt should seame) of that he had formerlie done, and to fre himselff of such slavery as he lyved in, did att Cambaia both convey himselff away and likewisse the pursser, who came to Suratt, butt the feight was begun and we putt of[f] to sea. Mr. Caneinge haveinge delivered the Generall whatt he knew concerninge the Porttingailles, came abord of our shipp, where he was recceved with greatt gladnesse. Our Generall came this morneinge to see our shipp and feights. All things was to his conttentt. He maid a speech unto the company, the effectt wherof was this: that allthough ther forcces weere more then oures, yett they were both basse and cowardlie, and that ther was a sayinge nott so comon as trew: Who so cowardlie as a Porttingall? and that after the first bravado was past, they were verie cowards, as he in former tymes had found them by experience. [He] did therffore perswad everie man to be of good courage, and shew oursellves trew Englishmen, famoussed over all the world for trew vallour; and that God, in Whom we trusted, would bee our helpe. [He urged us] to trust in God, and nott to feare death, allthough for death we weere ordayned; and in a better accion we could nott die then in the behalffe of so worthy a counttrey as we have, the comon wealth of our land, the estaitt of our masters. For death, sayth he, is the passage to Heaven. He shewed a sayinge of David, in his 16 Pssallme (towards the latter end): I will sett God allwaies before me, for He is on my right hand; therffore I shall nott fall. My hart is glad; my glorie rejoced. My flesh allso shall rest in hope Thou shalt shewe me the path of lieffe. In Thy presence is the fullnese of joie, and att Thy right hand ther is pleassure for evermore. In this manner haveing encouraged our men, [he] furder tould them that, if yt should pleasse God that any of our men in feight weere dismembred or laymed, he faithfullie promissed, upon his creditt and reputacion, in the hearinge of all the company, that he would be a meanes unto the Worshipfull whom we serve, in ther behalfes for reasonable mayntenance to keepp them as long as yt should please God they lyve, and himselfe to be the petetioner upon his knees till his request weere grauntted; butt that we should nott need to feare, for that we served a religious and worthy company of masters that would never see a man go to decay or wantt by any harme susteyned in ther servicce. Haveing endeed his speech, he tooke a cupp of wyne and drounk to the master and all the company, and desired God to give us His blessinge; and so rettourned abord his ownne shipp to sermon. We wentt to prayer, Mr. Caneing beinge speaker. We all joyned with him that God would asist us against our aproaching enemies. After praier we wentt to dynner, [and] drunk one to another, thinking tyme longe till they were come upp. We had weid apike[1], and was redie when the *Dragon* weyd, and [we] kept of[f] hir wither bowe. We had the wynd of them, which we aymed to keep. [We] stood right with them, with flags, ancientts, and our pendantts att everie yardarme. Ther viceadmerall was the headmost shipp. The *Dragon* steered direccttlie with hir and, haveing hailled hir with a noisse [i.e. flourish] of trumpetts, gave hir a sallutting peecce under hir sterne. She answered hir agayne. Then the *Dragon* came up with hir and gave hir a holle [i.e. whole] broadsid for a wellcome; which we did see to raik hir thorow and thorow. We heerd ther people make a greatt crie, for that yt could nott otherwisse bee butt that

[1] Hauled in the cable sufficiently to bring the ship immediately over the anchor, so as to weigh the latter expeditiously.

they had recceved greatt spoille and harme from the *Dragon*. She shott att the *Dragon*, butt shott over and did hir no harme, save onelie the sinkeinge of hir longboatt; which that night they freed and maid theitt [i.e. tight] agayne. The *Dragon* did so plague the vicce-admerall that the admarrall and the rest rune away afore the wynd. We weere reedy to second the *Dragon*, butt could nott, for that they rune away. The *Dragon* had a shott in the mainemast, which ther stuck fast. Another shott she had upon [her] stterbord boowe, butt no harme (the Lords name be praised). The vicce-admerall bore upp with hir consertts; the *Dragon* and we came to an anker, hallffe a lleague of[f] them to windward. This night we see the vice-admerall upon the carrene, with all the frigotts aboutt hir, thinking she had recceved some shott under watter. This feight was in the sight of the shoare, wher both our English and the counttrey people did behold us, allthough this afternone[s] worke were butt a preparittive to that ensewed.

30 November. This daie (being St. Andrewes Daie) we weied earlie in the morneing, keepinge the wynd of them, [and] bore right with them. The *Dragon*, being ahead, steered with the ammerall and gave hir such a breakfast as Nuno de Cuno litle expecctted, and sent him such tokens as maid the shipes sid crack wheere he was. All of them this morneinge more or lesse hard from the *Dragon*. We weere nott farr from hir, to second hir in the best manner we could. We sent them tokens to lett them tast of our curttesey. We came so neere that we never shott butt prevailled, being amongst them, where they all did shott att us. We had a hott conflictt this morneinge, butt no harme recceved (the Lords name be praissed). For the spacce of 3 or 4 houres our feight endured. We stood of[f] intto the chennell for deeper watter, [and] ankered in 7 fadom watter, aboutt a league from the enemie. They spoilled us some tacklinge, butt no more harme as yett. Att afternone, with [the] flod we weid. And the *Dragon* weid likewisse, and wentt up with thre of them; where she plaid hir partt couragiouslie all this afternone. One beinge from the rest a good distance and (as we did think) was aground, we came upp close upon hir steerbord sid, within ½ a stons cast and lesse of hir. With this shipp we spentt all this afternone in feight. We

made 100 greatt shott this day—langrill[1], round, and crossebar[2] —besides our small shott. They maid many shott att us, butt shott many over. We lost our boattson [Richard Barker *in margin*] this day, slayne by a greatt shott upon the forecasle. Our tackleing and sailles turne [i.e. torn], butt no more harme this day (the Lords name be praissed). Our boattson had one of his armes taiken away, with other towe mortall wounds, one in his bodie, the other in the other arme. I did my best endevour to give him cumportt [i.e. comfort]; butt being broken clene in sunder (the wound in his body more daungerous) ther was butt small hop of his liffe. So that yt pleassed God to call him within 2 houres he had recceved his hurtts.

Our master and cape merchantt, after the feight was ended, went abord the *Dragon* to see our Generall, and to know if all ther men were well. The Generall tould them that all his company was well, except one man slayne right outt with a shott in his bodie, wherupon he died instantly. Another with the same shott lost one of his armes. This was all the harme the *Dragon* recceved this daie, saveing his tackleing and sailles something torne. This night, in the begineing of the first watch, our men espied a frigott verie neere the shipp, which had rune ttoo and agayne dyvers tymes aboutt our shipp. The watch gave our master nottice of hir, and she being verie neare, our master caussed the guner to maik a shott att hir. The ordinance being reedy primed, he maid a shott att hir, which to our judgmentt was verie faire over hir. He maid another, and after that the third. She presenttlie putt furth tow lights for the other frigotts to come to hir, butt we did think she sunk before the frigotts came to hir; as afterwards, when we came to Sualley we did certaynelie understand, as the countrey people likewisse did affirme, for that they had found a greatt number of Christians drove upon the shoare, to the number of 30 or 40. We did think that this frigott was by the Generall sent to do some mischieffe against us, eyther by burneing of us or cutting of our cable; butt they maid a pitt for us and fell intto yt themselves. They knew

[1] Formed of irregular pieces of iron fastened together. This was intended to damage the rigging and sails of an opponent.

[2] A ball with a bar projecting on each side.

they had no hoppe to taik us by feighting with us, as they had reasonable well tried; and therffore they meantt by trecherey to betray us. Butt the Lord, who was our chieffe capttayne, both by daie and night, would nott suffer ther trecherous prettence to taike effecctt.

1 December. This daie we rested and did nott feight. Our Generall sentt us a new boattson in the place of Rychard Barker, who was slayne the daie beffore.

2 December. We weid and stood more to the southward, to seek deepp watter; they keeping in sight of us. This night we ankered in 10 fadom watter, neere untto Daman.

03 December. We weid and stood towards Sualley Rood agayne, thinking to meett with them, becausse thatt the last night we had lost sight of them. Our compa[n]yes [i.e. crews] both was sorie, for they had greatt desire to trie yt outt with them. Our Generall was fulley resolved to have fought withe them, if they had followed him wher he might have bene bold to have banged yt outt with them in deepp watter; they being lesser shippes then wee and light withall, that they drew butt litle watter. The Generall seing all the company so willing, yt did much move him to mayntteyne feight with them; allthough he was deswaded from yt by the chieff in his shipp, and withall to leave them and put to sea, to see if we could take any Ormus men bound for Goa; which if the Generall had consented unto, he never had nor could have had any trad att Suratt. The Generall, upon ther perswasion, put to sea and left them [i.e. the Portuguese].

4, 5 December. Becaumed att sea.

6 December. We had sight of Dua. [Being] Saboath Daie, we wentt tto sermon.

7 December. We putt in with the bay of Semeer[1]. Went ashoare with armes and gott fresh vittualle. Thes people are the Porttingailles neighbours.

8 December. We both weid, and stood alongst the coast towards a place called Madoffrabaud[2], about 12 leagues from Dua to the southwards[3].

[1] Simar Point is nine miles to the eastward of Diu. The town of that name is a little way inland.

[2] Muzafarābād (see p. 37).

[3] He means that Diu lay that distance to the southwards.

9 December. We ankered in the mouuth of the river, in 8 faddum watter. Our boatts sounded the barr, and found 3 fadum att flod. Heere we filled watter, and gott fresh vittualle. The people verie poore, but verie willing to lett us have anything the place would afourd. This Mudoffrabaud hath bene a greatt huge cittie, butt much ruinated and decayed; the walls overgrowne with wood. Yt hath a good ryver for small shippes. The Mallabars and Porttingailles sometymes with ther frigotts putt intto this river, and then the people and the inhabitantts therof doth flie away upp into the counttrey, for that they have bene many tymes ransacked and robbed by them, which is the reasons that maiks them so poore; butt verie harmeles people to them that offereth unto them no violence.

10 December. We with the *Hossiander* wentt to the ills of Mortt [see p. 37], to sound them, but found no place worth nottice, butt full of roccks and shoolds. We retourned to the *Dragon* agayne [and] shewed the Generall of our procceedings.

11 December. We had both fresh vittualle and watter from Mudoffrabaud.

12 December. The merchantts of the *Dragon* heere in this place maid saille of some iron to the Benians[1]. The *Dragons* longeboat had bene ashoare this daie to fill watter, [and] thre[2] of ther men this daie rune awaye, William Perfey chieff (who went furth our boattson) and other thre yong men, entycced by him. The Generall, after he knew they were gone, sent the master ashoare to the merchaunts to will the Governer to pursue them and, iff he tooke them, he should have 20 doll[ars] and a peece of English cloth. The Governer with much expedecion did fitt himselff, accompanied with a dossen souldiers, both horsse and foott; and that night did aprehend them, butt nott with his ownne force, butt by the helpe of a townne who did asist him. Perfey maid them flie as long as his powther and shott lasted; butt being all spentt, yiellded unto the Governer, who promissed to be his frend unto our Generall. And so in the night brought them bound, and kept them till morneinge.

13 December. This morneing both our boatts wentt ashoare to bring the Governer and his presoners abord; wheer he, being

[1] Banyans (Hindu traders). [2] '4 men' in margin.

att the wattersaid, loossed them and brought them into the boatt, with himselff and ½ a dossen of his souldiers. [He] repaired abord the *Dragon*, where the General did verey kindlie enttertayne the Governer and gave him whatt the master had promissed him to the uttermost, with mony to the souldiers. The Governer took leave, and tould the Generall the townne and himselff was att his comaund and servicce. The presoners [were] comited to [the] bilbowes. Being Saboath Daie, we repaired to sermon.

14 December. The Generall comaunded most of our men to come abord the *Dragon*, and sent for all the people ashoare with haist to repaire abord; where we weere all called and comaunded unto the ½ deck, wither presentlie the Generall came and maid a speech, the effecctt wherof was: wheras of laitt we had bene in feight with 4 men of warr, Porttingailles, and shipps both of fourc[e] and great burden, some 7 or 800 tons the shipp; and nott in respectt of the great unequallittie ther was bettwixt us, butt that we weere merchaunntts, we had refussd to maynetayne feight with them. They shewed such cowardize that we were glad to come upp with them allwaies to begin, or ells they would have rod att anker and never have budged. The General demaunded of both companyes ther opinions wether they thought yt were better for us to go over to Sualley agayne and feight with them, or to staie heere and spend our tyme, without doing of anything for the Worrshipfull Company our masters; and whether or which of thes towe resolucions might redound to our masters creditt, [our] counttres fame, and furderaunce of our presentt vaig we have in hand. Both the companyes with one accord gave ther voicces that they thought yt was better to goe over to Sualley agayne; and if the shippes weere there, they would feight yt out with them so long as they weere able to stand, if yt should stand with his likeing. Wherupon he promissed them that, over a day, 2 or 3, he meantt to go over, after he had discovered a place called Mea or Mocha[1], for by reportt yt was a good place or herber for shippes (butt we found yt otherwisse). After our Generall had ended his speech concerning our retourneing for Suratt, both our shippes companyes joyned to-

[1] Mahuwa (see note on p. 38).

gether in sewtt unto our Generall in the behalff of his 4 prisoners which the Governer had taken and brought him; butt he seamed loth to graunt them any favour att all butt what the lawe would doe, and for Perfey he meantt absolutlie to hange him, for an example to all the rest of his men, to rune away att such a tyme and to so a basse a people as the Porttingaille, and utterlie deffame himself and banish himself from his native counttrey and his wiffe and chilld, and to be so trecherous to rune to them to feight against us. Yett nottwithstandinge all this, both the companyes was so importtune, and did so earnestlie entreatt for them, that att last he was content to give liberttie unto thre of them, if we would be conttentt to lett him hange William Perffey, the chieff ringleader, who could never answeer the factt without his life. Both the companyes was verie constantt, and still entreatted the Generall; all generallie, except Mr. Bonner and Sallmon, and they two would nott condiscend [i.e. agree] to save him. Yett att length the Generall, seing both the companyes so importtunatt with him, tould them they should have ther requests, and grauntted the presoners should all have libertie. The Generall tould them that, if they had asked his right hand, he could nott deny them yt, for that they had proved themselves so faithfull and stoutt to resist the enemie. The presoners, haveing ther irons taiken of[f], gave thanks to both companyes for ther kyndnesse towards them; and allso unto the Generall upon ther knees, promisseing to became [*sic*] new men and to endeavour themselves in ther placces to give content unto our Generall. So this being done, the cooper was called to fill some beare; and haveing drunk, we of the *Hosseander* repaired abord our ownne shipp.

15 December. This morneing we weyed and stood towards Mea, allias Mocha; and ther we ankered in the mouth of the bay, in 7 fadum watter. Both the masters wentt to sound the bay, butt found yt verie shoold, and fitt for no shippinge. In this placce we gott fresh vittuall, both muttons, goatts, and watter. Riding in this place, we herd greatt ordinance go of[f] verie fast. The [interpreter?] that the Generall entertaynd att Suratt tould him that about 3 leagues of[f] ther was greatt warrs bettwixt the Mogole and the Mallabars, and that the Magolle had besieged a

place called Castelletta[1], a fortt verie stronge and faire, which the Mallabars had possessed and holden valientlie by forcce of armes. This castle was the chieff, and allmost an illand environed about with the sea. The Magolle had besieged this place with 7000 horsse and foott, and laid sieg to yt 2 monnth, butt could nott prevaille, for they wantted ordinance. They had 4 peecces, wherof one was a canon[2]; yett could nott batter ther walles. The generall of the army hard of our being att Mocha, and sent a letter unto our Generall to send him one of his chieffest officers, for that he greattlie desired to conffer with some of our people. We wentt ashoare to by vittuall, butt could gett none, and so retourned abourd agayne.

16 December. The *Dragons* skiffe wentt ashoare, wherin wentt Mr. Caneinge and Mr. Oliver, with other merchantts, to see this place, which was aboutt a league within the land; where we[3] see the walls and religues of a gallant cittie, which of laitt yeares was surprized by the Greatt Mogolle[4]. Att night [we] retourned abord agayne, all verie wearie with journeyinge from Mocha. Our merchantts wentt abord the *Dragon*, where after super they had confference with the Generall concerning our goeing over to Suratt and the dispatch of our shipp away for England; for the which Mr. Caneing had excceedinglie labored and, findinge the Generall so sudenlie allttered from his purposse, seamed much discontented. For that tow or thre daies before, he [i.e. the General] had called both shippes companyes together and tould them he meantt absolutlie to go over to Sualley Roode and dispatch bussines from Suratt, and if that the Portingailles should come, then to feight yt outt and wynn the trad by force of armes; unto which motion both the companyes did verie willinglie yi[e]ld unto, and was withall verie glad to heare the Generall so well resolved. Butt betwixt spirittuall and temporall tymeservers,

[1] In Lavanha's map (see note on p. 37 above) 'Castellete' is marked as ying on the shore above halfway between Mahuwa and Salbet. It does not appear in modern maps, and was evidently a mere fort.

[2] The ordinary cannon had a bore of about eight inches and threw a shot of 60 lb.

[3] Evidently Standish was one of the party.

[4] Mahuwa has a long history, for a sketch of which see the *Bombay Gazetteer*, vol. VIII, p. 536. This, however, gives no account of the capture of the town by the Mughals.

the Generall was cleare of another mynd, to the greatt grieff and discontent of some of our chieffest wellwishers of the vaige.

17 December. This morneing we see a counttrey boott standing towardes our shippes with a flag of truce. They could hardlie fettch the shippes withoutt greatt labor, and therfore the Generall sent his boott to hir and brought 2 of the chieff messengers and retourned abord. They did in discrett fashon carrie themselves, [and] tould the Generall that ther lord and master, the Governer of the army, had sent them in his name to salut him and to wellcome him into those partts; and that ther lord and master did greattlie desire to see him and his shippes, and to conferr with him touching the buying and sellinge of some comoditties that he or wee should wantt. This messag was by our Generall kindlie accepted, and [he] dettermined that Mr. Caneinge and Mr. Oliver should go with thes messengers into the army unto the Governer, to give all the contentt that might bee unto him, after ther sallutation; and for that he understood him [i.e. the Governor] to be a frend unto the Governer of Amedevar, he would be the more willing to do him any favour wherin he might, for that he had concluded with him for divers artticles in the establishing of a facctorie or trad att Suratt. The messengers took leave. This day the Generall was fullie dettermined to have sentt our shipp to Goga[1], to sound the herber and to taike nottice of the place; butt the messengers thatt came from the army deswaded the Generall to staie the shipp, and tould him they knew the place verie well, and did assure him that yt was no herber for neyther of our ships, for att lowe watter they did affirme the rood to be drie: that 3 leagues of[f] the shoare, of[f] into the sea, our shippes might ride, butt neyther recceve nor discharge any goods butt the Porttingaill might entterceptt yt (nott careinge for the shippes). The Generall gave creditt to what they had reportted, and staid our vaige to Goga. This newes pleased Mr. Caneing well, for that he thought we should protractt lesse tyme and the soonner go over to Sualley, wher some bussines might be performed, eyther by feighting with the

[1] Gogo (Gogha) was rising into importance, as, owing to the gradual silting up of the port of Cambay, the larger Indian vessels usually anchored at the former port and thence sent over their cargoes to Cambay in lighters.

Porttingailles (they being there) or in the dispatch of our merchantts affaires (they being absentt).

18 December. We had fresh vittuall from shoare. Our Generall sent his boatt, with a dossen shott [and] Capt. Hermon, to examyne a boatt [that] was heere comed into a kriek, laden with mealle and rice. I was specctator in the perfformance of this message of Mr. Hermons; which was done with too much severittie, for allthough they said they came from Dua, yett they did affirme that they were Benianns and that provission they had was for the army; butt Capt. Hermon, giveinge butt little creditt to what was spoken, caussed them to be hanged upp upon a tree by ther hands, fingers, and heads, to maik them confesse themselves to be Porttingailles; butt could not, becausse they were nott so, nor could nott speak a word of Porttingaille. His dealling was verie extreame, in my opinion, they being such harmles creattures.

19 December. Rettourned Mr. Caneing and Mr. Oliver from the army, with ther enterpretter the Indian. They had bene verie curtteouslie entertayned, and so much they gave the Generall to understand: that from the Governer of the army they had many salutacions; who much desired to see his person, in respecctt of the peace he concluded and agreed upon with his frend the Governer of Amedebar, which he hoped should continew unto the worlds end, for the comonwealthes sake of both our counttres; and that the causse wheerfore he sent unto us was for the love he had unto our Generall and our countrey, and the worthy reportt he had of our nattion, for that the English was allwaies a people famous over all the world in martiall exploitts. The Governer in this manner comending our nattion, a souldier came runeinge in greatt haist and did entterupt him in his speech, and tould him that the Mallabars was conttentt to yield up ther castles, upon condition that His Honor or Lordshipp would give unto the Captayne and some of ther chieffest ther lyves, and for the rest they should be ther slaves. The Generall comaunded the souldier to retorne the enemye this answeer: that they should feight for ther lives, and further that the English was his frends and would bringe ther shippes to asist him in any accion wherein they could, and if yt weere so that he could nott with his ownne

foorcces beatt downne ther walles, he had that intterest in the English as to hope they would be assistauntt untto him, and for ther satisfaccion they should nott onelie have the castle butt allso all the goods that was found therin. The souldier retournd the enemie this answeer, to ther small chumfortt. The souldier being gone, the Governer begun to procceed in his speech to Mr. Caneinge and the rest, his associatts. [He] tould them the kingdome was thers, for trad or to do them any servicce they should require; and tould them, asoone as he had taken the castle, he meant to give yt unto our Generall, and likewisse all the goods that was found therin, if yt would pleasse him butt to come upp with his shippes and countinaunce him, and shew him his shippes, which he greatlie desired to see; and that the Mallabars might see he had a frend of us; yt would be a meanes to maik them yield the soonner. Mr. Caneinge did acceptt of his gift, and gave him thanks; nott that our Generall did care or esteeme of any gift, save onelie free accesse to trad in ther kingdome, to maike saille of such comoditties as we had and to maik our rettourne in such comoditties as we thought would be vendible in our partts; and for his gift offered, he did accept of yt in the Companyes behalffe, for if yt should pleasse our Generall to asist him in the takeing of the castles, the pillag was aperteyneing unto the Company, and in ther behalffes he did accept of yt. The Generall further tould Mr. Caneinge that what comoditties eyther that partt of the counttrey or Amedevar or Cambay or any other place would afford, he would be a meanes we should have yt, the prise reasonable, and reedy conveyaunce to our shippes withoutt intterrupttion, for he hoped that our peace should continew unto the worlds end with much love and amitty; and that they had suffered a basse people to creepp into the chieffest portts and to inhabitt ther kingdome, with whom he understood we had of laitt bene in feight with 4 of ther best shippes and had done them greatt spoille to ther shippes and men; for that a gentleman being then present had laittlie beene at Daman when thatt the Porttingaille frigotts brought ashoare ther to be buried all ther maymed, slayne, and hurtt to be cured, if yt weere possible, to the number of 80 or 90 men. The Porttingailles did reportt themselves they had recceved greatt hurtt, and specciallie that shipp which fought with the litle shipp, and called hir a devell. After much confference and many curtteses offered and promissed in our Generalls behalf, tow cavelleroes was apointted to conductt them unto a tentt fitted for them, to maik them enttertteynementt in the best manner thatt might bee. Heere they remayned all night; and in the morneing the Generall sent for them agayne, still urging them to perswad our Generall to come upp with his shippes. Mr. Caneing promissed to do his endevour to perswad our Generall, and he thought he should so much prevaille with our Generall as to graunt his request to come upp and asist him in anything wherin he mightt. Horsses was prepared for everie man upon the Generalls charge, and of ther best horsses; and likewisse 2 or 3 pillotts for the bringeinge upp of our shippes in more saiftie against the castles, if yt should pleasse our Generall to condescend thertto. Mr. Caneing with his company took leave of His Lordshipp, and with much expedicion repaired abord the *Dragon*, where at larg he delivered unto our Generall his disscoursse with the Governor of the army, [whom he ?] did comend to be both wisse and descreett, and highlie esteemed of by the kinge the Greatt Magolle, and one of his chiefest nobles [see p. 38 *n*.]. Which when the Generall had throughlie understood by Mr. Caneinge the effecctt of the sending unto him, [he] gave order to Mr. Sallmon, our master, to wey att flood with him and stand for the castle, both of us having pilotts to conductt us into the roodstead.

20 December. This morneinge the *Dragon* and we ankered against the Mallabars castle. The *Dragon* saluttted the Governer of the army with 9 peecces, and we with 5 peecces. We repaired abord the *Dragon* to sermon, weid, and stood in with the shoare. The Generall recceved a present from the other Governer, wherof we had a share.

21 December. In the morneinge the Governer of the army sent 4 of his chiefest gentlemen abord the *Dragon*, to be ther as pledges till our Generall retourned abord againe. Our Generall landed, with 40 men attendantts. [The] *Dragon* shott 7 peecces, [the] *Hosseander* 3 peecces. The Governer of the army sent a dossen or 20 horsse to the seaside to recceve our Generall and his followers, and with trumpetts sounding repaired into the

campe amongst the trenshes, where the Governer of the army had his tentts; where he was with great curtesey enttertayned, wher many carpetts and rich clothes weere spreed upon the ground to sitt upon, as the manner of the counttrey is. The Governer of the army tould him he did much desire to see him: that the countrey was his, eyther for trad or wherin he pleassed to use them. Thus itteratting of his former proffessed kindnesses, att length tould our Generall his desire was that he would bring ashoare 4 or 2 of his best peecces and help him to maik a breach in the castle walles, and his souldiers should entter; butt for what goods should be found within the castle shoulde be att our Generalls disposseinge. Our Generall retourned His Lordshipp many thanks for his kindnesse; butt for to land any of his ordinance he could nott, for yt was contrarie to his comission; butt in anything wherin he might pleasure him he should comaund him and his men in any servicce. Our Generall tould him he did nott like his plattfforme where he had plantted his ordinance, and did advise him to allter it, and one of his men should stay ashoare with his guner for to direcctt them. The Governer retourned our Generall thanks, and apointted men for allteringe of the plattfformes, to be by the English direccted. Our Generall tooke leave for a whille, and wentt to see the castle, round about the walls, and after took horsse and rood over a great hill into a valley where the campe was, a mille distantt from the castle; where he was by the Governers apointtment riallie entertayned into his tent and all his followers tent richlie spred with clothes (as afforessaid); where pressentlie was brought greatt sstore of vittualls, sett upon the ground, where our [Generall] called all his chieffest attendantts to sett downne and eatt. Our drink was fresh watter, both could and sweett; many Moores tending upon us. The Generall, haveing dyned, caussed all the rest to sett downe, for ther was no wantt of vittuall. Our Generall was presented with a faire horsse and a skarffe; the merchantts, precher, and chiefest officers presented with skarffes. After a whille he had repossed himsellfe, rewarded the offeccers for his entertaynement, took horsse, and rood back agayne to the Governers trench; wher in breif he tould him so much he would nott break the Kinges comission. And when they see they could not prevaill in ther sewtt with our Generall, they desisted. Our Generall would have begged the Capttains liffe of the castle, and his son and his doughter; which att last they grauntted. Our Generall desired yt under writtinge and sealle, butt they reffussed yt. Our Generall tould them that, if they would give him the castle and all the goods within yt, he would nott pley with them[1] withoutt his licence or writing under his sealle. The daie being farr spentt, our Generall craved licencce to retorne abord; haveing left them ashoare 2 smithes to help them to maik greatt shott, with other towe of our men for to direcctt them in the maiking of a new plattfforme. This [daie?] a Porttingaille tould some of our people ashoare that the gallions was comeinge, and shewd them a letter from Dua to the same effecctt. The Generall did understand of yt, butt gave verie little creeditt unto such reportts; yett nottwithstanding comaunded both our shipps to be fitted for feight.

22 December. This morneing we see the 4 gallions standing towards us. We weere in reasonable good readinesse beffore; yett what might be done was done, in the best manner we could, for feight, and everie man was reedy with good resolucion to stand to yt, as beffore they had done. This morneinge Mr. Caneinge and Mr. Oliver went ashoare to speak with the Governer of the army from our Generall, to intreatt him to releasse our men, for that his enemy was in sight and he should have greatt occasion to use his men. [They] caried him a present from our Generall, with many salutacions and thanks for all his kindnesses, and wished that tyme would permitt to do him any pleasure wherin yt lie in his power to do for him; and that now he might both see and know whatt prejudice might have redounded to him if he, according to his request, should have landed any of his ordinance, the enemie being approaching to assault us. The Governer replied them this answeer: that he was glad we did nott, seeinge whatt had happened. The Governer of the army, the Governer of Cambaia and all the chieff of the Moores did advise our merchantts to diswade our Generall from feightinge with them, they being men of warr and of greatt forcce, and greatt unequallittie betwixtt us; moreover, we were merchantts, and might by that

[1] Urge the garrison to surrender.

meannes overthrow our vaige, we being farr from our ownne counttrey and they att ther ownne doores, where they might furnish themselves of everie wantt. Mr. Caneing rettourned them this answeer: that there was a Godd in heaven would feight with us and for us; He was our capttayne, and under His banner we did feight; and those that constantlie and faithffullie trusted in Him, He would deliver them in the day of battell. Which speech they liked verey well, and tould Mr. Caneinge that, if our Generall wanted eyther powther, shott, or vittualle, or anything ells whattsoever, we should have yt from abord his frigotts, which then att that tyme was ridinge in the roode, laittlie comed from Cambaia with all provissions for the armye. Mr. Caneing retourned him many thanks for his kindnesse and many favours exttended towards us, and tould him we weere nott destittuett of anythinge thatt was needfull; and allthougthe ther was but litle equality in our shippes and thers, and the number of ther men and ours, yett he should see, and all his company, thatt we would give them the best wellcome we could, and thatt nott in word butt in accion, and his eyes should be wittnese of yt. Thus, tyme not permittinge to stay longer, they tooke leave of the Governer and repaired abord.

23 December. In the morneinge we weid both, and steered right with them, they being att anker; the *Dragon* with the ammerall, and we with the vice-ammerall. We did maik them such a breakfast as I do verielie think was neyther in the way of curttesey or unkindnesse was well accepted. The *Dragon*, being ahead, steered from one to another, and gave them such banges as maid ther verie sides crack; for we neyther of us never shott butt were so neere we could nott misse. We still [i.e. continually] steered after the *Dragon*, and when she was with one we weere with another. And the truth is we did so teare them thatt some of them weere glad to cutt cables and be gone. This morneinges feight was in the sight of all the army, who stood so thick upon the hills, beholdinge of us, that, the number of them being so many, they covered the ground. We lost no tyme nor spared neyther powther nor shott, as our specctators ashoare can well wittnesse how this day we paid them, and maid them rune away aboutt 2 leagues of[f] into the sea; wither we followd them, re-

joceing and payinge them, to the greatt honor of our Generall and the creeditt of our nation, to have 2 merchantt shippes to beatt 4 men of warr. We ankered in the wynd of them. Being comed to anker, our Generall sentt Captain Hermon abord of us to know if we were well. We tould him all was well, saveing one or tow lightlie hurtt in the head. Captain Hermon tould us they had one man slayne, and some lightlie hurtt. This was all the harme that both our shippes recceved this daie. The Lords name be praissed, that did so wounderfullie preserve us; for some of our men escaped this daie verie narowlie from a cullverin shott thatt came in under our half deeck.

24 December. This morneinge verie earlie with daie we weid and sett saille towards the enemie; we being in the wynd of them, and nott alltogether without the sight of the army. This morneing they weid too; and comeing upp with them, we did so lett yt flie att the vicce-admerall (the *Dragon* being with the ammerall) as we maid hir beare upp helme and go from us; and in the self-same fashion we served the admerall. The *Dragon* haveinge geven hir the first *Bon jour*, we gave hir the *Besa los manos*; but she unwilling to complementt any longer with us, did *ander per atras*[1]. Our men this daie did shew greatt vallour, everie man in his place. One of our men threw a ball of fire into ther admerall, that bussied them all to putt yt outt agayne; and if they had nott seene yt when they did, yt had fired ther shipp. This day we tore them most cruellie. We see swiming by our shipp sid peecces of tymber, boords, and ould hatts and clothes. Ther sailles weere allmost torne from [the] yards, some of them, and ther tackleing cutt in peecces. Mr. Caneing did much encourage our men, and [was] verie redy himself to do what service he might. We spentt, thes 2 daies in feight, furth of our shipp 250 greatt shott. Our fight being ended and they comed to anker, all our company joyned together and maid a petetion to our Generall, [to] the effecctt that, wheras we had divers tymes bene in feight with thes four gallions, and had spent the greatest part off our provissions, as munition, shot, and powther, which was by the Worrshipful our masters apointed for the accomplishinge of our vaige: and

[1] Evidently Standish had picked up a little Portuguese. *Beijar as mãos* means to kiss hands (salute); and *andar para traz*, to go backwards.

for that our enemies were at home at ther owne doores, where they myght furnish themsellves with all such provissions as should be needfull for them, both with vittuall, men, and munition; and we being here far from home and from our ownne countrey, our provissions much spentt, that then we should be desolate and lefft naked and frustrait of all good hopes, and more-over subject to everie shipe that might assault us; therffore the effectt off our petetion is that we may undertaik some exploitt or entterprisse, wherby we maie spoille or burne some off ther shipes; which all our company is willinge to venture ther lives to performe, for our counttres sake, our masters proffitt whom we serve, and for the creditt and honor off yowe our Generall; or ells that we maie be gone furth of this counttrey whilst we have somethinge lefft to deffend oursellves withall against thosse who affterwardes might assault us. And thus the petetion ended. Our Generall, before he had recceved our petetion, had wrott a lletter unto our master and company, tending to the verie same effectt of the petetion, thatt, forasmuch as his shott and powther was greatt part of yt spentt, he meantt that night to put over to the rood off Sualley and leave them [i.e. the Portuguese]. I did verielie think they meantt to goe for Dua and ther repaire ther shippes and taik in fresh men. We did them great spoille in ther shippes, tackleing, sailles, and men. The Lord did mercieffullie defend us, under whose banner we did feight, seing whatt shotts we had recceved; but yt was the Lords glorie in preserveinge of us for His Gosepells sake and His truthes sake, that His light might shine amoungst us and His wounderfull blissings appeare unto us; nott for any goodnesse that was in us, butt for the miritts of Jesus Christ, whose name God grauntt may be glorified amongst us unto our lives end. Our Generall sent his skiffe to know if all our men was well, and tould us they had recceved no harme that daie, save onelie one man shott into the legge. Our master guner cast upe the expence off his stores this night. We had shott awaie 27 barrells off powther and 300 great shott (crosbar, langrill, and round); and delivered this account to our master to give unto the Generall.

25 December. We steered over the chennell E. by S. and E.S.E. till we came into 6 or 7 fadum watter, neere the shoolds,

and then we steered away S.E. by S. and S.E. This night we had sight of the land, and wee weere [by] estimaçion neere unto Daman; where till flod we ankeered.

26 December. We stood along the coast E.N.E. and N.E. by N. till we came to the barre [of Surat], where we ankered in 9 fadum watter. The Generall came abord, and gave our company thanks for ther last service with the Porttingailles, and [promised ?] for his partt to procure ther sattisfaccion, if yt did please God to permitt him lif to rettorne for England: as much as in him lied to doe in ther behalfes to the Worrshipfull Company should nott bee undone, for that he had found them all verie proper and stoutt men and had deserved to be well rewarded by the Worrshipfull Company; which he maid litle doutt of to the contrarie in ther parts to be performed, for they weere a worthy and woorrshipfull company towards men of desertt. And for ther pettition, he had perussed yt and did verie well like of yt: that we had shewed ourselves both honest and carefull to forsee such an inconvenience: and for the exploitt they had offered to maike, he could nott expecctt for more vallour and good service in us then he had allreedy found by us we had performed. And moreover tould us that, if yt weere so they did come agayne, we should spend one other daie with them for a farwell, and then putt in practtise what we had formerlie pretended [i.e. intended], which was, by Gods assistaunce, to sett one of them on fire with our skiffe. Our Generall gave the company many thanks, and tould them, if he did live, they should be well rewarded for ther servicce allreadie performed. Taiking leave off the company, he repaired abord the *Dragon*.

27 December. This morneinge before daie we ankered in the rood [of] Sualley without the barr, and with our skiffe sett ashoare Edward[1] Temple, the Generalls man, with letters for the merchauntts att Suratt, and Anthony Starkie, the steward and purser, sent ashoare to provide fresh vittuall. We left the *Dragon* att the barr, but att flod she came upp to Sualley, and ankered in her ownne birth wher she rood before. This daie

[1] A mistake for Richard (cf. p. 147). He was sent to Agra with Canning, but quarrelled with him on the way and returned to Surat, where he died on 27 June 1613 (*Letters Received*, vol. 1, pp. 300, 304).

came downne from Suratt the pursser [i.e. Christian] who had bene prisoner with the Porttingaille and was rune awaie with another English of Sir Henrie[s] company, whose name was Chamers. Thes 2 came downne from Suratt; and Thomas Carridge, by whom we did understand that in the first feight we had killd the Porttingailles 150 men, and did for certtaine averr yt from the countrey people, which had seene them driven ashoare, and partlie by thes Porttingailles themsellves. In our absence from Suratt, we hard that their (?) Governer was slaine by his brother, who should posesse his place. And for the Kinges firma, we understood yt was nott comed, butt everie daie expected. Our master and Mr. Caneing wentt abord the *Dragon*, with the merchaunt and the purser, whom this daie used greatt discourtesey thone towards the other[1], aboutt the enttertaynementt of Mr. Sallmons boy. The Generall did understand of this unkyndnesse, and took yt with greatt distast, for that his name had bene used. The Generall tould Mr. Caneinge playnlie that he was dishonest, with much more which is too tedious; butt in my opinion Mr. Caneinge was much wronged, as the matter, trewlie examyned, will att large declare. The Generall comaunded him to keepp the shipp, upon his displeasure, and nott to goe ashoare.

28 December. The merchauntts retourned to Suratt, to send awaie the goods that was ther reedy, with as much expedicion as possible might bee. This daie we filld watter, and did protractt no tyme, least the enemie should persue us. Medejopher came from Suratt to see our Generall. [He] did seame to rejoce of our good forttune against the Porttingailles, [and] tould us we had killd verie many of ther men and done them greatt spoille in the first feight. Medejopher offered our Generall powther, shott, or whatt ells Suratt would affoorde. This day we filld 4 tonnes watter.

29 December. Medejopher staid att Sualley, wher our Generall went ashoare to accompany him; wher they did discoursse of our feight, both att the barr and att Castelletta, and

[1] Meaning Canning and Salmon. The boy who was the cause of the dispute was evidently the one who had stolen a cup belonging to Canning and had run away, only to be recaptured (see p. 117).

of the kindnesse offered unto us by the Governer there. After the discoursse of the feight, falling into speech of trade, our Generall demaunded of him if the firma weere comed, for that the Governer of the army tould him att Castelleta that yt was comed to Amedevar. Our Generall craved the dispatch of the firma; yt was promissed him. Newes was brought unto our Generall the enemie was in sight agayne. [The] Generall tooke leave of Medejopher [and] comaunded the drume to call together all his men and repaire abord [the] bootts, being loaden with watter. [He] repaired abord, and afterwards came ashoare againe for the men. This newes proved not trew; so Captayne Hermon staid ashoare with his souldiers. This daie the goods came from Suratt, [to] the quanttittie of 21 bailles [of] callico.

30 December. Our Generall sent to Suratt [and] craved the dispatch of the firma. The matter of contraversie betwixt the master and Mr. Caneinge was brought in question, and divers of our company examyned of both sides; butt for my part, I had a privatt examynacion ashoare by the Generall, wherin I did resolve him as much as I knew concerninge this contraversie; butt I do think Mr. Caneing was imputed cullpable of many things more upon envie then truth. The councell being ended, Mr. Caneing went for Suratt.

31 December. Provissions of vittualle came from Suratt [and] went abord the *Dragon*. We sent emptie cask ashoare to be filld, according to former tymes; but our boott rettourned as she wentt, without any, and those that was to go to Szuratt durst nott, butt retourned abord agayne, for that Medejopher, one of the chief, had taken some disconttentt att our Generall, and therfore had comaunded the Mocodom nott to lett us have anything, neyther vittuall nor watter. Mr. Caneing came from Suratt and tould us the causse of the unkyndnesse was becausse our Generall would nott lett him have 20 clothes[1] without money, which beforetyme he had promissed him. Mr. Caneing tould us the firma was comed within 40 coursse[2] of Suratt; and for Medejopher, he had parttlie pacieffied him, and turned all

[1] Bales of broadcloth (about 30 yards in each).

[2] The *kos*, the usual measurement of distance in India, was variously reckoned at this time as one and a half or two English miles.

matters of greif into kyndnes againe. Butt whether our Generall would so accept of yt or no, the sequell will declare.

First Jenuarie. Mr. Caneing wentt abord the *Dragon*; where, after sermon was ended, the matter of contraversie was had in question; but how matters past I know nott, for that I was absentt. Butt this night Tobias Oliver came abord with our master, to be in Mr. Caneings place and to posesse his cabin; Mr. Caneinge himself detayned abord the *Dragon*, to go ther as an ordinarie merchauntt. With many other disgracces, he was exempted from the Generalls table, and his servantt prefered before him. But in my opinion he is a man verie wisse and descreett, and farr more fitting for the place he had then he who now hath yt; and I am affraid that if Mr. Caneinge should lyve discountenanced, the Worrshipfull Company our masters would nott be well served in this bussinesse.

2 Jenuarie. Our Generall came abord us, and calld our men together concerning Mr. Caneing and Mr. Sallmon, and tould them that he must seperatt them. [He] demaunded generallie of them all wether they would have ther master go into the *Dragon*, or Mr. Caneinge. They, for feare of displeassing the Generall and the master, and Mr. Caneing being absentt, did yield that Mr. Caneing should rather be displaced then the master; which he tould them he would do, and caussed the pursser to maik a writtinge tending to such effecctt, that the company might assigne unto yt. Butt for my partt I was absentt; and allthough I had bene there presentt, I would not have firmed to itt. But the company did yt more for feare then upon any dew desertt of Mr. Caneinge. This night Mr. Caneing came abord to dispatch some bussinesse about the packinge upp of a chest of money that he had opened for the use of the Worrshipfull Company; about which chest some discontent was taken by the Generall[1]. Mr. Caneing this night repaired abord the *Dragon* againe.

3 Jenuarie. This day went abord [the *Dragon*] to heare the sermon. Our boattsons matte [was] comitted to [the] bilbowes, for staying so longe ashoare, contrarie to order.

[1] This incident seems to be referred to at p. 290 of vol. II of *Letters Received*, where it is alleged that Salmon took 100*l*. of the Company's money to employ for the benefit of himself, Oliver, and Croft. Possibly Canning was blamed for allowing this.

04 Jenuarie. We filld fresh watter. This daie the Generalls goodes[1] came downne, and letters from the merchaunts that goodes would be downne this night, butt no firma comed.

05 Jenuarie. This day Mr. Coupland the preacher and divers of our merchants went to Suratt to dispatch bussines [and] to speak with the chief concerninge the firma; if no hope of yt, then to perswaid Mr. Aldsworth to repaire abord. This night came abord the *Dragon* 19 bailles of goods. My matte [was] sent for by the Generall; who had bene in the bilbowes about 30 hours, upon words given to the boattson, wherupon he was both beett and comitted to the bilbowes. The Generall, understanding how he had bene wronged, relleassed him [and] advissed him to patience and to keep himself free from such brawlles.

6 Jenuarie. Mr. Cowper[2] in the bilbowes for quarelling and calling one of the masters mattes flatt sheett. Our Generall rettourned the signett which he had from Medejopher, for that he had proved himselffe so unconstantt towards him. I prey God Sir Henrie Midlettons sayings be nott verefied in thes people. This daie Mr. Aldsworth wrot our Generall that, whether the firma came or no, he would nott come from Zurat.

07 Jenuarie. Newes came unto our Generall that the firma was comed to Zurat; the which newes was litle expeccted, for both our Generall and merchantts was quit out of hope yt would nott come, butt was packing upp and maikinge way to repaire abord, all butt Mr. Aldsworth, the Companies chief agent; and he would never consent to come away. He was nott a litle joyfull of this newes, for that he might more securelie remayne in the counttrey and in the trad att Suratt. I hoppe we all that are well-wishers unto the vaig shall have causse to praisse God for the establishing of a facctorie heere, and for the peaceable trad our merchantts is like to have heere att Suratt; for that heere many and sundrie of our English comoditties have bene vented att reasonable rattes and reedy money, wher[as] in other partts of Indea [i.e. the East Indies] yt is nott so. I beseech God give a

[1] Presumably goods bought by Best on his own account. Kerridge afterwards avowed that the General invested about 200*l*. at Surat in blue baftas for sale at Achin, Bantam, etc. (*Letters Received*, vol. II, p. 110).

[2] The name does not occur elsewhere, and probably we should read 'the master cowper' (cooper).

happie countynnaunce of this trad, long to contynew to the glorie of God, our masters profitt, and our Generalls creditt. Mr. Coupland, Mr. Caneing, and Mr. Oliver came from Suratt, with the cavellero that brought the firma, acompanyed with Cashavalley [Kāshif Ali?], a merchauntt of Suratt. Heareing the[y] weere comed to Sualley, the Generall sentt Mr. Bonner and our master to meett them and entreatt them in the name of the Generall to repair abord. So both the masters, haveing seene the firma, retourned abord with the merchantts, together with Mr. Alldsworth, who had nott the enttertaynementt that he expecctted he should have had att the Generalls hands. The Generall stood in doubtt wether yt was the firma or no, for that yt was brought in no statt nor fashion, nott beseameing the letter of so greatt a kinge as the Magolle was; for he expecctted Medejopher and all the chief to have comed downe with yt, and to accknowledge yt to be the Kinges firma. Wherupon a messenger was presentlie sent to Suratt to the same efect, to speack with the chief, in the name of our Generall, and retorne ther answer

8 March[1]. The Generall kept Mr. Aldsworth and Mr. Caneinge abord the *Dragon*, hourlie expectting newes from Suratt that the chief would come, according to his desire, and accknowledg the firma.

9 March. Mr. Ceredg came from Suratt and certified our Generall that most of the chief would come downne to Sualley, according to his desire, and deliver him the Kinges firma in the name of their Kinge. Wherupon Mr. Aldsworth and Mr. Caneinge was sent to Surat as pledges, till the chief rettourned againe from Sualley.

10 March. The Generall recceved letters from our merchantts that the chief had consulted together, and that absolutlie they meant to come downne and give our Generall all the content that might bee.

11 March. Our Generall had intelligence they were comed to Sualley. He prepared himself ashoare with 30 shott and other attendantts, and att Sualley found the Sabendor, and most of the chief presentt with him, save onelie Medejopher; and the newes was brought that he was comeinge. Neere at hand they

[1] An error for January (and so in the following three entries).

[*sic*] Generall took horsse and meett him, with another cavellero in the coach with him. After salutacions they went to the Mockodoms housse, wher all the rest of the cavelleroes staid the Generalls retourne. Wher allso the cavellero that brought the firma from the courtt was, in verie rich aparrell, reedy with the firma in his hand, covered with read silke and maid up in cloth of gould. [He] did, in the presence of all the chief, deliver yt unto our Generall. Wheer he demaunded to know the contents, yf they weere curespondent to the articles concluded upon with the Governer of Amedevar or no. The chief affirmed yt to be the same, and so our Generall in all reverencce and curttesey recceved yt; our trumpetts afterwards soundinge, and a value [i.e. volley] or towe of small shott. And for the undkindnesse betwixt our Generall and Medejopher, yt was tourned to greatt kindnesse and love againe, and there all discontentts was ended betwixt them. Our Generall tould them that presentlie he would apointt a merchaunt that within 6 or 7 daies should be reedy to taik his journey towards Agro with our Kinges present, which beforetyme they had seene, and allso our Kings letter; wherupon the Moore that brought the firma was contented to staie so longe, that he might have his company whom the Generall would apointt, which I do think wilbe Mr. Paulle Caneinge. They offeered our Generall great curtteses and privilidges for trad all ther counttres over, nott onelie att Suratt butt all ther counttrey over, as Amedevar, Cambaia, or any other part of the countrey that would afford us any comodities to our content; and for those people he meant to leave att Suratt, eyther merchantts or ther asistants, ther care should be such over them as if they were ther ownne native counttrey people, and to asist them in all accions whatsoever or whensoever they should have occasion to use them. And so, yf yt should pleasse God (as both we and they are mortall) to call them awaie furth of this world, look, what goods, moneys, or debtts were to them belongeinge or found dew unto them, yt should be by them maid good to a peny, and that there cittie should be answerable for yt; as beforetyme they had done unto the Dutch nattion, for that, all ther people resident being dead, they took inventorie of all ther goods, mones, and debtts was found dew unto them, and repaid yt unto ther nacion

to the vallue of a penny[1]. Our Generall yielded them many thanks, and for a whille took leave of the chief, [and] gave them 2 valley of shott and threw amongst the souldiers tow handfulls of money; and with the sound of the trumpetts repaired downne to the watterside, and there in his tentt dyned with such vittualls as the *Hossiander* did affoord; being verie mirrie and joyfull, nott onelie he butt all the merchantts and company generallie, that this bussines was in such desent maner accomplished. Being att dynner, newes was brought him that a Porttingaille frigott was comed within shott of the *Hossiander*, she rideing close by the shoare. He comaunded [our] guner to shott at hir. He, according to order, shott att hir thre tymes, and att last shott hir thorow the saille; yett she would not strik. Our boatts maid after hir; but the Generall gave order to call them agayne, for that they could not fetch hir. After dynner the Generall wentt upp to Sualley agayne, to accompany the chief. Att his comeing he did understand how Medejopher had cruellie skallded himselffe upon his bodie; wherupon the Generall apointted me a horsse to come downne in all haist and goe abord for stuff to dresse him withall. I retourned to Sualley and dressed him; and he would have had me staid all night, but I refussed, and about 12 acloke went abord our ownne shipp; and afterwards everie morneing and evening contynewed to dresse him, for the space of 8 or 10 daies, till yt pleassed God he was well agayne. The Generall took his lodging abord our shipp.

12 Jenuarie. Our Generall wentt ashoare, in manner afforessaid, to see Medejopher and the rest of the cavelleroes; and did entreatt them abord his shipp. They came first abord of our shipp; and haveing vewed hir in everie partt, she gave them greatt

[1] A Dutchman named David van Deynsen, with two companions, arrived in Surat in May 1606. The two juniors died, and Van Deynsen, in consequence of a dispute with a Portuguese, proceeded to the headquarters of the Khānkhānān at Burhānpur. There he learnt that the Portuguese had secured a monopoly of the trade at Surat, and a promise that Van Deynsen would be surrendered to them on his return. In despair he shot himself; and his effects were taken possession of by the Mughal authorities at Burhānpur and Surat. The latter, however, fearing reprisals, wrote to the Dutch at Masulipatam, offering to deliver the goods to anyone who might be sent to receive them; and this offer was renewed in 1613. It was not until 1615 that two Dutchmen arrived at Surat for this purpose, and then only a part of what was due was actually obtained. See *Roe*, p. xxix, and Terpstra, *Opkomst*, p. 22.

contentt. Afterwards the Generall conducted them abord the *Dragon*, being as many as the bootts would carrie. Ther the Generall gave them verie kynd entertaynementt, and shewed them his shipp and ordinance; which they did much admire to see such a shipp. The Generall accompanyed them all ashoare agayne, and gave them 7 partting peecces; and when they came against our shipp, we gave them 3 peecces. Our souldiers ashoare gave them att ther landing 2 valley of small shott. They offered to taik leave of our Generall att the watersid; butt he tould them he would accompany them to Sualley. So they in ther wagons, our Generall upon horsseback, repaired towards Sualley, and partted verie curtteouslie, [with] 2 valley of small shott [and] trumpetts soundinge. The Generall retourned abord his ownne shipp. He had bene enformed by the chief this daie of 340 Porttingailles we had slayne in both feights, as they did averr.

13 Jenuarie. Medejopher went abord to see the *Dragon* and the Generall, with divers other cavelleroes to see the shipp. Att ther departure the *Dragon* shott 5 peecces. This daie we had sight of 4 shippes, thinking them to be the Porttingaille men of warr. Allthough the Generall was perswaded they weere nott they, yett nottwithstanding we maid reedy both our shippes as beforetyme, and stood of[f] to the *Dragon*. This last night Mr. Aldsworth and Mr. Caneing came abord and ended all ther bussines with the Generall, and imediattlie retourned ashoare and so to Suratt; the Kings presentt being gone before. Feareing the wurst, greatt dispatch of bussines was maid, with as much expedicion as might be, that we might bee reedy to sett saille, and give them a farwell, if they should assault us.

14 Jenuarie. We did certtaynelie maik them to be the enemie. [The] Generall maid great dispatch with the merchantts, and apoynted Mr. Caneing for the courtt, with tow of his men for his attendantts. Our Generall did much rejoce he had ended his bussines with the merchantts and landed them such goods as he thought was convenientt. The enymie [was] daylie expectted to come upp with us, for that they rood in our sight upon the barr, but durst nott come upp with us.

15 Jenuarie. We filld watter with quick retourne, for that we

expecctted the enymy to come upp with us everie flod. Medejopher sent our Generall from Zuratt the quanttittie of 4 barrills of powther.

16 Jenuarie. Anthony Starkie was by the Generall apoynted to sell his goods att the mast, to pay 3 for one in Ingland, and he to go overland for England with letters unto the Worrshipfull Company from our Generall, and to taik alongst with him a Moore the Generall entertayned heere, a good linguest (Mamoud his name). Haveing dispatched with the Generall, [he] was this night sett ashoare, and with him Rychard Temple and Edward Huntt[1], who are apoynted to go Mr. Caneings attendantts to the courtt with [the] present and [the] Kings letter. Mr. Caneing and Mr. Carridge came from Suratt, and brought 8 bailles of callico abord the *Dragon*. They had delivered ashoare earlie this morneing a porttion of iron and a quantitie of lead, in lew of the goods they brought. Mr. Caneing and Mr. Carridge staid abord till sermon was done and dynner done, and then took leave of the Generall and repaired ashoare. The[y] had one parttinge peecce. Our Generall haveing to his full contentt dispacched all his bussines this night, within night [i.e. after nightfall] we weid and stood towards the enemy as farr as tydd would give leave.

18 Jenuarie. In the morneinge we were faire by the gallions, allmost within shott. We ofered nott to medle with them, butt stood our coursse. They weid and sett saille after us aboutt an houre or ½ an houre, for a bravado more then for any greatt desire they had to feight with us. They ankered; we stood our coursse. And thus we partted from thes valient champians, that had vowed to do so [*sic*] such famous acctts, butt yett [were] content [to] give us over, with greatt shame and infamy re-

[1] Another of Best's attendants. Like Temple, Hunt quarrelled with Canning on the way; and, appropriating the latter's horse, returned forthwith to Surat. Subsequently he was sent to Agra with Kerridge; brought down a caravan of indigo from thence; and went home in the *Hope*. When, in 1617, Best contracted with the Company for a second voyage, he agreed to take Hunt out with him again; and Best's dismissal, after Hunt had spent his money on an outfit, left the latter stranded. Thereupon he applied to the Company for employment; but on hearing his past record and being told that he 'is noted for a very deboist person, a ringleader to drawe others to loosenes,' the Company, 'dealinge moderatelie with him, wisht him to take for awnswere that they would nott employe him' (Court Minutes, 2 December 1617).

dounding unto themselves. Butt this was the Lords doinges, and God graunt us grace to give Him the glorie.

19 Jenuarie. Standing over the chennell, in the morneing before daie we had sight of a junk, so neere us that, 1 or 2 musketts being at hir discharged, she strok saille; and we sent our longboatt, with 10 shott, for the capttain and master to come abord our shipp. Our men staid there (most of them) and steered with us. Demaunding of the captain of whenc he was, [he] answereed, of Cananoer, and bound for Suratt: that there was 4 [of] them in company, and laden with cockernutts. Daie being light, our master caried the capttain and master abord the *Dragon.* Att which tyme all the other 3 were in sight, and could by no meanes to gett awaie, towe of them; butt one being so farr to wynward, they could nott fetch hir. The other three was, by the Generalls order, pelliged, and most part of yt carried abord the *Dragon*, as vittualle, sweettmeatts, pikes, and sping[ardos][1], apparell (as lyneing [linen]), with much other good luggidge. The Generall took from them a pinis. Afterwards they stood ther coursse for Zuratt after ther consertt. I praie God our people att Zuratt susteyne nott reveng att the hands of thes people for this daies worke[2].

20 Jenuarie: We gave chasse to 5 frigotts and a shipp, butt they rune in with the shoare, and night came on. [So] we left them and stood our coursse.

21. We gave chasse to 3 junks and a frigott. The 3 junks was taken and pelliged, being Mallabars. All the pellige was caried abord the *Dragon*, as yt was before, save onelie some musketts and other ould thinges, of which I took nottice of. The Generall took furth of thes junks 7 slaves which spok good Porttingaille, butt they leapt overbord and swim abord the junks agayne.

Allmost att night, we took a greatt junk of Callicuitt, which had the Porttingailles passe. This junk was pelliged by ours both (but the *Dragon* chief). The best thinge that came abord the *Hossiander* was about 25 spingardos and 32 targetts [i.e. shields], with other small matters nott worth the

[1] Port. *espingarda*, a musket.

[2] A few years later the capture of Malabar junks bound for Surat caused much friction with the authorities of that city, who objected strongly to such action as damaging the trade of the port.

writtinge. Hir principall ladeing was cocckernutts; with which we did nott meedle.

22 Jenuarie. The *Hossiander* took a junk and pilliged hir. After she was pelliged, another came fowlle of us, and we used hir in the same fashon; the *Dragon* being 2 leagues ahead, allmost outt of sight. Both thes junks was of Callicuit, and had the Porttingailles passe; ther loading was cocker, and bound for Cambaia. Being comed upp with the *Dragon*, the Generall sent his skiffe abord us to know what they weere we had pelliged, and allso to give order to our master nott to medle with any more suchlike vessells, exceptt they were shipes.

23 Jenuarie. Our Generall came abord us himselffe, and called our company together, and tould them that, forasmuch as they had ventured ther lyves and shewed themsellves so full of courage against the enemye, he did, in regard of that, suffer them to pellige thes junkes, that some small profitt might redound unto them in respectt of ther paines they had taken; and further tould them yt did much greve him to heare that his company and ours could nott agrey in pelliging, but to go together by the eares for pelige abord the prises, in the sight of the counttrey people, to ther great shame and infamye; for which causse he meant no more to molest or trouble any suchlike vessells; butt if yt did forttune we should meett with some shippes, then ther should be a better order taken for the conttentment of both shippes companies; for which purposse six of our chiefest officers, in the behallfe of our shipp, went abord the *Dragon* to agree and conclud upon some better orders then formerlie had bene taken for the sharing of such pellig as afterwards should or might be taken by eyther of us.

24 Jenuarie, Saboath Daie. We espied a Porttingaille shipp riding att anker about a lleague from shoare, and 20 leagues or therabouts to the southward of Goa. The Porttingailles and the chieff, seing us stand with them, imbarked themsellves, with all ther mones, jewells, and the best thinges they had, into a frigott and rune ashoare. [They] left abord the shipp the countter[y] master and aboutt 30 slaves and 2 women. They did nott resist, butt yiellded themsellves unto us, and tould us ther shipp was of Couchin and laden with ricce: that the Porttingailles was all

gone ashoare. We found all ther chests openned and all things of any worth or vallue taken outt, save onelie some coursse sewger and dried sewger and ould aparrill. Thomas Hounsell was by the Generalls order apointted the master of hir. He had out of both shippes 30 English to staie with him. No man was admitted to go of[f] abord the price [i.e. prize] unsearched. The slaves were verie glad, for that therby they were like to be freed from much misserey. 5 brasse basses[1] the *Dragon* had.

25 Jenuarie. We took furth of hir as much as we thought fittinge for the vaige, for that yt was verie go[o]d and well condicioned. All the pillage of this shipp was caried abord the *Dragon*. Ther was some powther, sweett oille, and other thinges. We had furth of hir 83 kanisters[2] of ricce, 5 kanisters of sewger. The *Dragon* had hir sailles and masts. And haveing taken out of hir all thinges of any worth, our people sett hir of fire. The people might perceyve the smoak ashoare. We had 3 Moores abord of us; the rest abord the *Dragon*.

26 Jenuarie. A boatt came of[f] from shoare and went abord the *Dragon* with a present to our Generall, and withall to entreatt him for the liberttie of some of those Moores he had taken furth of the Porttingaille shipp. Our Generall gave them all leave to depart, except 5 or 6 of the yongest fellowes he keept, and those three that we had. And so the boatt departted, with many thanks unto our Generall. This day came from the *Dragon* $\frac{1}{5}$ part of the pillage in the Porttingaille shipp. Our company cast lotts for yt, and one measse[3] wonne yt and shared yt, being a matter of very small worth or value.

27. This daie the *Dragon* took a junk; but being far ahead, we could nott tell wether they pelliged hir or nott, but they say themselves they did nott.

28 Jenuarie. Our master had bene abord the *Dragon*, where the Generall shewed him a Porttingaille letter which was found in a chest, written by a cavellero of Goa unto his frend att Couchin. The postscripttum was that Nuno de Guno had taken towe English shippes that was att Suratt, with 3 shippes of Goa

[1] A base was the smallest kind of cannon in use, throwing a half-pound ball.
[2] Canister has here its old meaning of 'basket.'
[3] The crew was divided into messes of four men each.

and a small shipp of Chaulle, and heere they are expecctted everie daie.

30 Jenuarie. We weere by estimacion about 30 leagues to the norwardes of Cape Comorin. We stood in with the shoare, and ankered att a place called Bringa. We rood a cables length of[f] the shoare in 10 fadum watter. Heere ashoare was a llittle village, inhabited by fishermen. Thes people came abord of us in litle gundells[1], and brought us greatt store of provission abord, as hens, planttains, coccker, and fresh fish; and all thinges att a verie cheapp ratte. Heere we filld watter, and had yt brought unto us in potts by the counttrey people, as att Sualley. They people goth naked, save onelie so much cloth as will cover ther members. Yt is a verie fruittfull place. We had anything we needed, for money, as peper, synamond, sheep, goatts, wild fowlle. Nothinge was wanttinge unto us in this place.

1 Febbruarie. An ambassader came from ther kinge to confer with our Generall from the king of this counttrey, which is from Comorin southwards untill Malldevas [i.e. the Maldives] north-westarwardes. He offered unto our Generall greatt kindnesse and trad, both for peper and sinamond; and tould him that the Kinge himselffe would come and confer with him, for that he greattlie desired trade with our naccion. In the meanetyme [he] promised watter or whatsoever ells the shoare did afford. Our Generall retourned him thanks for his curttesey, but the tyme of his abod in that place was uncerttaine, and therfore could not resollve him.

4 Febbruarie. We weid and stood our coursse towards the Cape, haveinge bene heere 5 daies and well reffresht our companyes and sick men. As yett we have nott found in the Indes a place of better reffreshing then this hath bene.

5 Febbruarie. We weere aboutt 2 leagues from the shoare. The countrey people came abord of us with 2 loggs tyed together[2], [which] served them for a bbott. We bought ther fish they had to sell, and sett them goinge, for that yt was like to blow. I did never see such a boatt put to sea. We could nott double the Cappe, but stood in with the land and ankered in 30 fadum watter. All this night verie much wynd.

[1] Gondolas (see note on p. 65).

[2] A kind of catamaran.

6 Febbruarie. In the morneinge we weid, with much wynd and rough sea; and in weying our anker the cable brok, and ther we partted with an anker of 700 weight [i.e. 7 cwt.]. We had lost the sight of the *Dragon* this night; butt before 12 aclock we gott sight of hir agayne, and both stood in with land as neere as we could lye.

8 Febbruarie. Fynding the wynd contrarie, we could nott doubble the Cape, butt, haveing endured 4 or 5 daies of fowlle weather, we putt roome for the rood of Bringae.

10 Febbruarie. We had sight of 50 frigotts comeinge from the norwards. They ankered a lleague to the norwards of us, close by the shoare. We putt outt our ordinance, butt they in the night stolle awaye and stood towards Cape Comorin to give nottice unto the China shipp[1] of our being upon ther coast and of what we had allreedye done.

11 Febbruarie. Our Generall sentt his skiffe for our cooke, for that William Flaille, the master cook of the *Dragon*, this last night decceassed; John Patteson to be master cooke in the *Dragon*. Our Generall promissed our master a cook furth of his shipp.

13 Febbruarie. Thomas Browne, a mariner in the *Dragon*, who in former tymes had performed the place of a cook, was by the Generalls order apoyntted for our master cook in John Pattesons place. We filld this daie 2½ tonnes of watter.

22 Febbruarie. We had 2 men ducktt in the *Dragon* for drinking drunk of the Saboath Day and in the sermon tyme: John Isack, a quarttermaster, and Christopher Bodam, the cockson. The Generall apoyntted Bodam to bring his clothes and goe in the *Dragon*.

23 Febbruarie. Gabriell Daves, our boattson, was by our Generall displaced, and Sillvester Percie apointted in his place. We had from the *Dragon* one whose name was John Chooke, to be a quarttermaster in Sillvester Peerccies place. This morneinge we weide and put to sea, haveing rood heer 7 daies about 7 leagues to the southward of Bringa; where we have had plentie of fresh vittuall and arack brought us abord by the countrey people, verie good and reasonable, untill the Porttingailles did

[1] A Portuguese vessel coming from Macao to Goa.

threatten them to burne ther housses, if they any more brought us anythinge.

26 Febbruarie. We doubled the Cape Comorin and stood our coursse for the iland of Seylon. We see fish heere in such aboundance as was wounderfull to behold; and likewisse many snakes we see swiminge by our shippes side. Our men cruellie plagued with flies and muskettous, [that] they were nott able to take rest eyther night or daie.

27 Febbruarie. We had sight of the illand of Seylon, and stood longst the coast.

1 March. A man [was sent] furth of the *Dragon*, by the Generalls order, to be one of our quarttermasters; his name William Hiedon.

5 March. We stood longst this coast of Seylon 4 or 5 daies, but could nott double Cape Galla. We stood in with the shoare to the norward of the Cappe. Close abord the shoare we found 30 fadum watter, and so stood of[f] to sea agayne.

8 March. 56 spingardoes taken in pillage [were] distributed amongst the company, everie man his share according to his place (haveing 37 men in the shipp). This daie the Generall wrott a letter unto our master, purposselie brought unto him by the *Dragons* pinis laitt att night, how he had seene two shippes which he thought was they he had so long looktt for[1]. [He] did will him to stand in with the shoare, and he would stand of[f] to sea, and so (he thought) they, beinge to wyndward, could hardlie passe us both; and if in the night he should chaunce to see them, then to shott off a peecce for warneinge to him; and if he should chaunce to see them, he would do the like; and then to putt outt a light upon the poupe.

9 March. We had sight of both the shippes. [The] *Dragon* gave chasse to one, we to another. Butt when we came to maik ours, she proved a Flemeinge; and she the *Dragon* gave chasse to was hir prize, which the daie before she had taken, a small shipp comed from Bengalla and bound for Pegu. Hir ladeinge was most part rice. Being comed upp with the Flemeinge, we hailled him. He tould us he was of Ancerdame [Amsterdam].

[1] Probably he was hoping to intercept some Portuguese vessels from the eastwards, bound for Goa (see p. 152).

We tould him of whence we were, [and] desired the capttayne and master to come abord. We haveing saluted each other with thre peecces, they came abord of us, [and] tould us they had bene att Meslopatania [Masulipatam]: that 4 mounthes ago there was English there: how they thought we had bene Porttingailles, and was glad, thinking to have had some purchasse [i.e. booty]: [that] ther shipp was a shipp of 140 tonnes [and] 10 peecce[s of] ordinance: and that they came upon this coast purposselie to look outt for purchasse. [They] desired to know what the name of our amerall[1] was, and tould us they had known hir in the Indes before. They promissed us anything that eyther ther shipp or prize would afford; and so retourned abord ther owne shipp with our master and merchauntt.

10. This morneing we lost sight, both of the *Dragon*, the Fleming, and his prize, by reason of bad lookinge outt; for many of our men were far outt of the waie of our chiefest, and those that should have had the greattest care had none att all. Butt this nights workinge procured variable opinnions to passe over us, to our greatt shame and infamie, yt [yf?] yt had proved as the Generall was creediblely incenssed of us by some of his chiefest.

12 March. We came into the company of the *Dragon* agayne. Our master and merchantt wentt abord to shew our Generall of what newes we had understood by the Flemeinge. Yt was generallie reported abord the *Dragon* we weere rune awaie, and much money both wonne and lost. Our Generall would nott belleve yt, nor give creditt unto anythinge was spoken to that effectt. We stood in with the shoare upon this coast of Seylon to seek for watter. We ankered in 17 fadum watter, maned our bootts with eyther 6 or 8 musketts, and sent them ashoare; butt the counttrey people, being frend to the Porttingailles, resisted our people and would nott suffer them to come ashoare. And so, seing no remedie, [they] retourned abord and lost ther labor.

13 March. We weid aboutt daielight, and stood of[f] to sea agayne. Yisternight our Generall was abord, examyned some matters of contraversie, promissing punishement for the next, and tould the company of runeing awaie.

14 March. We wentt to sermon abord the *Dragon*. After

[1] The *Dragon*.

dynner, stood in with the shoare within a cables length. We ankered, in hope of watter. The boatt was manned and sent ashoare with an Indean or tow to speak the language. Butt heere was no watter to be gott, nor the people to be spoken withall, for they rune awaie from our people. Our boott retourned. We weyed and stood of[f] agayne, without watter.

15 March. We had the sight of the Flemeing agayne. We stood with hir; and being comed up with hir, she gave the *Dragon* 3 salutinge peecces; the *Dragon* gave hir one. Our Generall sent his pinis abord hir for the capttain and master. They tould the Generall how they had peliged ther price [prize] and burned hir hull: how he had thought to have landed most of his prisoners ashoare this daie upon Seylon; but haveing sett ashoare 2 or three, they [i.e. the country people] presentlie cutt ther throatts; the rest cried out, and desired to be landed in some other place; so [he] took compassion over them and keept them att his shipp sterne in his prizes pinis. After some discoursse with our Generall, becausse yt was laitt the Flemeing tooke leave, haveinge bene verie curtteousslie by our Generall enttertayned. [He] retourned abord, promisseing the Generall to come next daie abord and dyne with him, and to bringe with him some of his frends to be mirrie.

16 March. The capttain of the Flemeinge, the master, and other ther officers came abord the *Dragon* and dyned with the Generall. Wher they did att large discoursse of ther vaige and [the] fleett they come furth with, and wither they inttended to go; and tould our Generall of a verie good place for watter, [and promised ?] to keepp company 7 or 8 daies. The Generall gave the capttain a bast cable[1] we had in the Porttingaille shipp. This daie we past Cape Galla, the wyndes begineing to change.

17. The master of the *Dragon*, his matte, our master and merchantt was invitted abord the Fleminge. He shott 8 peecces.

18 March. The capttain, the steersman, the merchantts of the *Dragon*[2] were invitted abord the *Hossiander*. She gave them a partting peece.

[1] One made of bass, i.e. prepared from fibrous bark.

[2] Apparently a slip for 'the Fleming.' By 'steersman' is meant the pilot (*stuurman*), equivalent to the English 'master.'

21. We lost company of the Flemeinge, haveing had from him towe black boyes, which he gave, one of them unto our Generall, the other unto the preacher, with certayne other things. We stood our coursse for Achin.

31. We wentt to straitt allowaunce of watter, in regard of calmes we were subjectt unto.

5 Aprill. Our master, by his reckninge, was in the height of Sumatra; butt we saw no land untill the 10th, and had everie daie a fyne gaill. The reason why they came so farr shortt of ther reckninge they afirme was becausse of the curantt setting so stronglie against them; and likewisse ther platts [i.e. charts] were found with the shorttest.

5, 6, 7. Much rayne and lightning, with gusts.

10. We had sight of the illand of Sumattra, haveing bene from Surat twelve weeks.

12. The *Dragon* and we ankered in the rood of Achin; wher we found towe great junks att anker, the one of Suratt, the other of Goga. Our men all verie healthfull (thanks be to God). The *Dragon* gave 7 saluting peecces; the *Hossiander* thre peecces. A boott came abord the *Dragon*, and then to us. This boott brought the Sabendor of Achin abord the *Dragon*, as the custome is; when shippes comes in, the King sends an officer to know what they are. The Generall recceved him verie curteouslie; and falling into parley, the Sabendor tould the Generall that from the King he had authoritie to bide him wellcome, and that the King did greattlie affecctt our nation, and what favour or kindnesse they could do for us, wee should have yt; promisseing next morneing to meett some of our English, whom the Generall should apointt, att the casle, and to go with them unto the Kinge. The Generall sent the King a present, and so parted. [The] *Dragon* shott 5 peeces. Heare we herd the Flemings had a facctorie.

13. This morneing our Generall, according to his promisse, sent one of our merchants, and tow or thre others to beare him company who had bene ther before, ashoare to the Sabendor, who promissed to conductt them to the Kings presence. They retourned agayne this night (butt verie laitt), and certified the Generall that the King was gone ahunttinge, butt one of his

chiefest nobles did recceve them verie kindlie, and promissed trad or what the townne or counttrey would afford, and that the King greatlie desired to have commercce with our nation. [He] apointted us a housse. Our people was entertayned by the Fleminges at ther housse; of which the Generall allso understood, and of ther bad carraidg ashoare heere. The King hath verie good ordinance of brasse, both about his pallace and in his castle.

14. The Generall sent the purser and one of the merchants ashoare to prepair and fitt the housse for the Generalls comeing ashoare. This daie the Captayne of the Flemeings came abord the *Dragon*. Our Generall did riallie entertayne him, and shott 12 peeces in healthes[1]. Butt being *minim*[*e*] *procax*[2], he could nott go ashoare that night.

15. The Sabender came abord the *Dragon* with a messuag from the King unto the Generall, to desire him to come ashoare, for that the King greatlie desired to speak with him; and in great haist all things was prepared and all provissions sent ashoare; and, with 50 or 60 of his chiefest men to attend him, he went ashoare to the King, with the Sabender and the Capttain of the Flemings. The *Dragon* shott 9 peecces; the *Hossiander* 5 peeces. The people of the cittie recceved him with all joie and mirth that might bee; butt the King was absentt ahuntting of wild ellofants, in which sportt he taiks greatt delight. Butt by some of his chiefe the Generall was entertayned. This daie tow of the *Dragons* men went into the field[3], and the one laymed the other; butt both were put into the bilbowes.

16. [The] King was expecctted from huntting, butt came nott. Carpenters [were] fitting the housse ashoare. A lletter was recceved from Priaman from the *Thomas*; the conttentts I know nott.

17. The Generall sent for both the masters ashoare, thinking this daie to speak with the Kinge touching trad. This day greatt dissorders abord our shipp, both with our ownne men and the

[1] This practice is referred to in *Hamlet* (Act I, sc. 2). In Sir Henry Middleton's commission (1610) the Company forbids 'all unnecessary expence of shooteing of ordinance at drinking of healthes' (*First Letter Book*, p. 344).

[2] 'Not in the least eager.' The inference is that he was too much overcome by Best's hospitality to be capable of moving.

[3] To fight a duel.

Dragons men, first by drinking drunk, and then by fighting with fists, in the sight of the Guzuratt junkes, to all our greatt shames and disgrac to our counttrey and nation.

18. This daie[1] our Kinges letter was sent for by the King of Achin, with an ellofantt and a share [chair] of statt[e] in the forme of a casle [i.e. a howdah] upon his back. After wentt the Generall to the courtt, where he presented the Kinge with a rich present from our Kinge; and the King likewisse did give unto our Generall a vest, with Mr. Moore and Mr. Oliver. He entertayned us with the fightinge of ellofants, buffeloes, and greatt rames; and afterwards was provided a greatt banquett, with many dishes and greatt store of arack. The banquett was served in dishes of pure gold and sillver. [They] brought in towe chests of gould, which they do use to keep ther beettle[2] in,[which] they use to eatt of verie much. Great curtesey by the King was offered, and that the countrey was att our comaund; butt our Generall as yett nott alltogether satisfied, for that he hopeth of furder commerce with the King, and att larg to deliver his mynd unto him.

25[3]. Our Generall went to the courtt, with the chief of our people [and ?] his accustomed attendants.

26. Keeptt housse.

27. Our Generall went to the embassador of Sian[4]; with whom he did converse of such comoditties as in ther countrey were vendible, and likewisse of the quallittie of such comoditties as were ther to be rettourned for England. The embassador did afirme that the quantittie of 2000 clothes would vent ther in the spac[e] of 2 mounthes, with divers other comoditties highlie esteemed of. Rialls of eight to be worth ther *7ss. 6ds.* the riall. Raw silk ther is greatt store and cheapp; and likewisse benjamyn [benzoin] better then thatt of Achin, and the weight greatter, for that 4 bahars of Achin maiks but 3 att Sian[5]. Callicoes of Suratt

[1] Best says the 17th.

[2] The chewing of betle leaves (generally mixed with areca-nut, etc.) is an old and widespread custom in Southern Asia.

[3] Best says the 24th.

[4] This is actually a more correct form than the usual 'Siam,' which seems to have come to us from the Malay *Siyăm*.

[5] This appears to be incorrect. The weight of the Achin *bahar* is given on p. 175 as 385 lb. and in Best's letter of 12 July 1613 (printed below) as 386 lb. The Siam *bahar* was equivalent to three pikul, i.e. about 400 lb. (cf. Floris, p. lxix); so there was but little difference between the two.

sells well there; black and read hatts, lookinge glasses, [and] birding peecces of the smallest sortt (being well damaskt[1]). All this the embassador for certayne did afirme unto our Generall, and offered to firme yt with the Kings sealle; seameing verie desirous to have comerce with the English. This daie he had a chilld circumcized[2], with greatt seremonyes after ther fashion.

29. This daie the Generall went to the courtt, butt could nott speake with His Majestie, for his nobles affirmed he was sick.

30. The embassador of Sian dyned with our Generall; butt sent his ownne cooks to dresse his vittualls, and brought his drink with him, being watter in greatt flagens of sillver.

1[3] Maie. The King went to recreatt himselfe, accompanyed with our Generall and the Dutch merchants; wher they went to a river, about 6 or 7 milles from the towne, the King riding upon an ellofantt, in a chaire of statt upon his back. They came to a place wher they washed themselves; the King sitting upon a seatt in the midst of the river, with our Generall and the Dutch merchants and all his nobles aboutt him in the watter, with aboundaunce of people that were specctators on the shoare; his nephew poureing watter upon him as he satt, with a golden buckitt, for the space of 5 or 6 houres. Then afterwards they had a greatt banquett, with aboundaunce of vittuall and arack, dressed after ther maner. Haveing ended the banquett, they retourned to the Kinges pallace, with our English trumpetts sounding before them, and women playing and singing before the Kinge. And thus they came to the pallace, wher att that tyme our Generall took leave of His Majestie.

2, 3, 4 daie. The Generall keept house, dispatching other bussinesses.

5 daie. Went to the courtt, and retourned all weett.

6. The Turks dwelling in Achin desired our Generall to go abord our shippes to see them, and was caried in our ownne bootts. Att ther retourne the *Dragon* shott 5 peecces, the

[1] Inlaid with gold or silver.

[2] Surely a mistake. It is true that the Siamese monarch had some Muhammadan subjects and might have chosen one of these as envoy to a Muhammadan state; but that the ambassador was really a Buddhist is strongly suggested by the anxiety he displayed to save the life of Fen.

[3] Best says the 2nd.

Hossiander 3 peeces; wheratt the Generall was much discontented, for that yt was without his order, the shotting of guns.

11. The Generall went abord, with the embassador of Sian; and the chief of the Guzuratt shippes haveing promissed, which afterwards came. When they had seene the *Dragon*, the Guzuratts departed and came abord the *Hossiander*. The *Dragon* shott 7 peeces. The Generall and the embassador, haveing dyned, repaired ashoare; and likewisse the Guzuratts from the *Hossiander*. [The] *Dragon* shott 13 peecces; the *Hossiander* 7 peeces.

14. The Generall went to the King [and] gott lycence to gitt[1] wood upon one of his illands. This daie newes came to our Generall thatt ther was a Porttingaille junk comed, but she lay behynd a pointt of the land to eastward, and some of the Porttingailles went to the King to carie newes of ther arivall, with the embassador which he had sent to the King of Joar, joyneing to Mallacca. The Generall gave order to Christian, with a nott[e] under his hand to Mr. Sallmon, to go abord the *Hossiander* and, when he should fynd a fitt oporttunittie, to weigh anker and to go wither Christian should direcctt him.

15. The Generall upon a suden wentt abord, and took all provissions with him, and left ashoare about 20 men, and some of them sick, and apoynted Mr. Hermon captain. This night, before the Generall came downne, they [*sic*] *Hossiander* had weid, and came to anker fast by the Porttingaille junk, with the *Dragons* pinis. In the meanetyme the Guzuratts with ther shalloppe had bene abord the Porttingailles and gave them intelligence of our comeing, and promissed them, for six mass[2] the man, to taik in themselves and ther goods, and land them in saiftie. Butt all the Porttingailles weere gone ashoare save one, and he said he would referr himself to ther curttesey, butt putt into them some certayne goods, which they went awaie with. And we, doubtfull of such a prettence [i.e. intention], shott 2 peecces att hir, and keept hir from the shoare, and with our boott fetched hir abord agayne the junk, where we delivered the goods in saiftie agayne. The junk had in [her?] certeyne chests and bailles of goods to us unknowne, which they said was for the Kinge. We brought the junk to the *Dragons* steerne; wher

[1] Possibly the copyist's mistake for 'cut' (as later). [2] See p. 175.

Thomas Hounsell had the charg given him of hir by the Generall.

16. This daie the King sentt unto our Generall to know whatt he [had] done and to know wether he weere his frend or no; and if he weere his frend, to shott of[f a] peece; otherwaies none. Whereupon the Generall comaunded the gonner to give fire to a hole cullverin. The messenger rettourned, satisfied that the Generall was his frend, and that next morneing the Generall meantt to come ashoare and speak with His Majestie.

17. The Generall came ashoare, with the Kings embassador. The *Dragon* shott 7 peecces. The Generall, after his comeing ashoare, with all expedicion prepared himselfe for the courtt. [He] gave unto the King the junk, and nott the value of *2d.* deminished. The King did kyndlie acceptt the gift, and retourned him thanks. This daie the Generall bought of the King 40 bahars of benjamyn, att 25 taill the bahar. This daie the ould man that served in the housse (becausse of his languag and knowledg in cookerey [he] was entertayned) was most cruellie murdered, and had both his leegs cutt of[f], through the mallice of the Sabendor. If yt had nott bene done sudenlie, the Generall might have saved his life. The onelie causse was the deniall of the Kings work, becausse he was then emploied by us.

18. We buried John Cransbie, a merchantt[1].

19. The *Hossiander* wentt to an illand, lycenced by the King to cutt wood; and had 2 Guzuratts for pillotts, with 12 of the *Dragons* men to help them. Upon which illand we found a great many people, with ther armes and leegs cutt of[f] for offences (which is the Kings lawe)[2]; haveing one chief apointted governor over them, in regard they should nott bee idle, butt be imploied in the Kings service for the maiking of brimston. And in the tyme of our wooding we found certayne spiders whose weebs weere perfecctt silk; the which our chirurgion hath one to showe.

[1] Cransby had come out as 'servaunt' to Paul Canning (Court Minutes, 21 April 1614).

[2] 'A thief, detected, is punished with the loss of a member (from a finger to an arm) and banish'd to some of the islands off the Head. Pulo Gomes and Pulo Way are the chief receptacles of these unfortunate wretches; whence they often return to the city, and are common in the streets without hands or arms (the greatest badge of infamy).' (Lockyer, p. 38.)

Heere our shipp had like to have rune upon the llee shoare. [She] brok hir anker; a sheatt anker was lett fall, butt would nott hould. Hall was chief abord att this tyme. The master and his matt, being ashoare, came abord with all expedicion, seing the shipp drive and in such danger, and likewisse myself, being with them att that tyme and verie sick of a fever. [They] hoissed ther foreyard and instantlie sett saill, and doubled the pointt or lee shoare. The people abord, being so amassed, knew nott whatt they did, but wrought the contrarie waie. Butt trewlie yt was no small danger the shipp then escaped; but yt was more Gods providence then our mens carefullnes. We gott aboutt 10 tonne of wood.

20. Recceved benjamyn from the courtt by the *Dragons* skiffe; weighed yt with English weights, and found the bahar to conteyne 395[1] ll. suttle [i.e. net].

21. Nathaniell Fenn had his triall by a jurie, and was found gilltie of death for rebellion against the Generall, as allso drawing his sword and threattning his death. Presentlie after the jurie had geven in ther verditt, came the embassador of Sian and beegged him of the Generall, and att that instantt caried him away from the place wher he ly in, bound in irons. Otherwaies next morneing he had bene hanged or shott to death.

22. We recceved benjamyn; weighed yt as before, and packed yt in cask. The Generall wantted 100 dollars per Fens accountt, which he chargeth him withall. The other denieth such a matter.

23. Saboth Daie. Nothing done.

24. Benjamyn recceved; weighed and packed as before. The Generall gave order to the purser to come abord and taik nottice of goods to be recceved from the *Dragon* into the *Hossiander*; to whom I did minister more phizick before his going of[f] abord agayne, for that here ashoare I had geven him phizick and caussed him to keep a diett the space [of] 27 daies, for that myself being sick abord and nott able to goe ashoare.

25. This daie we recceved from the *Dragon* abord the *Hossiander* 257 ends [of] iron.

26. This daie came into the rood of Achin a junk of Suratt,

[1] This is probably a copyist's error for '385,' the figure given later (p. 175) by Croft. Best, in his letter from Achin, said that the *bahar* was 386 lb.

which brought letters from our merchantts there unto our Generall; by which letter we understood thatt Mr. Caneinge in his journey to Agra was assaulted by theves, and in resistaunce recceved a shott in his bodie with an arowe and [was] dangerousslie wounded: and likewisse of Robertt Trullie, one of his attendantts, was shott into the arme: and how Mr. Canninge and his company had convicctted [i.e. vanquished] the theves and sentt them awaie, some kild, some laymed: allso how Mr. Temple and Mr. Hunt afte[r]wards in ther journey rune awaye from Mr. Caneinge, and took one or tow of his best horsses with them and great store of money[1]. Thes towe men, Temple and Huntt, weere the Generalls servantts, and he prefered them to Mr. Caneinge to be his attendantts to the courtt of the Great Magole, and in his greattest necessittie [they] did give him the slipp, to ther great shame and infamie. We understood likewisse by thes letters how that Nuno de Gunno was by the Vice Roie imprisoned at Goa[2], for retourninge without comission; allso of the price of cloth to be att 25 or 30 mamowdas. Furder, we understood how that Chaull, Bassee[n], and other placces where the Portugalls have inhabitted weere besieged, scince our departure, by the Greatt Magolle and the Decannees[3]; in which proceedinges God give them hapie successe.

30. The 30th the capttain of the junk of Dabull dyned with our Generall.

31. Our Generall [went] to the courtt.

1 June. Mallum Guinee, the capttain of the junk that brought letters to our Generall from Suratt, dyned with our Generall.

2 June. Our Generall, with all our chieffe[4], wentt to the courtt; where before the Kinge we see an ollephantt and a tiger maik a cruell feight; His Majestie siting upon an ollephantt beholdinge the sportt. Which beinge ended, the Generall accompanied His Majestie to his pallacce, and so took leave.

3 June. Keept housse.

[1] For all this see *Early Travels*, p. 200.

[2] This was quite contrary to fact: see Bocarro's narrative (given later).

[3] The forces of the King of Ahmadnagar, who was frequently at war with the Portuguese.

[4] Here, and elsewhere in the narrative, 'chief' is used as a plural (chief men).

4. The Sian embassador came to conferr with our Generall.

5. Our Generall, with his chieff, wentt to the courtt to procure the Kinges letter for tolleracion of trad att Priaman, a placc[e] about 110 leagues of[f], within his dominions.

6, 7. Keept housse.

8. [Five] of our men this daie was, per the Generalles order, taiken into the *Dragon* to help to suplie the wantt of his men deceassed, videllceett John Daves, John Choak, Robert Morton, Thomas Hoomes, William Hoidinn.

9. The Guzuratts wentt abord this daie to see the *Dragon*. She gave them for ther wellcome 7 peecces. The *Hossiander* shott 3 peecces.

10. The Generall this daie went to the courtt to move the Kinge for his letter to Priaman; which was promissed unto our Generall over a daie, towe or three. This daie att the courtt we understood how that about 3 or 4 daies past a nobleman, for lookinge att one of the Kinges concubynes, was judged by the King to have one of his eyes puld outt. Another, for wearinge a turband extraordinary, had a peecce of his skull cutt awaie.

11 June. The Generall was, by one of the capttains of the Guzurattes, invitted to dynner; by whom he, with all his followers, was verie curtteouslie entertayned. He was of Dabull.

12. Our Generall keept housse[1].

13. Itt pleassed God of His merccie to call awaie Raph Standich, master surgion. Beinge in perfecctt memorie [he] did dispose of his goods by the maikinge of a will (as per the tenur apeareth) by wittnesse[2]: Henrie Rudes and Rychard Layne supervisors.

14. The Generall wentt to the courtt, with the chiefe; where he presented the King with 4 murderers[3], 4 tergetts [see p. 148], 6 launces; which the Kinge recceved in great curttesey, and tould the Generall he would prepair a present for the Kinge of England, whom he called his brother; and that he would send yt by

[1] Here (or possibly a little earlier) Standish's journal must have come to an end, and Croft took up the story.

[2] I.e., he declared his wishes in the presence of witnesses. No will has been found at Somerset House.

[3] A small kind of cannon.

him. Our Generall retourned many thanks to His Majestie in our Kinges behalfe. Att our comeinge awaie from the courtt, without the gaitt we see a man lyinge slayne, and was to lie there till the dogges had eatten his flesh, for comittinge adullterey with another mans wiffe.

15. Keeptt housse.

16. Raph Standich his aparell sould att the mast. His principall goods reserved till order from the Generall.

17. The Generall, with our chiefe, wentt to the courtt, [and] presented the Kinge with an English shipp[1]; in which shipp he took greatt pleassure, and did acceptt of yt and esteeme yt moore then a matter of greatter worth. The letter was promissed within a daie or towe; and many promisses of honor and creditt to our Generall, for the fame of our nation. This daie the Capttain of the Flemings deceassed. Our Generall, att his retorn from the courtt, wentt, with all his followers, to his burieall, our trumpets sounding his knell. This daie heere arived in the rood of Achen a junke which came from Messapotania [Masulipatam]; wherin came a Fleminge passenger, by whom we understod newes of the *Globe*: of the death [of] Capttain Anthonye Hippen, and one Mr. Brownne: and how one Mr. John[2] Essington was maid capttain. We understood of hir distresse by drinkinge salt watter, and allso of hir going to Pattania.

18. Our Generall went to the Rassedor[3], one of the Kinges chiefest subjecctts, to whom the Kinge doth referr all his chiefe and waightie matters of statte; by whom our Generall was curteouslie and with greatt respecctt entertayned, and promissed the letter att whatt tyme himselfe would apointt.

19 June. This day, for the badnesse of the weather, nothinge was done.

20. In the mourninge we were in the way to the Rassedors housse for the dispatch of the letter, butt we meett one of his servants in the waie, who brought the letter. Our Generall re-

[1] Obviously a model, possibly made by one of the sailors.

[2] An error for 'Thomas.'

[3] This was possibly the interpreter's attempt to convey the status of the official, not his title. In that case it may represent the Persian *rāzdār*, 'a confidant.' He was probably identical with the 'Kings deputye' mentioned on p. 54.

tourned baik agayne with the messenger to our housse, and there the letter was by our jurabassa[1] enterpreted. The effecctt wherof was that our Generall should att his pleasure disspose of a facctorie at Priaman or Tecowe, and his merchantts to be by the people curtteouslie entreatted: a bargayne, beinge once maid, should stand, and neyther partie revolt: and ther to have the same weight of Achen, which we may carie with us, in all such comoditties as we shall transportt for those placces, without any contradiccttion of the chiefe. This daie the Kinge [him]selfe came downne by watter from his pallace, attended of both sides the river with greatt store of ollephants [and] horsses; many of his nobles being in the praw[2] with His Majestie, and a multitud of souldiers and people which did accompany him to the fortt or castle; wither he went, partlie for recreacion, and partlie for profitt, for this daie he did confiscatt a junk of Suratt which was worth 100,000 crowns, and maid all the people slaves, for that they had bene att a place called Pera[3], which people are enemies to this Kinge of Achen. This beinge done, the Kinge retourned to the courtt by land, ridinge upon an ollephant, which had a chaire of pure gold upon his back. Our Generall accompanied His Majestie to the courtt, [he] promissing the next daie to go abord and see our shippes.

21. Our Generall, earlie this mourninge (as his accustomed manner was) tooke ollephant and with his chiefe went to the Rassedors house; where our Generall informed him of some dislike he had found in the Kinges letter, beinge enterpreted unto him by his brooker. One principall and chief causse was for the remittinge of customes and tributes, according to the articles concluded and agreed upon betwixt His Majesties uncle[4] deceassed and Sir James Lankaster; the tenur wherof was that all

[1] Malay *jurubahāsa*, 'language-master,' i.e. an interpreter.

[2] Malay *prāū*, a boat.

[3] Perak (pronounced Pera), on the western side of the Malay Peninsula.

[4] This should be 'grandfather,' as on p. 53. The monarch with whom Lancaster negotiated was Alā-addīn Riāyat Shāh. He died in 1604, and was succeeded by his son Ali Riāyat Shāh. The latter survived only three years, and the throne then passed to his sister's son, Iskandar Muda, who was reigning when Best arrived. He died in December 1636. (Information from Dr Blagden, who refers to an article in *Bijdragen tot de Taal-, Land-, en Volken Kunde van N. Indië*, 1911, deel 65, pp. 135–265.)

our nation should be priviledged to trad in any part or portt of this illand, without paying tribut or custome for any goods we should maik saille of; and that the chief go[vernors] of Priaman and Te[c]owe had scince that tyme, wrongfullie and far contrarie to the conclussion of peace and trad maid and agreed upon betwixt His Majesties uncle deceassed and Sir James Lankaster, forcced some of our nation to pay tribute; for which wrongs recceved our Generall craved redresse, and that His Majesties letter, which now he should have, might import so much, and quit us from our former wronges ther recceved per the chieffe. The Rassedor promissed to move the King concerninge this bussines in our Generalls behalfe, and withall [return ?] absolute answeer next mourninge. Our Generall retourned him thanks and, with expect[ation] of answeer next morneinge, took leave. This daie our Generall receved the capttains son of the junk confiscatt into our housse, and keept him privat till night, and then he conveyed himselfe awaie (by the help of a frind) into some privat place prepared for him; for the King had maid search for him, his father being then prisoner and all his poor men slaves.

22. Our Generall kept housse, expeccttinge the Kinges comeinge to go abord and see the shippes; and had caussed both the masters to prepare ther shippes for his entertaynement. But yt was so much labor lost.

23. The Generall sent one of our merchants to the Rassedor to receve his answeer from the Kinge touching the bussines before mentioned. His answeer was that he had moved the Kinge in the behalfe of our Generall, but could nott prevaille. [He] promissed many kindnesses to our Generall, but could not do whatt he required. With this answeer the merchant retourned to our Generall from the Rassedor.

24. Our Generall went to the courtt for the dispatch of bussines. And this daie our Generall prevailled so much that the Kinges present and his letter was obteyned. This daie the Generall sould the Kinge 168 bahars of iron att 5 taille the baharr, to be delivered with expedicion. The present and letter was brought to our housse by a nobleman riding upon an ollephantt, accompanied with other towe of the Kinges chiefe nobles, with

muzick plaieing before them alongst the streetts, as ther customes is in such affaires which concernes the Kinge. The present was a rich creast [*kris*] of pure gold, set with pretious stones, 8 campheer dishes, 4 peecces of fine stuffe, [and] a launce enameld with gould. Att the receitt of this present and letter for our king, our Generall did present the 3 nobles with [each?] of them of [a?] book of fyne callico; who, taikinge leave, retourned to the courtt.

25. Our Generall keeptt house, for dispatch of bussines.

26. Our Generall went to the courtt, accordinge to the Kinges desire unto him the daie before; where we see the Kinge in most royall estait, comeinge unto his church in most rich array, accompanyed with his nobles and chief of his kingedome. From the church [he] retourned unto a grene before his pallacce gaitt, wher he did sitt in a rich chaire of statte of pure gold. His nobles, standinge before him, was called one by one in ther degres to taik ther placces, which was done by greatt obeysance, in bowing downe ther bodies to the grownnd and holding upp of ther hands above ther heads[1]. In the midest of the nobles our Generall was called, and all the rest of the forraine and strang imbassadors, as the honor of ther Kinge and country did deserve. After all the nobles were seatted, inferiours took ther placces. The Kinges gard was 200 greatt ollephants, compassing the place where he satt; a multitud of people aspeccting [i.e. beholding] the fighting of ollephantts, which are the greattest and strongest beasts in the world, haveing teeth a yard and a half longe. The feight of the tame ollephants were both fiercce and furious; butt the wild ones did far excceed them, for before they could be gotten together, they rune amongst the housses and [by] vehement force of there teeth and trounke[s] did pull them downe. Butt beinge once meett, they maid a most furious feight, and did gore and wound one another with ther teeth most cruellie. Growinge weak, the Kinge caussed them to be partted. After them came buffelos, a beast verie fiercce and stronge, which maid a worthie feight and gave greatt content to the speecctators. After them came in

[1] Purchas says (*Pilgrimage*, p. 612): 'In saluting the King, they lay their hands folded on their head; which in other salutations they lay on the forhead.'

greatt rames, which allso maid a good feight. Ther was more sportt to be seene; butt growing laitt, the Kinge did pretermitt the rest. The sportts being ended, all the nobles in ther degree rose uppe and came before the Kinge, kissed his hands, and so with lowe obeysaunce going backwards from his prescence. The King satt still till they all had done in forme afforessaid, and then he himself rose upp and took ollephantt and repaired to his pallace in greatt pomp.

27. The King went by land to his castle or fortt upon the seaside. Our Generall followed him; and ther they staid the space of an houre or towe. Our Generall accompanied His Majestie to the courtt, and ther partted.

28. This mourninge earllie we herd ordinance shott of[f] att the courtt; wither our Generall presentlie repaired, with his trumpetts allwaies sounding before him. The King, hearing by his trumpetts thatt he was comed to the courtt, sent for him by his chopp; without which chopp no man can bee admited into the Kinges prescence. The Kinge tould him att that tyme he could nott confer, for that his army was retourned from Joar, and had brought the King prisoner, and that att that tyme many of his nobles were assembled for to confer of matters of staitt. Our Generall, percevinge and under[standing] before of the arivall of this fleett, left them to ther afaires. For we had understood before of the procceed of this bussines: how the King of Joar was convicctted [see p. 163] and brought presoner, with other tow inferiour kinges, one his brother in lawe, who was the King of Ziak[1], and the other his frend, the King of Paun[2]; who was both brought with the Kinge of Joar[3]. Greatt solemnitye was maid, both in courtt and cittie, for the vicctorie. His army was 100 small frigotts and gallies, some haveing ordinance, some none; the number of souldiers 20,000. A Flemish shipp att this tyme hapened to be att [the] ille of Joar, tradinge there; which did, in the King of Joars behalf, resist and shott att the army of this Kinge of Achen and Sumatra. Butt in the eend, for hir moore

[1] Siak, a state on the eastern coast of Sumatra. Netscher says (p. 29) that its chief was an illegitimate brother of the Sultan of Johore, and that the eldest son of the latter had married a daughter of the former.

[2] Pahang, a kingdom on the eastern side of the Malay Peninsula.

[3] Rāja Sabrang is meant (see next page).

saiftie, she put to sea, withoutt losse of goods or men. Butt the Capttain of the Flemings[1] and his merchants ashoare burned ther housse and fleed, haveing taken with them ther best jewells, and fleed to the yonge Kinge[2], and in his behalfe resisted against the army and killed divers of ther men, some of them beinge likewisse slayne. Butt the yong King of Joar yielded, and they weere taken and brought hither to Achen prisoners, mariners and merchantts, to the number of 20. Our Generall, hearinge of ther comeinge, went to see the Cappttain and to encourage him; and after some discourse touchinge ther bad fortunne, our Generall was inquisitive to know some newes from Bantam. The Capttain tould him that 4 mounthes past they had beene att Bantam: of Sir Henries Midletons being there in the *Trad*, and most of his merchantts and men dead: of hir sheathinge there: of the *Sallomons* beinge there: and of the death of Mr. Ward [see p. 12]: of the *Hecter* and *Thomas* ther goinge for England: of Generall Saires goinge to Jappan in the *Clove*[3]. No newes we could understand of the *James*. God, if yt be His will, blisse hir and preserve hir; for our Generall stands in greatt doubtt of hir[4]. Our Generall, havinge endeed discoursse with the Capttain, took leave, and promissed his best meanes to the Kinge in ther behalfes.

29. The Generall, with his chief, wentt to the courtt, where instanttlie he had accesse unto the Kinge. Falling into discoursse, the Kinge, beinge possessed with some good humor, did of his ownne accord promisse unto our Generall the remitt of customes att Priaman and Tecowe, accordinge to the articles concluded and agreed betwixt his uncle (the ould Kinge) and Sir James Lankaster, with many other kindnesses [and] the offer of the confiscatt goods att an indifferentt ratte. Our Generall did accept the kindnesse, for that the merchantts had a quantitie of Achen gold which they determined to imploie rather then to loosse by the exchange of yt for rialls. Our Generall promissed His Majestie to ssee the goodes; and so at this tyme partted.

[1] Apparently this was Abraham Theunemans.

[2] Rāja Sabrang seems to be meant. He was a brother of the Sultan and the real ruler of the kingdom.

[3] The *Hector* left Bantam on 11 December 1612, and the *Thomas* a month later. Saris sailed for Japan on 15 January 1613.

[4] See note on p. 11.

30. The Generall sentt tow of our merchauntts downne to the fortt, where the goods was, to see the sortts; with whom wentt Mallu[m] Guinee (the master of the junk that brought letters from Suratt to our Generall), to geve his advisse in the sorttes and goodnes. But haveinge sene the goodes, our merchanttes and the Kinges officers could nott agrey of pricces.

July 1. Our Generall went to the courtt, where he found the Kinge with his nobles and his newe surprized subjectes. But our Generall, perceyveinge ther occassions to be serious, gave waie to ther affaires, and retourned home.

2. Our Generall by His Majestie sent for. Wher we meett His Majestie in most rioall staitt in the waie to the church with great solemntie. He had, for his guard [that] went before him, 200 greatt ollephantes, 2000 small shott, 2000 pikes, 200 launces, 100 bowmen; 20 naked swordes of pure gould caried before him. 20 fencers went before him, plaiinge with swordes and tergettes. A horsse leed before him, covered with beaten gould, the bridle sett with stones; at his sadle crutch[1] a shaff [i.e. sheaf] of arrowes, the quiver of beatten gould, sett with pretious stones. Before him went his towe sons, of 8 or 9 yeares ould, arayed with jewelles and rich stones. His Majestie rode upon an ollephant; his sadle of pure gold; his slave behynd him in rich arraye, with his beetle boxe, and a fann of pure gould in his hand, to keepe the flies from the Kinge. The Kinges robbes weere so rich that I cannott well describe them. He had a turband upon his head, sett with jewells and prettious stones invalluable; creast and sword of pure gold, the skaberd sett with stones. Before him went an ollephant with a chaire of staitt, covered all with beatten sillver, that, if yt should chaunce to rayne, he might change ollephants[2]. This ollephant had casses maid of pure gold, to putt upon his teeth. From the church he retourned to a place of pleassure prepared for his entertaynementt. Where His Majestie

[1] The raised parts of the saddle.

[2] Purchas, in his *Pilgrimage* (p. 613), gives a less prosaic reason for the spare elephant: 'Once every yeere they observe a solemne ceremonie of going to church, to see if Mahomet bee come. Then are there fortie elephants, richly covered, and on them the nobles; one spare for the Prophet; and another whereon the King rideth with much pompe. When they have looked into the moskee and not seene their Mahomet, the King returnes on that spare elephant.'

beinge seatted, all his nobles, according to ther custome, was called, and all forreyne embassadors, as the fame of ther countrey did deserve, were seatted amongst the nobles; which being done, we see the fighting of wild and tame ollephants, buffolos, and rames. Thes pleasures being past, all the nobles in greatt obedience saluted His Majestie att his rissing upp, and did accompany him to his palla[ce], where we left him to his concubynes. This day the Sian embassador sett saille furth of the road of Achen; butt left Nathaniell Fen, whose life he begged, behind him.

3. Our Generall wentt to the courtt; where the King maid a second offer unto him of the Guzuratts confiscatt goods. The merchants went to the castle to see thes goods, butt could nott agree with the Kinges officers who had comission for the saill of them.

4. To the courtt, [and] certified His Majestie that his [i.e. the General's] merchantts and his officers could nott agree of pricces, and so did ceasse to medle any more in this bussines; butt moved him for the dispatch of his letter to Tecowe and Priaman.

5. To the courtt for the dispatch of the letter. Att our retouren from the courtt, we see a man executed for some offence comitted in the warrs. He was first laid upon the ground upon his back, and both his eyes puld outt; and after, a stak[e] was drove in att his foundementt, through all his bodie, and out att the crowne of his head[1]; and being dead, his corppes were burned. Another souldier, the daie before, had his eyes puld out, his bodie cloven in tow peecces, and then burned with a doge in his bellie. I was specctator to this misserable tragedie. Another was boylled in oille this daie; which was as cruell a torttuer as the other. Thes men had comitted some offence in the warrs, wherby some prejudecce had happened. The generall of the army, for his wellcome, becausse he did not bring the ould King of Joar, who was an ould decreped man and had assigned his kingdome to his sone[2], was by the Kinge forcced to eatt a platter of turdes, and afterwards to wash his bodie in them, to the Kinges greatt infamie and dishonour, for so base a thing to

[1] On this method of punishment see a note on p. 118 of Floris.
[2] 'Brother' is probably intended (see p. 170).

be published amongst forreyners and strangers. Allthough this seeme strange, yett yt is trew, as God is in heaven.

6. Our Generall went to the courtt, but could not speak with the Kinge; but one of his chiefe was sent to our Generall to certifie him that yt was His Majesties pleassure that he should have the confiscatt goodes att his ownne prisse. Our Generall certtified the nobles yt was nott so; for that severall tymes he had sent his merchauntes to that purpose to the fortt, but could nott effectt nothinge but upon unreasonable pricces, and for that causse he was absolutlie purposed to give yt over.

7. To the courtt. This daie our Generall pressented the Kinge with tow English fowllinge pecces, [and] obtayned the letter for Tecowe and Priama[n], butt customes nott remitted, to his greatt dishonor and breach of former promisses with our Generall. This daie the Flemings that was taken prissoners at Joar was by the Kinges officers ransacked of many jewells and aparill.

8. Our merchantes bargayned with the Guzurattes for call[icoes] and other goodes of severall sorttes, to carie for Tecowe and Priaman; the Generall haisteninge the merchauntes for dispatch. This daie a China junk came into the rood of Achen. [She] was at Bantam, and had Sir Henrie Midletons passe.

9. This daie Henrie Miller, one of our saillers which rune awaie from the shipe 2 or 3 daies scince, was found agayne att the Porttingailles housse[1]. After his punishment [he was] apoynted for the *Dragon*.

10. Our boatt came to [*sic*] ashoare, [and] took in 4 bailles of goodes for the *Dragon*. No man admitted to come ashoare, but with haist to repaire abord. The Generall [was] sentt for by the Kinge to come to the courtt; wither he instantlie repaired, and caried him a peecce for a pressent. [He] could nott be admitted to his pressence, but, haveinge attented an indifferent tyme, he came awaie agayne. Of which the Kinge understandinge, sentt his chope for him agayne. Where fallinge into discoursse, our Generall moved him in the behalfe of the Guzurattes, and offered

[1] Probably this refers to some private Portuguese trader. There is no evidence of a Portuguese factory at Achin at this time.

him a faire peecce of ordinance furth of the *Dragon* for the liberttie of 4 of the chieff of them, vidz. the ould man and his sonne and the towe pillottes; but the Kinge refused to do yt under a greatt some of money. Wherupon our Generall took leave, haveinge found him allwaies reedie to promisse much and in thend to performe litle. But his bassenes hath not onelie bene evident to his owne subjectes butt allso unto us, in nott performeinge whatt formerlie he had promissed unto our Generall. He diverse tymes shewed us his glorie, but never his loialltie nor fidellitie; and therfore we will leave him to that infidellitie he doth professe.

11. Our Generall, hasteninge bussines, sentt abord 4 or 5 slaves, bought here at 4 or 5 taille. The percer [Christian?] comaunded our boatt ashoare next mourninge.

12. Earllie in the mourninge our longe boat [went] ashoare to fetch downe provission. This daie we gave upp housse at Achen. Our Generall comeinge abord, in the waie at Pega [*sic*] was his ould servantt, Nathaniell Fen, who craved of the Generall licence to passe in the shipe for England. Our Generall, to be shortt, did condicionallie grantt him that favour, that if he would go as a mariner, to taik his turne at hellme and roowe in the longe boatt. He answered he was willinge to doe yt, but he wanted money to defraie his lodginge and diett. The Generall tould him he would not furnish him, but, if he could maik meanes of himselfe to come abord, he should, upon the condicions before mentioned; and thus the skiff put of[f] and left him to his wittes. Saillinge downe the river, certayne of the Guzurates which was stolne awaie came swiminge abord the skiffe and was caried abord the *Dragon*; who, to wellcome our Generall abord, shott 5 pecces. The *Hossiander* shot 3 peeces. Comaund was given to both the maisters to gitt upp ther topmastes and to bringe ther sailles to yardes, to maike reedie for the next opertunitie to weye. This daie Patterick Naren was by the Generall apoyneted master sirgion in the *Hossiander*. We had from the *Dragon* 4 litle kides and 20 hens. Our maister went abord the *Dragon* to wellcome the Generall. At his retourne he brought with him 6 Indeans and a boye, [and?] Hewgh Gittinges, our cape merchant.

13. In the mourninge the Flemish Captain came abord the

Dragon, [and] brought letters for Bantam. Our Generall comaunded his cockson to sett him ashor at the casle. At his parttinge, gave him 3 peeces.

14. We sett saille furth of the rood of Achen, haveinge bene here 3 monnthes and 2 daies; in which tyme we have lost, furth of both shipes, 25 men. Our Generall bought and entertayned here about 25 or thereabout Indeans, for to suplie the want of our men deceassed. Nathaniell Fen left behynd at Achen.

The quallitie of money and weightes at Achen.

Yowe have a great weight called a bahar, which doth conteyne 385 ll. English. Yowe have allso a small weight called a cattee[1], which maikes 2 ll. English. You have gould, ther coyned, called masses[2], at 9*d.* the peece, and 5 goes for a pece of 8. Yowe have also lead money, of which 1000 maikes a masse, called casse[3]. Ther also doth larres[4] go currant, at 9*d.* the peece, and 5 to a peece of 8. Sometymes they go at a higher ratte. This money is curant all the Indes over, and much profitt gotten by the exchange of them.

This illand of Sumatra, alliis called Ophir[5], from whence Sallomon had his gould, as the Scriptures in divers placces maikes mention. They do professe Mahamatts lawe, as for the most part of Assia and Affrica doth. They have no church[6] nor churchyard, butt buries ther dead in the corner of streettes[7]

[1] Malay *kati*, varying from one to two pounds.

[2] *Mas* is the Malay word for gold. The coin so called was a small and thin one of gold, reckoned by John Davis in 1600 as equivalent to about 9½*d.* (*Purchas His Pilgrimes*, vol. I, p. 117). Sixteen of these made a gold *tael* (an imaginary coin). See a note on p. 314 of *Letters Received*, vol. III.

[3] The Chinese coins known to the English as 'cash.'

[4] The *lāri*, so called because it was first struck at the Persian city of Lār, was a small rod of silver, stamped, and then bent double (see Pyrard, vol. I, p. 232). Its popularity in the East was due to the purity of its silver.

[5] See a note on p. 116 of Mundy, vol. III. Purchas (*Pilgrimage*, p. 613) says: 'They have a tradition that Achen is Ophir.'

[6] Yet Croft has already described (pp. 168, 171) two visits of the king to his 'church' (i.e. mosque). Purchas (*Pilgrimage*, p. 612) says: 'In Acem [Achin] mesquits of timber and reed, with vessels of water at the entrie, for them to wash, accordinge to the Arabian custome.'

[7] 'They bury their dead in the fields, with their head towards Mecca; laying a freestone at the head and another at the feet, with signification what the deceased had beene. The kings have them, not of stone but of gold; and this king had two made for him, each weighing a thousand pound, enriched with stones.' (Purchas, *ut supra.*)

This cittie of Achen lieth within 6 degrees of the Equanoctiall Lyne; which maikes yt so exceedinge hott. Yeet the people countynually goeth bareheaded and barefootted; and so doth the Kinge and all his nobles and chieff of the land. Thes people are greatt swimmers and divers in generall, women as well as men. They teach ther chilldren this artt in ther infancie; so they become verie exquisite in ther perfectt aige. This swiminge they hould to be a great preservacion of ther health; for which causse they dailie exersise yt, as the custome of eattinge and drinking. This illand [is] verie rich, and plentie of fruit; yett the comon sortt of people laies upon an erbe called beettle, by which they fynd greatt sustenance; so that this aforesaid herbe and tobacco is the ordinarie food, both to men and women. The Kinge hath one loyall [i.e. legal, or legitimate] wiffe, whosse chilld doth posesse the croowne. He hath allso threskore concubynes; for where he heres of a proper woman, eyther in cittie or countree, he sendeth for hir to the courtt. Allthoughe she bee maried, she must come; and if hir husband seeme unwillinge or loath to partt from hir, then he pressentlie comaundes hir husbandes prick to be cutt of[f], and oftentymes worsse punishments. If the Kinge have more sones then one, when he dies they are all put to death save the elldest, or conveyed furth of the kingdome into some other countree, becausse they shall not contend for the croowne after the Kinges death. If a subject die without heire malle, his goodes and landes falles to the Kinge, and the wiffe, with hir doughters, maye go begge. Many nations have trad for this illand, more for the comoditties yt affordes then the affabillitie of the people; for they are both inhumayne and basse, and much unworthie to inhabite so sweet a countree.

17. Thomas Sicklyne deceassed, and by will gave unto his brother in lawe, John Stronge, all his goodes and waiges; some legacies exceptted, mentioned in the will.

20. Fowlles as bigge as a raven came flieinge into the shipe and light upon our mens shoulders; but smelled so stronge of fish, they could nott eatt them, neyther rost nor sode [i.e. boiled].

22. Raphe Standiches goodes sould at the mast; came to 115*ll.*

26. From the 25 till the last of this instant verie bad wether; much wynd and rayne, with lightninge. Divers of the *Dragons* men and ours fall sick by intemperat and corupted aire.

First [August], beinge Saboath daie. We lost the sight of the *Dragon* this afternoone. Being betwixt the towe ilandes of Niptan [see p. 63 *n.*], we meet with a currant sett against us, that, haveinge litle wynd, we could nott stem the currantt, but drove in with the shoare. Our master, seing litle good to be done, did, by the consent of the company, alter his coursse and stood awaie S. by E. and S.S.E., to go about the southward end of the illand, and so to stand in with the mayne of Sumatra. The *Dragon* she gott about the norward end of the illand. Our master had the directions of Capt. Keellinge and Daves ther journalles[1].

4. Sailling alongst the mayne iland of Sumatra, we sse a sulphir[2] out of a mountayne, which caussed vehement lightninges in the night, as if the sea had bene of fire.

7 of August. We arived in the rood of Tecowe, where we found the *Dragon* at anker.

8. We went abord the *Dragon* to sermon. We understood of the death of thre men in the tyme of our absence, which was 8 daies. After dinner, towe officers came from shoare, sent by the chieff to knowe wether our Generall had the Kinges letter or no. The letter was shewed them. After some disscoursse with our Generall, they tould him he was nott in the right roodstead, for that he might come nearer the shoare and ride under the northermost illand of the three in five fatham water, for that ther Sir Henrie Midleton had rood in the *Trad*, the tyme of his being ther. Likwisse they did sertifie our Generall of the *Trades* beinge aground[3], and allso of another shipe of his fleet[4] beinge here aground. They did likwisse sertifie our Generall of the death of Sir Henrie at Bantam, since his departtinge from Tecowe, with many or most partt of his merchants and mariners. They did affirme Sir Henries death to be after a verie strange manner,

[1] As regards John Davis, see a note on p. 10. William Keeling visited Priaman in 1608, and extracts from his journal will be found in *Purchas His Pilgrimes* (vol. I, p. 188).

[2] An eruption of sulphur from a volcano.

[3] See *The Voyages of Sir James Lancaster*, p. 211.

[4] The *Darling* (Jourdain, p. 231).

which to discribe yt, yt would seeme incredulous[1]; but I omitt to speak any more of yt, beseechinge Gȯd yt be nott so as is by them affirmed; but what the truth is, the sequell will declare.

9. Our Generall sent our chieff ashoare with the letter and to conferr with the countree people and the Governer, who seemed verie dessirous to conferr with our Generall. Our people retourned abord, and tould our Generall that the Governer and the chieffe ashoare had assembled themselves and was comed downe to the seaside, where they greatlie desired disscoursse and receitt of ther Kinges letter. Upon which newes our Generall prepared himself for the shoare, with 30 or 40 men forth of both shippes attendinge upon him. The *Dragon* shott 9 pecces, the *Hossiander* 5 peeces. A shipe of the Kinges of Achen, wherein was Guzurattes, shott 3 peeces. The chieff meett our Generall upon the sandes, where they curteousslie saluted him after ther countrey manner, and caried him to a sumerhousse, wher they all satt downe to conferr. The Kinges letter [was] by our Generall with greatt obeyssaunce delivered them, and by them on ther parttes loiallie acceptted with great reverence, as beseemed the letter of so greatt a kinge. The copie of yt by them was taken, after yt was published in the hearinge of all the multitude. The chieff tould our Generall the countree was free for him to trad where he best pleassed, upon reasonable pricces. The chieffe tould our Generall they would send a messenger to Priaman to give notice unto the Governer ther, for that the letter concerned them, and that our Generall was free to trade ther likewisse. Our Generall answered that, if they pleassed, they might send ther messenger to Priaman in his small shippe, for that he was determined to send hir thither within a daie or towe. The chieff certiffied our Generall of the death of Sir Henrie Midleton, and did affirme yt, butt nott in such manner as was first reportted, butt onelie upon grieff and sorowe for the death of his merchantts and mariners, that, haveinge brought his vaige to such effectt, [he] could nott acomplisse yt for want of men. Our Generall promissed the next morneinge to send his merchants ashoare

[1] Used in the now obsolete sense of 'incredible.' The story hinted at is not on record; but it may be connected with the diabolic apparitions mentioned in *Letters Received*, vol. III, p. 320, and Floris, p. 84.

with trad. They promissed entertaynement. The chief intreated our Generall to go with them to ther cittie, a mille or twayne within the land, to taik such entertaynement as the countree did yield. Our Generall excussed himselfe by the vehemencie of the heatt and badnesse of the waie. The capttain of the Guzurattes offered him the like curtesey. Our Generall did returne him thankes, but he refussed his kindnes. Our Generall tould him of thee [*sic*] successe [which] had hapened at Achen to his countremen ther, by the confiscatinge of ther shipe and goodes and the captivatinge of themselves. [He] tould him also he had moved the Kinge divers tymes in ther behalffes, but could nott prevaille. After disscoursse, the capttain gave thankes to our Generall for his kindnes towardes his countremen. Our Generall took leave of the chieffs, and, after a litle recreation by walkinge ashoare, repaired abord the *Dragon*.

August 10. The merchauntes ashoare, providing a housse and maikinge waie for trad. This daie came abord the cavellero that Sir Henrie Midleton, in his tyme of beinge here, loved so well that he offered him 1000 dollars to go with him for England.

11. Our merchanttes ashoare; where they understood the pricce of peper to be betwixt 18 or 16 rialles the bahar or there-aboutes; butt no pricce as yeett certaynlie maid. This daie the Generall dispossed of the merchantes for imploymentes. He apoynted Mr. Olliver to go with us in the *Hossiander* for Priaman, to understand of newes ther and to pressent the Governer; Mr. Moore and Mr. Gittinges, with other asistauntes, to staie at Tecowe for the dispatch of bussines for the *Dragon*.

12. In the morneinge we sett saille for Priaman, but, beinge calme, we came to anker agayne before we sailled furth of the rood of Tecowe; but, haveinge a litle gaille, we weyed agayne and stood our coursse for Priaman S. [and] S. by E

13. We ankered in the rood of Priaman[1], [and] sent our skiffe with John Chambers ashoare to learne newes; by whom we understood the Governer seamed much discont[ent]ed becausse we came not first to Priaman, for that yt was the chieff portt of those parttes and that the Kinges letter was directed to them. This night we went ashoare to an illand cloosse by where the

[1] '3 salutinge peces to the towne' (marginal note).

ship rood, upon which iland we found a tombe of 18 foot, where afterwardes we understood a giant had bene intombed. We found fresh watter and cocker nuttes.

14. Tobias Olliver, our cape merchant, went ashoare. Our shipe shot 5 pecces. The Governer and the chieff had assembled themselves, and meett us att the seaside; wher, after salutacion, the letter was delivered [to] the Governer; which was, both by him and all the rest of the chieff, verie loiallie and with great homage receved. The Governer, with Mr. Olliver, took ollephant and rood up to the towne; where, comeinge to a housse fitted for the same purposse, they lighted and satt downe; where the letter was published and the copie taken. The Governer tould Mr. Olliver yt was suffecient he had sseene the letter, and that he had privilidge from the [King?] to admitt him trad, where himselfe best pleassed: peper they had some quantitie reedie, and more in tyme they would provide. Mr. Olliver was inquisitive of letters left by our English, but none the[y] would acknowledge but one left by Capttain Keellinge to be by them conveyed to the Kinge. They tould us the names of divers English [who] had bene ther the last yeare or year last past—Mr. Paycok[1], and one Mr. Ball[2], Mr. Quin, and of one Beamant[3], who was there interpreter; butt could tell us no newes of Sir Henrie Midleton, of whom we most desired to learne newes. Mr. Olliver pressented the Governer with towe fowllinge peeces, 2 vests, towe bookes of callico. In lewe of this pressent the Governer gave Mr. Olliver a buffello and towe rawe hens broilled upon the coalles. We went with Mr. Olliver to ssee one of the chieffe who was sick; by whom we were curteousslie entertayned. We still enqueared of letters, but none we could heare of. From thenc we went to the Governer agayne, to knowe the pricce of peper and to know wether they would bringe ther peper to Tecowe or no. The Governers answeer was that the people of Tecowe in former tymes had brought ther peper to Priaman, but for them, they never att no tyme had

[1] Tempest Peacock, cape merchant in the *Thomas*. He went afterwards to Japan with Saris.

[2] George Ball, another of the merchants in the *Thomas*.

[3] The John Beaumont of *Letters Received*, vol. 1, pp. 200, 204–6, 208. He was one of those seized and tortured by the Dutch at Amboina, but was released and got safely back to England.

caried thers for Tecowe, nor would nott yield to yt; but if our Generall weere so pleased to send one of his shipes thither, they would maik reedie ther peper within towe monnthes tyme, to the quantitie of 2000 bahars, and that they would eyther sell yt for rialls of 8 or truck for callicoes; but ther [price ?] they had nott yeet brooken, but promised the next daie to maik him a pricce. The daie beinge farr spent, we craved licence and repaired abord. Bad landing we found here.

15. We acompanied Mr. Olliver ashoare to Priaman; where fallinge into perley [i.e. parley] concerninge the pricce of peper, we found them resolved that, accordinge as our Generall did conclude with thee people of Tecowe, for ther peper, so they would sell thers, and deliver yt at the seaside, where Capttain Keelling and others in tymes past had recceved thers; but by no meanes they would condiscend [i.e. agree] to transportt anye for Tecowe. And this we found to be the effectt of ther answer. We repaired abord, [and] left Mr. Olliver ashoar verie sick, [with] the surgon to attend him; butt, the extremitie of his fitt beinge past, [they] came abord.

16. In the mourninge earlie we weied, and stood for Tecowe; but the extremitie of wether forced us to putt roome into the roode of Priaman agayne, wher we ankered.

17. This mourninge we weyed, and stood for Tecowe.

18. We arived in the rood of Tecowe. The Generall sent his skiffe for Mr. Olliver; by whom hee understood of our proceedinges at Priaman. He retourned abord agayne this night, and tould us the Generall had certaine newes of the death of Sir Henrie Midleton, and the losse of his mainmast. This newes came by Chinezes laitlie comed to Tecowe from Bantam.

19. Mr. Olliver this mourninge, per the Generalls order, went abord the *Dragon*, [and] caried with him his beed and provissions; and Hewgh Gittinges came in his place. The chief this daie was expeccted to come abord and sse goodes and conclud with the Generall of pricees; but the badnesse of the wether hindered them.

20. This morninge verie earlie the Generall sent his boat and shallope to warpe us in nearer the *Dragon*, and to fill watter upon an illand for us, for that he had determined we should go for

Bantam. We recceved this daie from the *Dragon* at severall tymes 2900 bars of lead, [and] 3 chestes of fowllinge pecces (conteyning 51). This daie I gave a receitt for 22 peces, for that we delivered 2 chests before att Achen and had no receitt for them; which 2 chests did conteyne 29. We recceved this daie more from the *Dragon* one butt [of] stronge beare, [and] a hawccer of 7 inches. More, we delivered this daie furth of the *Hossiander*, per the Generalls order, one chest of money, for which I had a recceitt under his owne handes. This daie I gave Mr. Olliver a receitt for 90 pair [of] shewes, 40 shirttes, 50 shewttes [i.e. suits], [and] 60 ll. of sope. We recceved from the *Dragon* the tymber of the pinis maid att Deedfurth [i.e. Deptford][1].

21. This morneinge earlie Mr. Christian, the pursser[2], came abord us, with his provissions, apoyntted per the Generall to bee our chieff faccter for Bantam; Gilles Hilles, his attendant; Watter Staccie; and 2 Indeans. This last night we had 3 Guzurattes swim ashoar and rune awaye. We weied and stood our coursse for Bantam. We gave the *Dragon* 3 peeces for a farwell. She gave us one; and so we partted.

26. Beinge in 3 degrees or theraboutes to the southward of Priaman in our vaige to Bantam, we had most cruell and fearfull wether, by thunderinge, lightninge, and raine for many daies together, but esspeciallie one night and a daie. I maie trewlie saie that the greattest cannon in all the world, when yt was fired, did never roare as the thunder heere did; with lightninge and rayne in such aboundaunce as I never in my life hard the like. And I do furder think that in England yt never rayned so much in 6 daies as here yt did in 24 houres. Yt was both wounderfull and miraculous to behold, and did justlie veriefie the sayinge of that worthie profitt David in his 107 Psallme, where yt is said that they that go downe to the sea in shipes and ocupie by great watters, those men doth see the wounders of the Lord. And God of His mercie graunt that we all, that hard and ssee thes wounders and workes of the Lord, maie to His glorie maik usse of the 31 versse of the same Pssallme.

29. This daie by extremitie of wether we splitt our maine-topesaille; and this night sunk our skiffe att the shipp[s] sterne[3]

[1] See note on p. 65.

[2] Of the *Dragon*.

[3] Here the journal comes to an abrupt conclusion.

EXTRACTS FROM THE JOURNAL OF NATHANIEL SALMON

MASTER OF THE *HOSIANDER*[1]

I

Munday, the 31th of August 1612. At 6 a clock in the morning, by my judgment, with the way that wee have runn wee are in the latitude 20° 15′. And now seeing the water to bee chaunged, wee heaved overboard our lead and found 19 fadom water, saft ozie ground; but yett could see noe land. Therfore I cannot judge but that our shipp is a great deale to the eastward of my reckning, for the land of Due [i.e. Diu] beareth N.E. and by East 60 leages of[f], and I knowe wee cannot bee so farr of[f], by the depth of water which now wee find, and also by the culler of the water, which is so suddenly changed. This 24 howers wee have [run ?] 36 leages with the wend at the west and by south, and faire weather; and now from [12 ?] to 4 a clock wee steared E.N.E. 6 leages ½, and shoulding our depth from 18 fadom to 9 or 10 fadom, very good shoulding. And so running a glasse[2] further, wee had presently 19 or 20 fadom. Soe wee continued our course E.N.E. untill 6 a clock, and wee stered E. till 2 a clock in the morning, the water shoulding from 20 to 12 fadom, very good shoulding.

September first.

And at 2 a clocke wee stood to the southward, and lying S.W. and by S., and shewed 2 lights to the *Dragon*, and shott of[f] a peece. But before wee had tackt our shipp, wee weare in 9 fadom. And soe standing till 4 a clock the same morning, being the first of September, wee spide the land under our lee, some 4 leages of[f], as wee did judge, bearing E.N.E. of us; and I judge[d] it to bee the land of Due. But in the morning, when I see how the land laye alongst, wee found it to bee the land towards the

[1] I.O. *Marine Records*, no. XVIII, f. 15. My reasons for attributing this journal to Salmon are given in the introduction.

[2] Both the hour- and the halfhour-glass were used, but the latter is probably intended.

south of Damon, having then but 6 or 7 fadom. And at 8 a clock wee tackt to the northward of Daman, and the same day, at 1 or 2 a clock in the afternoone, wee came to an ancker somewhat to the northward of Daman, in 7 fadom water, in the sight of the tower of Daman, and soe [rode ?] ther all night.

2d day. The next morning, betweene 4 and 5 [a] clock, wee wayed and stood to the southward into deeper water, and ankred. And the same day the Generall called a counsell to send our shipp to discover the barre of Surat and to bring a pylot for the *Dragon* to bring her upp also. And in the afternoone at 4 a clocke wee sett sayle, and steared E.S.E. in with the shoare till wee had but 6 fadom water; and then wee haled it up to the northward and stered N. and by W. and N.N.W. untill wee came so hye upp as the river of Gundeve[1], as wee did judge and as the Indians tould us which wee brought out of the *Dragon*. And so, being night, wee came to ancker, being then an hie water.

Thursday, the 3d of September. In the morning wee waied and stood up for the barr of Surat; but being little wind, and tide of flud being then done, wee came to an ancker againe, in 7 fadom water, having sayled some 5 or 6 myles N. and by W. [The] same day at low water, the wind being westerly with a gale, wee waied againe for the bar. And having not stered above 2 howers but wee weare in sight therof; but not knowing of it, wee weare perswaded that wee [weare] above it by the foresaid Indians; and so wee bore downe and came to an ancker against Nunsore[2], a river that lyeth some 3 leages to the southward of S[urat].

Fryday, the 4th day. Wee rid still against Nunsore, and sent our skiff abourd of a boate that came out of the foresaid river; and shee tould us that [wee][3] weare not against Surat, but against Nunsore. So wee asked a pylot to [con]vey us up; who being very loath, yet at last he was willing, so that wee would leave [one of our ?] men for a pawne; the which wee agreed unto, and left one of our carpenters. [Then ?] the *Dragon* came up to us and, thincking that wee had rid at the barr of [Surat], came to an

[1] Gandevi is at the head of the estuary of the Ambika River.
[2] Nosari, 8 miles up the Purna River, and 18 miles south of Surat.
[3] The MS. is damaged in this place.

anckor some halfe a myle to windward of us; blo[wing a ?] gayle of wind, so that wee could not rowe abourd of her.

Saterday, the 5th. At 10 a clock wee waied; but the wind being so farr notherly that wee could not hall it of[f] the shoare, but weare fayne to come to an ancker againe. And at the very same tyme ther came a boate of Surat abourd of us, and brought us newes that Sir Middleton had bene ther, but was gone, with all the marchannts with him, and Captaine Hawkings and his wife with all the rest; and also he brought us a lettre which Sir Henry Middleton had left to bee delivered unto the next shipps that came thither. The which wee receiving, presently shott of[f] a peece, that the Generall might come aboard; for it blew so that wee could not rowe ahead, shee riding to windward of us. So presently he came to receive the could newes with the letter, which came as warme to his stomack as a cup of coole water in a frosty morning. This day it blew so hard that the Generall was constrained to lye abourd of our shipp all night.

6 day, Sunday. In the morning the Generall went abourd of the *Dragon*. And at the same tyme wee waied, and went of[f] to the *Dragon*; the wind being then at W., and faire weather.

7th day, Munday. At 10 a clock in the morning wee waied, and stood up for the barr of Surat, with the wind at W. and by S. And the same day, about 4 a clocke in the afternoone, wee came to an ancker in 7 fadom water, some ¾ of a myle without the barr; but the *Dragon* rid about 2 cables length without us. The pagot[1] bore E.S.E. of us. This pagot is a great white howse, that standeth in a thickett of bushes; and the further you bee of[f] it, the plainer you shall see it. This pagot is an image that the Gogerts [Gujarātis] and the Bangans [Banyans] doe worship, and is a great thing as bigg as a church without a steeple. Ther is also a great tree that standeth a little to the southward of the foresaid pagot, the better for your knowledg and the finding of the foresaid barr. The boint [point ?] that lyeth to the northward of the foresaid bar bore N. and by W. of us, as wee ridd. This day the *Dragon* sent her skiff ashoare, with the purser and some other;

[1] They were off the mouth of the Sachin River, and the 'pagot' (pagoda) was the Hindu temple, dedicated to Hanumān, on the south side of the town of Bhimpur, which stands on the north side of the river entrance. This temple is still a conspicuous landmark.

which I doe not knowe who they weare, for they came not neere us.

This barr lyeth in latitude (found by severall observations) 21° 15′. Swally lyeth to the northward of the barr of Surat about 3 leages of[f], bearing N. and by E. from the barr and the roade of Swally. But as you goe from the barr to Swally, you must steare N.N.W., by reason of the pointe which lyeth out to the northwards of the barr; and so stearing you shall have deepe water about a myle of[f] the shoare. And when you are past this point, you shall steare more northerly (as occasion shall serve) untill you come to the shoulding of the shoare; which you must have a great care of, for it shouldeth of a sudden. For when you come into 9 fadom, in running of a cable further into the shoare you shall have but 5 fadom; and running a little further, you shall have but 3 fadom; and within a cast or two you shall bee aground, for ther is [a] sand that lyeth betweene the shoare and you. For within this sand ther is 8 or 9 fadom water, but upon this sand you shall have at low water 5 foote in the best of the channell; for both to the northward and also to the southward of this foresaid channell it is adry at low water. Therfore a shipp of any great draught cannot goe and ride within; for they that ride within this sand, ride within muskett shott of the shoare; but they that ride without, ride a myle of[f] the shoare. The most water wee found upon this sand at a high water was 21 foote at a spring tyde. A W.S.W. moone [i.e. monsoon, wind] maketh a full sea, and hyeth 18 foote water. Without this sand lyeth also another sand, about 3 or 4 myles of[f], and lyeth also adrye at lowe water. Betweene these 2 sands ther is 15 or 13 fadom water. The marks to knowe when you are so hie as the road of Swally is a wood that lyeth to the southward of the towne of Swally. This wood the southermost parte therof must beare south-east; and so bearinge, you [may] ancker in what depth you will, from 5 fadom to 10 or 12 fadom, if you will.

The variation of Swally is 16° 30′, and the variation of Surat 16° 20′. If you sayle from Surat [roads] you shall steare S.W.; and so stearing shall come into 15 or 16 fadom; and then you may steare S.S.W., and shall find noe lesse water, if you keepe in the channell. For to the westward, and also to the eastward, you shall have lesse water; for wee tryed both sides. For of[f] Damon wee runn in with our shipp within a league of the shoare, and the least water wee had at $\frac{3}{4}$ flud was 6 fatham; and the more wee hauld of[f] the shoare, the deeper the water. For in running thus to the westward, the water will deepe[n] till you come to 18 fadom water; and then it will begin to should. For ther lyeth sand[s] all alongst from Cambaia till you come so farr to the southwards almost as Daman, which hath 2 fadam water upon them at $\frac{1}{2}$ ebbe. In running in the depth aforenamed, and keeping of the channell, yf you bee above Daman you shall hardly see the land, but the trees that growe theron. But if you bee bound for Suratt and fall with Due (which is the best place to fall withall, if possible you can), you must steare away east for Daman; which beareth E. and W. on[e] of another, neerest of any other point. And if you find any should water, you must halle of[f] more southerly, and then the water will deepe[n]. For the depth betweene Damon and Due is 18 and 20 fadam water; which is the most, but sometimes you shall have but 10 or 12 fadom, and then presently deepe[n] againe till you come to the shoulding of the shoare, which is very good shoulding.

The towne of Daman lyeth in latitud 20° 20′, and is to the eastward of Due 40 leagues. If you bee north 3 leages or 2 leages and $\frac{1}{2}$, that you can any waye see the towne, you may know [it by ?] this marke: you shall see a steeple that standeth in the towne (for all the [townes] to the northward have not the like). Also ther is an hill that standeth a little [to the ?] northward; and from that place to the northward is all low land, without any hill, either small or great, on that side of the bay; for if you bee anything of[f] the shoare, you shall think that all the trees standeth in the water; for it is very low land. But to the southward of Daman it is reasonable hie land; which is a great means to knowe whether you bee to the southward or to the northward of Daman. The variation of the compas of Daman is 16° and 20′. From Daman to the northward ther is a towne called Gundeve; also to the northward therof ther is a towne called Nunsore. This towne also hath a small river that belongeth unto yt; but not fitting for any shipp, but for frygatts or suchlike. This river is 12 myles to the southwards of Suratt.

II[1]

Sunday, the 17th of January [1613]. About 7 or 8 a clock in the evening [waied, we][2] riding in the road [of] Swally, bound for Achene. I pray God bee our good sp[eed. At] 12 a clocke wee came to an anckor againe, about 3 or 4 myles to the north [ward] of the barr of Surat, by reason that it was calme and also the tyde done.

Munday, the 18th. In the morning, about 6 a clock, wee waied; and as wee ca[me] thwart of the barr of Surat, 4 gallownes waied and stood after us, giving us chase till 10 a clocke, and then came to an ancker. But wee stood awaye. This [day] at 6 a clock the hye land to the southward of Daman bearing S.E. [ ] of[f].

Twesday, the 19th. In the morning wee mett with 4 Mallabars shipps, layden with cokernuts, being bound for Surat. 3 of them wee tooke and pilledg[ed] them, and so lett them goe. This day wee weare in latitud 19° 35′, and the variation from N. to W., 15° 55′.

Wednesday, the 20th. At noone, in latitud (by observation) 18° 45′. This day in the afternoone at 2 a clock wee steared E.S.E. in with the shoare; and at 6 a clocke wee saw the towne of Challe [Chaul], bearing E.N.E. 4 leages of[f]. Wee sawe a shippe riding in a baye to the southward of Chaule; but being night, wee lett her alone and went not to her, but stood alongst S. and by W., with the wind at N.N.W. Wee sounded, and found 17 fadam water.

Thursday, the 21th. In the morning before day wee halled in with the shoare, and the *Dragon* in the offin. Wee saw 3 Mallabars shipps, and spake with them, and they tould us they weare bound for Cambaia and belonged to Cuchen [Cochin], having the Portugalls passe with them. This day wee weare in latitud (by judgment) 17° 15′, and the compas varyed from N. to West 15° 40′; the wind continuing still northerly, with fayre weather.

[1] This portion occurs at the beginning of the volume containing the preceding section.

[2] The MS. is damaged at the edges of the pages, and many words have been lost. As far as possible, the missing words have been supplied (conjecturally) within square brackets. Otherwise a blank is left.

Fryday, the 22th. At noone wee weare faire by the ilelands that lyeth to [the] northwards of Goa. Wee came within halfe a myle of them, and sounded and had [ ]. This day, at 6 a clock in the evening, wee weare thwart of Goa, sein[g the] ileland of Goa very plaine, bearing E. and by N., 6 leages of[f], and lyeth in 15° [ ]. From Goa to the southwards the land lyeth S.E. and by S. ½ sotherly; but y[ou must] have a care of small ilelands that lye alongst this coast, a myle or 2 of[f] the sh[oare].

Saterday, the 23th. At noone in latitud 14° 10′. This 24 howers wee steared S.S.E. [ ], with the wind at N.N.E. This day the compas varyed, from N. to W., 15° 20′.

Sunday, the 24th. In the morning wee weare thwart of a small ileland that ly[eth] of[f] the shoare[1]. This iland wee spyed in the night, almost right ahed of us. [Wee] steared S.W. 3 or 4 glasse to goe cleare of it. Wee saw 60 sayle of frygatt[s, which] went within this ileland. They weare Portugalls, bound for Cuchene. About 2 or 3 a clock wee spied a shipp at an anckor, which was a Port[ingal] shipp, layden with rice. But as soone as they saw what wee weare [the] Portingalls went away with their boate, carrying all that was any [thing of] worth, leaving 40 Indyans aboard of her. So wee went abourd of [her, cut] her cables, and stood of[f] the shoare with her.

Munday, the 25th. In the morning, being calme, wee went abourd with our boa[t, the] Generall with us, to see what was in her; but finding nothing but rice th[ ] thing, wee tooke so much as wee thought good of, and then wee burnt h[er].

Tewsday, the 26th. In the morning, being little wind, wee spied a M[allabar, and brought her] abourd of the *Dragon*. Shee was also layden with cokernutts; and in her w[ee put the men] that was in the Portingall shipp, to sett ashoare, saving 8, which w[ee took along in our] shipps.

Wedensday, the 27th. At noone wee weare in latitud (by observation) 10° 56′; the variation, 14° 30′ from N. to W. At eight a clock in the evening wee lay a hull till 5 in the morning, and then wee sett saile and stood alongst (being to the southward

[1] Probably Hog (Shirali) Island, which lies a mile and a half off the coast, about four miles north-west of Bhatkal.

of Cuchen[1]), for wee had intelligence of 2 ships that rid ther; which weare gon in before wee came thither.

Thursday, the 28th. At noone in latitud (by observation) 10° 56′. This day wee observed the variation, from N. to West, 15° 00′. This afternoone wee stered S.S.W. of[f], for a refe that lyeth in this latitud (or somewhat more to the southward) and lyeth 6 or 7 leages of[f] by reporte; but wee saw none. From 8 a clocke to 12 a clock at night it was little wend, and then the wind came southerly.

Fryday, the 29th. At noone in latitud (by observation) 8° 15′. This day in the fornone it was calme, and in the afternoone the wend came to the S.S.W., and wee steared E.S.E. and S.E. and by E. in with the shoare. This day the variation, from N. to W., 15° 15′.

Saterday, the 30th. In the morning wee steared in with the shoare; and at 2 a clocke in the afternoone wee came to an anckor at a place called Bringon[2]. Wee anckred within muskitt shott of the shoare, in 16 fatham. In this place wee had fresh water and henns, with other refreshing wee had ther in great aboundance.

Thursday, the 4th of February. Wee waied to goe for the Cape. And at 6 a clock in the afternoone wee came to an anckor about 5 or 6 leages to the southward of the place wher wee waied (the place called Ballenga), in 22 or 23 fadam, 3 myles of[f] the shoare.

Fryday, the 5th. In the morning wee waied, with the wend of[f] the shoare, and stood alongst for the Cape. But about 10 a clock the wind came easterly, with a storme of wend. This was as soone as wee came open of the foresaid Cape. This was the munsone that blew soe fearce. Wee having stood of[f] thus some 5 or 6 leages, wee found the wind to bee more feirce. Soe wee tackt, and stood in for the shoare; and in the evening wee came to an anckor in 30 fatham water. But wee had not beene at an anckor 2 howers but the wend came easterly, with a storme of wend, that wee ridd very easily, by reason of the currant that setteth to the S.

Saterday, the 6th. In the morning wee tryed if wee could way

[1] A slip for 'Calicut' (see Best's journal).
[2] Brinjaon (see p. 43 *n*).

our anckor. The wind continuing very fresh, wee weare afraied wee should loose our anckor. And in waying, when our ancker was apeeke, with the force of our mens heaving the cable brake; so wee sett sayle to gett in with the shoare. The *Dragon* (shee waying in the night) gott into the shoare before day; but wee, not seing of her, rid still. This day wee plyed it to an[d] agayne, with little wind; soe that the currant was stronger then the wind. So in the evening wee came to anckor.

Sunday, the 7th. In the morning wee wayed, with little wind of[f] the shoare. And at noone, when the breese came, wee gott into the shoare, and came unto an anckor about 3 leages to the southward of Bellenga, in a bay, a myle of[f] the shoare, in 15 fatham water.

Munday, the 8th. In the morning wee wayed, with the wind of[f] the shoare, to goe for Bellenga; and at 3 a clock in the afternoone wee came to an anckor.

Saterday, the 13th. At a eleven a clocke wee waied, riding at Bellenga with the wind at W.S.W., and wee stearing alongst the shoare. And at 8 a clock in the evening wee came to an anckor about 7 leages to the S. of Bellenga, in 19 fadam water, a myle of[f] the shoare.

Sunday, the 14th. In the morning wee waied, with the wend of[f] the shoare, to plie for the Cape. But as soone as wee came open of the Cape wee found our old wend to blowe. So wee made one boarde [i.e. tack] of[f], and then wee stood in againe for the shoare, seeing it was but folly to strive against the streame (my meaning is, to get about the Cape so long as the easterly munson bloweth). And standing in with the shoare, wee came close by a rocke that lyeth 4 myle of[f] the shoare. Within the shoare and this rocke ther lyeth 2 small ilands. The rock and the 2 ilelands lyeth in forme of a tryangle, 2 myle on[e] from another. By this rock, within a cables length, ther is 20 fadam water. [This roc]ke is noe bigger then a great boate, and lyeth close by the waters edge; which [is very d]aungerous for them that doe not knowe it. From this rocke wee run about [ ] to the N., and so came to an anckor, in 17 fatham water, but fowle ground.

Wednesday, the 24th of February. In the morning, before

day, wee waied, ri[ding about] 15 leages to the northward of Cape Commorene, in a bay. This bay is foule ground [ ] any thing neere the shoare; for wee rid 4 myle of[f] the shoare in 17 fadam water [and had] fowle ground, for our cable was almost cut asunder; not knowing of it till wee waid our anckor. This day at 6 a clock in the afternoone Cape Commorene E.N.E., 6 leages [off]; having little wind, at W.S.W.

Thursday, the 25th. At 6 a clock in the morning Cape Commorene bore N.N.W., about [ ] of[f], and wee stearing S.E. and by E., with the wend at W.N.W. This cape lyeth in latitud [ ], and the compas varyed, from N. to W., 14° 15′.

Fryday, the 26th. At noone in latitud (by observation) 7° 50′; the Cape bearing N.N.W., about 14 leages of[f].

Saterday, the 27th. At noone in latitud (by observation) 7° 20′. This 24 howers wee steared [ ] 15 leages. The wind variable; and the variation of the compas, from N. to W., 14° [ ].

Sunday, the 28th. At 6 a clock in the morning wee had sight of Sellone. And in the [evening] about 7 a clock wee weare in 11 fadam water; so wee came to an anckor, thinking that the [*Dragon*] had come to an anckor also; but shee stood of[f] to the westward. This place, wher wee c[ame to] an anckor, was to the northward of a towne of the Portingalls, called Collombo.

Munday, the first of March. In the morning wee tackt, and stood in for the shoare. But being [little] wind, wee could not gett neere the ileland before night. And at 10 a clock wee stood of[f] againe to the westward, lying W.S.W., with the wind at S.

Tewsday, the 2d. At 6 a clock wee weare a faire birth of[f] the ileland of Sellone, a little to the southward of Collombo. Standing in with the shoare till 10 a clock in the evening, wee stood againe to the westward (the wend continuing to the southward); wee now perceiving th[at the] Generall was minded that wee should plie to windward, to gett aboute Cape Galla. Th[is day] the compas varyed, from N. to W., 13° 25′.

Wednesday, the 3d. At 8 a clock in the morning wee weare in sight of Cape Galla, bear[ing] E. and by S., about 10 leages of[f]. The wind on this side the ileland is most comonly variable as [long] as the easterly munson bloweth.

Thursday, the 4th. At 9 a clock in the morning wee weare open of Cape Galla. But as so[on] as we came open, the easterly wind blowing so feirce that wee weare faine to tack and [to] stand in with the shoare; tarrying there, plying to and againe, untill such tyme as it plea[sed] God to send us a slent[1] of wind to carry us about. This day wee observed the latitude and found [it] to bee 5° 55′.

The 9th of March. In the morning, the sun rising, wee sawe 2 sayles, the one to w[indward] and the other to leward; the *Dragon* going to the windermost, and wee going to her that [was to] leward. But when wee came up with them, the one proved to bee a Fleming, and the other [a Portin]gall that came from Batgalla[2], laiden with rise. This Portingall was the Flemin[gs prize], which shee tooke of[f] Cape Galla, and lay ther of[f] and on to looke for shippes that was to c[ome from] Chenie [China].

Fryday, the 11th[3] of March. At 3 a clock in the afternoone wee came to an anckor abo[ut] to the northward of Cape Galla, to see if wee could gett any fresh water. So wee went [ashoare] with our boate. But when wee came ashoare, wee sett an Indian ashoare to aske the [country] people whether wee could have any or noe; but they tould us that wee should hav[e none. The] reason was because ther was Portingalls amongst them. So, having this answere, we c[ame aboard].

Saterday, the 12th [13th]. In the morning, by breake of day, wee wayed, with the wind of[f] the shoa[re until] clocke; and then the wind came out of the sea. This afternoone, at 6 a clock, Cape Galla bore [N. of us,] leages of[f]. Cape Galla standeth in latitude 5° 45′; and the compas varyeth, from N. to W., 13° 15′.

Sunday, the 13th [14th]. At 12 a clock the wind came westerly. And wee being to the eastw[ard of Cape] Galla, wee stood in with the shoare to see if wee could find any place to water in. [Being] neere the shoare, wee spyed a baye, wher wee came to an anckor in 15 f[adam]; but it was fowle ground. So wee sent the boate ashoare. The people [would not come] neere them; so they darest

[1] A slant, or gust of wind coming obliquely.

[2] A slip for 'Bangalla' (Bengal); see pp. 46, 153.

[3] An error for 12th. The journal continues to be a day out until 20 March.

not tarry, but came presently abourd agai[ne and we] stood of[f] againe to the *Dragon*, that was in the offin.

Munday, the 14th [15th]. Wee spyed a sayle to windward of us, which came unto us, and in the afternoone wee spake with him; which proved to bee the foresaid Fleming that wee spake withall the 7th of the same moneth. This evening at 7 a clocke wee steared E.S.E., and East and by South all night, with the wind at W.N.W., and much raine.

Tewsday, the 15th [16th]. At noone, in latitud 5° 40′, and the variation, from North to West, 12° 45′. This daye, being calme, the Generall sent for the captaine of the Fleming abourd of him to dinner.

Wednesday, the 16th [17th]. The wind coming easterly, wee stood in with the shoare, lying N.E. in, having a fresh gayle. And wee standing in till 4 a clock, and then wee spyed a breach that lyeth 3 leages of[f] the shoare. Wee runn in till the breach bore E.S.E. Wee sounded, but founde noe ground. Soe wee tackt to the southward, lying S. of[f].

From the 16th till the 20th wee plyed to windward alongst the shoare with the easterlye wind, faire weather. And the 20th at noone, being Saterday, the wend came up southerly, a fresh gayle, and wee stearing E.S.E. and E. and by S., and wee being to the eastward of Cape Galla 30 leages, the land falling away to the northward. This point of the ileland at 6 a clock in the afternoone boare N.W. and by W., 5 leages of[f]. This day the compas varyed, from N. to W., 12° 30′.

Sunday, the 21th. At noone, in latitude (by observation) 6° 10′, and in longitude, from Cape Galla to the estward, 2° 12′. This 24 howers wee steared E.S.E. and E. and by S., 16 leagues.

Munday, the 22th. At noone, in latitude (by observation) 6° 15′, and in longitude, from Cape Galla to the eastward, 2° 53′. This 24 howers wee steared E., and E. and by S., by our compas; but the variation being from N. to W., therfore wee have made our waye but East ½ Notherlye 15 leages. This day the variation of the compasse, from N. to W., 11° 45′.

Tewsday, the 23th. At noone, in latitude (by judgment) 6° 25′, and in longitude, from Cape Galla, 2° 56′. This 24 howers wee steared N.N.E., 5 leages, with the wind variable, but most commonly calm. This day the compas varyed, from N. to W., 11° 20′.

Wednesday, the 24th. At noone, in latitude 7° 15′, and in longitude, from Cape Galla, 3° 12′. This 24 howres wee steared N.W. and by N., 12 leages, with the wend at E.S.E., and the compas varyed, from N. to W., 10° 35′.

Thursday, the 25th. At noone, in latitude (by observation) 7° 10′, and longitude, from Cape Galla to the eastward, 3° 2′. This 24 howers wee steared N.E., 3 leages, and S.S.W., 9 leages, with the wind easterly. This day the compasse varied, from N. to W., 10° 25′.

Fryday, the 26th. At noone, in latitude (by observation) 6° 25′, and in longitude, from Cape Galla to the eastward, 3° 22′. This 24 howers wee stered S.E. and by S., 15 leages, with the wind betweene the N.E. and E. and by S.

Saterday, the 27th. At noone, in latitude (by observation) 5° 40′, and in longitude, from Cape Galla to the eastward, 3° 56′. This 24 howers wee steared S.E., 18 leages, with the wind betweene the N.E. and the E.S.E. This day the compas varyed, from N. to W., 10° 25′.

Sunday, the 28th. At noone, in the latitude (by observation) 5° 6′, and in longitude, from Cape Galla to the eastward, 4° 15′. This 24 howers wee steared S.E. and by S., 13 leages, with the wind at E. and by N. This day the compas varyed, from N. to W., 10° 15′.

Munday, the 29th. At noone, in latitude 5° 8′, and in longitude, from Cape Galla to the eastward, 4° 24′. This 24 howers wee steared S.E. and by S., 5 leages, and N. and by E., 3 leages, with the wind easterly. The compasse varied, from N. to W., 10° 20′.

Tewsday, the 30th. Calme.

Wednesday, the 31th. At noone, in latitude (by observation) 5° 12′, and in longitude, from Cape Galla to the eastward, 5° 6′. This 24 howers wee steared 13 leages East ½ a point Northerly, with the wind at W.S.W. This day the compasse varied, from N. to W., 10° 30′.

Thursday, the first of Aprill 1613. At noone, in latitud (by judgment) 5° 12′, and longitude, from Cape Galla to the eastward, 5° 15′. This 24 howers wee steared E., 3[1] leages, with the wind most commonly calme. The compasse varied, from N. to W., 10° 38′.

Fryday, the 2d. At noone, in latitude 5° 15′, and in longitude, from Galla to the eastward, 5° 50′. This 24 howers wee stered East somewhat Northerly, 12 leages, with the wind variable and calme.

Saterday, the 3d. At noone, in latitude 5° 10′, and in longitude, from Cape Galla to the eastward, [ ]. This 24 howers wee steared East ½ a point Southerly, 15 leages, with the wind southerly. [The] compasse varyed, from N. to W., 9° 30′.

Sunday, the 4th. At noone, the latitude (by observation) 5° 05′, and in longitude, from Cape [Galla] to the eastward, 8° 00′. This 24 howers wee steared Est Southerly, allowing the variation; but wee found that wee have made an E. and by N. way, 30 leages, with the wind [at] S.S.W. And the compasse varyed, from N. to W., 8° 50′. This 24 howers for the most part wee had, as it weare, many riplings, as it weare overfalls[2]; which wee suspect to bee a currante [which] setteth into the northward into the Baye of Bangalla. For wee find one [our ?] shipp to bee further to the northward today then wee weare yesterday by 10′ [*sic*], although wee steared a southerly course.

Munday, the 5t. At noone, in latitude (by judgment) 5° 05′, and in longitude, from Cape Galla to the eastward, 9° 24′. This 24 howers wee steared Est, 28 leages, with the wind at S.W. and much raine.

Tewsday, the 6th. At noone, in latitude (by observation) 5° 10′, and in longitude, from Cape Galla to the eastward, 10° 20′. This 24 howers wee steared Est ½ Southerly, 18 leages, with the wind from the S. to the W. and by N., with much raine and gusty weather.

Wednesday, the 7th. At noone, in latitude (by judgment) 5° 10′, and in longitude, from Cape Galla to the eastward, 11° 20′, which is 20′ to the eastward of Achene. This 24 howers wee steared E., 20 leages, with the wind at W.S.W. by W. Our shipp

[1] Best says 8, and this is the more probable figure.

[2] Breakers, caused either by the sea running over a submerged reef or shoal, or else (as here) by the meeting of contrary currents.

is 20′ to the eastward of the meridian of Achene by my account, and yett wee can see noe land; therfore I judge the currant to sett to the westward, which keepeth us backe, as hereafter wee shall prove by our falling with the land.

Thursday, the 8th. At noone, in the latitud (by observation) 5° 30′. This 24 howers wee steared Est ½ a point N., 10 leages, with the wind variable; and the variation, from N. to W., 7° 25′. This day wee looked out for land, but could see none, although wee weare ashoare by our reckoning; which makes us all to marvell.

Fryday, the 9th. At noone, in latitude (by observation) 5° 20′. This 24 howers wee steared Est and by S., 8 leages, with the wind variable. Our eies are still towards the shoare, but can see none. I thinck wee shall bee at Mallaca, with our reckoning, before wee shall see the land.

Saterday, the 10th. At 5 a clock in the morning wee saw the land. Although it weare long, [at] first the northermost parte boare est of us. This morning the variation of the compasse, from N. to W., 6° 30′; and at noone wee weare in latitud 5° 50′. This 24 howers wee ster[ed] N.E., 15 leages, with the wind at S.E. and S.S.E., faire weather. And at 7 a clocke in the evening wee tackt and stood of[f] till one a clock after midnight, and then wee stood in[to the land], lying E.S.E. in.

Sunday, the 11th. At 6 a clocke in the morning wee weare faire by a little ileland [which] lyeth to the northward of the baye of Achene; and having little wend, the currant drove [us at] a great pace to the northward of him. This ileland is called Gums-paulla[1]. In the evening wee weare betweene the ilelands that lyeth without the baye of Ache[ne], with the wind variable, and much raine and gusty weather.

Munday, the 12th. At 8 a clock in the morning the wind came northerly, and at o[ne a clock] in the afternoone wee came to an anckor in the roade of Achene, finding 2 jon[cks lying] ther at an anckor. Before wee came in they tould us they weare of Surat.

[In the] roade of Achene you may anckor in what depth you will, ether 7, 8, 9, or 10 [fadam], or more or lesse if you please, and ride within saker shott of the shoare. [If] you goe about

[1] Pulo Gomes (see p. 50).

2 myle of[f] the shoare, you shall have noe ground at a 100 [fadam of] lyne, nor any sounding if you bee once 2 or 3 myle of[f] the shoare, not all [ ] about; for wee, being betweene the ilelands in the night, kept the lead going, [but] could have noe ground at 50 or 60 fadam of lyne.

EXTRACTS FROM
ROBERT BONNER'S ACCOUNT OF THE VOYAGE[1]

Notes taken out of M[r]. Robert Boners journall, who was then master in the Dragon.

The first of February [1612], having received in all provisions for so long a voyage, we set saile from Gravesend, and the same day at ten of the clocke we anchored in the Hope.

Aprill the thirteenth, wee had the generall [i.e. trade] wind. Note that you shall seldome meete with the generall wind till you come in two or three degrees to the southward of the Line; and then, when you come to meete with the Ternadoes[2] (as you shall be sure to meete them in two or three, and sometimes in foure degrees, to the northward of the Line), you must be very diligent to ply to the southward, for therein lyeth the mayne of your good or bad passage. And likewise for the health of your men, or they are very unhealthfull. And for passing the Line, order it so, by your course from Maio, that you may passe the Line betwixt seven and ten degrees of longitude from the Lizard. But covet not to come within sixe degrees, for feare of the calmes upon the coast of Guinea[3]; and not without ten degrees of longitude from the Lizard (if it be possible), for feare of meeting with the west-north-west streame that sets alongst the coast of Brasil, and so into the West Indies. And so passing the Line in seven, eight, or nine degrees to the westward of the meridian of the Lizard, you shall not feare the flats of Brasil[4]. For the generall wind will blow at the east-south-east and at south-east; so that you shall make a south-south-west way commonly, and so keepe the ship good full, that she may goe through; for there is losse of time in

[1] From *Purchas His Pilgrimes*, vol. I, p. 479.

[2] Tornadoes (violent tempests common in those regions at certain seasons).

[3] 'This endangered and much hindered the *Dragon* and *Hector* in the Third Voyage, as you may read in the relations thereof' (note by Purchas).

[4] The Abrolhos (or Brazil Bank), a dangerous shoal off the Brazilian coast, extending from lat. 17° to 20° S.

hawking[1] of the ship crosse by the wind; therefore give her a fathome of the sheete.

Note, he that comes out of the sea, bound in for the bay of Soldania, let him keep himselfe betweene thirtie-three degrees, fiftie minutes, and thirtie-foure degrees, twentie minutes, of latitude; so shall you be sure not to come much wide of the bay. If, seeing the land, you find it high, then you are to the south-westward of the bay; if low sand hils, then know that you are to the northward of the bay of Soldania. But falling with the high land to the southward of the bay, which is betwixt the Cape and the Bay, the land lyeth north-north-west and south-south-east from the Cape seven leagues, and then it trents away north-east and south-west, towards the point of the Sugarloafe, some foure leagues; and from this point of the Sugarloafe lyeth Penguin Iland. But keepe faire by the point; for two miles from Penguin Iland lyes a shoales [*sic*]. It is from the point to the iland some seven or eight miles north and south. And so borrowing on the said point, at eight or nine fathome, your course south-east and east-south-east, untill you bring the Table south-south-west and the Sugarloafe hill south-west and by west; and so you may anchor in sixe and an halfe or sixe fathome, as you will. And then will the point of the land by the Sugarloafe beare from you west-north-west, and Penguin Iland north-north-west some three leagues off, and the point some two miles off. The latitude of the bay of Soldania (I meane of the point going in) is thirtie-foure degrees, five minutes[2]; the variation of the needle is fortie minutes easterly. When you come in with the land heereabouts, although it be thicke, feare not; for the land is bold within a cables length.

I am of opinion that the current neere Cape Das Aguilhas sets southerly not past fiftie or sixtie leagues off the land; and therefore, being bound to the eastward, haule off the land sixtie leagues, after you are to the eastward of Cape Das Aguilhas; so shall you find no current. The land lyes from the Cape Das Aguilhas ninetie or one hundred leagues east-northerly, and not, as in the cards, east-north-east.

[1] Mr G. S. Laird Clowes suggests that this is a mistake for 'yawing.'
[2] See note on p. 13.

Ino [*sic*] de Nova is a low ragged iland, about foure miles in length, lying south-south-east and north-north-west. This iland hath latitude seventeene degrees, thirtie minutes, and longitude from the Cape of Good Hope nineteene degrees, fortie minutes etc. Wee had no ground at one hundred fathome. We can perceive no danger from it; only at the south-south-east end of it lies a small breach about a mile off. Therefore feare not to haule in sight of it, being bound this waies; for if you shall haule over for the maine, you shall be mightily troubled with a strong current setting to the southward; and there are likewise many dangerous bankes, whereon many Portugals have lost their ships. Wherefore be sure you haule not much to the westward of this ile Ino de Nova; for you may very boldly haule in sight of it without danger, and so shall you not meete with the current.

The eight and twentieth day of November, we received a letter from M[r]. Canning and our purser concerning foure gallions of war, with thirty saile of frigats, which were comming to fight with us. And this day we saw them some two leagues to the southward of the barre of Surat. This day the Sabandar of Surat came aboord to veiw us, as wee judge, being a friend to the Portugals. But the more he looked the worse he liked, we having all things readie, etc.

The nine and twentieth day, at two in the afternoone, wee set saile and stood with the foure gallions and frigats, which were come within some two leagues of us. The first which we met withall was the vice-admirall. Wee gave her such a welcome as that she was glad to haste unto the rest with all speed. Night being neere, and our long boat sunke at our sterne with an unluckey shot, we anchored.

The thirtieth day, early in the moorning, wee set saile and stood with them; and after some houres fight put three of the gallions ashoare on the offermost sand; and then wee stood into deeper water, and anchored. Their frigats were straight aboord the ships aground, and shoared them up with their yards, or els I thinke they had never come off. As soone as the floud came wee weighed; but they were afloate ere wee could get to them. Wee fought with them till it was darke, and had one man kild and another hurt.

The first day of December 1612, we roade within a league one of the other. Alwayes we had thought they would have come to us, we having gone to them three severall times; but they are not so hastie. I thinke they have more minde to goe for Goa againe.

The nineteenth day, there came a second messenger from a great lord of the Great Mogols, from a place called the Castellet; which place this great man lyes in campe against; sending our Generall word that, if he will but come thwart that place with his ships to grace him, hee will be a sworne friend unto the English for ever. The Generall, hearing that hee was a great man in favour with the King, resolved to goe spend a day or two with him, to see what his desire was.

The twentieth day, we anchored thwart of the campe, beeing close by the seaside, for the castle besieged butted upon the sea; they in the castle being a companie of rebels and rovers on the sea.

The one and twentieth day, upon the receipt of good caution for his person, our Generall landed; and at three returned to ship.

The two and twentieth day, we saw the foure gallions and frigats againe in sight; having beene at Diu for more fresh souldiers, to have a bout more with us. At night they anchored within a mile of us.

The three and twentieth day, by daylight we were under saile and stood with the admirall; and so fought till two of the clocke, at which time they cut their cable and began to runne, the admirall having received a shot under water; but the helpe of the frigats brought her upon the carine presently, and stopped it. And so for this time fled; all the campe standing by the seaside looking on us, within a league or two miles of us. For a great commander did there just by us besiege a castle holden by rebels and pirats, and were willing spectators of this sea-fight.

The foure and twentieth day we stood with them againe, and fought with them till two or three of the clocke in the afternoone. They fled, and, being light ships and cleane[1], went from us. One man kild, and no more hurt; praysed be God for all His

[1] Not encumbered by weeds, etc. adhering to the hull.

mercies. Note that wee have spent sixe hundred [and] eightie great shot and three thousand small shot out of the *Dragon*, and some sixtie barrels of powder. Their admirall had thirtie-eight peeces, and the rest thirtie by ship; very good ordnance. This night we steered for Surat south-east, to haule without the sands. South from Mea[1], some sixe leagues off, lyes the first spit; on which sand the *Ascension* was lost.

The fourth day of February 1612 [1613], wee set saile[2] and stood to the southward; wind at north-north-west.

The fifth day, being some eight leagues short of Cape Comorin, wee met with the wind at east; very much wind. So that we plaine see there is no going to the eastwards, the easterly monson not being done. Heere we anchored at a point of the land; from which point the land trents away east-south-east with the Cape of Comorin, and distant eight leagues. But beware how you come neere this point, for thwart of it foure miles off lyes two sunken rockes close by the edge of the water, and lyes in the streame of twentie or twentie-two fathome; wherefore keepe off in twentie-eight or thirtie fathome, and feare them not. But bee sure that you keepe within thirtie-five or fortie fathome; for the current sets off south with the Maldines[3], and being calme some Portugall ships have beene driven to the Maldines[3], and beene in great danger. You shall know this point from the which these two sunken rockes lye, by this. Thwart of the point lye two bigge rockes, a good heighth above the water. A league right off from the eastermost of the dry rockes lye the two sunken rockes. Where we roade, the two dry rockes did beare from us south-east and by east, foure miles of[f] the northermost. Here the people will come aboord of your ship every day with provisions, as hens and hogges, with linnesse [*sic*] in their little canoes.

The five and twentieth day, at foure a clocke, the Cape of Comorin did beare north-north-west some four leagues off. Note, that the Cape itselfe is very low land, with two craggie rockes lying a little from it; but up in the countrey, high ragged land. The Cape of Comorin hath latitude seven degrees, fiftie minutes; and longitude from the meridian of the Cape of Good

[1] Mahuwa (see note on p. 38). [2] From Brinjaon.
[3] An error for 'Maldives.'

Hope, fiftie-seven degrees, twentie minutes east. The variation is foureteene degrees, thirtie minutes westerly[1]. We have very faire shoalding off from it, twentie-foure fathomes; foure leagues of[f], sand. From the Cape the land trents away east-north-east.

I doe thinke that the Gulf of Cambaya is the worst place in all the Indies for wormes; and therefore the ships which goe for Surat must have good provision. The barre of Surat hath latitude twentie-one degrees, ten minutes; and longitude from the Cape of Good Hope, fiftie-three degrees, thirtie minutes easterly. Variation, sixteene degrees, fiftie minutes westerly[2]. Latitude of Swally is twentie-one degrees, twentie minutes; variation, seventeene degrees, no minutes.

The road of Achen hath latitude five degrees, fortie minutes south; and longitude from the Cape of Good Hope of seventie-three degrees, thirtie-foure minutes east, and from the Cape of Comorin about sixteene degrees, twentie minutes east[3]. The variation is sixe degrees, thirtie minutes westerly. As you ride in the road, one high great iland will beare north of you, distant some sixe leagues; and the two other bigge ilands will beare from the west-south-west to the north-west and by west. Anchorhold good. In the westerly monson you shall have many times very much wind, with gusts of raine; but you shall ride very well. There goes a small current to the eastward and westward, in manner of a tyde, but not so certaine, and heights and fals some five or sixe foot water.

The King loveth our Generall exceeding well; insomuch that hee maketh no sport but hee commands some one of his nobles to goe for the Arrankaia Putee; for soe hath hee named him, so that all the citie through is he called by that name. And all our men by the common people very kindly entertayned, more then ever any strangers heretofore have beene.

In steering north-north-west from the little iland which lyes south-west and by west seven leagues from Priaman Iland, wee saw a shoald bearing from the said little iland south-east and by south, five miles off. We sent our boat to it, who found it but

[1] His figures differ from those of Best (p. 44).
[2] See note on p. 27.
[3] The correct figures are 5° 35′ N. latitude, and 95° 20′ east of Greenwich.

three fathome rockes. From this shoald the homockes of Tecu beare north and by west. Wherefore, beeing bound for Tecu, keepe off so that the homockes may beare north, or north and by east, and feare not. The homockes are two round hils standing upon the low land close by the sea-side. At two a clocke we saw the three little round ilands of Tecu; which ilands you must ride under. They beare of[f] us north and by east, some foure leagues off. Wee steere[d] north, keeping the ilands open on our starboord bow. Note, that by good looking out you shall perceive any danger, by this: it will shew itselfe in white spots. For otherwise the sea is of his perfect colour, as in the maine ocean.

At night wee anchored within two leagues of the two outermost ilands of Tecu, in thirtie fathomes; the ilands bearing north and by east and the homocks north-easterly. Note, the homockes doe stand some three leagues to the northward of the ilands of Tecu; there being in all three of them, but the northermost of the three homockes doth not shew itselfe so perfectly as the other doe.

The seventh of August, in the morning, weighed and plyed in, the wind at the north-north-east. Of[f] the land we see a shoale, bearing from the two offermost ilands of Tecu southwest and by south, foure or five miles off, right in the faireway. We sent our boat to it, and found it but two fathome and a halfe, being a rocke of two cables length long. This is the unluckey rocke whereon the princely *Trade* received her destruction[1], as we understand by those people. About eleven of the clocke we anchored on the easter-side of the uttermost iland, in nine fathome, soft, ozie (praysed be God). Riding under this outward iland of the three, we saw a breach, bearing south halfe easterly, and another south and by east, some three leagues off; which breach, as you come for this place, you must leave betwixt you and the shoare. Wherefore keepe this outer iland north and by east, or north-north-east, and feare nothing. But beware when you come within two leagues of this iland; for south-west and by south, two leagues or five miles off, lyes the rocke whereon the unhappie *Trade* grounded. Wherefore keepe this iland north and

[1] Meaning that by grounding thereon the *Trade's Increase* sprung the leak which led to her subsequent loss at Bantam.

by east, and upon life feare not. Your depth, as you come neere the iland, will bee from thirtie to ten, nine, and eight fathomes, soft, ozie. You shall have nine fathomes within your ships length of[f] either side of the iland.

The ninth day, some people came aboord. We find them very base and subtile.

The eleventh day, the *Hoziander* departed for Priaman, to shew them likewise that wee have brought the Kings letter of Achen, without the which you cannot trade. Note that, as wee ride here, upon the poope we see the foure ilands of Priaman bearing south-east and by south, some seven leagues off.

This day, at nine of the clocke, wee sailed into the inner roade, which is betwixt the mayne and the innermost iland, halfe a mile from the mayne and a cables length from the iland; your depth foure fathome, soft, ozie. Our depth in was twentie-two foot, beeing halfe tyde. It highes and fals some five or sixe foot water. The tyde, as I perceive, runnes twelve houres north-north-west, and twelve houres contrarie. To the northward of all the ilands, in comming in, you shall have foure fathomes and an halfe; but keepe neere the inner iland, for from the mayne on that side lyes a shoald. The ilands are all of one bignesse, being halfe a mile apiece in circuit. They will beare from the south-west and by south to the north-west. Your best water is on the iland; digge a well, and presently [i.e. immediately] water comes[1]

[1] In John Davis's *Ruter* (*Purchas His Pilgrimes*, vol. I, p. 450), he says: 'Upon this ile under which you ride, is a well, made artificially by those that have used to water there.' He adds: 'The people here are covetous and still begging for one thing or other....Here is good trade from Java with junkes; for their pepper they bring them salt, which is verie scant upon this side of the iland. And about September and October there commeth every yeare a Guserate [junk] with cotton cloth to serve this side of the iland, and ladeth away pepper and carrieth away some gold; for gold is more plentie there then silver, as we might plainely see by the countrie people, for they are very desirous of rials of eight. Here is some benjamin to be had, and verie good storax, with other commodities.'

THE NARRATIVE OF THE REV. PATRICK COPLAND

Remembrances taken out of a tractate written by Master Patrike Copland, Minister[1].

In the tropickes are seldome or no stormes, but a smooth sea, with soft gales. Flying fishes are frequent, as bigge as a small whiting; they flye twice the length of a ship. Turnados (gusts within two degrees of the Line) cause all things, specially cloaths, to smell. They had ninetie or a hundred sicke, the rest weake, before they came to Soldania.

The bay of Soldania and all about the Cape is so healthfull and fruitfull as might grow a Paradise of the world. It well agrees with English bodies; for all but one in twentie dayes recovered as at the first day they set forth. They had then, in June, snow upon the hils; the weather warmish. The countrey is mixed: mountaines, plaines, medowes, streames; the woods as if they were artificially planted for order. There is freestone to build with, plentie of fish and fowle, wilde geese, partriches and duckes, antilopes, deere, rivers [*sic*]. They had thirtie nine beeves, one hundred and fifteene sheepe for a little brasse cut out of two or three old kettles. For the sheepe worth one penny, or one penny halfe penny, the piece; the beeves twelve pence. The people are loving; afraid at first, by reason of the unkindnesse of [the] Dutch which came there to make traine oyle, who killed and stole their cattell; and at our returne more kind; of middle size, well limmed, very nimble and active. They dance in true measure. All naked; only weare a short cloke of sheepe or seale skinnes to their middle (the hairie side inward), a cap of the same, and a kind of rats skinne about their privities. Some had a sole on their feet, tyed about. Their neckes were adorned with greasie tripes, which sometimes they would pull off and eat raw. When we threw away their beasts entrailes, they would eate them halfe

[1] From *Purchas His Pilgrimes*, vol. I, p. 466. The 'tractate' does not appear to have been printed, and nothing is known as to its fate.

raw, the bloud lothsomely slavering. Bracelets about their armes they had, of copper or ivorie, with many ostrich feathers and shels. The womens habit is as the mens. They were shamefac't at first; but at our returne homewards they would lift up their rat-skinnes and shew their privities. Their breasts hang to the middle; their haire curled. Copper with them is gold; iron, silver. Their houses little tents in the field, of skins, moveable at pleasure. Their language with doubling the tongue in their throat.

There is a high hill, called the Table, overcovering all the adjoyning territories one hundred miles. Some went and discovered many bayes and rivers. The negroes behaved themselves peaceably at Sinon[1], yet seeme of little or no religion. They cut their skinnes like Baals priests. One seemed (by making price) to be commander.

The Guzerates tooke sea-coale to carry for a wonder to the Mogol. The Portugall fleete was two hundred fortie sayle of frigats (merchants bound for Cambaya, which furnish the carracks), foure gallions, with twenty-five or twentie-sixe frigats. The admirall was Numo de Ancuna[2]. When the Sabandar perswaded him to keep between us and shoare, he answered proudly that he scorned to spend a weekes provision on his men in hindering us, being able to force us to yeeld in an houre. They had all red colours displayed[3]. After three fights they manned a frigat with sixe or seven score best men, to fire us, which were all sunke.

Medhaphrabads[4] is now ruined by the Mogols warres; which sometime hath beene a faire citie and walled. Here was a castle

[1] It may be conjectured that Copland wrote 'sermon.'

[2] To Copland's narrative Purchas (vol. I, p. 478) appends the following extracts from the journal of Nathaniel Salmon: 'The Sabandar counselled the Admirall, Nunha del Cunha, to cause his frigats to ride betwixt the shoare and us, so to keepe us from watering; which he refused. Yea, M[r]. Canning (which had been taken by them) was delivered at our house [in Surat] in scorne, they professing this their only feare and care, least we should run away. The three that were driven aground had there perished, but for their frigats. Out of the fire-frigat were taken up eightie-foure men drowned. The *Dragon* in these fights hath spent sixe hundred [and] thirtie-nine great shot and we three hundred [and] eightie-seven.'

[3] The usual signal that no quarter would be given.

[4] Muzafarābād (see p. 37 *n*).

kept by the Ratspuches [Rājpūts], in which at that time a strong rebell to the Mogoll was besieged by the Nabob, with fiftie or sixtie thousand people in his campe. The Nabob had a stately and spacious tent, covered above with cloth of gold, beneath spread with Turkie carpets. The Generall would not stirre till he had taken the castle. He sent a horse and two vests wrought with silke and gold to our Generall, and foure vests for foure other. They have store of good grapes; yet none but rasin wine[1].

The three and twentieth and foure and twentieth of December, in view of the whole army, we had a second fight, and forced them, first to cut their cables, and then flee from us, being better of saile then we.

I rode to Surat in a coach drawne with oxen (which is most ordinary, though they have store of goodly horses). Here in the way was the goodliest spring and harvest together that ever I saw; the fields joyning, one greene as a meadow, the other yellow as gold, ready to bee cut; their graine wheat and rice. They have excellent bread. All along were goodly villages, full of trees yeelding taddy, like new sweet wine, much strengthening and fatting[2]. Surat hath stone and bricke houses, faire, square, flat-roofed; goodly gardens, with pomegranats, pome-citrons, limons, melons, figs, continuing all the yeere, with curious springs of fresh water. The people are grave, judicious, neat, tall, goodly cloathed in long white callico or silke robes.

The Sabandar assured us that we had killed of the Portugals above three hundred and fiftie. We heard after that there were spoyled and killed above five hundred. The Generall sent letters by land, and the messenger with his Indian were poysoned by two friers homewards; but a second letter was delivered to a mariner, which came to their [i.e. the East India Company's] hands.

The twelfth of Aprill they anchored in the road of Achen,

[1] Wine made from raisins (probably imported from Portuguese India). For an account of the cultivation of grapes in Western India see Watt's *Commercial Products of India*, p. 1112.

[2] Purchas, in his *Pilgrimage* (p. 539), adds, on Copland's authority: 'A smith, which loved his liquor, said hee could wish no other wages but a pot of this taddy alway at his girdle.' For references to the making of toddy see Mundy, vol. II, p. 32 *n*.

where the King welcomed our men. The arancaia came riding in a tent [i.e. howdah] on an elephants backe, with two or three of the Kings boyes (for he is attended with boyes abroad, women within), holding a bason of gold, to receive the Kings letter. Our Generall followed, with fortie or fiftie men. After the letter and present delivered, the King told us we should see some of his pastime, and called for his cockes; which after they have fought about once or twice, they take them up, bath them, picke their feathers, and sow up their wounds. After an houre thus spent in cockfighting, his rammes fought, very fiercely; then his tame elephants, more cruelly; then his buffles, most stomackfully. Finally, our antilopes, wherewith our Generall had presented him; whose fight best pleased him. Hee all this while drinkes tobacco in a silver pipe, given by his women, which are in a close roome behind him. After this, supper was served in by young boyes of foureteene or fifteene yeeres, in swasse[1] (a mettall halfe copper, halfe gold). This supper continued from seven till almost twelve; in which we had foure hundred dishes, with hot drinkes. The next day the King sent the Generall an elephant to ride on, and appointed one of his chiefe arancaias to attend him alwayes. They had continuall free accesse granted, without the Kings creese (which is used as a scepter), and promise to ratifie the articles agreed upon by his predecessors and Sir James Lancaster.

The second of May all strangers were invited to a banquet sixe miles off; for which purpose two elephants were sent for our Generall. Here were all the dishes brought by water; the boyes holding the dish with one hand and swimming with the other (so did they carrie the strong drinke also); whereof when they had tasted (which they must of all), they threw the rest into the river. It continued from one till five. In it were five hundred dishes, well dressed. Our Generall, weary with sitting by the King thus long in the water, was dismissed an houre before the rest. The Captaine of the Dutch house, taking there his bane, either with hot drinke or cold sitting so long in the water, soone after died.

The second of June they were entertained with a fight of foure elephants with a wild tygre, tied at a stake; which yet, fastening on their trunks and legges, made them to roare and bleed ex-

[1] Malay *suasa*, gold alloyed with copper.

treamely. This day we were told that one eye of a nobleman was plucked out, for looking on one of the Kings women washing in a river. Another gentleman, wearing a shash[1], had his head round cut so farre as that was too large. Some he is said to boyle in scalding oyle; some are sawne apeices; others their legges cut off, or spitted alive, or empaled on stakes.

The twentie-fifth [*sic*] was before the King a fight of wild elephants; which would quickly kill each other, but that some tame are made fast to them, which draw them backe; sometime eighty or an hundred men helping. They set one wild betweene two tame to tame them.

He sent the King a letter (for painting and writing most stately), a creese, etc., for a present.

The letter is thus Englished[2].

Peducka Sirie[3] Sultan, King of Kings, renowmed for his warres, and sole king of Sumatra, and a king more famous then his predecessors, feared in his kingdome and honoured of all bordering nations: in whom there is the true image of a king: in whome raignes the true methode of government: formed (as it were) of the most pure metall and adorned with the most finest colours: whose seat is high and most compleat, like to a christall river, pure and cleare as the christall glasse: from whom floweth the pure streame of bountie and justice: whose presence is as the finest gold: King of Priaman and of the mountaine of gold, viz. Solida[4], and lord of nine sorts of stones[5], king of two

[1] Turban (see p. 164).

[2] Purchas reprints the letter in his *Pilgrimage* (p. 614).

[3] This (Dr Blagden tells me) is an honorific title commonly used in the Malay region, in the form *sĕri paduka*. These two words are derived from the Sanskrit *śrī*, 'splendour, luck,' and *pādukā*, 'shoe'; the monarch being so exalted that the ordinary mortal dares not lift his eyes beyond the royal footgear. The King of Achin's formal title is given as Sultan Raja Iskandar Muda Johan Bĕrdaulat; though in a letter to James I in 1615–16 (Bodleian Library, *Laud Or. b.* 1 (*R*)) he appears to style himself Sultan Perkasa Alam Johan Bĕrdaulat (see an article by the Rev. W. G. Shellabear in the *Journal of the R.A.S., Straits Branch*, July 1898, p. 123).

[4] Sillida (Talang), south-east of Padang, in Sumatra. The Dutch started gold-mining there about 1670, but discontinued it in 1694, as the results were not commensurate with the great expenses incurred. See Elias Hesse's *Gold-Bergwerke in Sumatra*, 1680–83 (The Hague, 1931).

[5] Sanskrit *nava ratna*, an arm-ornament composed of the nine precious stones, viz. diamond, ruby, emerald, sapphire, topaz, pearls, coral, hyacinth, and carbuncle.

sombrieroes[1] of beaten gold, having for his seats mats of gold, his furniture for his horses and armour for himselfe being likewise of pure gold, his elephant with teeth of gold and all provisions thereunto belonging, his lances halfe gold, halfe silver, his small shot of the same, a saddle also for another elephant of the same metall, a tent of silver, and all his seales halfe gold, halfe silver, his vessels for bathing of pure gold, his sepulchre of gold (whereas his predecessours had all these halfe gold, halfe silver)[2], his services compleat of gold and silver: a king under whom there are many kings, having taken the king of Arrow[3]: all the countrey of Priaman, Tecoo, Barouse[4], beeing subdued by him, is now under his command: seventie elephants and much provisions carried by sea to make his warres at Arrow, where God gave me more victory then any of my predecessors. This great king sendeth this letter of salutation to James, King of Great Britaine, viz. England, Scotland, France, and Ireland, to signifie the great content he hath received by His Highnesse letter, delivered by the hands of Arancaia Pulo[5], Thomas Best, His Majesties embassadour: at the receipt whereof his eyes were surprized with a celestiall brightnesse and his spirits ravished with a divine joy; the opening thereof rendred a savour more fragrant then the most odoriferous flowers or sweetest perfumes in the world. For which cause I, the great King of Sumatra, doe profese myselfe to bee of one heart, of one mind, and of one flesh with the most potent prince James, K[ing] of England, and do earnestly desire that the league begun may be continued to all posterities. And herein I take my greatest felicitie, there being

[1] State umbrellas (Port. *sombriero*).

[2] See note on p. 175 and the royal letter mentioned on p. 211 *n*. In the latter, as translated by Mr Shellabear, the monarch calls himself 'the king who has provided for his own monument with a monument of gold, styled Mĕgat Ālam, descendant of the kings with monuments of gold alloy.' 'Mĕgat Ālam' in this connection is difficult to understand; and Dr Blagden thinks that we should read 'Makota Ālam' ('Crown of the World') and take it as referring, not to the monument, but to the monarch himself.

[3] Aru was at one time a powerful kingdom on the north-east coast of Sumatra, extending from Achin to the river Rokan, but after a long struggle it was conquered by the Achinese in 1612.

[4] Baros (or Barus), on the western coast of Sumatra, in about 2° N. latitude.

[5] Read *puto* (for *putih*; see p. 56 *n*).

nothing in the world more pleasant or joyfull to me. And for a testimony of my desire that the league and amitie begun may be continued betwixt us, I have returned this letter unto Your Majestie, making also my prayers unto the Great God for the continuance of the same. And it shall be my greatest honour to receive memoriall from so great a potentate and so remote a nation. And for a pledge of my love and honour, and continuance of our league, I send Your Majestie a creese wrought with gold (the hilt thereof being beaten gold), with a ring of stones, an assagaya [see p. 58] of swasse (halfe copper, halfe gold), eight purslan [porcelain] dishes (small and great) of camfire [camphor], one piece of sowring stuffe, three pieces of calico lawne: which Your Majestie accepting as from a brother, I shall rest satisfied and much honoured. And so, with my prayers to the Great God, creator of heaven and earth, for Your Majesties long life, with victory over your enemies and prosperitie in your land. Given at our pallace of Achen, the 1022 yeere of Mahomet[1], by the accompt of the Moores.

This king of Achen is a proper gallant man of warre, of thirty-two yeares, of middle size, full of spirit, strong by sea and land. His countrey populous. His elephants many, whereof wee saw one hundred [and] sixtie or one hundred [and] eightie at a time. His gallies and frigats carry in them very good brasse ordnance, demicanon, culverin, sakar, minion, etc. His building stately and spacious, though not strong. His court at Achen pleasant, having a goodly branch of the maine river about and through his pallace; which branch he cut and brought sixe or eight miles off in twenty dayes, while we continued at Achen. Sumatra is very mountainous and woodie. The people courteous; wept at our departure, leaving little[2]. Without his chop strangers may neither come at him nor depart from him. He desired the Generall to commend him to the King of England and to entreat him to send him two white women; for (said hee) if I beget one of them with child, and it proove a sonne, I will make him King of Priaman, Passaman, and of the coast from whence you fetch your pepper; so that yee shall not need to come any

[1] A.H. 1022 began on 11 February 1613 (O.S.).
[2] Something seems to have been omitted here.

more to mee, but to your owne English king for these commodities[1].

July the twelfth we tooke leave of Achen. The ninth of August they went on shoare at Tecoo. Here they stayed eleven weekes; bought one hundred [and] twenty tunne of pepper: buried twenty-five men, which got their death at Passaman, for Tecoo is healthfull. Pepper growes most at Passaman and the countrey about.

[1] This remarkable proposal quickly bore fruit. On 9 November 1614 a 'gentleman of honourable parentage' presented himself at a meeting of the Court of Committees and offered to send out his daughter—described as 'very beautifull and personable' and endowed with 'most excellent parts for musicke, her needle, and good discourse.' The Committees were unwilling to lend themselves to the scheme, and, on the application being renewed three weeks later, shelved it by referring the gentleman to King James. As nothing more is heard of the matter, we may conclude that wiser counsels prevailed. (See *John Company*, p. 22.)

EXTRACTS FROM THE NARRATIVE of NICHOLAS WITHINGTON[1]

Havinge provided all thinges necessarye for soe longe a voyage, wee wayed anchoure on the firste of Februarye 1611 [1612] from Gravesende; from whence wee sailed with prosperous wynds and wether[2] untill the eighth of June followinge, when wee came to the Cape Bona Speransa, where our Generall wente on shoare. And havinge manye of our men sicke, hee caused the tents to bee pitched and our sicke men to bee brought on shoare. The people of the countrye brought us downe some sheepe and cowes, which wee bought of them, givinge for a sheepe a little peece of brasse and for a cowe three peeces; which brasse may be vallewed at 2*s*. the three peeces. Theire sheepe have noe woole on their backs, but haire verye large; beeinge reasonablye well fleshed, with exceedinge greate tayles. Theire beeves [oxen] are like ours; verye large of bone, but leane for the moste parte.

The people of that countrye are negrose, with woollye pates, flat nosed, and verye straight of bodye. The men have but one stone apeece; the other is cutt out when they bee younge. They goe apparrelled with a skinne about theire shoulders, which reacheth downe to theire waste. They have the skinne of a ratte to hange before theire privie members, and another on theire buttocks; or else all naked. Some of them weare capps of leather made

[1] Withington had come out as an attendant upon Captain Best. His original narrative was available to Purchas, who paraphrased or quoted from it in his *Pilgrimes* (part I, book IV, chap. 8). It was again made use of in 1735, when another series of extracts was published as an appendix (itself dated 1734) to a narrative of the Central American travels of John Cockburn. The anonymous editor of that volume states that he made use of Withington's original manuscript, but says nothing regarding the whereabouts of the document; nor has it since been traced. In the text the 1734 version has been followed, as being much fuller than that given by Purchas. Since, however, the extracts made by the latter include some passages omitted by the eighteenth-century editor, these have for the most part been restored, either in notes or as interpolations (between square brackets).

For a complete account of Withington's remarkable adventures see my *Early Travels in India*, p. 188.

[2] 'The eleventh of April 1612 we crossed the equinoctiall. Foule weather eight daies together, wind and raine' (*Purchas*).

close to theire pates, and shoe-soles tyed to their feete, much broader and longer then theire feete. Theire armes wherewith they fighte are launces verye small, with heades artificially [i.e. skilfully] made. They have likewise bowes and arrowes, but of little or noe force. They are verye experte in throweing theire darts, for they would runne into the sea by the shore-syde and kill much fishe with flynginge of theire darts, in a small tyme, and come and sell us them for little snippes of brasse or copper. They weare aboute theire neckes fatt gutts of sheepe or oxen, which smell unsaverilye; and when they are hungrye, will eate them. They will eate any garbage, bothe rawe and fowle. When wee had killed an oxe or a sheepe at anye time, they would scramble for the offall, like doggs, and eate yt.

In this baye of Saldama[1] lyeth a lowe iland called Penguye[2] [*sic*], by the name of the aboundance of penguins that are theron; which are fowles without wings, aboute the bignesse of a goose. They are good to eate, but somewhat ranke. There is allsoe in this iland aboundance of seales; whereof wee coughte some. In fyne, the inhabitants of the place live like miserable people, as indeede they are.

The 28th of June 1612 wee departed from the baye of Saldama with prosperous wyndes, saylinge on in our voyage[3] untill the 13th day of Auguste, when wee crossed the equinoctiall lyne. And the 30th daye wee sawe snakes swyminge in the sea, beeinge in the height of eighteene and a halfe degrees to the norward of the equinoctiall[4]. And soe wee sayled on untill the fourth of September, when wee came within foure leagues of the barr of Suratt; where wee mett with the *Ozeander*, beeinge one of our fleete, whoe was rydinge at an anchoure there, havinge gotten a pilott out of a boate of the countrye and lefte one of our carpenters mates in hostage for him; whoe, unwiselye carryinge some moneye aboute him, when the Moores were from the

[1] Doubtless 'Saldania' in the MS.

[2] Robben Island (see p. 13).

[3] 'The six and twentieth of July they had sight of Saint Laurence' (*Purchas*).

[4] 'The first of September they saw land. The second anchor against Daman towne, inhabited and conquered by Portugalls. The fluxe [i.e. dysentery] infested them all that remained on land at Surat; Mr Aldworth was sicke forty dayes' (*Purchas*).

shippe, they cutt his throate and tooke what hee had (as afterwards wee were certaynlye informed).

Uppon the 7th of the same moneth wee arrived at the barre of Suratt in the East-Indeases; and the thirteenth day wee came to Suratt, and were kyndlye entertayned of the Governor and the chiefes of the cittye. There is an order in this cuntrye that strangers cominge to visite an inhabitante (bee hee a man of anye fashion) doe presente him with somethinge or other, and not to come to him emptye-handed; insomuch that our people which wee sente firste on shore, having nothing but money aboute them to give for presents, were fayne to presente the Governor of the cittye, and other chiefe men, with each a royall of eight; which they kyndlye accepted, takinge yt for a greate honour to bee presented, though the presente bee but small.

[Notwithstanding Sir Henry Middleton taking their ships in the Red-sea, yet they promised us good dealing, considering else they must burne their ships (said Mill Jeffed [Mīr Jafar], one of the chiefe merchants of Surat) and give over their trade by sea. Impossible it was to have any trade at Surat, by reason of Portugall frigats in the rivers mouth; therefore the Generall repaired with his ships to Swally, whence he might by land go and come without danger. The third [*sic*] of October Sheke Shuffe[1], Governour of Amadavar, chiefe citie of Guzerat, came to Surat and so to Swally, and agreed upon articles. Master Canning had been taken by the Portugals, but the Vice-Roy commanded to set him ashoare at Surat, saying: Let him goe helpe his countrymen to fight, and then we will take their ship and the rest of them altogether. But the purser made an escape and so came to us on land. Master Canning was set on shoare at Surat, according to promise, and so went aboord.]

Here wee remayned trading untill the 29th of November; when the same daye, our shippes lying in the mouth of the river of Suratt, fower Portungale gallioons, with a whole fleete of frigotts, came in sight of our two shippes (or rather one shippe and a pynnace). Then our Generall (in the *Dragon*) presentlye

[1] Kerridge writes the name as 'Shekisuphe,' 'Shekysuphe' (both in *O.C.* 170) and 'Sheak Isuph' (see his letter of 26 May 1616, below). These spellings, and the one in the text, suggest that it was really 'Shaikh Yūsuf.' As noted on p. 31, he was only the acting 'Governour.'

wayed anchoure, and worthelye encouraged our men not to feare them nor the greatnesse of theire shippes or fleete, but to shew themselves true Englishmen; and soe mett their admirall and vize-admirall, and shott not one shoote till hee came betweene them, and then gave each of them a broadsyde and a brave volleye of shott, which made them give way and come noe more neare her that daye. The other shippes were not as yett come uppe, and the *Ozeander* could not gett cleare of her anchours, soe shee shott not one shoote that daye; but the *Dragon* supplyed her wante verye well. And it drawinge neare night, they all came to anchoure within sight of each other; and the next morninge wayed anchours againe and beganne theire fight, in which the *Ozeander* bravely redeemed the tyme shee loste the daye before. The fyrye *Dragon*, bestiringe herselfe, in some three howers hott feight drove three of the gallions on the sands; and then the *Ozeander*, drawinge little water, daunced the haye[1] aboute them, and soe payed them that they durste not shewe a man on theire deckes; killinge and spoylinge their men, and battered theire shipps exceedinglye. In the afternoone, the flud beeinge come, the gallionns, with the helpe of the friggots, were aflote agayne, and receaved a brave welcome of our shippes; with whom they continued feight about foure howers, but much to theire disadvantage and our greate honour. It beeinge nowe night, wee came to our anchours, and theire rode that night and all the nexte daye, without meddling each with other. And the daye after, the *Dragon* drawinge much water, and the baye shallowe, the Generall wente from thence and rode on the other syde of the baye, at a place called Mendrofrobag [see p. 37]; where all that tyme Sardar Chaune[2], a great nobleman of the Mogulls, with 2000 horses, was beseidginge a castle of the Rasbooches [Rājpūts], a caste of Gentills[3] and formerly (before the conqueste of Guyseratt by the Mogull) greate nobles of the cuntrye, but

[1] A country dance, in which the performers wound in and out. Purchas (*Pilgrimage*, 1626, p. 525) repeats the phrase, and goes on to amplify it by saying that the *Hosiander* 'played like a salmon (my friend, Mr. Nathaniel Salmon, was master and commander in her), swimming, frisking lightly (but not with light effect), leaping about these huge whale carkasses.'

[2] See note on p. 38.

[3] Hindus; from Port. *gentio*.

nowe live by robbinge and spoylinge poore passengers by the waye. Of this nobleman was our Generall verye honourablye entertayned, and presented with a gallante horse and furniture; which horse our Generall afterwards presented to the Governour of Goga, a porte-towne to the westward of Suratt.

About ten dayes after the shippes staye, where they had trade and commerce with this people, the Portungale shippes and friggots, havinge replenished theire wants with store of freshe men, came thether to our shippes; which made Sardar Chaune, allthough he had heard wee had put them to the worste on the other syde in our former fighte, yet, seeinge theire greate odds, bothe in bignesse and quantitye, through his love to our Generall was verye fearfull of the [e]vente of the fighte and counselled our Generall to flye; which hee smyling at, tould him that (God willinge) hee should see theire greate number should not avayle them against him. And soe, havinge all his men aboard, wayed anchoure and with a brave resolution sett on them, beatinge and spoyling them in such fashion that theire whole defence was in flyinge away; and in fower houres space wee drove them cleane out of our sight, and retorned and anchored with perpetuall honoure; this fight beeing before thowsands of the countrye people, whoe (to our nations greate fame) have devulged the same farr and neare. Sardar Chann, after the rasinge of his castle and takinge the rebbells, repayringe to the Greate Mogull, related to him at large the discourse of this fighte; which made the Kinge admire much, formerlye thinkinge there had bin noe nation comparable to the Portungale by sea.

The 27th of December 1612 our shippes, retorninge againe, came to Suallye, havinge loste in all the fightes with the four Portungales only three men, and those saylors; and one man loste his arme, shott off with a greate shott; not anye else of our companye either hurte or wounded (thanks bee to God). But the Portungales on the contrarye (as wee have ben since certaynlye informed by those that sawe moste of them buryed) had slayne 160 men. Some reporte 300 and odd, but themselves confesse 160; but sure theire losse was more then they will confesse.

The 13th of Januarye 1612 [1613] I, beeinge in Suratt, was

sente for aboard by the Generall; where, by a counsaile, I was entertayned and bounde to the Worshippfull Companye of Marchaunts, and in regard of my languadge[1] (which others of theire factors wanted) I was appoynted to remayne in Suratt as a factor. And having entred into a bonde of 400*l.* for the accomplishment of my service, I was this day dispeeded from the Generall and retorned to Suratt. Theis and manye other things accomplished, wee for the cuntrye were set on shore; and the 18th of Januarye 1612 [1613] the shippes departed for England; the gallionns never offering one shott at them, havinge ridden manye dayes in sight of them.

[1] In a letter of 9 November 1613 (in Brit. Mus. *Egerton MS.* 2086, f. 10) Withington refers to his having been at Fez (Morocco) 'some three years past.' Presumably he had there acquired some knowledge of Arabic.

BOCARRO'S ACCOUNT OF THE FIGHTING IN THE GULF OF CAMBAY[1]

Although Nuno da Cunha received his instructions from the Viceroy Lourenço de Tavora, yet the outcome of his expedition fell as it were within the viceroyalty of Dom Hieronymo de Azevedo, with which this work begins; and therefore it is our business to give an account of it here.

Nuno da Cunha set out from Goa in November 1612, with a squadron of four galleons, being himself in command of one, while the captains of the other three were Francisco de Miranda Henriques, Gaspar de Mello de Sampaio, and Manuel de Andrade Beringel...[2]. The vessels had been fitted out as well as time permitted—quite well enough to deal with all other nations[3], but leaving much to be desired in a conflict with a European enemy. Thus, proper ordnance was lacking, for none of the galleons except the flagship carried as many as twenty-eight guns; of the others, one had eighteen, and the remaining two still less. There was also a great deficiency of gunners, especially of skilled men. Few Portuguese sailors were available, and hence it was necessary to employ in their place Moslem lascars—sailors who, as they go to sea merely for gain, do their best to avoid fighting, because it does not profit them. Finally, the galleons, although large and strong, were very sluggish in comparison with their opponents—a matter of importance in naval warfare. The only things they did not lack were good leaders and soldiers of tried valour.

The fleet proceeded to Surat, without any incident on the way worth mentioning. The same day on which it arrived, the English, who were lying in the Pool [of Swally] with one ship and a pinnace (*patacho*), at once came out, fearing lest they should be boarded if they remained in the Pool; and, trusting in the swift-

[1] *Decada* 13, pp. 24–31. Professor Prestage has kindly revised my translation of the Portuguese text, which is not free from obscurities.

[2] Then follows a list of Portuguese gentlemen who embarked in the fleet.

[3] Meaning, probably, all *Eastern* nations.

ness of their vessels, they encountered our galleons at four o'clock in the afternoon and fought with them until dark. In this fight they killed many of our men; though none of our vessels failed to do her part and to give as much as she received. On our side there died this day thirty[1], more or less, according to the small information I could obtain on the point. Nor could I discover the names of the dead, in order to perpetuate their memory, or for their honour and for the satisfaction of those bound to them by friendship, by blood, or even by acquaintance. The soldiers, seeing the slaughter made by the enemy's artillery and finding themselves denied the time or opportunity to show their valour in the vengeance they wished to take and could have taken, cursed the first inventor of that contrivance, which is the consumer and destroyer of all the valiant men of the world.

Night having come, the combatants separated, and our galleons anchored, owing to the great currents there are in those latitudes. And at daylight the ship and the pinnace again attacked the galleons, and the artillery combat was renewed, and was fought on both sides with all possible fervour. And as the galleon of Gaspar de Mello was putting its bowsprit on the stern of the enemy pinnace, in order to board her, the galleon went aground, and the pinnace saved herself over the shoals or sandbanks that are in the sea around the Pool of Surat. The same misfortune happened to Manuel de Andrade Beringel, when he endeavoured to overtake and board the English ship. The reason was that, as the enemy vessels were more *apatanadas*[2] than ours, they drew much less water, and thus could retreat when necessary or attack when they pleased, not making it a point of honour never to show their backs, as our men did in fighting with them; for, being ships of war, we should feel it a great disgrace to avoid an encounter; while they, relying only on artillery fire from a dis-

[1] Meaning, probably, thirty of the Portuguese (ignoring the losses among the lascars).

[2] I owe to Captain C. R. Boxer the ingenious explanation (confirmed by two Portuguese experts) that this is a misprint for *apatamadas*, meaning '*patamar*-like'—*patamar* being a well-known Indian term for a light sailing vessel. This applies very well to the *Hosiander*, which was doubtless built specially for service in shallow waters; and Bocarro may naturally have concluded (though wrongly) that the *Dragon* had been constructed on similar lines.

tance, withdrew or came on as they pleased, being enabled to do so by the handiness of their vessels, which were well fitted and better sailers than ours. If ours were placed on a footing of equality with theirs in these respects, better results might be expected; but in India this can rarely be attained, seeing that, as the voyages[1] are so numerous and the seamen receive such good wages, all devote themselves to those expeditions, and nothing can prevent them, owing to the vast extent of the Portuguese territory[2]. But as war is only an invention to enable each man to get the better of his enemy, all who can should make use of every possible means to that end, save those that are infamous.

Nuno da Cunha and Francisco de Miranda, seeing that the two galleons had run aground, themselves steered away from the sandbank and anchored; and the enemy ship was now far off. When the tide turned in the afternoon, the galleon of Gaspar de Mello floated off before that of Manuel de Andrade, and rejoined the flagship. The latter, together with the galleon of Francisco de Miranda, while the other two were aground, was attacked by the English ship alone, and both sides fought briskly with their guns. In the meantime the [English] pinnace was sent to engage the galleons that were on the sands; and since she drew little water, she got very near to Manuel de Andrade's vessel (which was more firmly aground), and from both sides poured in many shots, spending all her force upon this ship and doing her great damage. However, at the turn of the tide she got afloat and went to the flagship. Dom Francisco Soutomaior, with the Fleet of the North, was present at this day's action. He was in command of twelve vessels; but, as he had no orders to fight with ships and pinnaces, he did nothing except render aid to our galleons in whatever manner he was directed to do or thought would be to their benefit. As they saw that any pinnace of ours, armed with its four falcons, could pass all along the coast of India in defiance of large squadrons of native boats, which attack with all resolution and courage, it seemed strange that we could not do more

[1] *Viagens*. These were the ventures to China, the Moluccas, etc., granted or sold by the Viceroys, in trades which had been declared monopolies.

[2] Bocarro's meaning seems to be that the expert pilots and seamen devoted themselves to these profitable voyages to distant ports, and consequently it was impossible to secure their services at Goa in an emergency like the present.

against these enemies. Nevertheless, the resolution of the Portuguese in this particular exceeds everything, and they are so eager and desirous to try any way with these enemies except artillery fire that they even board sailing ships with oared boats, a plan which many times has not been attended with good success.

The battle on the second day ended when our four galleons were re-united, for when the enemy saw them together, knowing that our aim was to board them and thus deprive them of the advantage of their ordnance, they sailed off to the opposite coast of the gulf. Thus at daybreak they were out of the sight of our fleet; and on Luiz de Brito de Mello arriving from Diu, of which he was Captain-General, he brought intelligence that the English were making for that coast. Thereupon the Commander-in-Chief, Nuno da Cunha, made the signal to weigh anchor and sailed in pursuit, ordering Luiz de Brito to find out exactly where the enemy was and come to inform him. This Luiz de Brito accomplished successfully; for when Nuno da Cunha was lying with the galleons off the bar of Diu, Luiz de Brito came to him with the news that the English were at Castellete, which is on the coast [*blank*] leagues below Diu. Nuno da Cunha proceeded without delay to that spot, ordering the other three galleons of his squadron to board the enemy at night. But afterwards he countermanded this order, on finding that the English were anchored in three fathoms only of water, a depth far too shallow for our galleons. This the enemy had purposely done, for fear of such an attempt on our part.

At daybreak, when they saw our vessels, they at once came to meet them. This they did for fear of losing reputation with a captain of the Great Mogul's, who was beleaguering the fortress of Castellete and was bombarding it with two pieces of heavy ordnance, which we had lent him for that purpose from the fortress of Diu. Our reason for doing this was that it would suit us well to have this nest of [piratical] craft destroyed. These boats were continually at Castellete, and the black captain of that place favoured and aided them, on account of the money they paid him when he rose in rebellion against his own king. The result was that all this coast was notably infested by the pirates, and suffered thereby great detriment.

Our galleons fought with the enemy for two days from sunrise to sunset, without once having an opportunity of boarding, by reason that the English ship and pinnace were much more agile than the galleons; and moreover, they were careful not to fight unless they had the weather-gage, and every time that we endeavoured to get near them they turned to windward. Thus they slew many of our people, while we could not learn what loss we were causing them. When you cannot see, you can never be sure, and can only rely on inferences from the fact that our galleons did not cease from shooting; and as the hulls of the enemy must have received many shots, there must have been loss of life.

On the second day of the fight the flagship was struck by a shot which caused a fire in her lower deck; and so burning, as could well be seen, she turned towards the land. Her three consorts came up to her to help as far as they could and learn her condition. When they reached her, they found that she had already managed to extinguish the fire, though with great labour; two cabins on that deck having been burnt out and much damage done. At this time the enemy ship hoisted a square black flag, as a sign that their chief commander was dead[1], and made sail again for Surat. The pinnace did the same, abandoning the fight and crowding on sail.

The Captain-General, Nuno da Cunha, returned to Castellete, to see whether he could induce the Captain of that fortress to surrender to him rather than to the negro forces that were beleaguering and bombarding him. He sent the Captain a message to this effect, by a soldier named Hieronymo de Figueiroa, who negotiated in such wise that the negroes thought it better to yield to Nuno da Cunha than to the Moguls, who would, they feared, put them all to death. But, as wicked men are fearful and suspicious of all, the Captain of Castellete, thinking that, as he had obtained security from Nuno da Cunha, the Moors would not interfere with him, refused to surrender to the Captain-General; and one morning at daybreak he and his associates forsook the fortress and, mounting their horses, fled into the country. However, the Moguls pursued and slew them all,

[1] This was, of course, an error. Possibly Best was signalling to the *Hosiander* to break off and follow him.

without sparing one. It is the just judgment of God that those who in their wickedness will not trust anybody find succour in none.

The next morning the Moguls entered the fortress, and sent word to Nuno da Cunha that he had better go speedily in search of the English, as there was nothing more for him to do at that place. And they proceeded to pull down the fort, leaving not one stone on another, in order that it should not be used again or rebuilt, nor any opportunity be given to cause them similar trouble in future.

Nuno da Cunha, without making any delay, sailed for Surat in search of the English in the direction he had been told they had gone. He arrived in the afternoon, when it was too late to attack. Next day at dawn he sighted the ship and the pinnace, which thereupon set sail, keeping in shallow water (having no cargo on board) and showing no willingness to come to a fight. Nuno da Cunha followed them vigorously with his galleons as far as he could, until, being so much swifter (as already mentioned), they were lost to sight. Then, recognizing that further pursuit would be useless, he returned to Surat, and there consulted with his captains how he could attack the factory which the English had established in that city. It was decided to send someone up thither to ascertain how matters stood, in order that they might then judge what course to take; and so Gaspar de Mello was despatched in disguise, to look into and consider the whole situation with his usual prudence and judgment. His report was that the situation was such that nothing could usefully be done. At the same time he confirmed the news that we had slain the enemy's commander-in-chief and many of their people.

Nuno da Cunha, seeing that he could do nothing more there, set sail for Goa, calling on his way at the fortresses of the North, to ascertain whether he could perform any service to His Majesty at those ports. Arriving at Chaul, he found that they were at open war with the Melique[1], on which account he was begged to leave there some of his people. He accordingly put on shore four companies, each of thirty men, under the command

[1] Malik Ambar, the generalissimo of the King of Ahmadnagar and the real ruler of that part of India.

of Pero Gomes de Sousa, Pero Gomes o Villão, Gonçalo de Proença, and Luiz Tello de Meneses. Then setting sail for Goa, he arrived there in March 1613, and was received with every token of joy by Dom Hieronymo de Azevedo, then established as Governor. And although some said that, in view of Nuno da Cunha's reputation, he had not accomplished much in that expedition, yet, as such persons had not much experience of fighting with the English and the Dutch in large vessels, and considering the differences already pointed out and the defects on our side, as well as the advantages possessed by the enemy in sailors, gunners, and artillery, it was afterwards considered, for these reasons and taking into account the successes we afterwards had against the enemy when we were stronger, that Nuno da Cunha had well discharged the duty entrusted to him and had not disappointed expectations; for if he could not capture the enemy, for the reasons given, he compelled him to leave the harbour, flee, and go away without cargo, all in sight of the people of the country. If such a result could always be obtained, it would be for this State one of the greatest benefits it could receive.

A REGISTER OF WILLS, DEBTS, ETC. IN THE *DRAGON*[1]

Thirty-one pages of accounts of debts due from various members of the ship to others. Most entries are undated; in others the dates range from 30 October to 2 December, 1613. The following names occur: John Amian, Robert Balderston, Phillipp Bardon, Thomas Best, Christopher Bodam, Robert Bonner, Thomas Browne, Georg Burgen, William Burneett, John Bushnell, Thomas Carrwell (master cook), John Choak, Aldaine (or Alban) Clarke, John Coockins, Raph Croft, Gabriell Daves (boatswain), Thomas Daves, William Diamond, John Dier, William Ellmes, Robert Fenny, John Filder, William Finsh, Pearccc Flod, Georg Frie, Georg Furnacce, John Gonsallv[e]s (Indian), John Gray, William Gressam (master trumpeter), James Hadellsey, Richard Harrolde, Davee Hewghes, Gilles Hilles, William Holmes, Thomas Hounsell, John Isack, Francis Johnson (of the *Trades Increase*), Thomas Joones (merchant), Petter Jooson (Dutchman), Henrie Longe, Christopher Luther (merchant), Hermon Lyne, John Mahomeett, John Mapletton, John Marichurch, Rychard Marrow, Robert Marshall, Henry Miller, Robertt Mortton, John Murfitt, Patterick Naren, William Nealle, William Newball (master surgeon), Tobias Olliver, John Patteson, Thomas Patteson, Robart Percie, Thomas Percie (or Percce), William Perfey, Henry Pokinghorne, Georg Power (surgeon's mate), Edward Ravens, Edward Roads, John Rosse, Henrie Rudes, Nathaniell Sallmon, John Santh the elder, Thomas Settcoale, John Simes, Man Smith, Watter Staccie, Raph Standich, Rychard Tatten, William Tuck (Scotsman), Anthony Tuttie, John Wattson, James Weebber, John West, John Windress, John Yeamans.

After the index are entered the wills of (1) Robert Healo (dated 29 September 1613), (2) Olliver Judson (dated 1613), (3) Robert Porttman (dated 18 October 1613; he died 29 October). The witnesses include John Whitter, John Daves, Robert Abell, and Patterick Coupland.

[1] I.O. *Marine Records*, no. XVI. On the third page is the title: 'The acco[unt] of Inventoryes in the *Dragon*, 29 Occtober.'

CORRESPONDENCE

Thomas Best at Swally Road to *the Governor and Company of the Merchants Trading to the East Indies*

14 January 1613[1]

Worshipful Sir and the rest of the Company,

I let Your Worships know that, leaving the Isle of Wight on 21 February, on the 27th our mainyard broke. It was not until 5[2] March that we fixed it again, and meanwhile we had to keep our mainsail lowered. On 21[3] April we crossed the Line, and on 22 May the mainyard broke once more. On the 29th of the same we got it again into position, and in the interim we were forced to use our topsail only; yet we managed to keep company with the rest of the fleet.

On 8 June we entered the bay of Saldania, together with the *Hosiander* and the *Solomon*. The *James* had lost company with us at the Cape of Good Hope, within sight of land, in a very great storm, two nights before we reached Saldania. Since then we have had no news of her. Here we refreshed, and departed on the 28th of the same month. The *Solomon* left us, with the intention of making her way to Bantam; while I, with the *Dragon* and the *Hosiander*, directed our course for Surat. On 13 July our mainmast was endangered by the weight of the mainyard; on which account I took down our topmast, and did not dare to keep the mainyard aloft, but lowered the mainsail. This state of things continued until we reached Surat; so we sailed two thousand miles without using our mainsail.

We arrived on 7 September, and the same day sent on land three or four merchants. On 17 October the governor of all these parts came to the seaside with a great following. On the 19th I landed, having first received on board four principal men of the country as hostages for my person. On the 22nd [*sic*] we concluded an agreement, the conditions of which are contained in thirteen articles. This having been done, he [the Governor] came on board my ship, where he showed much satisfaction; and two days later we bade each other farewell, with presents given on either side, and much to the satisfaction of the people in general. At this place we obtained a good quantity of wood to repair our mast, and so I have now hopes that it will be

[1] Translated from the Spanish version printed in *Documentos Remettidos da India*, vol. III, p. 73. Professor Prestage has been kind enough to revise my translations of this and the other documents extracted from that work.

[2] This does not agree with the date given in Best's log (see p. 3).

[3] An error for '11.'

quite safe. Out of two small yards I have made one large one; and thus everything is well repaired.

On 29 [*sic*] November four great galleons and thirty or forty Portuguese frigates came in sight. On the 30th, after dinner, we weighed anchor and met them in the middle of the roadstead. We began a fight at three in the afternoon, which lasted until night; and then we were obliged to anchor until the following morning, at the distance of a cannon shot from the Portuguese admiral's ship. Before the sun rose we lifted our anchors and renewed the fight. I will not describe this in detail; but, briefly, in four separate days we had five separate fights, in which we [the *Dragon*] discharged 640 or 650 great shot and 3000 small; while the *Hosiander* spent 370 or 380 great shot. In the first three combats we killed 150 of their men and wounded many more; and in the other fights they suffered still greater loss. The enemy ships were much torn and broken, and the men were discouraged and unwilling to resume the fight. Up to the present only two of our men have been killed and one has lost an arm; in the *Hosiander* one was slain, but no one else was hurt. So our total loss was three men, thanks to the Lord, who has been our guard and salvation. And since leaving England, in both our ships (containing 220 men) we have lost 14 or 15; the others are as well as when they came from England. As for myself, up to the present I have had no illness.

Your Worships will receive a copy of the articles with the merchants' letters. And on the 11th of this month we received the *farmān* of the King, confirming and approving the peace we had made. Although the *farmān* is not all it should be, nevertheless it is sufficient for securing our trade in these parts; for, in addition to the King's *farmān*, I have the signature of the governor with whom I concluded the treaty, and those of the Governor of Surat and four other great men, the chief ones of the city, including the Shāhbandar, whom Sir Henry Middleton held as a prisoner. I think that Sir Henry's capture of those ships was the real cause of the grant of commerce to us; for they are as a people base and servile, and at sea are at the mercy of all nations, yet have a great trade and are very rich. The country is very fertile and abounds in commodities suitable for England and Turkey; so that, if Your Worships can provide forces sufficient to drive away the Portuguese and defend this roadstead, you may count upon obtaining all that is to be hoped for from the East Indies. I have made trial of their [i.e. the Portuguese] forces, and they are in truth very weak. Notwithstanding all this, we have been, and still are, in some danger from their stratagems; for, despairing of prevailing by force, they had recourse to fireships, even sacrificing vessels for that purpose; and if they were men, instead of beasts, they might easily destroy our ships, for theirs sail better than ours. We have had a thorough experience of them, and it is my opinion that, if four of your finest ships were to come out here, they could hold this road, despite all the efforts the Portuguese could make, and would be able to discharge and load at pleasure. I believe, however, that the Portuguese would never leave them in peace, unless the sovereigns of the two countries were to come to an agreement to that effect. If that cannot be arranged, it would be well for Your Worships to procure from His Majesty letters of marque. Could such be obtained, no better trade could be desired in the East Indies than here; and then a small amount of money would suffice to lade your ships in these parts. If Your Worships think fit to continue to trade in these countries, it will be necessary to provide a larger supply of guns, powder, and shot, because otherwise they [the Portuguese] will tire them and force them to expend their store, as they have done to us. Moreover, our supply is so limited that, were there to be another fight, we could not afford to expend more than 300 shot, and we have kept in reserve 350. Of powder we have no lack; and, given a little time, our smiths will provide a fresh supply of cannon balls. So I am not afraid of being in want.

As regards the sale of cloth and other merchandise, I refer, as to price, to the merchants. As to quantity, I think we may sell here each year from 700 to 800 pieces of cloth, at the prices for which we have now sold, viz. forty rials[1] per yard (*bara*); also 4000 to 5000 weight[2] of quicksilver at from 70 to 80 crowns[3] their weight[4], which is 33 lb. But if no greater care be taken in future in the packing of the quicksilver, it would be better not to send any; for, besides the trouble it has caused us, I think we have lost more than a fourth part. Of vermilion we may sell four to six barrels, at the same price as the quicksilver. Some small quantity of lead will vend, at 40 rials the kintal[5]. There is no sale here for iron. As for the colours of the cloth I refer me to the merchants.

Touching this coast of Cambay, both to the north and to the south of the Bar [of Surat], it is quite good, although it has hitherto been held to be dangerous for anchorage. I have made trial at two points, the one as far as the Swally shore, the other up to within eight or ten leagues of Goga; and I have found no danger worth speaking of, especially on the Goga side, for there our ships may ride in great safety, if they arrive before the end of the winter, that is, before the 10th September (and I counsel Your Worships not to permit your

[1] Equivalent to five rials of eight.
[2] Forty to fifty cwt.
[3] *Escudos*. Rials of eight are probably meant.
[4] *Peso*. The maund is of course intended.
[5] Probably 'cwt' in the original. As before, '40 rials' means five rials of eight.

ships to come to the Bar of Surat until that time). After the 10th or 15th September there is no danger.

I am now about to sail for Achin, Priaman, etc., in order to sell there the goods I have laden here. The particulars of all these Your Worships will understand from the merchants, who have been disposed in the following manner: Mr. Aldworth, Thomas Kerridge, and William Biddulph[1], with Aldworth's servant [i.e. John Young] are to reside in Surat, Cambay, and Ahmadābād (this city of Ahmadābād is the chief city of all these parts, and it was the Governor of that place who concluded the treaty with me in the name of his king); while Paul Canning is to go to Agra to the King, accompanied by one or two more (I know not yet who these will be), and will take with him the present and letters from our sovereign.

We have just received news that the galleons mean to attack us again, and some of my people say that they have already sighted them. Should this prove to be so, it may upset our affairs and prevent us from arranging matters suitably. And therefore, if there should be any deficiency in things of minor importance, Your Worships must excuse it.

All other matters I leave to the merchants, who have now more leisure and less work than I. May God guard Your Worships.

Your Worships' loving servant,
THOMAS BEST.

Ralph Croft, aboard the Hosiander *at Swally,* to *Sir Thomas Smythe*

14 January 1613[2]

Worshipful Sir,

In accordance with my duty, I pray earnestly to our Lord for Your Worship's health, which I beg His Divine Majesty to augment, for His service and Your Worship's own benefit.

The other letter I wrote to Your Worship was from the Cape of Good Hope on 27 June, by the *Solomon*. On the 29th we put to sea, in company with the *Dragon*, leaving in port the *Solomon*, which, however, was on the point of departure and the General was much offended that we did not get her to sea at the same time as ourselves. After our coming away we had the weather and wind so favourable that on 30 July we had got into the latitude of St. Lawrence. On 3 August we came in sight of certain islands, and that same day reached the island of Molesio [i.e. Mohilla]. We endeavoured to enter into a

[1] The names are much mangled in the Spanish version.

[2] Translated from the Spanish version printed in *Doc. Remett.*, vol. III, p. 78.

harbour there, but could not find sufficient depth of water, and so were forced to put to sea again, sailing directly for the port of Surat. On 1 September we sighted the coast of India and arrived near the port of Daman, a little to the west of it. On the 6th of the same month, together with the *Dragon*, we reached the Bar of Surat in safety; thanks be to the Lord for all His mercies. Here we were visited by certain Moors of the said port of Surat, and among them was one who called himself Chadon Abroger[1]. He told us that he had formerly served the English, and recently Sir Henry Middleton, from whom he brought a letter for our General, which in brief intimated as follows: that our General should not expect any trade at Surat, nor should he trust the merchants of that place, for he (the said Sir Henry Middleton) had found them a people very inconstant and fickle, who did not keep their word. Another letter from the same gentleman was found at Swally in the charge of the Mondame [i.e. the Mukaddam] of that place, which lies about two leagues from the Bar of Surat, where, as we learnt, the said Sir Henry had spent some time with his ships. Here we found very good provision, both of water and of other necessaries. From the Moor already mentioned we heard that Captain Hawkins and his wife had departed with Sir Henry for his own country, being out of hopes to establish any trade in this place, and that all the rest of our Englishmen had dispersed, each shifting for himself.

This news troubled our General very much, for he knew not what to do, and did not dare to send ashore either men or goods. Nevertheless, the said Moorish agent encouraged him very much, urging that he should not so much distrust the people of this land nor conceive so bad an opinion of them, for he assured him that his men would be as safe on land as in the ship; and furthermore he promised him that he would himself assist them to buy in that port of Surat all that was required for the ship and would return them on board in safety. At length the General trusted to the Moor's promises, and sent with him his steward and purser, together with a man called Davis, carpenter of the ship. On arriving they were received by the Governor of the city, accompanied by many of the principal persons, with much courtesy and friendliness; and after spending two days in the city, they returned to the ship in a country vessel, bringing bread, rice, sugar, flour, lemons, etc., which much refreshed our men.

Seven days after our men had been in the port and in the city of Surat, the Governor, with other gentlemen, came to visit the *Dragon*, and presented the General with sheep, goats, and sugar; and with much courtesy and affability they welcomed his coming into these parts, promising not only trade but also the supply of all things that

[1] This appears to have been the Spanish translator's rendering of 'Jadou, a broker.'

the city and country would yield. Our General repaid them with good treatment, and ended by presenting a handsome piece of plate. And with the said Governor and gentlemen he sent to the city of his own people Mr. Aldworth, Mr. Canning, and Thomas Kerridge, with some of the crew, to reside there and to hire a house; and the day following he despatched to the city two frigates laden with merchandise.

When we had rid fifteen days at this anchorage, the Portuguese sent from Goa a number of small ships, about sixteen in all; but these did not dare to attempt anything or even to approach us. They took refuge in the river's mouth and there remained. Because there was no water there deep enough for such large hulls as ours [we could not attack them?], and for this reason our ships departed for Swally. However, the Portuguese still remained in the river, with the result that we dared not send merchandise to Surat, fearing the Portuguese would capture it, as they did capture some of our men, viz. Mr. Canning, Edward Christian, and a musician of the name of Chambers; these, coming to visit us with certain of the country people, were taken by the Portuguese. The latter gave the Indians their liberty, and they, on reaching Surat, informed Mr. Aldworth, who immediately sent notice to our General. At this moment there arrived from Meca [Mokha], in the Red Sea, a large ship of 300 tons, which lay in the port with a very rich cargo. Our General at once ordered our master to weigh anchor and approach that ship (which belonged to Gujarāt); at the same time directing him to use all courtesy to the captain of the said vessel and to desire him to bring it under the lee of our ship. Should he refuse to do this peaceably, our master was to shoot and oblige him by force. He acted accordingly; and since the captain was unwilling to do as we requested, we fired two great shot, and nolens volens we took him under the lee of the *Dragon*. This vessel had 12 great pieces of artillery on each side, and had more than 300 sailors and passengers on board. The General was much troubled about having sent his goods and merchants on shore, wishing them all in safety again, that he might better carry away that Portuguese[1] ship. He therefore wrote a letter to Mr. Aldworth; but the latter, having seen the place and the people, was so highly pleased that he refused to return to the ship. Indeed, he endeavoured by all means in his power, both with our General and also with the Governor of the place, to establish commerce with them, although our General was of a contrary opinion.

When the merchants and the principal men of Surat heard that the General had taken their ship, they did everything in their power to regain the favour and friendship of our General; and for this purpose

[1] Possibly the meaning is that Best affected to regard the Gujarāti ship as an enemy vessel, because she was provided with a Portuguese pass.

they sent for the Governor of Ahmadābād (who under the King holds the chief control over this land) for him to make peace with our General and confirm and establish a perpetual trade between us and them. The General, however, still kept possession of the ship, and her captain remained aboard the *Dragon*. On 4 [*sic*] October the Governor of Ahmadābād and the Governor of Surat, accompanied by all the merchants and chief men of the city, arrived and pitched their tents on the seashore at Swally. The General would not land unless hostages were sent on board, and so the Governor of Ahmadābād despatched three gentlemen of high standing amongst them, who remained in the ship until his safe return. When the General set foot on land, he was presented with a horse on behalf of the Governor of Ahmadābād. The latter received him with much courtesy in his tent; and they proceeded to discourse regarding certain articles and stipulations. The Governor displayed the authority he held from the King, as also his commission as Governor, which he caused to be brought and shown to the General. And finding that his credentials were valid, they proceeded and agreed upon many points. The following day they came to a conclusion; and the King's present was shown to the Governor and was then sent back to the ship. The General declared that on the arrival of the King's *farmān*, confirming what had been treated and agreed, he would at once despatch the royal present and letter to the court, by one of the merchants appointed to reside there. The Governor forthwith sent off a courier to the court, promising that within forty days the King's *farmān* should arrive. The General sent the Governor and his son Sendas a present; and they did the same to him, with great demonstrations of friendship on both sides. The General then restored their ship, without removing a single thing from her. These matters having been settled, the Governor bought from the General 2000 covados [*codos*] of broadcloth at 20 mahmūdīs a covado, half to be paid in cash and the rest in other goods (which was done in calicoes and a small quantity of muslins). Having received his cloth, the Governor departed, promising (as already mentioned) a *farmān* from his sovereign.

Broadcloth sells here fairly well, much of it for cash down. Quicksilver is highly esteemed, and fetches a good price. Swordblades, unmounted, have been sold to much profit; for blades which have cost in England 8 rials have here been disposed of for 30. We have sold to advantage everything that Your Worships sent in the ship, except the elephants' teeth, which are only worth as much as they cost in England. Calicoes and other products of this country the merchants buy at a good price, according to time and occasion.

At certain courts held aboard the *Dragon* by the General and our merchants (who came from Surat for the purpose), it was decided that the *Hosiander* should go back to England from this place, and choice was made of those to whom this duty should be entrusted, with instructions to go about it with all possible diligence and haste. For this purpose some were sent to Ahmadābād and others to Cambay, in order the more quickly to procure the goods to lade and dispatch the ship, so as not to lose time and occasion.

Two days after the merchants had returned to Surat, supplied with all necessaries for the accomplishment of this journey, and when they were on the point of starting, each one with his commission, the General received two letters from Goa, the one from Mr. Canning and the other from Edward Christian. The latter was a prisoner in one of the frigates, and the letters came by means of a man named Chambers, who, although he too was a prisoner in the same frigate, had greater liberty than Christian, and so sent secretly the letters of the other two to Surat, from whence they were transmitted to the *Dragon*. Both were to the same effect, namely, to give notice to our General that four war galleons, well provided with all necessaries for fighting, were about to sail for the port of Swally to capture our ships; and that their commander, named Nuno da Cuña, had received the blessed sacrament, vowing to capture us and carry the *Dragon* to Goa and our ship, the *Hosiander*, to Cherille [Chaul ?]. Also that they knew already very assuredly all that we had done, that is to say, that the General had concluded peace with the Governor of Ahmadābād and that we had established a trade with those of Surat (which benefit they hoped to deprive us of). Moreover, they had also learnt what goods we had in the ship, how much money and all other things, as though they had seen them. They had already sold us before they set out from Goa, and had arranged for the distribution of the broadcloth among their friends, as though they already had it in their hands. But the Lord ordained that all should turn out to the contrary of what they thought, as the sequel will show.

The General, having well weighed the contents of the said letters, at once despatched a messenger to Surat, giving advice thereof to the merchants and commanding them to refrain from action until they received further instructions. In the meantime he prepared for fight, clearing away all that might hinder and getting together what was necessary. He then awaited the galleons; having put his ship in such a state that it cheered his men to see a vessel so well prepared to fight as was the *Dragon*. Of the *Hosiander* I will say nothing, as I might be suspected of partiality; but I leave it to the good judgment of Your Worship and the rest of the gentlemen of the Company to guess how well she would play her part. And I doubt not Your Worship will hear before many more days what at present I have no time to write.

The day after we received the letters we sighted the ships in the roadstead, with 25 frigates following them. Our two were ready for battle; but the enemy showed no eagerness to engage, approaching the land with the flowing tide and not using their sails. This morning Mr. Canning came on board, before the fray commenced, and told us that the Portuguese had set him at liberty, saying that they scorned to keep any of our men, since before long they would have both ships and men (as they declared and reckoned upon). Mr. Canning told us that Edward Christian and John[1] Chambers had fled from the Portuguese in Cambay and gone for Surat. Mr. Canning, after some speech with the General, came aboard our ship; where he remained during all the fighting, and much encouraged our men in the combat. After eating we commended ourselves to God, for the enemy was already approaching, so much so that both of us weighed anchor and went to receive him. Of the battle that followed there was no lack of spectators on land, for many had come from Surat solely to see the outcome. The leading ship of the enemy was the vice-admiral, which the *Dragon* dealt with in such a manner that the others, fearing a like reception, fled. We in the *Hosiander* followed them as long as the high tide lasted, leaving the *Dragon* with her first antagonist, with whom she so dealt as to punish her well before leaving. Before departing, all the frigates surrounded her and carried her away to rest, by reason that she had received much damage by our shot.

This night we anchored a league from the enemy. And the next day (being St. Andrew's Day), with the wind against us we pushed into the middle of the Portuguese, saluting them with broadsides, first on one side and then on the other, for the space of two or three hours. When the tide turned we again anchored, all in safety and with no loss of life. After dinner we once more weighed, as soon as we had sufficient water, the tide having come. This time we engaged only one of our opponents, and spent all the afternoon in the fight. During this afternoon we fired 100 shot, and pounded that vessel so effectively that she judged it advisable to take refuge with her consorts. The *Dragon* on the same day fought alone with the other three; in which fray they killed three of our men, without any further damage worth speaking of (the Lord be praised for all).

The General now determined to cease fighting and to go over to the opposite coast, where are situated Diu, Simar, Muzafarābād, and Mahuwa[2], and as far as Castelleta, which was being besieged by the Mogul's forces, about 1000 valiant warriors, engaged against the Malabars, who were holding that fortress. The commander of the besieging army sent to beg our General to come on shore, and sent hostages for his safe return. The said commander also desired him to

[1] On p. 109 his name is given as William.

[2] 'Dua, Asemur, Amedosfrabard, y Amocha.'

lend the services of two of our larger pieces of artillery, to help in demolishing the castle of the Malabars [*alárabes*]; but this our General refused to do. Meanwhile we saw the Portuguese coming once more against us; and there, in the sight of the commander and all his army, we fought with them two days, and in the end forced them to withdraw into the open sea, while their flagship fled. On this occasion the *Dragon* had one man killed and another wounded.

We then returned again to the road of Swally; where ten days later they brought us the royal *farmān*, which had been sent from court and was now delivered to the General with great solemnity. All the principal men of Surat then took note of our merchants who are to reside in Surat, and they despatched goods to the town. And in the midst of these affairs the Portuguese have appeared once more, to fight again with us; but the Lord, who has hitherto defended us, will, I trust, in His divine goodness continue to assist us. For myself I am under a particular obligation all the days of my life to praise Him and acknowledge His great mercy and heavenly care in saving me from a cannon ball, from which, I confess, I escaped by His special protection. During our first fight we sank one of their frigates, and all those on board were drowned. We have killed, in all the skirmishes we have had with them, more than 300 persons, according to their own admission and the reports of the country people; yet despite this they are now coming with reinforcements to attack us again.

We met off St. Lawrence two carracks, who fired at us and we at them, with the result that three of their men were killed. The captain of one of the carracks gave this information to Mr. Canning in Goa.

This night the General will have finished all his business here; and on the morrow we shall be ready to meet them [the Portuguese] and then to pass on to Priaman.

There have been some differences between Mr. Canning and Mr. Salmon, with the result that the former was ordered to transfer himself to the *Dragon*, and is now to go to Agra with the present for the King.

The *Dragon* has lost, out of her original crew, [including those killed] in these encounters with the Portuguese, a matter of 25, and the *Hosiander* 5.

I have no space for more; and so, with my daily prayers for the safety of Your Worship, I cease[1].

Your Worship's servant,

RALPH CROFT.

[1] In the Spanish version is here added the date '29 November, Sabbath Day.' This is obviously a transfer from an earlier portion of the letter, the bulk of which was doubtless written at that time, and brought later up to 14 January.

The Rev. P[atrick] Copland at Swally Road to *[the Rev. John] Randall*[1] *in London*

14 January 1613[2]

Very Reverend Sir,

I send my greetings to you and to the rest of my friends.

These are to inform you that now, as always since we set out on our voyage, I am enjoying good health, praise be to the holy name of God for everything.

We arrived in our port of Surat at the beginning of September, and have there established a factory, with much benefit to the Worshipful Company and all the English nation, if we may continue to trade in peace; for the land is very healthful and fertile, and abounds in rich commodities. It seems like another Egypt, or, to say better, a terrestrial Paradise; such is its abundance in all earthly things. But so great is the power of the Portuguese along all this coast that they hold the people in such slavery that they do not allow the country ships to sail without a pass, for which they pay them tribute. We have felt some of their malice and strength by the fleet of frigates, or small boats, which they sent from Goa (the chief city they have in the Indies) to stop our trade; and also by four great galleons, accompanied by 26 frigates, with which we have already fought five times, putting them to flight on both sides of the Gulf of Cambay, in the sight of the chief nobles and best soldiers of the Great Mogul, with no small damage to their ships and the loss of 200 to 300 men. In these encounters the *Dragon* and the *Hosiander* (our smaller ship) have lost between them only three killed and one wounded. We fired 1000 great shot (little more or less) and 10,600 musket balls. The fighting was very obstinate, for the first three skirmishes lasted 5, 6, and 7 hours respectively; the other two about 14 (rather more than less). And in all these combats God has worked miraculously and wonderfully on our behalf, in the view of one of the chief nobles in all the land, who, accompanied by 6000 or 7000 soldiers, was besieging a castle on the seashore, where this fight occurred. In all these encounters I have seen God sending us troubles and placing us in them as He set the three young men in the fiery furnace; and we have felt His divine assistance therein and His subsequent delivery of us in an extraordinary manner out of the said difficulties. For, since our ships were merchantmen of not much more than 200 men, they were in great danger to be de-

[1] Addressed as 'minister of the church of St. Andrew.' Randall was the celebrated Puritan preacher, who was rector of St Andrew Hubbard in London from 1599 to 1622. For a notice of him see the *Dict. of Nat. Biography*.

[2] Translated from the Spanish version in *Doc. Remett.*, vol. III, p. 85.

voured alive by the royal fleet of four war galleons, sent on purpose to sink or burn us. The smallest of them was a ship of 700 or 800 tons, while the greatest was larger than the *Dragon*; and each had as many men on board as all ours put together. In addition, they had the aid of 26 frigates, to assist them on all occasions. But our God fought for us, as He did for the Israelites.

I am forced to be brief, for the four galleons have again come into the sight of our men, after having spent 20 days and more in their ports, refitting their ships, refreshing their men, and taking in new ones. And the General is obliged with all haste to set on shore the merchants of the port (*Pe.*) and other factors, who have been consulting about their affairs and the despatch of our ships.

I am suitor unto you for your prayers to God for me (as I know you do) until we see each other again face to face, when it pleases His divine majesty. And I do know, and have learnt by more than a thousand experiences, who is our God, and in troubles He is quickly found. Pray to Him that He may deign to increase His gifts in me, and that He may bestow upon me the requisite words and open my lips, in order that I may propagate His kingdom in the hearts of the many who belong to Him here.

I have found our General to be a man of much determination and valour; and moreover, as he promised Your Worship, he has been as a father to me, with the result that I find in him great comfort, despite many weaknesses in myself.

Commend me to each of our friends in particular, as if I mentioned them all by name.

P. COPLAND.

Thomas Best at Swally to *Sir Thomas Smythe*

16 January 1613[1]

Honorable Sir (with the Worshipfull the Companie),

A former, 2 dayes since, I wrott all in hast. Tyme then (neather at present) so permitted me to wright such thinges as I would; our enimyes, the 4 gallions [of] the Portingalls, ridinge so fayre by us that every tyd we expected to be in battle with them. Thearfore you must

[1] From a copy in *Factory Records, Miscellaneous*, vol. xxv (p. 67). This is one of several documents copied into his note-book by Thomas Elkington, prior to his departure for the East in 1614. He notes that Best's letter was 'sent by the waye of Aleppoe, and received hear in London the 7th December 1613.' This is confirmed by a letter of the following day (*Cal. S.P. Dom.*, 1611–18, p. 214), which shows that intelligence of the doings at Surat had then come to hand.

be pleased at, this tyme to accept of that I send, though nether so full, ample, nore large as you desier.

Arrivinge at the Cape Bonasperanca the 8th of June, with [the] *Osiander* and *Sollomon*. The *James* loosinge our company the second night before; since which tyme we have not heard of hear. Beinge hear well refreshed, we departed Soldania the 28th June, and arived at the coast of Cambaya the first of September, and at the bar of Suratt the 7th September; having in my passadge undergone much truble by reason of a rotten mayneyard, which brake twice before I came to Saldania. And in Soldania, to make my yard substantiall and stronge, I aded so much waight unto it that the 14th of July, in some reasonable fowle weather, with rowlinge sprange my maynemast so much that I could not indewer my maynetoppmast upon it, nether yet the foresaid mayneyar d, but onely the maynetopsaile; with which I continued till I came to the bar of Suratt, and so havinge sailed (before I came to the Cape and since) 2000 leagues without a mayne-saile.

Hear at the bar, the day of my arivall, I landed 2 or 3 merchants. Som 4 daies after, I landed Mr. Aldworth and Mr. Canninge; and presently after, som small quantitie of goods of all sortes. The 27 or 28th of September, Mr. Canninge, Edward Christian, and one of my musitioners wear taken by the Portingalls frigatts, thay cominge from Suratt to the ship in a litle boate by night. The 17th October, the Governor of Amadevas (the chefe cittie of all those parts) came downe to the watterside at Swally to me; [desiring me ?] to com unto him, which I refused to doe. But so, he beinge accompaned with the Governor and all the principall men of Suratt, and a great troope atending upone them, beinge settled in ther tennts, the said Governor of Amadavas sent to me to com; but I did refeues so to doe, but so as he would send mee 4 pri[n]sipall men aboard to be pledges for me; which, after 2 daies, he graunted. The 19th, havinge received my pledges, I landed. And beinge placed before the Governor and the rest of the great men, the Governor tould me that his cominge was to wellcome mee into those partes and to entertaine mee with all kindnes and curtesey. I demaunded of him of what authoritie he came unto mee, eather of himselfe or by the Kinge sent. Hee answeared me: by order from the Kinge. And withall shewed mee the Kings letter, with the greate seale unto it; the coppie whearof I presently requiered, that so to us and to our nation it might apeare that he had authoritie to trade with mee; which was presently graunted, and by his secretary presently performed. Which done, he requiered mee to demaund what I requiered. I tould him: nott a present trade, but a league and fellowship with ther Kinge, the settlinge of a factory att Suratt and in all other places in the Magolls dominions at my pleasure. In fine, by the 22th we concluded our league and pease with them, upon such conditions as ar contayned in 13 articles, which for this porpose I had prepared; the coppie whearof hear inclosed ar sent you. The present busines finished, 2 dayes after both myselfe [himselfe?] and his sonn, with divers other great men, came aboard my shipp; whear thay received much content, and the next day departed, with presents given one both sids, to the great joye of all the people.

About 5th[1] November, 4 gallions of the Portingalls came unto us; with whome wee have had 5 severall fights in 4 dayes, and upone them have spent out of the *Dragon* 640 or 650 great shott and 3000 small, and the *Hosander* 370 or 380 great. And so one both sides, beinge both well wearied, we parted company.

One Christmas Eave we came to the bar of Suratt, allias Swally, and thear continued 20 dayes all quiett. The 11th January, the Kinges firma was brought unto mee by the cheefe men of Suratt. And 2 dayes after, the 4 gallions, with the frigatts, came agayne in sight, anchoringe at the bar of Suratt (we at Swally); whear thay have continued to this present, givinge us convenient tyme to finish and end our busines hear. Insomuch as we ar now eaven redie to saile, and do perpose (God willinge) by tomorrow at night to depart. [W]heather in the meane tyme we shalbe trubled with them, we know not; but ther devotions [i.e. inclinations] ar but little, and ther stomackes less, to medle with us, and we, every man, as well prepared as when we first begun with them; our courages much more, havinge now experience of a couardless [*sic*] enymy.

Departinge from this place, I purpose (by the grace of God) for Hehill, Briania[2], etc., with some fayre quantitie of goods, the particulers and sortes whearof from the marchants you shalbe enformed, as likewise for both the quantitie and quallitie of those goods we leave in Suratt, under the charge of Mr. Thomas Aldworth, Thomas Kerridge, and William Biddulph; whome (with Nycolas Withington, whom hear we have entertayned into your servise for 7 years) wee have settlett [*sic*] in Suratt. And Mr. Paule Canninge, with 2 other young [men] (whose names I doe not knowe), we have appoynted for Agra; and ther to be resident at courte, to encounter the Jesusitts [i.e. Jesuits], our enimyes, whear[3] thear and in all those partes ar studious to bringe us agayne into disgrace and dishonor with the Kinge and country. But the acction of Sir Henry Midleton in the Red Sea hath possessed them with such a generall fear of us, I take it thay will neaver dare againe in grose manner to offend us. For besides the Kings seale that I have, I have the 2 Governors aforesaid seales to the

[1] Probably 'the fine' (i.e. end) in the original.
[2] In the original, doubtless, 'Tecow, Priaman.'
[3] A slip for 'who.'

articles agreed upon, and allso the seales of 4 principall men in Suratt, whearof Yabaulor[1] is one, whome Sir Henry Midleton som tyme heald as a plege. In fine, it is simplye my opinion that you have the substance and som, for so much as Kinge and country can give you; so that which resteth or is behind to stablish current and good factory and trade in thease countryes is to be performed by yourselves: in the first place, that you make a care principally to send fitt and sufficient men to take the charge of your busines, both in Suratt and the court. Yf, after my much care and great desiers to settle you a factory hear upon good tearmes, and yf afterwards I should betray it, wear more to wrong you then in the former I have donn you servise; and thearfor lett not myne advise offend any, sith I intend onely and aym att nothing but the profitt and gaine of the Worshipfull Companie. Mr. Aldworth is a very honest man, but no ways fitt to be an Agent and Cheef Factor in Suratt. To aledge reasons would grow tedious. Some proper, sollid, and experienced marchant, that hath lyne sometymes in Turkey or in Barbary, would be best fittinge for thease partes. And such is the pleasure, the content, and ritches which this country yealdeth, with holsomnes of ayre, that yf the treue knowledge therof wear certainely knowne in London, you would then be as much trubled with the seuts of good men to lye in Suratt, Cambaya, Amadavas, and Sorall[2], as now you are overladen with the peticions of foolish and idle boyes, which neather hath creadit nor quallitie fitt to serve nearer hom. How Mr. Canninge will prove att courte I am doubtfull. Jealouse I am not, [if] such as he should be, he may for the Worshipfull Companie obtaine and procure all that he will; but it is tyme that must t[r]ye him, for though [he hath] many good partes, he hath [them] accompaned with som ill. Sewer I ame, yf with the Kinge he prove such as he should be, he may obtaine of him what hee will. Amongst us he is the fittest of all for thease places, and a nessecitie to send one, and with hime one to speake for him (for he hath not the language), and to waight one him only one, and not otherwise. For his provissition and jorney we have appoynted 150*l.*, at 5*s.* the doller, and afterwards (for monyes needfull) to take[3] in Agra and to charge Mr. Aldworth with it by bill of exchange; requiringe in all to be frugall, not prodigall and lavish, seinge the stocke is small that is now in the country; which he hath promised, namely to be a good husband to the Worshipfull Companie.

Now, for that which concearneth the Portingalls, which is the mayne cause or obstacle that heare may hinder you trad, the forces ar smalle which thay wilbe able to make agaynst you. Ther men of all sortes more couardly, at least as much as migh[t] an armey of women

[1] Probably the original had 'Xabandar' (Best's spelling of *Shāhbandar*).
[2] Probably the copyist's error for 'Baroch' (Broach).
[3] Borrow.

in our land. Suer[l]y, yf myne eyes had not seene, I could not [have] beleved ther basenes and couardlynes. Then thease 4 gallions that rid by us thay have no better in all thease countryes. In burden thease 4 ar from 700 to 900 and 1000 tonns; good ordnance (better then we have any), but so small use thay make of them, with so little skill, that a man would never desier a better an enymy. In a word, it is myne oppinion that 4 of your lesser[1] sort of ships, espetially yf eather the *Trades Increse* or *Dragon* myght be one, certainely thay will beat all the forces the Portingalls can send heather against them. And for ther carrackes, thay will neaver com; the channell hearabout not very broad, and the tides stronge. Thease 4 gallions cannot hear worke with sailes; much less can ther carrickes. Now yf you shall send 3 or 4 ships, thay shall not need now hear to make any longe stay, not to exceed above 50 or 60 dayes at the uttmost; in which tyme the companies in the ships wilbe refreshed, good provision of vitualls provided, and all goods prepared laden into the ships; makinge this your reconinge, that every year you may have one of 3 or 4 ships retorned you home the same year, [and] the others, with ther goods received, to proseed to ther severall places whear by Your Worships thay shalbe directed and appoynted, with those comodities which thay shall hear receive in. And with thease will torne you to as good accompt as any thinge that from England you shall send, espetially then when your factors have hear gathered som experience and knowledg in the comodities of this place; which at this present thay understand nott.

Tyme permitteth me not to bee so large as I would; and therfore you must with patience undergoe the want of divers particulers that I could wish to advise you of. Yett I hope what is wanting one my parte wilbe supplyed by the merchants. To be laden yearly, to send and to land in Suratt to be disposed of for Cambaya [and] Amadavas, 700 or 800 clothes. For the collors I refer to the merchants; onely your stametts and Venice reds ar the best. You must packe them better then thease wear that wear sent by us, or elce your spoyle and damidge will be such as it hath bine now with us. You must packe them with somthinge that can defend the droping of the ships overlopes[2] upone them. Som good quantitie of quicksilver; twice or thrice as much more, so sent, will sell hear to a great reconinge. For all other comodities fittinge, I doe refer you to the marchants. Onely, for presents fitt to be given in thease countryes, that you send yearly 5 or 6 cases of bottles filled with hott waters [i.e. spirits], some faire lookinglasses, and good store of pictures, espetially such as discover Venus and Cupids actes, for thease ar presents fitt for the Great

[1] Probably we should read 'better' (cf. p. 231).
[2] The orlop was the floor or deck covering the hold.

Magoll and greate burds [*read* lords?] of that country. Also som fayre knives; at present [one] of thease, of 8 or 10*l.*, is of them more esteemed then 2 or 3 of your broadclothes or your great peeces of plate, which the Governor tells us the Kinge would not esteeme.

The factors which proseed with mee upone my voyadg ar Williame Mare [i.e. More] and John Cransbay in the *Dragon*, and in the *Hosander* Tobye Oliott [i.e. Oliver] and Hugh Gittlings [i.e. Gittings]. I should have writt to you of the retorne of Mr. Paull Canninge and Edward Christian to us againe in his right place, but it was forgotten. 2 monnth[s] thay wear from the ships. Near to Cambaya Edward Christian, with one C[h]ambers, that had run away from Sir Henry Midl[e]ton, rann away from the frigotts; and a day or 2 after, Mr. Canning was sett ashore at Suratt.

Thus havinge [given] you my weake judgment in the premises, prayinge you to accept it with like goodwill, I send it to your service. My desiers ar the same with yours. It is onely God that can give the blessinge; whose mercies to me in this present voyadge hath bine great; in the continuance whearof resteth my comfort and hope that the end wilbe corespondant to the begininge, namely, glory to Himeselfe, honor to our land, with gaine and profitt to the wholl body of the great and worshipfull Company.

Thomas Aldworth etc. at Surat to *the East India Company*

25 January 1613[1]

Right Worshipfull,

Our duties remembred, etc. From Cape Bona Esperansa wee wrotte you particular letters, per the *Sollomon*, of what till then had passed; whom wee left beehinde us, ready to departe within a day or two. And now Your Worshipps shall perceave what hath passed since our comminge thence.

Wee departed from Saldania the 28th of June, with prosperous windes; had sight of St. Lawrance Ilande the 26th [July]; and the 30th ditto mett with 2 Portingall carrickes bounde for Goa, som 60 leagues shorte of Mosambige [i.e. Mozambique]. Wee thinkeinge to have spoken with them, but comminge neere them thay shott att us, and wee one peece att eatch of them; the *Ozeander* discharginge some 15 or 16 peeces att the admyrall likwise, slew (as since wee have bin

[1] *O.C.* 102 (I.O. records). This is apparently a signed copy of the letter first sent. It has been printed, with modernized spelling, in *Letters Received*, vol. 1, p. 233. It was probably drafted by Aldworth, and merely signed by the two juniors.

enformed) 3 of their men; who likwise shott divers shott att her, but did noe hurte att all (thankes bee to God). And soe partinge, wee helde on our course; and 2 dayes followinge had sighte of them agayne, but came not neere them.

The 13th[1] of August wee had sighte of an ilande called Mall Illa, where wee thoughte to have anchored for refreshmente, as allsoe to have fishte our mast (beeinge halfe broken); but founde the place full of suncke rockes, which caused us to alter our purpose and continue on our course. And the 13th ditto wee crossed the Line, and had very temperat weather; our people (thankes bee to God) all in good health. The first of September wee came into very white water, and presently after had sight of lande, which our Indians and other our people affirmed to bee the coast of Damon. Where wee came to an anchor, and a counsell [was] caulled by the Generall. Itt was ordred that Mr. Thomas Aldwourth and Thomas Keridge should goe aboarde the *Ozeander*, whereby to seeke meanes to goe or sende to the citty of Suratt, the sooner to learne the state of the country. But havinge nonne aboarde us that directly knew the place, wee anchored att Nunsery; where 3 dayes followinge the Generall, with the *Dragon*, came and anchored by us. And the nexte day, beeinge the 5th, a boate from this citty came aboarde of us, wherein was one Jadowe, a broker to the English, who broughte with him a breefe letter (unsealed) from Sir Henry Middleton, wherein hee advized all our countrymen not to expecte any trade heere, the people beeinge trecherous, and hee referringe us to a larger letter left with the Muckadam of Sually (some 4 leagues to the norwardes of Suratt). And havinge taken a pilott out of a boate which passed by us, the nexte day wee sett sayle towardes Suratt, and the 7th ditto anchored att the barre.

Wee beeinge now att anchor att the barr of Suratt, a counsell was called, where itt was ordered that Thomas Keridge, Edward Cristian, Anthony Starky, and Thomas Davis (carpenter in the *Ozeander*) should repare to the citty, to bee informed of the country, as allsoe to procure Sir Henries letter beefore specified; which thay receaved and sente aboarde (the coppy whereof wee heerewith sende you). Which letter caused our Generall much to suspecte the setlinge of any trade heere, notwithstandinge the greate incoradgmente given us by those that weare sente ashore, who weare all kindely entertayned by the Governor and cheefes of the citty; who allsoe, att our peoples demaunde, sente their firmaes for warrante of our secure tradinge with them. Upon receyght whereof, the 12th ditto, Mr. Thomas Aldwourth and Mr. Paule Canninge came allsoe on shore, and weare kindely entertayned by the Governor and the rest. The same night

[1] An error for '3rd.'

some 14 Portingall frigatts entred into the river; but 2 dayes after departed. Whereupon wee wrotte to the Generall for the sendinge on shore of some quantitie of goodes for tryall; who sente us nonne, but wrotte us a letter willinge us to come on boarde; which the 15th ditto wee did. Where a counsell beeinge called, itt was ordered that a good quantity of our goodes should fourthwith bee landed. And soe wee returned the nexte day on shore agayne; Mr. Thomas Aldwourth beeinge fallen sicke att that time, and soe continued very weake some 40 dayes.

The 22th wee dispeeded away 5 boates for the goodes aforesayde; whereof 3 the 24th ditto retourned with 4 bales cloath, 1 bale keirsie, 1700 barrs lead, 600 endes iron, 3 barrells quicksilver, and 1 smalle vessell of vermellion. The other 2 boates sente empty, by reason of a shippe of this place which came from Mecha, arrived att the barr and broughte newes that Sir Henry Middleton, with 3 or 4 English shippes, had taken them, with divers others of this country, and forsed them to deliver him goodes, in trucke of cloath and other things, att such rates as pleased him; as allsoe that hee tooke divers other things without givinge anythinge for itt. Heereupon wee remayned doubtfull of what mighte beefall us and our goodes, for that heere was a gennerall murmoringe in the citty aboute this newes. But wee founde the people very reasonable, and the cheefes came unto our howse, desiringe that this newes mighte noe way dismay us, and notwithstandinge this injury donne them by Sir Henry, wee should finde all honest respect from them unto us; and withall requested us to write home in their beehalfes for restitution of their losse that way sustaned; which wee promised them to doe. Of all which wee certified the Generall and wrott him to sende us the residue of the goodes beefore determyned; but his answere was hee would sende nonne, wishinge us with our goodes on boarde agayne, doubtinge the peoples dealinge with us; and heereupon sente for Mr. Canninge and the purser to repare unto him; who accordingly wente, and weare taken that nighte by the Portingall frigottes within the mouth of the river, and weare detayned by them untill the fine of November.

The 29th of September heere arrived another shippe of this place from the Red Sea; which our Generall possessed himselfe of, and wrott unto us hee woulde detayne her untill hee had receaved us, and the proceede of those goods landed, aboarde agayne. Whereunto wee answered wee saw noe cause to the contrary but that wee mighte settle our factory heere, having newes that the Governor of Amadabaz was shortly to come, with order from the Kinge for our peaceable entertaynemente. Wherefore havinge advized the Generall, hee repayred with his shippes to Sually; and soe accordingly the sayde Governor came unto Suratt. In the meanewhile wee made sale of those goodes wee had heere on shore, viz. cloath att 20 ma[hmūdis] the covado [see p. 34], northernes att 6 ma. the covado, lead att 7 ma. the maen, quicksilver and vermellion att 300 ma. the maen, to bee payde in comodities fitt for Achin. But our iron would not yealde above 3½ ma. per maen; which yett remaneth the greatest parte unsoulde. After this Thomas Keridge fell sicke, and soe continued for the space of a month.

The 14th of October the aforesayde Governor wente unto Sually; where, after 3 or 4 dayes conference with our Generall on shore, these articles, which heerewith wee sende you, weare concluded on; and made a bargayne with him of 40 thowsande ma. for cloath, att our former price, to pay halfe mony in hande, the other halfe in blew callicoes; which accordingly was accomplished. In the articles aforesayde it was agreede on that within 40 dayes the Kinges firma for confirmation of the sayde articles should bee sente us. Notwithstandinge, itt came not in 20 dayes after the time prefixed; which was the cause that our Generall doubted to lande any more goodes untill hee receaved the aforesayde firma from the Kinge; in all which time heere was little donne, excepte some few things sould on shippeboarde att Sually, allthough this people much desired our comodities, and noe cause to doubte them.

The 25th of November wee receaved letters from Mr. Canninge and Edward Cristian, wherein thay advized us of 4 gallions ready to departe from Goa, on purpose to take or to fire our shippes; which proved true, for that the 28th ditto the frigottes, in number 25, who came in company with the sayde gallions to assist them, sett Mr. Canninge on shore att the citty of Suratt; Edward Cristian havinge escaped from them (by their joynte consente and plott) att Cambaya some 4 dayes beefore. The 29th ditto Mr. Canninge repared aboarde, wee accompaniinge him to the waterside to see the evente of this busines. And this afternoone the galliones, with 6 frigotts to eatch of them towinge, came neere our shippes; who allsoe wayed anchor and mett them, in sighte of us and many other people standing on the shore to looke on them. Where the *Dragon* alone, att the first encounter, made their admirall and vize-admyrall turne backe and fly beefore her; their other 2 shippes not beeinge come up, neyther was the *Ozeander* att this time come to the *Dragon*. And havinge exchanged some 40 greate shott of eatch side, the nighte beeinge come, thay anchored in sighte of eatch other. And the next morninge our shippes wayed agayne and beegan their fighte with them; which continued some 3 owres, in which time thay drove 3 of their gallions on the sandes, and soe our shippes came to an anchor. And in the afternoone wayed agayne; in which time, the floud beeinge come, the gallions, with the helpe of the frigottes, weare afloate agayne. With whom this third time our shippes havinge fought some 4 owres, with much honnor and advantadge of their enimies, itt beeinge now nighte, came to an anchor, and there rodd this nighte and all the nexte day, without medlinge eatch with other. The 31 ditto, our shippes sett sayle and departed; whereupon wee much doubted some great hurte to bee donne aboarde them; but (thankes bee to God) itt proved contrary, wee havinge had but one man slayne in these 3 fightes. What passed with them in their fightes on the other side, wee referre you to their particular letters who weare presente att them.

Beefore the comminge of the sayde gallions itt was concluded, by a counsell aboard the *Dragon*, that the *Ozeander* shoulde bee dispeeded directly for Englande, and order given for the buyinge of such commodities as should bee fittinge. But their sudden departure in that manner, and not heeringe what was beecome of them, caused us to desist from executinge what was determyned.

The 27th of December our shippes returned hether agayne; att which time wee sent aboard all such goodes as wee had ready. And now the Generall, seeinge the Kings firma was not itt [i.e. yet] come, was throughly resolved to leave this place; and wrott his letter for Mr. Thomas Aldwourth and the rest to repayre on board, and to bringe with them all such goodes as weare in their power. Whereunto Mr. Aldwourth answered hee would not come on boarde untill the Kings firma came (for that the Generall had given out speeches aboarde the shipps that, if hee had him on board, hee would carry him alongst with him). Heereupon the Generall called a counsell, and soe required the sayde Thomas Aldwourth to come on board; which hee agayne refused to doe, for that hee harde certaynely the firma was comminge. And in the interim of these things (itt pleased God) the firma came; and heereupon Mr. Aldwourth, with the rest, wente on board. After this, 7 dayes weare spente in receivinge the firma, for that the Generall was doubtfull whether itt was the Kings firma or not; and beeinge resolved, would not receive itt untill some of the cheefes of the citty should bringe itt downe unto him to Sually; which in fine thay did. And the very day followinge the receight of itt (beeinge the 14th d[ay]) the gallions weare agayne in sighte, but came not neere to proffer fighte. Notwithstandinge, the Generall resolved not to make any longer stay heere, but tooke in such goods as weare ready, and landed the rest of the cloath, quicksilver, and vermellion, all the ellephants teeth, and some 1200 barres of lead; carriinge the rest alongst with him, as allsoe all the peeces of eyght and iron. And soe, the 18th presente, departed, not havinge received from hence above the some of 3,500*ll.* sterling, in goods fittinge Achin, Priaman, etc.; intendinge to returne therehence directly for this place aboute October or November nexte, havinge left with us, in goods and monies to bee invested in commodities fitt for Englande agaynst his returne, to the vallew of 4,000*ll.* sterling or thereaboute. Since which time wee have bin busied in furnishinge Mr. Paule Canninge with things nessessary for his journy to Agra with the Kings letter and presente, beeinge thereto appoynted by the Generall and counsell aboarde the *Dragon*. Likewise by the sayde counsell itt was there ordered that Anthony Starky, the bearer heereof, should bee dispeeded for Englande, with letters to give notice to Your Worshipps how things stande heere with us. And soe have furnished him with nessessaries fittinge such a journy, which will amounte unto 1950 ma., as appeareth.

Wee are in all remayninge heere 10 persons, whereof 5 are att presente goinge for Agra, and 5 of us remayne heere, viz. Thomas Aldwourth, Thomas Keridge, William Biddulph, Nicholas Withington, and John Younge (servante to Mr. Aldwourth). The sayde Nicholas Withington, beeinge one of the Generalls men, is entertayned by consente and bound to the Worshipfull Company for 7 yeares. Those for Agra: Mr. Paule Canninge, 2 of the Generalls men[1], and 2 muzisions[2]....

Your Worships to bee commaunded,

THO. ALDWORTHE.

WM. BIDDULPH.

NICH. WITHINGTON.

Aboute a month hence, heere goeth a shippe to the Red Sea, by whom wee will allsoe write[3].

[1] Richard Temple and Edward Hunt.

[2] Lancelot Canning and Robert Trully.

[3] To this letter the writers have appended: (1) information about goods suitable for sale at Surat, viz. '500 Venniz red cloathes (whereof 30 or 40 stammells), 100 poppengie [popinjay] greenes and light grasse greenes, 100 strawe cullers, yallowes, and horseflesh, 100 lighte blewes, commonly called hulings, 200 murries in grayne and other plesant cullors that will hold, of divers sortes; more, 500 peeces of Devon kersies, of the cullors abovesayde, of 50*s.* per peece price'; (2) a statement of advances of money made at Surat to various factors; (3) the following note of weights, etc.: 'Their wayghtes are a maen and a seire. Their maen is 40 seire, and of English wayght 32 ll. 15 oz. Their seire is 13 oz., or thereabouts. Their measures are two, which thay call covados. On[e] is a longe covado, qt. [i.e. containing] within one inch of our English yard; wherewith thay measure cloath [i.e. broadcloth]. The shorte covado is for silkes, and contayneth just [i.e. exactly] as the Portingall covado.'

[*Thomas Aldworth*][1] *at Surat* to *Sir Thomas Smythe*
25 January 1613[2]

In the general letter we have described what has taken place here. Now I will give Your Worship an account of the importance of this port of Surat, which is, as it were, the fountainhead from whence we may draw all the trade of our East Indies; for we find here merchandise which we can take and sell in nearly all parts of these Indies and also in England. For this reason the Portuguese resent very much our entry into this city, and they have worked hard, both by craft and by force, to prevent us. But, thanks be to God, their efforts have not been successful; and I trust that we have here laid such firm foundations that the Portuguese will no longer attempt to drive us out; especially if His Majesty of England be pleased to favour us in this design, by which I think His Majesty will benefit his royal treasury by more than 200,000 crowns every year, besides the advantage to the whole kingdom by the sale of the goods that come from thence, especially broadcloth, at a higher price than in any other part of India[3]; inasmuch as in future it will be unnecessary to send out any money, but only such things as are mentioned in our general letter.

But for the security of this trade, it has seemed to me desirable to acquaint Your Worship of one thing which appears to me to be of great importance, and that is to establish a settlement at the Cape of Good Hope. This might easily be effected, if every year the ships bound for these parts were to bring out a hundred men and leave them there on the way. During our stay at Saldania, which lies near the Cape, I went, with four or five more, two leagues into the country; and I assure Your Worship that never have I seen a better land in all my life. Though it was the middle of the cold season, the grass came up to our knees. The land is full of woods and beautiful rivers of fresh water, with abundance of deer, fishes and birds; while the number of cows and ewes was astonishing. We bought forty cows for less than four bronze rials apiece, and sheep, as many as we would, at half a bronze rial each. The climate is very healthful, insomuch that, though we arrived with many of our people sick, they all regained health and strength within twenty days. Moreover, it is a place so protected by nature that a very few men can defend themselves against a large number. And we found the natives of the country to be a nation most courteous and tractable, and we had no trouble with them all the time of our stay. Also, as touching its situation, it lies almost in the

[1] The name of the writer is not given; but internal evidence points to Aldworth. [2] Translated from *Doc. Remett.*, vol. III, p. 71.

[3] The East Indies.

middle of the track from Europe to the Indies, and would prove no less serviceable to our voyages than Mozambique is to the Portuguese. And if His Majesty were pleased to give a commission to four or five prudent persons in London to select a hundred men each year from those condemned to death and send them out to found a settlement, without doubt the said convicts would not lack friends who would find eighty ducats for each man, and this would defray the cost of their transportation[1]. Thus they might be established there without any expense to the King or to Your Worships, beyond the artillery necessary for their defence. This I venture to represent to Your Worship, in fulfilment of the obligation I am under to serve my king and my country.

We experienced some difficulty in setting up the factory here; and principally because the General was so incredulous. He could not be persuaded that we should have here a peaceful commerce, even when the King's *farmān* arrived; and this has been a cause of much loss to us. Furthermore, he has departed with not even half the merchandise he might have taken. He is a man of good understanding, but too much inclined to his own will. However, I hope that from henceforth our affairs will go with a smoother current.

Nothing more offers at present. May God keep Your Worship. [PS.] The General told me nothing about the movements[2] of the fleet until we came in sight of St. Lawrence. For this reason I was unable to send a letter about it[3] from the Cape.

Thomas Kerridge at Surat to *Sir Thomas Smythe*

25 January 1613[4]

Right Worshipful Sir,

From the Cape of Good Hope I wrote briefly by the *Solomon* of all that had happened till that time. Now I let Your Worship know that, by the special favour of God, we have set up our factory in the

[1] Apparently as a result of this suggestion, a number of 'condemned men from Newgate' were sent out in the fleet that took Sir Thomas Roe to India (see *The Embassy*, p. 6), but the experiment proved a failure. Long before, the Portuguese had taken out convicts for similar purposes (Prestage, *The Portuguese Pioneers*, pp. 280–1).

[2] The Spanish text has *mit°*, with a query. Apparently what the writer wished to convey was that Best gave him no warning at the Cape of the impending departure of the ships, and in fact said nothing to him of his plans until they were in sight of Madagascar.

[3] The proposal for a settlement at Table Bay.

[4] Translated from the Spanish version printed in *Doc. Remett.*, vol. III, p. 77.

city of Surat. I hope that it will subsist many years, and I pray God that such may be the case, for I think that in all India there is no place so suitable for the sale of the commodities that come from England. It is now desirable, in order the better to establish this commerce, that the Worshipful Company should send hither so many and such fit ships as may resist the forces which the Portuguese have in these parts. They have lost much of their reputation here, by the poor spirit they displayed in their combats with us; while in the same proportion our credit has increased.

The Portuguese will do their utmost, both by gifts and by force, to expel us from this place. It is therefore necessary for us to gain the goodwill of the King and of certain principal persons; the which may be obtained with some trifles from our country, rather than by the gift of other things of much greater value. And of such Mr. Canning, who is to reside at court, will have much need. The ships came out without any provision whatever of the kind.

Some are of opinion that it would prove of great utility to send out people from England to inhabit Saldania, at the Cape of Good Hope; for it is a land very fertile and pleasant, and has great abundance of cows, sheep, deer, birds, and fishes, besides whales and other such creatures, from which each year a great quantity of oil could be obtained. There are also many other commodities to be had there. Only wheat is lacking; and of this it would at first be necessary to bring some quantity from England for sowing, and soon we should have abundance. Such a settlement would doubtless afford great relief to our people, and no less honour to our king and to Your Worships for achieving it.

Since all other matters are dealt with in the general letter, I will say no more, save to recommend Your Worships to God.

Your Worships' obedient servant,
THOMAS KERRIDGE.

Thomas Kerridge at Surat to *Sir Thomas Smythe*

12 March 1613[1]

Right Worshipfull and Honored Sir,

My humble dutye beinge remembred, etc. You may be pleased to understand thatt per the *Sollomon* from the Cape of Bona Esperansa

[1] *O.C.* 105 (I.O. Records). It is in Kerridge's own hand, and is headed 'Copye of my letter of the 12th of Marche, written from Suratt by waye of the Red Sea.' A modernized version of the whole letter appears in *Letters Received*, vol. I, p. 256. Here only the portion bearing on our subject is given. The present transcript is probably the one sent by Kerridge via Masulipatam with his letter of 20 September 1614 (see *ibid.*, vol. II, p. 110).

I wrote Your Worship a few lynes of whatt till then had passed. From whence wee departed the 28th of June, and arryved in saphetye att the barre of Suratt the 7th of September anno ditto. Where myselfe and others were sentt to the towne, and received all kynde usage from the inhabytantts, and incouragement for the settlynge of our factorye. Butt the daye followinge wee receaved a letter of Sir Henry Midletons, relatynge all his proceedings in this place; wherein [he] wished us nott to expectt any factorye here. With which letter I repayred on boarde; by meanes whereof, as also by the arryvall of a shippe of this place shortly after from Mecha, taken in the Red Sea by Sir Henry Midleton, the settlinge of our factory here by manye was helld unfitt; so thatt differences in oppynyons in thatt poynte caused some controversyes to arise betweene our chiefest. Nottwithstandynge, a certaine quantetye of goods was landed, and sould att the prices specyfyed in our generall letter. In the interim hereof the Governour of Amadabaz came to Suratt to buye of our comodities for the King, with order thatt the English showld be used with all kyndnesse and permytted to trade in any nature they showld require, eyther by settlinge factory or for the presentt. Whereupon the Generall propownded certaine artycles, which, after muche arguinge, were by the said Governor yealded unto, and confirmed in the Kings firma to the Governor; which confirmacion was delyvered the Generall some 2 moneths after there agreement (which hee caryed herehence with him).

The 28 of November there arryved att the barre of Suratt 4 gallyons and 25 frigatts of the Portingals, with purpose to have taken or fyred our shippes; and the 29th and 30th our shippes fought with them, with greate honor and advantage. Yett, in regaurd here are dangerous shoalds and some of the gallyons came agrownde, our shippes left the place and wentt farther of[f] to sea; where, wantynge freshe water, they repayred to another roade on this coaste, called Mondrafrabag, where laye incamped some 7 or 8 thowsand soldyers of this kings, beseeginge a towne revolted. Whereof the Portingals havynge intellygence, they wentt thether also. With whome our shippes fought againe this second tyme two severall dayes, and forsed them to a dishonorable flight, in sight of all the campe. And so returned to Suratt, where they road 3 weekes without any molestacion; havynge kylld (by reporte) some 200 of the enymyes, butt of ours (thanckes be to God) only 3 were slayne.

Our shipps havynge landed there comodities (there iron and the greatest partt of theire lead excepted) and havynge received aboarde some 3,500*ll.* sterling in comodities fitt for Achine, Pryaman, etc., the Portingals being againe (4 dayes paste) returned att the barre, the Generall resolved, contrary to his former purpose, to leave this place, for thatt the greatest partt of his provizyons of powder and shotte were spentt, and doupting att leaste the enymyes cuttynge of[f] his boates with theire frigatts in passinge to and from the shoare of Sualy. The 18th of January they departed, purposinge from Achine etc. to returne hether again. And for thatt Your Worship might have speedy intellygence of whatt here passed, the Generall appoynted the steward, Anthony Starky, to travell home by lande with letters; whoe departed from hence the 25th ditto. Per whome I wrote briefely a few lynes to Your Worship in partycular, referringe me to our generall letter; whereunto I was constrayned, tyme nott permyttinge other, by reason of the shipps so soddayne departure (contrary to expectacion), our goods in the costomehowse, and dyvers reconings and busynesses to end with this people....

The 20th of February wee receyved another firma from the Kinge, written in the name of the Generall; the former beinge to the Governor of Amadabaz; wherewith seeinge us nott well contented, hee procured this other to be written dyrectly to the English, in the Perseian tounge (as the former); the copye whereof, as also the translacion, wee herewith send....

Your Worships moste bownden in all duty,

THO. KERIDGE.

Thomas Best etc. at Achin to *Thomas Aldworth etc. at Surat*

12 July 1613[1]

Laus Deo. In Achin, the 12th July 1613.

Loving frinds,

Salutacions etc. These are to give you knowledge of all materiall occurrences past since our departure from Swallye, when (as you knowe) wee sett saile the 20th Januarie last, but passed by the gallions without any warlike greetinge. The nextte daye wee mett with certaine Malabar juncks, from whom wee tooke some powder and munition, and soe discharginge them wee passed alonge the coast of India, in sightte of most of the Portugall townes, till att the barre of Barselore[2], in sightte of the Portugall armada of aboutte 60 frigatts, wee

[1] I.O. Records, *O.C.* 107. A copy, probably sent home from Surat. It has been printed (in modernized spelling and with a few errors) in *Letters Received*, vol. 1, p. 269.

[2] Basrūr, on the Malabar coast, in lat. 13° 38′ N. It is now almost deserted, the trade having been diverted to Kandapur, four miles to the west, on the same inlet.

tooke a small shippe of theirs, laden with rice and jagra[1]; most of her men flyinge on shoare in their boatte. Wee tooke out of her good store of jagra and rice, and her mainemast, which made us a good mizonmast; and then, att the request of the people in her (shee beinge verie leake) wee fired her, tooke her men into our shippe, and sentte them on shoare by the nextte boatte wee mett.

Aboutte the 1 Feb[ruary] wee came to Brinjaon, a small towne some 20 leagues shortte [of] Cape Comorin; where wee were well entertained and had good reefreshinge of water, hennes, fish, cocos, and other fruitts. After 9 or 10 dayes staye, wee sett sayle and endevoured to passe the cape, but were constrained to retorne for B[r]injaon; findinge by good experience that itt shalbe needlesse for any of our shippes which shall heereafter arive att Suratte to proceed on their voyadge for these partts till the middest of Marche.

The 19th of Februarie wee passed Cape Comorin, and fell with Ceylan the 25th of the same[2]. And neere Punta de Galle mette with a smalle Dutch shippe, which keptte us companie 3 or 4 dayes, and then, the wind somewhatt favouringe, wee left them and putt from the coast of Ceylan for this place, where we arived the 12 of Aprill. And after two dayes had accesse unto the Kinge, whom, together with the people, wee find very gripinge, base, and covetous; our brokers very untrustie, intelligencinge[3] our busines, to our greatte prejudice; soe that, in case any of our shippes shall heereafter come for this place, itt shalbe requisitte that in Suratte they bee furnished with one, that can speake the Malaya. Our goods boughtte in Suratte are generallie improper for this place; noughtte beinge heere vendible butt fine whitte callicoes of Baroche [Broach], from 30 to 70 mamuthes per peece, and fine blewes, from 12 to 30 mamuthes. This place is nowe glutted, by reason all trade upon this iland is by the Kinge prohibited to the Guzeratts, save onelie att Achin. 4 of their shippes are nowe heere; whereof 2 wee found heere. Then arived our trustie frind, Malym Ghany; and lastlie the Sabindars shippe, beinge skared from Peracke by the Portingalls, who before had taken 2 of their shippes there, came hither; where instannttlie they were confiscatte, shippe and goods, and the people all made slaves to the Kinge, for goinge to Peracke (beinge the Kings enemies). By Malin Ghany wee receaved your letters, much rejoycinge att the ample firma receaved from Agra, butt more sorrowinge for the indiscreette demeanour of Paull Canninge, whose soe weake beginninge presagethe as unsound a continuaunce and unprofitable conclusion of the Worshipfull Companies affaires by him there to bee mannaged. God turne all to the best.

[1] Coarse sugar.

[2] These dates (like others in the letter) were probably given from memory; they do not agree with those in the journals.

[3] Revealing to others.

The 12 of Maye wee tooke a Portingall barcke, nott farre from this road, wherein came an ambassador from Malacca; but att the earnest request of the Kinge our Generall released her; for which he did him much honour, and gave him the tittle of Orancaya Pute, which is, whitte or cleare-hearted lord. The 2 of this presentte the Kings armada of frigatts came from Joor, bringinge the kinge thereof, with his brother, many of their people, and 22 Dutch prisoners (most of them of the factorie there, the rest of a Dutch shippe then there ridinge). By these we had newes of the *Globe*, of Sir Henrye Middletonne and Captaine Saris fleetts, of the *Solomon* and the *Pearle*; but of the *James* there is noe newes. The *Globe* came first to Mussilapatan, went thence to Bantam, thence to Patane, thence to Siam, and is nowe retorned to Patane, to come with this nextte monsoone to Mussilapatan, and soe home. They have lost Captain Hippon, and one Browne, their master. The *Salomon*, *Peppercorne*, and *Thomas* are gone for England, the *Hector* for Banda, Captaine Saris for Japon; and Sir Henrie Middleton, with the *Trade* and *Darlinge*, is nowe in Bantam, most of his men beinge dead. Of the *James* God send good newes. Wee found heere 2 ambassadors of Siam; from whome wee receaved letters in the name of their kings for the safe trade of our nation in his kingdomes, and from the chief (havinge his kings sealle) wee receaved a letter to the Kings Majestie of England, to move him to send shippes thither, assuringe good entertainementte; of which countries wee have also had good intelligence. Wee have heere sold onelie 168 bahars [of] iron (each bahar beinge 386 li. Englishe) att 5 taile the bahare, each taylle valuinge 16 masse or mamuthes; and have boughtte 23 bahars [of] benjamin, att 25 taylle per bahar. The gold receaved wee have heere ymployed in Suratte goods, viz. blewe callicoes att 80 masse per corge (equall to those cost in Suratt 74), blewe canakins att 26, 30, and 34 mam. per corge (the best beinge of Cambaya), blewe sela att 24 and 28 per corge, trockandias att the same ratte (according to their goodnesse), serasse pintadoes att 50, and some verie fine att 80 mam. per corge, chirans att 24[1]. Of these commoditties wee have boughtte to the valewe of 600 taylle, understandinge them fitte for Passaman, Tecoo, Baros, and Priaman; of which first places wee have heere had good intelligence and encouragementte, and have redeemed, to serve us for broker, a Guseratte

[1] For some of these piece-goods see a note on p. 66. 'Tröckandia' is apparently the Mahratti *trikanda*, meaning 'three sections.' A letter to Persia in 1619 (*English Factories*, 1618–21, p. 142), says that 'camnikeens' and 'tricandees' owed their names to 'theire shortnes and dying...the camnikeen beeing made of baftaes and tricandee of duttie' (*dhoti*). 'Sarasses' or 'serasses' are frequently mentioned among the piece-goods exported from Surat, and the addition of 'pintadoes' (Port. *pintado*, 'painted') shows that they were patterned goods; but their exact nature is not known.

(captive to the Kinge) for 10 tayll, who hath the Portuguese and is well acquainted in those partts. So that, wee hopinge there to lade, you cannott expect us to come any more for Suratte this voyadge; but principallie for that wee have lost 25 (?) of our good men heere (but none officers). The *Oceander* hath onelie lost Ralphe Standish, their surgeon.

Wee have receaved from this kinge his letter and presentte to His Majestie of England, together with his letter for trade att Priaman etc. Our Generall hath much endevoured to redeeme Abdela Cadir (father-in-lawe to Hoja Shan Allye); also Malyn Ally, Mea Hassan, Buggee Manate, Hassan Gematee, Algee Croudia, and Daud Bapon[1]. But the tirantte (though otherwise alwaies honouringe him) in this would nott bee moved, albeitt hee offred him 2 the fairest peeces of ordinaunce in the *Dragon* for a presentte to him; soe that of force they must have patience.

These nott servinge for other, wee cease, and commend you, with ourselves, to God, restinge

Your lovinge frinds,
T. Best.
Wm. More.
H. Gyttins.

Readie to sett saile. Mr. Oliver in health, but absentte att the sealinge.

The Company to *the Factors at Bantam*

3 November 1614[2]

...All our goods that came in the *Dragon* and *Expedition* are sould; the most parte of the pepper shipt out of the land by our owne adventurers, som four Italy, som four Germany, and som four Turkey. The price of the pepper sould, at 20*d.* the *l.* Bantam pepper and 23*d.* Pryaman, ungarbled. All our cloves sould at 6*s.* 11*d.*, ungarbled. All our benjamine at 3*s.* and 3*s.* 1*d.* It would yeald noe more, because it was very bad and evyll conditioned. All the abovesaid weare sould at 4 sixe mounthes tyme[3]....

[1] These names have for the most part been perverted beyond recognition; but we may guess that some of them represent Abdul Kādir, Mu'allim Ali, Miyān Hasan, and possibly Hasan Jamāli. 'Bapon' may be a mistake for 'Bapou,' i.e. Bāpū.

[2] From a copy in *Factory Records, Miscellaneous*, vol. xxv (p. 122).

[3] An explanation of this will be found at p. 269.

Thomas Kerridge at Ahmadābād to *Sir Thomas Roe at Surat*

10 October 1615[1]

... Touching the invaliditye of the articles agreed upon by Capt[ain] Best, wherof we wrote the Generall[2], you may please to understand that Shecksuph[3], Divon of Amadabaz, apointed by the Kinge for the concludinge of peace with the Eng[lish], and Merjafersola[4], who then was Governour of Surratt, and som other of the cheefes that subscribed unto the sayde capitulations, are deceased; which, beinge they were never confirmed per the Kinge, other then in a generall firmaen (he not understandinge the particulers), I conceave it fittinge that the sayd articles, with such additions for redresse of abuses bellowe [i.e. at Surat] as the quallety of the cawse requireth, be compendiouslye drawne into the Persian tounge in severall coppyes, that, at the tyme of Your Lordshipps gracious intertaynment (or soone after), the Kinge may confirme them, with his firma [i.e. signature] or seale annexed; that so they maye be disspressed [i.e. dispersed] and be continewally extant with our factories in severall places, therby to avoyde cavelation in any of the particulers; which elce will happen, by the often channge of governours, as myself have had experience in the tyme of lesse grace, for a principall counseller denyed that the Kinge had granted any suche particulers as are ther mentioned.

The originall in the Persian is not in our possession. Either Capt[ain] Best neglected to take them, or elce caried them home to the Compa[ny]; nor ever since could they be procured, though I often advized to Mr. Aldworth for them. The Shawbander is not without a coppy of them; but hee, I feare, is no great frindes to us, and therfor the more difficult to be procured. I have written a fewe lynes to our antient frinde Mier Giofer [Mīr Jafar] (who also subscribed them), if possible to procure and deliver them unto Your Lordshippe....

[1] From a copy in Brit. Mus. *Addl. MS.* 9366, f. 12.

[2] Referring to a letter of 26 September 1615 (*ibid.*, f. 6) from Kerridge and John Brown to Capt. Keeling, in which it is stated that 'the articles agreed upon by Captayne Best were never signed by the Kinge, otherwise then by a generall firmaen without knowledge of the particulers; and those (the Governours that signed them beinge dead) are of small vallidity.'

[3] Shaikh Yūsuf (see p. 217).

[4] Probably 'Mīrza Faiz-ullāh' is intended.

[*William Nichols*] *at Achin* to *Thomas Aldworth at Surat*

31 January 1616[1]

By the unsertayntye of this convayance[2] I ame discoradged for amplefying, as otherwise I would. In breefe, therefore, it maye please you, the 12 of April 1613 we arived with [th]e *Dragon* and *Hoziander* in this roade of Achein; where we contynued untell the 13 of July following, haveing heare buryed out of both shipps 26 men. And at last, with this Kinge[s] letter to trade at Tecoo or Pryaman, we arived in the roade of Tecoo the 7th of August. Where all the merchants dying, John Wattson and John Harman, with some 20 more marriners, it fell to my lott to be left prinsepall merchant for the sall[e] of the goods, and my mate captain of the *Hoziander*, to remayne abourd, espeatyally in the night. Thuse, fynding slacke salles, and knavery by the people ashore, who, haveing pepper, did detrackt tyme, which they knewe to be chargyable to us, at last, the 30 of October 1613, Gennerall Best departed for Bantam. Soe, after a 3 mounthes, Captain Christian was foursed to followe; the *Hoziander* provinge soe leaque thorowgh the worme (espeatyall growing, by there joudgments, thorough the fowlenes of the sea water at Sually). After 5 mounthes absence, haveing sheathed at Jackatra (nere Bantam), [she] retourned....

Thomas Kerridge and other factors at Surat to *Sir Thomas Roe at Ajmer*

26 May 1616[3]

...The inconstancy and infedillity of this people caused the breach betweene Sir Henry Myddleton and them and what theron ensued. In the interim wherof came Captain Best, whoe soone after, haveing knowledge of the passed, feared to settle heere and, haveing landed goods, would have had them returned aboard and soe departed; which the people [would] by noe meanes condescend unto (though hee surprised one of their shipps for that cause), but as it were perforce, with extraordinary kinde usage and protestacions (Mr. Aldworth beeing willing to harken therunto) detayned us. And soone

[1] From an unsigned copy in the India Office (*O.C.* 336). The whole letter is printed in *Letters Received*, vol. IV, p. 21.

[2] It was entrusted to the master of a Dabhol ship, bound for the Red Sea.

[3] From an unsigned copy in the India Office (*Factory Records, Surat*, vol. LXXXIV, part I, f. 36). The whole letter, in a modernized version, is given at p. 311 of *Letters Received*, vol. IV.

after Sheak Isuph, Dyvon of Amadavaz, by the procurement of some greater courtiers haveing received a firmaen from the King to that purpose, came to Swally, treated and concluded a peace with our nation, under conditions comprised in certayne articles, wherof Your Lordship hath a copy; which, for want of sufficyent linguists, were not translated into the Persian, as requisite, but their firmes [i.e. signatures] for assurance were taken to the originall in English, and others by them framed in the Persian; wherof (itt beeing then omitted) wee could never since obtaine a coppie. Captain Beste beeing departed, wee received a firmaend from the King, dyrected to the English, ratefieing in gennerall termes what had bine concluded by the said Sheak Isuph; which not beeing soe sufficyent as wee desired, Mr. Pawle Canning (apoynted to reside in courte) was injoynd to procure the Kings firm unto the said articles....

EXTRACTS FROM THE COURT MINUTES OF THE EAST INDIA COMPANY[1]

22 *December* 1613 (*A General Court*) (vol. III, p. xvii).

...Mr. Governour acquainted them...further that a letter was sent from Mr. Best out of the East Indies, signifying the setling of a trade in the mayne; which was forborne to bee red, because some thinges were therein that were nott fitt to bee publisht; yett, for the satisfaction of any of the Company which should bee desyrous to see the same in private, Andrewe Ellym, the Accountant, wilbe ready to shewe yt unto them; or, yf they thought fitt, they might have ytt read nowe, or att another Courte. But all rested satisfied with Mr. Governours speech, and would nott have yt red....

15 *April* 1614 (vol. III, p. 96).

...Mr. Governor acquainted them that Mres. Best had bene with him and entreated favour for 100*li*. of her husbands sallary, to releive her present occasions; beinge urdgd thereunto by reason that she fayled of such fraight as she expected to have received for her husbands parte of the *Pearle* and some other shippinge, which he had appointed her to receive, and some other rent which she should have had. And although yt were objected that Mr. Best was soe provident to leave her sufficient meanes of maintenance duringe his absence and would conceyve yt an indignitye to have her come and demand any parte of his sallary, yet they weyed withall that, wantinge those hopes she relyed upon, and the testymony of Mr. Governour, whoe averd that Mr. Best at his departure entreated him to be good unto her: they therefore at last resolvd to have 50*li*. sent unto her by Mr. Mountney[2]; and yf she should urdge her necessitie, then to have the other 50*li*. sent unto her by Mr. Mountney, presently or else 2 or 3 monnethes hence, accordinge to occasion....

19 *April* 1614 (vol. III, p. 99).

...The Company beinge enformed that Mres. Best hath discovered her wants to be soe greate as that lesse then 100*li*. of her husbands wages will not releive her as is fittinge: they were therefore contented

[1] Preserved at the India Office. A 'General Court' means a meeting to which all members of the Company were summoned. Otherwise, the proceedings are those of the 'Committees' (equivalent to modern 'Directors').

[2] Richard Mountney, the Company's 'Husband.'

to grannte the same, and ordered to have yt paid presentlie unto her; supposinge that he could not but take yt very kindlie and thankfullie at the Company[s] hands to be soe carefull to supplye her wannts in his absence, upon such just grounds as were formerlie layd downe and alledge[d] by her....

8 *June* 1614 (vol. III, p. 117).

...One Nicholas Banghman [*sic*] presented himselfe in courte (in company with a Scottishman[1], whoe hath served the Portugalls these 32 yeares in the East Indies) and brought newes of the saufe arrivall of the *Dragon* into the Downes: with letters from Captaine Best of the 7th of this instannt, dated betwixt the Nesse [Dungeness] and Dover, whereby they understood of the greate losse of the *Trades Encrease*, which miscarryed neare Bantam whilest she was carryninge [i.e. careening]; Sir Henry Middleton and most of his men beinge dead, but yett all her goods on shore at Bantam, and onlye the bare shipp perisht: a relation breiflie of his [Best's] voyage, and invoice of his ladinge: with his desier to bee furnisht with a pilott, men, and some fresh provisions. Whereupon they entreated Mr. Salmon[2] to under-

[1] This was William Carmichael, for whose remarkable career see the Introduction.

[2] Robert Salmon, son of Robert Salmon (1533–91) of Leigh-on-Sea, and brother of the Nathaniel Salmon who was master of the *Hosiander*. From the inscription on his monument we learn that he was born in 1566 or 1567; and he was probably the seaman of that name who was master of the *Pleasure* (then lading for Russia) in 1599 and again in 1606–7 (London Port Books). He was admitted to the freedom of the East India Company in November 1609 without fine, in consideration of 'the divers benefitts that might happen unto the Companie in the provisions to be made aboute their shippinge and hireinge men'; and he served as a 'Committee' from about 1613 to 1618. During part of this period he seems to have been paid a regular salary for his services (Court Minutes, 24 October 1617). After that he took no part in the direction, though from time to time his help was sought in the valuing or surveying of ships. In 1617 he was Master of the Trinity House, in this respect following in the footsteps of his father, who had held the same office in 1588. The coats-of-arms of both may still be seen in one of the windows of the chapel of the Trinity Hospital in the Mile End Road, in commemoration of their services; and according to his monument, the younger Robert was not only the Master of the Trinity House but 'the glory of it 24 yeares.' In 1640 he was chosen Sheriff of London, but declined to serve and was fined accordingly. He died in the following year (18 June), and was buried in the parish church of Leigh-on-Sea, where his monument, surmounted by a bust, is still extant. A drawing of it will be found at p. 137 of Barrett's *Trinity House*.

Salmon appears to have married twice. By his first wife (name unknown) he had a son Robert (who has been mentioned already as marrying the widow of Robert Bonner) and two daughters. His second wife was Martha (born in 1577), sister of Lancelot Andrewes, Bishop of Winchester. She had been

take the care thereof, and to hasten downe presentlie and use his best endevours to give him satisfaction in those his demanndes. Sundrie other letters were red (as tyme would permitt)...one from William More, dated at Tecooe the 14th of August 1613[1], relating the successe of there buysines at Suratt and setlinge a good trade for the ventinge of 4000 broadcloathes yearlie, with sundrye other materiall circumstances....

9 *June* 1614 (vol. III, p. 117).

A letter was red from Edward Cristen, dated from Tecooe on Sumatra the 27th of October 1613, and another from Nathaniell Salmon, of the same date[2]; wherein Edward Cristen maketh relation of his intended voyadge to the Molluccoes, with hopes of good successe....Lastlie, one other letter[3] was red, from Mr. Patricke Copland, dated the 7th of this instannt from aboard the *Dragon*, extollinge the zeale and care of the Generall and good government amongst his people, which mayntayned love betweene them, liveinge peaceablie and conscionablie all the whole voyadge....

17 *June* 1614 (vol. III, p. 121).

...Captaine Best presentinge himselfe in courte, and some congratulations past upon his saufe retourne out of the East Indies, hee made a breife relation of the Portugalls comeinge to Suratt to have putt him from trade; and acquainted them with letters and a present which hee hath to His Majestie from the Kinge of Achen; which Mr. Governour desyred him to putt in a readines against Sundaie next, to bee presented to His Majestie by him....Mr. Governor acquainted them that sixe grocers have beene abourd the *Dragon* in the Downes [and] bought 2400 waight [i.e. 24 cwt.] of pepper and 40*li.* of cloves; whoe affirme that the countrye was fild with spices, both at Rye, Dover, and Sandwich, which they had bought abourd, and, their goods beinge stayed by warrannt from Mr. Governour, they desyred favour from the Company; but beinge absent, nothinge was done in their buysines at present. Yett Captaine Best, beinge demanded a reason thereof, acquainted this company that, for his mens better encourragement at Suratt, upon the comeinge of the Portugalls, he tould them that they should have favour in layinge out their meanes upon comodities; and beinge afterwards at Achen, not expectinge to proceede to Bantam, hee gave them leave to buye pepper (because that

previously married to Robert Princep, by whom she had had a son, Thomas. By her second marriage she had two sons, the Rev. Peter Salmon and Thomas Salmon (Russell's *Life of Bishop Andrewes*, p. 542). She survived till 1653.

[1] Not extant.

[2] Neither letter has survived.

[3] Not extant.

place affourded nothinge else), provided that they did make entrye into the pursers booke of whatsoever they brought abourd, and the rest should bee adjudged unlawfull gotten and to apperteyne unto the Company; which are the goods (as he supposeth) that are nowe sould; referringe himselfe to the pursers bookes and excusinge none that is not soe entred. Butt yett the Company held yt reasonable that such as have bought those goods should nottwithstandinge paye fraight for them, before the goods be suffered to bee carryed away; or some such other course taken with them, as upon advise should bee thought fittinge. Upon enquirye made, Captaine Best certifyed them that he hath brought home in the *Dragon* sixe peeces [of ordnance] of the *Trades Encrease*; and the Hollander[1] hath 3 of them. The rest of her ordinnance were sould to the Dutch, to bee paid for in [Holland] or else to delyver as mony for them to the English, waight for waight[2]; which was the rather done, because the Kinge of Bantam was earnest for them. He acquainted them further that he hath remayneinge abourd aboute 36 hog[s]heads of beefe and porke, all very good, three butts of wyne, a butt of cyder, 5 or 6 barrells of oyle, and 2000 bread; haveinge sould to the valewe of 100*li.* sterling, in provisions and cordage, at Bantam: that at his comeinge away he brought 21 of the *Trades Encrease* men, and therefore tooke 16 hoggesheads of her beefe and porke, which he spent first, because yt was not soe good as his owne, butt all that is remayneinge nowe is of his owne store; which they desyred Mr. Abbott[3] and some others [to inquire?] amongst the shipps that are to goe for the Straicts[4], whether they will not buy any parte thereof. They entringe into consideration at what tyme [it] will be fittinge to breake bulke [aboard the *Dragon*], and understandinge by Mr. Mountney that loyters [i.e. lighters] are gone downe to take out her ordinaunce, cordage, emptie caske, and all other lumber, which cannot bee effected to cleire her untill Mondaie or Tuesdaie next, they therefore held yt fitt to have bulke broken on Thursdaye, and to entreate 2 Comittees dailie to goe abourd and see the hatches opened and shutt up againe, to beginne in course and soe to proceede untill she bee unladen. Because there be divers loose particulars aboord of good valewe, which cannott suddenlie be distinguisht to whome they doe apperteine, it was therefore ordered that Mr. Mountney should cause a close loyter[5] to be there ready, to have them

[1] Apparently a slip for '*Hosiander*.'

[2] From a reference in the Court Minutes for 3 March 1615, it appears that a settlement was to be made in Holland, either by delivery of fresh ordnance or payment of the value, at the choice of the English Company.

[3] Morris Abbot, then a 'Committee' and afterwards Governor (knighted in 1625).

[4] That is, for the Mediterranean.

[5] A lighter closed in, both for security and secrecy.

putt in and brought up to Mr. Governours, to be safelie kept there untill they may be considered of at better leasure.... The Company desyringe to be satisfied what goods were lefte at Suratt belonginge to the 10th Voyadge, Captaine Best awnswered that yt will appeare in the accompt of John Cransbye, which he promised to bringe with him at his next comeinge unto the accomptannts; supposing that there is a matter of 4000*li*. And [he will bring ?] alsoe the letters he received from Mr. Aldworth and the rest of the factours, sent to him and received by him whilest he lay att Achen; wherein they make noe mention of any troubles that did befall them after his departure, as is intimated in Mr. Gurneys[1] letter, but that they were well and the estate of their buysines likewise. They desyringe his opinion of leaveinge Bantam and setlinge in some other place, both in reguard of the ayre and exaction of customes, hee delivered his opinion that yt is fitt to leave the place and make their rendevouz at Jacatra[2] (soe they may have the Flemings to joyne with them to leave Bantam), a place aboute 5 leagues from thence, under the comannd of another kinge, the ayre very healthfull[3] and the kinge desyrous of them, profferinge all kindnes and that they shall paye butt $3\frac{1}{2}$ [per cent.] custome, and to be favorable in any other priviledges; whereas at Bantam the kinge hath exacted to $5\frac{3}{4}$ per cent, and more. Captaine Best likewise perswaded them to give dyrections that noe more divisions may be hereafter, by haveinge sundrye houses there, upon soe many severall accompts, for their chardge is extreame thereby. But he hath reconcyled the former division that was, soe that they joyne in love and dyett together, although they have three severall houses yet, kept by three severall personns, George Ball in one, William Sheppard in the second, and Cassarian [David] in the third[4]. And [he] certyfied them that elaphannts teeth are in noe request nor reputation at Suratt; but [broad]cloathes much desired (there measure in length 35 ynches), sould for double the value they cost in England; and [he] perswaded to send 1000 with their next shipps....

[1] John Gourney, a factor in the *James*. His letter is not extant.

[2] The Dutch had been contemplating since 1607 a removal from Bantam to Jakatra (about fifty miles to the eastward), and in 1610 they obtained permission to establish a factory at the latter place. In 1619, as the outcome of hostilities in which the English for a time aided the King of Jakatra, the Dutch destroyed the native town and built on its site the fortress of Batavia (Nova), which thereupon became their headquarters in the East. The English had in 1613 negotiated for leave to settle at Jakatra; but, though the King was willing, they were deterred from accepting his offers by the threats of the Bantam authorities. However, they frequently repaired their ships at that place, and for a time maintained an agent there.

[3] This was far from being true, as the Dutch found to their cost.

[4] Ball (see p. 180) and David were merchants of the Eighth Voyage, while Sheppard belonged to the Ninth.

20 *June* 1614 (vol. III, p. 125).

...God haveinge blest the *Dragons* retourne, which hath brought home a good quantitye of pepper, they entred into consideration what course were best to be thought upon to be determind of at next Generall Courte concerning the same. And Mr. Abbott...doth make noe question but they may give leave...that twoe capitalls[1] may bee delivered upon the 10th Voyage. But for the price and tyme, they referd yt to be determyned by the said Generall Court; as alsoe at what rates and tyme to sell unto the grocers, both case and callicoe[2], garbled....

22 *June* 1614 (*A General Court*) (vol. III, p. 126).

...Mr. Governour acquainted this courte that the espetiall cause of callinge them together at present was to lett them knowe of the retourne of the shipp the *Dragon* out of the East Indies (a thinge which they are not ignorannt of); in which shipp Captaine Best, the Generall, hath performed worthie service, both for the honour of this kingdome and English nation and for the setling of a beneficiall trade in Cambaia, for the good of this Company: a service of very greate moment and consequence, in the prosecutinge whereof he had many oppositions, assaults, and sundrie attempts made by the Portugalls, divers fights and encounters; in all which yt pleased God soe to blesse his endevours as that he repeld them, setled a factory on shore, upon good capitulations with the cheefe governours of those parts, authorized from the Emperour, and those articles afterwards confirmd under the seale of the lannd from the Grand Magore himselfe. Soe that he hath done as much for the present as could bee expected from him; which by Gods blessinge may prove a very proffitable trade, both to this Company and comonwealth. They caused sundry letters to be red (as tyme would permitt), one directed from Mr. Aldworth and others from Suratt unto Captaine Best[3], discoursing of their affaires after his departure and prices of comodities, hopinge to see his retourne backe againe unto them; one other from Nathaniell Salmon to Mr. Governour from Tecoe, extollinge the plenty and pleasantnes of the country of Cambaia, wishinge himselfe in England that hee might

[1] The adventurers in any particular Voyage received back their capital and profits in a series of 'divisions,' and often they were given the option of taking out these 'divisions' in goods at fixed rates, thus enabling them to make a further profit by retailing the commodities received. A 'double capitall' means of course a return of 200 per cent., viz. the amount originally subscribed and an equal sum in addition.

[2] These terms are explained on p. 269.

[3] None of the letters here mentioned is now extant.

proceede in there next shippinge into those parts; a letter from William Moore att Tecooe, likewise of advise of sundry particulars, as well for present as future trade; and another from Captaine Newporte, from aboard the *Expedition*....Some former letters haveinge mentioned the providinge of twoe drumlers[1] to remayne in the ryver of Suratt to secure the goods from the Portugalls frigotts that are to be past up and downe betwixt Suratt and their shippinge, Mr. Best his opinion beinge demanded therein, he replyed very confidentlie that yt was better cheape, and saufer for their goods, to have them carryed by carts from the shore (then by water), where their shipps did ride soe neare, as they might bee heard call from abourd unto the land; and the carryage soe reasonable as that yt would bee as cheape as by water; and the Emperour and the Governours beinge tyed by their articles to make good and secure all their goods on shore from any violence of the Portugalls, hee concluded yt farr more saufe then by water, where the Portugalls would alwaies be attempting against them and seekinge all advantage, both to their greate chardge, danger, and trouble....The Company, entringe into consideration howe to dispose of such pepper as God hath sent home in the *Dragon*, were desyrous to take some course for the dispersinge thereof before the Hollanders shipps should retourne, as that they might not loose the oportunity of the marketts abroad, and the rather because Captaine Newporte is expected very shortlie with more. And they beinge satisfied from the Comittees that the 6th and 10th Voyadges, each of them, will beare a double capitall, they resolvd to give leave to such of the Sixt Voyage as have taken out one capitall heretofore to take out a second now, and those that have had nothinge to take out twoe; and a double capitall for the 10th [in pepper], either case or callicoe, ungarbled, to be transported. And advising of the price, some were of opinion to sett the price lowe, in reguard the Hollanders are dailye expected, and such as shall disperse yt ought to bee encouraged by the price. Yet some others reasons being delivered, of the small quantitye that is like to come this yeare, either for Hollanders, Portugalls, or this land, the goodnes of this, and a condition that the Company doe tye themselves unto, that yf by any other occasion the Company shall sett lower price betwixt this and Christmas next, then such as have taken out upon their adventures shalbe abated accordinglie, and they shall pay noe more then the lowest price that shall be made. And the question at last beinge putt (after sundry doubts objected and cleird) betwixt 19*d*. without condition and 20*d*. with the former condition of abatement, it was resolvd by erection of hands to

[1] Small, fast vessels. 'She was immediatly assaulted by divers English pinasses, hoyes, and drumblers' (Hakluyt, vol. IV, p. 223).

sell the callicoe at 20*d.* and the case at 23*d.* per *li.*[1] ungarbled, to bee transported. Butt yf any shall take out more then twoe capitalls upon either Voyadge, he is to awnswere for yt with securytie att three six monnethes, or a yeares daie right out[2]. And yt was resolvd by the like erection of hands to make sale of garbled pepper, to be uttered in towne, the case at 2*s.* per *li.* and callicoe at 21*d.* per *li.*, noe lesse then sixe baggs at a time, to be paid for (with securitie) at 4 and 4 monnethes; but yf any be desyrous to take out a greater quantity, of 40 baggs or upwards, then to give tyme at three four monnethes for payment thereof, with securitie as before....

28 *June* 1614 (vol. III, p. 129).

...The Company findinge the greate damage that hath befalne them from tyme to tyme at Bantam, both by the mortalitie of their men and exactions made by the Kinge and Governours of customes and other duties, wherby they doe daylie encroach more and more, to the greate prejudice and disadvantage of the marchants, both English and Dutch, it was therefore recomended to their considerations to be dulie weighed, to thinke upon some other more convenyent place whether [i.e. whither] to remove and settle their factorye, both wholesome for ayre and more reasonable and conscionable for all other dutyes. And haveinge heard the opinion of Captaine Best, and dulie considered of the dangers that may befall in removeinge, and contrary wise the benefitt that is likelie to redound thereby, and the reputation that yt will bringe unto the Company, when yt shall appeare howe tender they bee over their mens lives, and bee knowne what care they take to remove them into a more healthfull place and settle elswhere, they all concluded, by erection of hands, of sendinge away a pinnace with all convenient speede, with advise and comission to such persons of good discretion as shall be further considered of, as well to conferr with the Kinge of Jacatra aboute a certaine place there for a factory and a setled course for the customes, with leave to build

[1] A comparison of the prices here stated with those given in the letter to Bantam on p. 258 shows that by 'case' pepper is meant that which Best had bought at the Sumatra ports, while that which he acquired at Bantam is distinguished as 'calico' pepper. The origin of these terms can only be guessed; but the most probable explanation seems to be that the Bantam pepper was brought home in sacks made of coarse calico, while the Sumatra, bought loose, was packed at Bantam in wooden chests or cases, partly to differentiate it and partly for convenience in stowage.

[2] Meaning that the buyer was to give bond that he would pay for the pepper in three equal instalments at the end of six, twelve, and eighteen months respectively (or, at his option, pay the whole at the end of twelve months), and was to find a guarantor as well. See note on p. 48 of *Court Minutes of the East India Company*, 1635–39.

a strong house, free from fire; as alsoe to conferre with the Flemmings, to have their consent likewise and resolution to leave Bantam and joyne with the Englishe in removeinge wholie to Jacatra or elsewhere, as they shalbe better advised. The managinge of which buysines doth require a man or twoe of good experience, wisdome, and resolution, to keepe his intents private and for the saufe conveyannce away of their goods without discovery or suspition to the Kinge or Governour of Bantam. And Captaine Best delyveringe his opinion therein, gave greate comendations both of John Jourdan and George Ball, both for their sobriety and understandinge, holdinge them to bee as fitt and sufficient personns to have the care of this maine buysines recommended unto their discretions, and better experienct then can bee sent from hence; supposinge that they will thinke much to submitt themselves unto any straunger not soe well experienct as themselves, whoe of necessitie must receive his directions and light from them; but the buysines once effected, then the Company may dispose of their principall affaires to whom they shall thinke fitt. Yett because one present here at their conferences may better be possest with the Companies intents then any other by relation and wrightinge, they advised of Mr. Nicholas Isaacke[1] and Mr. Francis Otley, personns well qualified for such a service; of whome Mr. Best delivered his knowledge of Mr. Isaacke, for his sufficiency; whereupon yt was resolvd to entertaine him for that action, yf hee may be had; desyring Mr. Governour to write his letter unto him to come up to London, where the Company will conferre with him, and conclude for the voyadge, or give him content for his jorney and paines taken in comeinge upp....

29 *June* 1614 (vol. III, p. 132).

...Mr. Best acquainted this courte with some observations that he had made abroad, which hee supposeth the Company may make good use of: that the Flemyngs have one that lyveth on shore in the Indies, whoe hath the title of Generall and is furnisht with absolute power and authoritie to comaund all the rest, as well for trade as government[2]; and is of opinion that their buysines will never bee well

[1] It appears from the Court Minutes that Captain David Middleton had wished to take Nicholas Isaac (or Isaacson) with him in his voyage for the First Joint Stock (1614) as second in command; but the latter, on being approached, demanded a salary of 200*l.*, and the Company refused to give so much, especially to 'a man that never was in the East Indyes.' On the present occasion (as will be seen) they also found his terms too exorbitant.

[2] The post of Governor-General had been created in 1609, but it was not until December 1610 that Pieter Both, the first occupant of the post, reached Bantam.

carryed untill this Company have the lyke, by one of countenance and sufficiency to give directions unto the rest for the managinge of their affaires into severall places, and that all the rest may submitt themselves unto government, without any opposition; which he referd to their wysdomes, to be more seriouslie considered of hereafter. And for the present buysines in hand, delyvered his opinion that such as shall be employed maye with discretion and secrecy conveye awaye their mony and remove yt by degrees, some at one tyme and some at another, and then the goods will never bee reguarded, butt that they may shipp them awaye, when and howe they will, without any exception or reguard taken thereunto by the Governour or any other in authoritie.

Mr. Middleton[1] propoundinge to knowe whether store of pepper may not be had at Pryaman and Achen, Mr. Best acquainted this courte that, yf they had a factory setled at Tecooe (which is under the Kinge of Achens comannd)—whereunto Captaine Best doth wholie incline and houlds yt most necessary and proffitable—they might then, in tyme of yeare, procure greate quantities of pepper for Cambaia goods; affirminge the value of 5000*li.* in cloth from Suratt will yeild a matter of 18 or 20,000*li.* in pepper; which will not bee much dearer unto them then the Bantam pepper, consideringe the first price that those cloathes doe cost, and that tyme and meanes to vent the same will make the natives plante greate quantities in the countrye, as they have done att Bantam; assuringe them that at Tecooe there is greate store of gould to be had, and the place very holesome to lyve in; soe that yf any reasonable quantity thereof bee brought for England, although yt bee but for small proffitt, yet yt will bringe a greate reputation unto this Company. And they, takeinge espetiall notice thereof, intended to have a factory disposed of there, soe soone as they could give directions for the same....

5 *July* 1614 (*A General Court*) (vol. III, p. 141).

...A letter[2] was red...from Edward Cristen, dated at Tecooe on Sumatra the 27 of October 1613, discoursinge his voyadge to Bantam in the Hollander[3] for intelligence and retourne backe to the Generall with heavie newes of the losse of Sir Henry Middleton, the *Trades Encrease*, and most of his men at Bantam, danger of fier there, the *Dragons* proceedinge thether, and the favour bestowed upon him by makinge him captaine of the *Hoseander* for an intended voyage to the

[1] Robert Middleton, one of the 'Committees.'
[2] Already mentioned on p. 264.
[3] A mistake for *Hosiander*.

Molluccoes, from whence hee hopeth to lade cloves, or better comodities, with Gods assistance, or never to see England againe.

. . . This courte was made acquainted that the espetiall occasion of their meetinge was to make choise of their Governour, Deputy, Comittees, and other officers appointed to bee elected as at this tyme. But before they proceeded to their buysines Mr. Governour made knowne unto them an accident latelye befalne, which perhaps might be censurd by some abroad, as too severaly prosecuted by him against young men, butt, the trueth beinge delyvered, he would leave yt to be construed by any indifferent judgment; giveing them to understannde that certaine grocers went aboard the *Dragon* in the Downes and bought pepper and other spices, to the quantity of 2400 waight and more; which being brought in a carte thorough Deptford, betwixt 2 and 3 of the clocke on Whit Sunday morninge, was staied by the constable and bailiffe of the towne, suspectinge yt by reason they whoe drave the carte could neither tell to whome yt apperteynd nor where yt should bee delivered in London; and beinge housd afterwards by these persons, Mr. Governour sent his warrannt as a Justice in those parts to have yt detayned untill they should have further directions. These younge men suinge for favour, the Company, one day being mett[1], were contented to passe over the wronge done unto them (although every tunne of such goods stood the Company in 40*li*. fraight at the least), conditionally they would paye the some of tenn pounds towards the paines taken by the officers of the said place, and yett had caused Mr. Westrowe[2] underhannd to procure a matter of 40*s*. from them for those men of Deptford, and they should have the goods delyvered unto them. Butt they, refusinge to contribute one penny in that nature, gave out that they would rather spend 20*li*. in lawe to justifie their courses then paye one penny by compulsion; and soe procured a newe certificate from Sandwich, and made the officers beleive yt was a warrannte and for the goods, which they would carry awaye, although Sir Thomas Smith were present to oppose them, and by that meanes gott them into their possession. Whereupon he caused them to be putt in suite, both in the Exchequour and Admiralty, to make them knowe themselfes and not to contest and brave yt in that manner, where[as] there actions are not justifiable. And because such as doe nott understand the manner and matter may bee readye to cast aspersions upon him abroad, he therefore desyred all present that, yf they should heare anythinge to his disparadgment, that they would awnswere for him accordinge to equitye and trueth. All that heard yt condempned them in their opinions, and gave Mr. Governour thankes for his paines taken therein, which may prove

[1] On 1 July 1614 (vol. III, p. 137).

[2] Thomas Westrow, one of the 'Committees.'

effectuall for an example to others for runninge into the lyke courses hereafter[1].

Mr. Governor gave a touch likewise of the action performed by Captaine Best, beinge sparing therein, because the Generall himselfe was present; yett could not passe yt over in silence without admiration that yt pleased God to give such a blessinge and courage to men to performe such fights with one shipp and a pynnace against 4 such gallions and soe many frigotts, soe well furnisht with store of munition and mand with such nombers of men; which never daunted the spiritts of our men, but that their courages rather encreast then quaild; which proveth the Companies care to provide good and sufficient men, and wipeth away some ymputation cast upon them, as yf they cared not whome they enterteynd. And desyred all present that, when shipps are to goe forth, they would endevour to assiste to procure good and sufficient men to be presented; wherein they should doe good service to the Company and ease the Comittees of a greate deale of trouble and care. And putt them alsoe in remembraunce howe much right they had done unto themselves, by takeinge awaye those disorders which happened thorough the disjoynted stocke, by reconcileing and drawinge all into one entire accompt....

5 *July* 1614 (vol. III, p. 147).

...The Company, findinge themselves much agreved with the private trade that is used by their factours in the country, cast an ymputation upon their comanders for permittinge and not hindringe the same; butt yett were well satisfied with Captaine Best his apologie, yeilding a reason whye hee permitted his men to buye of such comodities as the shipp did lade withall, which was, to encourrage them the better to fight, and for that there were noe other things to bee had but pepper, where they were, as he hath oftentymes heretofore trulie enformed them.

9 *July* 1614 (vol. III, p. 154).

...The occasion of Mr. Isaacks demand to have leave for private trade[2] caused some things to bee cald to remembraunce, that Mr. Aldworth and Mr. Canninge have offended in (in high measure) at their comeinge to Suratt, by sendinge their goods to Bantam and

[1] From entries in the Court Minutes for 18, 21, and 25 October and 4 November 1614 it appears that the dispute was finally settled by the offenders paying to the Company the sum of 20*l*.

[2] Isaac had demanded, not only a salary of 200*l*. a year, but liberty to trade on his own account to the extent of 200*l*. The Company refused to employ him on such terms, resolving that to sanction private trade would be 'a dangerous president.'

combyninge with the factours there to favour them in the retournes, as they will expect the like at their hannds; which they doe conceive to bee soe greate a wronge done unto the Company as that yt is not fitt to be endured, but (to terrifie others) to send for them home and call them to accompt for what they have done....

A letter was red from Mr. Francis Otley to Mr. Crispe[1], wrytten from Middleborough [Middelburg] the 27th of June 1614, desyringe to bee employed in the Companies service. Hee was much comended by many for his honestie and sufficiency, and therefore they did enclyne to yeild to have him conferd withall, yf hee did come to London; purposinge to have employed him, uppon good testimony of his sufficiency. But beinge enformed that hee hath a Dutchwoman to his wife, they distasted yt much, supposinge that hee may beate a trade privately and convey his goods home by the Dutchmen; suspectinge him the rather, because hee is employed in a course of lyfe which cannot but gaine him 3 or 400*li.* a yeare by brokeridge, and is (as is said) in bare estate. Whereupon, all things considered, yt was held the saufest course to forbeare him; and therefore wisht that some of his freinds would write unto him to forbeare to make preparation for that employment untill hee doe heare further from them by writeinge[2]....

Mr. Best acquainted this courte that the ordinance which they doe employe in most of their shippinge is too small, and the number too fewe; instancynge that the *Dragon* must bee furnisht with more hereafter, and greater. Which they intended to consider of, and take such course therein as should bee thought necessary and fittinge; and desyred the Comittees appointed for those buysines of the ordinannce to advise thereof, and enforme themselves in the meane tyme....

11 *July* 1614 (vol. III, p. 156).

...The *Expedition* beinge nowe retournd into the Downes, by the blessinge of God, Mr. Governour moved to have one sent downe to fetch her up. Mr. Salmon[3] was nominated; butt Mr. Best disswaded, advisinge not to permitt him to goe from the *Dragon*, but to take care of bringinge her to Wolledge or the Wall [i.e. Blackwall], beinge a buysines of greater dannger then the former. Mr. Salmon comended

[1] Nicholas Crispe, one of the 'Committees.' He was an active supporter of the East India trade from its commencement, and seems to have been closely associated with Sir Thomas Smythe (Dasent's *Acts of the Privy Council*, 1601–4, p. 267). The celebrated Sir Nicholas Crispe was his nephew.

[2] The question of employing Ottley was again raised at meetings held on 18 and 21 October 1614, but in the end he was rejected as 'altogether unfitt for their service.'

[3] Robert Salmon (see p. 263). He was present at this meeting.

the sufficiency of Mr. Bonner, the master of the *Dragon*, to be equall for that service with any manns that could bee employed; whoe may, yf he shall see cause, procure any one amongst many of his neighbours of sufficient experience to joyne in assistannce with him to effect the same. And they, haveing dulie considered hereof, resolvd at last to leave the chardge of bringinge the *Dragon* up unto Mr. Bonner as before; and Mr. Salmon to procure men, or any other provisions for the *Expedition* that shalbee needfull, and to take the chardge of bringinge her over.

...A letter was red from William Nicholls, whoe went forth purssers mate in the *Dragon*, dated at Tecooe the 30th of November 1613[1], extollinge Achen to be a most comodious place for a factory to vent Suratt comodities; where greate benefitt may bee made, yf policye may be used to pollicye, for the people of the countrye are very craftie and worke upon the advantage of the sudden comeinge and departure of our shippinge. He advised of the particuler comodities of Suratt that are most requested there, and howe the next shipps that proceede to that place should carry themselves towards those people, to drawe them on to good trade....A letter was likewise red from John Jourdan[2], dated the second of January 1613 [1614] at Bantam, expressinge the quantity of pepper laden in the *Expedition* for the accompt of the 6th Voyadge; and division that is falne againe amongst the factours at Bantam, in their severall houses, for superioritie; and howe the ordinannce and powder of the *Trades Encrease* is disposed amongst the Hollanders and the Kinge of Bantam. As also one from him to Captaine Best of the same date and matter[3]....

12 *July* 1614 (vol. III, p. 161).

...And lastlie was red one other letter from Edward Cristen, captain of the *Hosiander*, dated in the road of Tecooe the 8th of December 1613[4], relatinge his successe in his affaires att Tecowe after the departure of the Generall, the subtiltye of the people in holdinge up the price of their pepper, and condempninge the ignorannce of the factors of the *Expedition*, whose wilfulnes occasioned the price to bee enhaunct at that instant. And haveinge loste his monsone for the Molluccoes, he entended to gett his ladinge of pepper twice to Bantam, with some other comodities that those parts doe afford. He intended (God willinge) to shape his course for England in convenient tyme, hopinge yt will prove to Their Worships best proffitt....

[1] Not extant.

[2] No longer extant. Jourdain refers to it in his subsequent letter of 31 January 1614 (see *Letters Received*, vol. II, p. 14).

[3] Not extant.

[4] Not extant.

19 *July* 1614 (vol. III, p. 171).

...This courte was enformed that the pursers in this Tenth Voyage, more espetially then heretofore, have permitted some saylours to runn out upon their accompts more then their wages doth amounte unto, contrary to that article in their comission which prohibiteth all choppinge and changinge, butt onlye for a third parte of their wages; and soe the Company are likewise destitute of meanes to punnishe them for any wronngs they shall committ, in forsakeinge the shipp soe soone as they doe come neare the land. Mr. Best excused Abell [1], as one employed unwillingly, for wannte of other choise, whoe was nott acquainted with the other pursers proceedings. Edward Christen was taken prisoner at Suratt, and Nicolson [2] his mate contynuallye employed in the affaires of marchandizinge, whereby they could nott keepe such exact accompts as were fittinge and necessary. But seeinge the pursers have neglected their dutyes, whereby many poore men are wrongd that should have satisfaction out of their wages for sundrye somes taken up [i.e. borrowed] of them, it was therefore referd to the Auditours to consider howe to right the same; some supposinge that, seeinge the pursers expect poundage from men, they ought to make good those debts that shalbee made in their books, and the chardge to fall upon the poundage, which, beeinge nowe a matter of 54*li.* or thereabouts, ought to bee chardgd upon them that seeke to reape the benefitt of the said poundage; and soe lefte yt to the Auditers, to determyne thereof as in equitye they shall see cause. Butt greate abuses havinge happened by sale of dead mens goods at the mast, to the prejudice of their poore wyves and children, it was therefore concluded that the pursers shall hereafter take notice of the goods of any man that dyeth, and reserve them in some convenient place by themselves, to give accompt of them at his retourne to their wyves and others, and onelye there apparrell to bee sold at the maste, and such things as cannott convenientlye bee kept....

26 *July* 1614 (vol. III, p. 177).

Some occasion of speech beinge delyvered, whereby the actions of some comannders abroad were justlie censurde, and their prowde behaviours towardes their men much distasted, an ymputation was partlie cast upon some of the Comittees here, as a greate occasion to encrease in them [i.e. the commanders] an overweeninge opinion of themselves by usinge them with such extraordinary respect in giveinge place unto them in their courtes; which doth lyfte up the conceites of

[1] His Christian name was Robert, and he had been steward's mate in the *Dragon* (Court Minutes, 9 November 1614).

[2] A slip for 'Nichols.'

some that are not worthie of them, all beinge servannts unto the Companye and therefore not to bee soe extraordinarylie regarded as they have bene, butt in their places as is fittinge. Butt Mr. Best was much commended for the good service he hath performed, haveinge deserved extraordinary respect for the hopefull yssue which he hath effected, and yett is condempned for the greate private trade thatt hee used, and greate gaines made unto himselfe; blameinge him in that hee tooke noe more direct course for the Company in bringinge home the goods of the 6th Voyadge, that were offered unto him by some of those factours (as hath beene certyfied in their letters)....

9 *August* 1614 (vol. III, p. 192).

...Captaine Best desyringe to have his bond from the Company, seeinge hee hath performed his voyadge, some consideration was had of the manner of the carryage and performannce of the same. It was alledgd that he hath deserved extraordinarily well and yll: well, for the good service hee hath done, and yll, by his greate private trade, as well in his owne particuler as permission and example to others. Yet notwithstanding, consideringe howe the buysines was carryed amongst his men, and for some other considerations, [it] was advised to have as little speech made of the matter that is past as may bee; conceyveinge that yt is fittinge to tollerate this in him at this tyme, and remytt the offence, in expectation of his future employment; butt yet to lett him knowe what kindnes hee hath receyved from the Company, whoe hould the president to bee soe yll that, yf time should conclude [i.e. bring about] his employment, they held yt fittinge to binde him absolutelie from all private trade and give him leave to putt in what stocke he will with the Company. And hee expectinge a gratification for his service past, they wisht to have yt held in suspense for a tyme, untill his resolution might bee knowne for another voyadge; the Company having reguard to the service that may bee hoped, as well as that already performed, in the giveinge of their gratification; and therefore lefte yt wholie to Mr. Governour to treate with him aparte howe hee stannds affected for a newe voyadge and to disclayme all private trade, and soe to enforme this courte with his opinion of that buysines; and concluded to referre yt unto Mr. Governour to deliver him his bond and gratifie him in such manner as he should thinke fitt....

Mr. Bonner, whoe went forth master in the *Dragon* with Captaine Best, in the stead of Mr. Hunte[1], haveinge his wages mended at

[1] The loss of the Court Minutes of the period prevents our learning anything of this episode; but in the London Port Books (16/2) we find Edward Hunt entered (18 January 1612) as master of the *Dragon*, bound for the East Indies. The cause of his dismissal can only be surmised, but probably it was some discovery that he had secretly shipped goods for the purpose of trading on his own account.

Gravesend when he was made master, hopeth that the Company will bestowe some gratification upon him, in reguard his wages were but small (as he alledgeth). Captaine Best gave him greate comendations, both for his sufficiencye and honestie, haveinge never opposde the comand of the Captaine; esteeming him as fitt for the managinge of a greate shipp as any man can bee, and, beinge a batchelor, is the apter for their employment upon another voyadge. The Company, desyringe to give encouradgment to such as doe deserve well, held yt fitt to have him gratified; yett makeinge scruple whether to have yt done privatelie or publiquelie, producinge reasonns to contradict either. They therefore, to avoied all exceptions, referd yt to Mr. Governour to give him satisfaction, upon such tearmes as hee himselfe should conceyve most indifferent [i.e. just][1].

16 *August* 1614 (vol. III, p. 198).

...Captaine Best motionynge to have the weeklie wages of the Indians[2] here to bee delyvered unto him to paie unto them, the Company conceyved yt unfittinge to trouble him with the same, butt ordered that there officers [officer?] should make payment of them weekelie, as hee doth unto all other men thatt are employed in their workes.

John Gate beeinge dead, whoe went forth as midshipman in the *Dragon*, some question arisinge amongst his freinds for such wages as are due unto him, Captaine Best likewise motiond to have them paid into his hands, for him to delyver them to whome they shall appeare to bee due, and hee will dischardge the Company of them. Butt they beeinge unwillinge to make other men judges of their buysines, and esteemeinge themselves of sufficient understandinge to doe right unto all menn, resolvd to have the said wages kept in their owne hands, untill they may bee satisfyed unto whome they doe justlie belonge.

William Holmes, gunner of the *Dragon*, haveinge receyved certaine goods into his possession apperteyneinge to twoe poore weomen, which he unjustlie detayneth (as Captaine Best hath enformed), Captaine Best therefore propounded to have Holmes his wages delyvered unto his hannds, that hee may see the poore woemen satisfied out of the same, accordinge to equitie and conscience[3]. Butt the Company,

[1] What gratuity was given to Bonner is not on record.

[2] Asiatics brought home as sailors, and waiting to be repatriated in the next voyage.

[3] Best's persistence in such demands was doubtless not unconnected with the fact that in such cases custom prescribed that the distributing agent should retain a portion of the money as his commission.

conceyveinge yt injustice in them yf they should delyver their servannts wages (which they have earnd in their publique service) into any private manns hannds, upon any pretence whatsoever, would not give occasion to have such an ymputation cast upon them, and therefore intended to paye that which they owe, unto such to whome the same doth apperteine, and to leave the lawe to decyde all other differences and wrongs, yf any bee offered....

Accordinge to former resolutions, it was nowe lykewise thought fitt, and confirmd, to have Mr. Aldworth, Mr. Cannynge, and such other factours in the Indies as are knowne to have used private trade, to bee sent for home, to bee made examples unto others how hatefull those courses are unto the Companie....

19 *August* 1614 (vol. III, p. 202).

...Captaine Best haveinge brought home a younge youth, an Indian, whoe was taught by Mr. Copland, the preacher, to wright and reade, and is very apt to learne, the Company therefore resolvd to have him kept here to schoole, to bee taught and enstructed in religion, that hereafter, beeinge well grounded, hee might upon occasion bee sent into his countrye, where God may bee soe pleased to make him an instrument in convertinge some of his nation; and resolvd to have 20 markes per annum allowed for that purpose; and that, yf Mr. Coplannd, the preacher, should undertake another voyadge, that then this youth should bee permitted to goe and attend him....

Mr. Governour acquainted this courte that, accordinge to their order, he hath conferd with Captaine Best; whose awnsweare hee finds to bee very uncertaine. Whoe alledgeth that the Companie have good choise of sufficient personns for that service; himselfe doubtfull as yet whatt to doe, butt within a fortnight, after he is retournd out of the countrye, shalbee able to give a more certaine awnsweare; yet notwithstandinge is willinge to doe what the Company shall thinke fitt, and to bee at their command, yf they will have him and shall have neede of his service. They, considering all actions passed, commended the service he perfourmed in the fight: supposinge that more effectuall capitulations might have beene drawne and concluded (for the benefitt and strengthninge of the trade) with the Grand Mogoll and Governours of Cambaia: condempninge him exceedinglie for his private trade[1]. And comparinge him with some others, he was preferd in their opinions; butt yett some wisht that, yf he should goe, to have him tyed in strict points from all private trade, and not to lett him slipp hereafter, as nowe they have. And upon sight of his bond (before yt

[1] Captain Saris, taxed with private trade, alleged that 'Mr. Bests was double as much as his, whose voyage brought forth but twoe for one' (Court Minutes, 9 February 1615).

was delyvered up) Mr. Governor, haveinge laid open his faulte at large, made knowne the favour that hath beene showne him in remyttinge his offence, haveinge had soe greate and juste cause to take yt yll at his hannds for makinge soe large a retourne by his private trade, challenginge him in particuler for the greate quantitie of silke brought, and the manner of sellinge yt in towne, to the prejudice of some other brethren of this Companye, whoe had formerlie bought greate quantities of the Company and were nowe much prejudicte by the sale of his. And yett, upon due consideration of all circumstances, they conceyved him the fittest for thatt service, yf hee may bee had, butt nott to bee permitted to use private trade; wisheinge that hee should bee urdgd to a present and certaine resolution, that they might bee satisfied whome to rest upon; desiringe Mr. Governour to treate with him, and conclude upon such tearmes as he shall houlde most fittinge.

A motion beinge made in courte (by way of supposition) that, yf Captaine Best doe goe as Generall, yt is conceyved that Mr. Salmon wilbe willinge, and a fitt personn, to goe vice-admirall; haveinge some reasons to induce unto such a motion and to bee soe perswaded. The Company therefore referd the consideration thereof unto Mr. Governour, to treate with him likewise aboute the same. Yett some alledgd that hee could nott bee spared from the chardge he had undertaken here, butt that the Company should have a greater wante of him here at home then his service could benefitt him abroade.

This courte was informed that the benjamyn [i.e. benzoin] brought home by Captaine Best is soe foule and yll putt upp [that it] is nott held to be marchantable; and therefore wisht to have yt lookt into, seene, and considered of, before yt should bee offered to be sould (beinge a matter of soe greate moment). Whereupon they entreated Mr. Johnson[1] and Mr. Westrowe to undertake the care thereof, and to call unto them twoe others, of the generalitie[2], to assiste and bee witnesses thereof, and delyver their opinions of the same unto this courte....

1 *September* 1614 (vol. III, p. 209).

...This courte entringe into consideration of enterteyneinge Mr. Best, they were enformed thatt hee is much troubled aboute some speeches delyvered of him for his private trade, and in that hee had noe gratification given him; beeinge given to understand that hee insisteth upon haveinge leave to carrie a private stocke, and therefore (as Mr. Governor hath heard) propoundeth twoe severall offers—

[1] Robert Johnson, one of the 'Committees.'

[2] Ordinary members of the Company.

either that hee may carry 2000*li.*, to laye yt oute for himselfe in such comodities as hee shall bee able to provide, to bee brought home out of hould[1], and at his retourne the Company shall have the said goods (yf they please) for 6000*li.*: or else that they shall give him his 2000*li.* againe, and take the goods into their possession and lett him have the one halfe of the gaine that shalbe made of them, over and above the said 2000*li.* They, beinge dryven to this straict, either to have private trade with leave or without leave, thought his latter offer not fitt to be rejected, in reguard the Companie shall beare noe adventure, and wilbe a meanes to tie him to the greater and more extraordinary care, as well for procuringe comodities as preventinge his marriners from their private trade; and therefore thought yt fitt to have that motion further considered of heereafter, and desyred Mr. Governour to conferre with him and knowe his resolution, that they may proceede accordinglie, either to conclude with him, or for some other.

7 *September* 1614 (vol. III, p. 210).

...This courte beeinge desirous to be satisfied whether Mr. Best will proceede in their service with the next fleete att Christmas, Mr. Governor acquainted them in what manner he had proceeded with him; whose first awnswere was that the Companie are not unprovided of sufficient personns, butt yf they were, and would comand him, that then hee would goe. And Mr. Governor haveinge beene since entreated to presse a direct awnswere and resolution, he desyreth that they would provide themselves elswhere, yf they may, because yf hee goe, yt will prejudice and hinder him very much in his estate; and this is all that he can drawe from him as yet. Notwithstandinge, he acquainted him with reports which have beene brought unto him that he hath excepted againste the Companie and challengd them of unkindnes that he hath not beene gratified for his service paste; and tould him that hee was not forgotten, butt the Companie intended to doe things seasonablie, and in their gratifications to have respect as well to the future as the tyme paste, and therefore were the willinger to understand his resolution before they woulde resolve on anythinge; Mr. Governor giveinge them to understand that he expecteth a gratification accordinge to their former resolution, that whosoever passeth the West parts and putteth nott into any porte before hee cometh to the Downes[2] is rewarded for that service with 100*li.* Butt the Com-

[1] Private trade goods were never put into the hold (that being reserved for the Company's cargo), but were stowed in the owners' cabins or on the decks.

[2] The Company's objection to such calls was that they afforded opportunities of landing private trade goods. From 1610 onwards any call at Falmouth, Plymouth, or Dartmouth (except in cases of urgent necessity) was forbidden in the commission for the voyage (*First Letter Book*, pp. 346, 378, 418).

panie acknowledgd noe such order, butt reserve the power in themselves to gratifie where they finde desert; some alledginge that, yf hee will not goe againe, that he hath then beene sufficientlie rewarded in permittinge him to goe free with that extraordinary private trade which hee made, the fraight whereof is worth 300*li.* and more, and that in his service hee performed noe more then was expected from him: [he] setled a factory where one was setled before and was the overture of that which succeeded, and capitulated noe more for the priviledge of our people then was formerlie effected by others: and that he had made a very slender voyage yf hee had not reapt the fruicts of other mens labours, by that disaster which befell unto Sir Henrie Middleton and the *Trades Encrease*: that Sir James Lancaster and others did as well before him (Sir James haveinge broken the yce for trade in the Indies [and] setled a factory at Bantam and Achein) and yet reservd noe private gaine to themselves. But yt was awnswered for him that he made his trade with good advantage: carryed his men well forth, and brought them home in some good order: that he forcte and setled a factory there: and lastlie, purchaste to this kingdome extraordinary honor, by mayntayneinge such a valiante fight for the honor of this nation as never did any before in those parts, wherein he shewed resolution and judgment: and that his due is noe more then justice, haveinge deserved yt by performinge good service in the whole course of his voyage, and therefore ought to [be] well respected by them, or otherwise yt will fall as an ymputation upon the Companie, and the disgraceinge of him will prove a disgrace to themselves: butt yet could not excuse him to bee worthie of blame for taxinge the Company of ingratitude. And all confessinge that he hath done well in generall, and yett yll in particuler by his private trade (in remittinge of which and delyveringe his bond they have already done much for him): yett notwithstandinge, in respect of the honor of this Companie and for the encouradgment of others, it was held fitt, and soe resolvd (by erection of hands) to give him a gratification, and referd the some to Mr. Governor, to doe therein as hee shall thinke fitt, and to procure his further service hereafter, yf they may.

A motion was made to have Mr. Bestes accompts seene and audyted; and that hereafter extraordinarye care should bee had thatt comanders bee not permitted to breake comissions without comptroll, nor to have such offences remitted....

Mr. Governor certyfied this courte that, advisinge sometymes in private by himselfe in what manner the next voyage might best bee furnisht with a sufficient comander, yf Captaine Best should still persiste in his denyall, hee hath concluded in his thoughts that none can be fitter then Captaine Best in all respects, and whome he would rather have then any other, espetially for his knowledge in navigation, governinge a shipp at sea, and to mannage a fight upon occasion; butt yet for marchandizinge [he] doth preferr Captaine Keelinge farre before him, and one that hath good command likewise over his men abroad (whome they loved and respected for his kinde usage of them). And therefore hath thought upon employinge Captaine Keelinge as Generall to Suratt, and Captaine Newporte his vizadmyrall, whose resolution and knowledge in marine causes hath beene often and sufficientlie knowne, beeinge able to supplye the defect of the other for navigation: and Captaine Keelinge, haveinge disposed of all affaires att Suratt, and dispatcht away a shipp for England, then to proceede to Bantam and reside there (or at Jacatra) for some certaine tyme, as Generall on shore, to passe from porte to porte (where the Companie have any factoryes), take accompt of every factor, and reduce all there said accompts to some certaine place, and to consider what places wilbee fitt to mayntaine factoryes in, and which will nott: that, as Mr. Edwards and Mr. Emsworth[1] are esteemed fitt personns to bee cheife and principall for all the factoryes thatt are to bee setled in Cambaia and those parts there, soe he should bee cheife for all the other parts, of Bengalla, Jacatra, and those places aboute Bantam....

13 *September* 1614 (vol. III, p. 218).

...Occasion beinge ministred to have some speech of Mr. Bests goinge, and Mr. Governor acquaintinge them with his intents (as he conceyved it) concerninge private trade, they resolvd not to permitt him to have any; and thereupon he [the Governor] wisht them to consider of some other personn, for without private trade Captaine Best will not goe....

16 *September* 1614 (vol. III, p. 220).

...Upon Captaine Bests conference with Mr. Governor, Mr. Governor demanded his resolution concerninge his owne goeinge; whoe assured him he could not goe without his greate prejudice, and desyred the Companie to accept of that for an absolute awnswere[2]. And then moved Mr. Governor for allowance of wages for Mr. Bonner and his mates untill the dischardge of the shipp, haveinge given their dilligent attendannce aboard all that tyme; which he conceyveinge to be reasonable, did yeild thereunto, and this courte approved the same. But makeinge the lyke demand for himselfe, Mr.

[1] William Edwards and Nicholas Emsworth had gone out in Downton's fleet in the previous spring. Emsworth died at Surat on 23 November 1614.

[2] On 27 September the Governor informed the Court that Best had told him that, 'yf the Companie had nott had Captaine Keelinge for this voyage, he would then have gone; but he wilbee readye another yeare to doe them service, yf they shall be soe pleased.'

Governor wisht him to advise well thereof, before he propounded yt any further; supposinge that upon serious deliberation he himselfe would not thinke yt fitt for him to persiste in that demannd; and soe lefte yt....

21 *October* 1614 (vol. III, p. 251).

...Captaine Best propounded in the behalfe of one Anthony Wallys, a youth whoe was with him in his last voyadge and kept a booke of accompts with his owne hand (which was shewed in courte); and beinge nowe desyrous to serve the Company, the Captaine offered to become bound for him, and the youth referd himselfe unto the Company for the manner of his enterteynement and meanes, beinge a prettye scholler, and his father a godlie preacher (as Mr. Best enformed); whereupon they referd him to bee farther considered of, against annother courte....

26 *October* 1614 (vol. III, p. 255).

...A letter was red, wrytten by Richard[1] Larkin from Bantam, of the 10th of January 1613 [i.e. 1614]...accusinge Captaine Best to have taken certaine pepper belonginge to the 6 Voyadge at an underhand price; which by his authoritie he would have, and he [Larkin] durst not oppose (as he alledgd). Annother letter was red, wrytten by John Jourdan at Bantam, of the 31th of Januarye 1613 [1614][2], relatinge the estate of their buysines there at present: there joyneinge in better manner then formerlie they had done, for the benefitt and good of the Company: and intents to prosecute the effectinge of buildinge a house to secure their goods from fire, accordinge to the capitulations made by Captaine Best and Captaine Sayris with the Kinge of Bantam....

4 *November* 1614 (vol. III, p. 261).

...Captaine Best propounded to their considerations a matter worth note, as he conceived yt: that, seeing the Malabars are servannts and tributaryes unto the Portugalls, whether yt were not fitt to give order unto their shipps to make prize of them. But this Companie, haveinge hitherto proceeded peaceablie but where they have bene provokt, held yt fitt to contynue that course still, and not to meddle with them except they offend, nor to beginne any quarrells (nor yett to endure and putt [up ?] any wrongs); but yet to touch yt in their comissions, to beware of them.

Anthony Wallis preferd his petition; whoe had bene formerlie

[1] An error for 'Robert.' The letter is not extant.
[2] Printed in *Letters Received*, vol. II, p. 14.

referd (beinge a youth that kept Captaine Best his accompts abroad in his last voyage). And, beinge much comended againe by Mr. Best, was nowe resolvd of (by erection of hands) to be enterteynd for 7 yeares, and hereafter to be considered of, howe and in what manner to be disposed.

5 *July* 1615 (*A General Court*) (vol. III, p. 439).

...Mr. Governor gave this court to understand that, supposeinge the newes of receiveinge money is welcome to most men, he therfore thought fitt to make knowne the payment of sundrie dividents, which the Auditours have thought upon and are found may be made, as followeth:...And a whole capitall for the 10th [Voyage] the last of December; the last of which could not sooner be effected, because of greate somes paid forth for marryners wages and His Majesties customes....

18 *July* 1615 (vol. III, p. 448).

...A letter was red, wrytten by Mr. Patricke Copland to Mr. Governor, bearinge date the 6th of this instannt, giveinge to understannd howe much the Indyan youth recomended to his care had profited in the knowledge of Christian religion, soe that hee is able to render an accompt of his faith; and therefore desired to receive directions from Mr. Governor concerninge the baptizinge of him; beinge of opinion that yt were fitt to have yt publiquelie effected, beinge the first fruites of India, etc. This court, beinge desirous to understand the opinion of My Lords Grace of Canterburie before they would resolve anythinge in soe waightie a buysines, entreated Mr. Deputie[1] to speake with His Grace and knowe his pleasure therein. And for the other parte of Mr. Coplands letters, desiringe to have the yeares allowance for the youth to be paid unto Mr. Daniell Wight, they ordered to have yt delivered accordinglie.

...Mr. Governor made knowne unto them a greevannce and wronge unto this Companie (as hee conceyveth it), that some of the Comitties have delt with Mr. Best aboute his employment in the next shippes, [they] haveinge noe comission nor order thereunto; whereby he [Best], conceyveinge that the Companie doe seeke after him, will either stand upon his tearmes for private trade or expect such greate wages as will make a president nott to be tollerated; beeinge likewise of opinion that, although he bee bound in great bonds from usinge all private trade, yet that he will not forbeare it. And callinge to remembraunce his former courses, both of Achen and Bantam, besides the leaveinge of one of his shipps abroad at his retourne, they

[1] Morris Abbot (see p. 265) was the archbishop's brother. He had been elected Deputy Governor on 5 July 1615.

did much distaste them. And haveinge time enough to consider of a comander betwixt this and Bartholomewtide[1], they wisht that noe further speeches should bee made unto him or any other directlie, untill they might see whome yt would please God to send home of those are nowe abroad....

4 *August* 1615 (vol. III, p. 460).

...A petition was red, preferd by Thomas Carwell, whoe went out trumpeters mate in the *Dragon* upon the 10th Voyage and by the death of the cookes being made master cooke by Captaine Best, with promise of augmentinge his wages [by] a marke[2] a monneth for his said service, hee undertooke and performed the same by the space of sixteene monnethes, whereby there became due unto him (as he alledgeth) the some of tenn poundes, thirteene shillinges, and fower pence; and beinge prest forth into the Kinges shipps (as by a letter from Sir William St. John[3] appered), whereby he could not come to demannd the same any sooner, and Captaine Best haveinge subscrybed the said petition, affirmeinge it to be true which was conteyned therein, and that the partie would not otherwise have served as cooke, they held it just to performe the same, and ordered to have a warrannt made for payment thereof, accordinge to the said agreement formerlie made....

8 *September* 1615 (*A General Court*) (vol. III, p. 475).

...Mr. Governor acquainted this courte that, by the blessinge of God, Whoe hath given them the start before their neighbours [i.e. the Dutch], there are goods come home in these twoe shipps[4], upon severall accomptes, whereby the adventurers shall receyve some parte of the fruicts thereof, in pepper to be transported, namelie, upon the accompt of the 7th Voyage three capital[s], upon the Ninth one capitall and a halfe, and upon the Tenth 25*li.* upon the hundred[5] (which is a 4th parte more then formerlie hath bene delivered); which is done that the oportunitye of sellinge and caryinge out in due time may not be neglected. They then entred into consideration of the price of the said pepper, and time for such as shall take out more then their partes....It was resolved (by erection of hands) that the callicoe pepper should be at 21*d.* and the Priaman at 2*s.*, ungarbled, to be

[1] St Bartholomew's Day is 24 August.

[2] That is, 13*s.* 4*d.*

[3] Captain in the Royal Navy; knighted 21 December 1607.

[4] The *Globe* and the *James*.

[5] These divisions had been decided upon at a meeting of the 'Committees' held the same day (vol. III, p. 474).

transported; and for the overplus which shalbee taken out more then their proportionable parts, time was given for payment (by the like erection of hannds) at three six monnethes....

10 *October* 1615 (vol. III, p. 501).

...A letter was red, wrytten by Mr. Best unto Mr. Governor, wherein he complayned of some wronge supposed to have bene done unto him by some whoe have drawne an ill opinion of him from the Companie without any desert of his, and therefore desireth to have a time of hearinge appointed him, that he might cleare himselfe in a courte of Comittees; glanncing afarre of[f] as if he had bene motioned by some to proceede in another voiage. But Mr. Governor and all present excusde themselves from any such motion, or to have once sent unto him at any time. Yet seeinge he standeth upon his purgation, and knowinge well enough howe he hath demeasned himselfe, both abroad and since his retourne, they were willinge to give him a day of hearinge; and in the meanetime entreated Mr. Hanford[1], Mr. Westrowe, and the rest of the Auditours to peruse such letters and wrightings as have bene sent, and take Mr. Ellam unto them to take a collection of some of his misdeameanours, as well for breach of his comission [and of] his bond by private trade, procuringe the factours at Bantam to cull out the best of the Companies goods and convertinge of them to his private accompt, with the like notorious wrongs and abuses; that some heads may be in a readynes to be objected against him. And to present them unto this courte upon Friday next, that a day may then be appointed for his hearinge, accordinge to his desire; that, although many of these things be remytted and past, yet they may serve to shewe him his errours and wrongs done unto the Companie, which should make him the rather to knowe himselfe....

17 *October* 1615 (vol. III, p. 510).

...Mr. Best haveinge formerlie entreated for a tyme of meetinge to bee appointed before this courte to cleare some aspersions unjustlie cast upon him (as hee pretendeth), [he] was referd to a courte on Fridaye morninge, at which time they resolvd to heare his assertions....

20 *October* 1615 (vol. III, p. 518).

...This day beinge the time appointed for Mr. Best to come and bee heard before the courte, he entreated Mr. Governor, before the companie was come together, that he might be excused at this time, because he had some buysines of ymporte that cald him away. And

[1] Humphrey Hanford, one of the 'Committees.'

Mr. Governor tould him that he must then acknowledg it to be his owne acte, and not thatt he cannot be permitted to come and awnsweare for himselfe or that the Company are not willinge and readie to heare him. And soe for present he absented himselfe....

24 *October* 1615 (vol. III, p. 523).

Mr. Best presenting himselfe in courte, the letter which he wrote unto Mr. Governor was red, wherein he desired audyence, to be permitted to awnsweare for himselfe in court to some unjust aspertions cast upon him (as he intimated). Thereuppon one of the Comittees acquainted them that he never malicte Mr. Best in his lyfe, but, being at table with him, upon some occasion of speech ministred concerninge his goinge againe, he allegd that the Company had bene very ungratefull in recompencinge soe slenderlie his former service, by bestoweinge a hundred jacobus[1] upon him, supposinge that, if he had deserved that, he deserved more. But Mr. Governor, whoe delivered the said money (as from the Company), perceived noe otherwise but that he receyved yt in good parte, by puttinge yt up without any such exception, and gave him thanks for his paines vouchsafed therein. But Mr. Leate[2] puttinge him in mynde of many other kindnesses that he ought to acknowledge to have receyved from them, as the fraight of his goods brought home in private adventure (which was valued to be worth 3 or 400*li.* merelie in fraight, and yet tollerated by them), his drawinge and employinge of aventures for other private men abroad, notwithstandinge his bond (which tyed him from a greate penaltie from any such private trade for himselfe or others), and the Companies kindnes to passe over these thinges and bestowe upon him 100 jacobus. His awnswere thereunto was that he esteemed his bond as nothinge, neyther had he any intent to hould the same; nor could not acknowledge thankfullnes for the gratification given, because (in his conceipt) it did not deserve soe much; and [he] was alwaies allowed a tunne or 2 tunne fraight out of the Straicts[3] (as he said). The difference was approved to be greate betwixt the trade of the Straicts and the East Indies, and the Companies action towards him worthie of all due respect. But findinge him to insiste in comparison whether he hath bene thankfull to the Company or they kinde to him, stomackt a speech delivered in courte by a Comittee[4], which discouragd him

[1] Equivalent to 110*l.* The jacobus (unite) was a gold coin, issued in 1604 at 20*s.* but increased in 1612 to 22*s.* by statute.

[2] Nicholas Leate, one of the 'Committees.'

[3] Meaning in his voyages to and from the Mediterranean, on account of the Levant Company.

[4] 'Mr. Freeman' in margin; i.e. Ralph Freeman, who had been a 'Committee' in 1613–14 and 1614–15.

from all thought of any new employment: that if he went, he was worthie of a gratification, but otherwise he had receyved enough; which speech drewe him to speake more then otherwise hee intended. And therefore, this courte desiringe to drawe the buysines to a head, one of the Auditers haveinge collected some particulers out of wrightinges from the East Indies, hee divided his actions into three parts: 1, aboute setlinge the factory att Surat; 2, his proceedings at Achen and Bantam; 3 and last, his behaviour and carryage of himselfe towards the Company since his retourne; with some passages and errors in his accompts.

1, for Surat (which is the place he challengeth for his glorie), if he faile of haveinge perfourmed good service there, it will appeare to have bene noewhere. And there, by letters from Mr. Aldworth and Biddulph, in awnsweare of his sent unto them, yt is apparant thatt he was the onelye man that discouragd from remayneinge ashore, urginge the factours to quite the place and bringe away all their goods abourd; attempting twice to have departed with all the men and goods, and would have gone to have taken Guzaratts, whereby the future hopes of ever setlinge any trade there [would] have bene quite taken away, had not Mr. Aldworth opposed his intent, groundinge himselfe upon the Companies commission, which armed him with that resolution to settle a trade, in despite of his contradiction. Whereunto he awnsweared that formerlie he taxt Mr. Aldworth onely with weaknes, butt noe dishonestie; yet nowe he condempneth him for both, and unfitt to manage soe greate and waightie a buysines; confessinge that, at his first comeinge to Suratt, hee was discouragd from setlinge any trade there, beinge drawne thereunto by those reasons that moved Sir Henry Middleton, as he was possest [i.e. informed] by twoe relations which hee receyved from Sir Henrye, wherein he labourd[1] him not to land any goods. Yet hee thought fitt to send on shore some fewe packs, with 3 or 4 marchannts, whoe contynued there 16 or 18 dayes without notice of the worth of their comodityes. In the interim Sir Henryes action came to light; the marchannts were cald before the Governor; and Mr. Aldworth wrote a timerous letter, as one that expected none other but death. Within a daye or twoe came in the greate Guzaratts shipp, which Mr. Best tooke, translated some of their principall personns abourd his owne, and then sent for his marchannts. Thereupon came speech of the Viz Roye and Governor comeinge downe with aucthoritie to treate aboute setlinge of a trade, and then he receyved securitie for his men. Whoe sendinge for Mr. Best on shore, he refused, without good caution of sufficient men; and they beeinge tendred, hee went on shore, and presented the capitula-

[1] Used in the now obsolete sense of 'urged.'

tions unto them, which he had conceyved and made readye for that purpose. Assuringe them[1] that the simplicitye and weaknes of their factours, wannt of good securitie, sufficient warrannt, and good ground, with the discouradgments he receyved from Sir Henry Middletons relation (which hee promysed to send unto Mr. Governor) were the onelie motives that occasioned that stopp and doubt in setlinge a factorie there.

2. Att Achein he putt the Company to extraordinary expences by his greate guiftes and pompe hee used in his carryage; wastinge a greate deale of tyme, without doinge anythinge for the Companies good, [not] soe much as renewinge the ould capitulations; bought noe comodities butt a parcell of very bad benjamyn for the Companies accompt, and very good for himselfe. His awnsweare thereunto was that there comission caryed him thether, where the porte, people, and charge[2] weere to him unknowne: that, there factours beeinge landed att Suratt, he had butt fewe of judgment with him: and beeinge there, he could not departe without leave of the Kinge, whoe, beinge absolute, will detayne and give leave to departe at his pleasure, and they, beinge under his comand, must obey: affirminge that the Kinge would nott confirme the capitulations his father[3] had formerlie made; for a trueth whereof he referred himselfe to the reporte of those that were there with him. And saith that hee was noe marchannt, and therefore knewe not howe to make choise of good benjamyn for the Company; and in excuse of his owne (if he had any, as then he was verye doubtfull), hee did noe more therein then Mr. Johnson or any other would have done in the like case; assuringe himselfe thatt the Company expect not [only?] that their servannts should be beneficiall unto them, but to be benefitted by the Company.

3. Att Bantam, findinge all things out of order by the death of Sir Henry Middleton, he neglected to goe to the Molluccaes (accordinge to his comission) butt dealt with the factours for the goods of the *Trades Encrease*; buyinge parte thereof for the Companies accompt, and appropriatinge a greate [part?] to his owne particuler, makinge good use of fishinge in that troubled water[4]; which casualtie if it had nott befalne, he had made the worste voyage for the Company that ever any had done which retourned saufe. But by his power he wrought his owne endes for the best comodities, and laded of the

[1] Meaning the assembled Committees.

[2] I.e. pecuniary expenses.

[3] A slip for 'grandfather.'

[4] In the Court Minutes for 14 November 1614 mention is made of accusations against two of the factors at Bantam of 'cullinge out the best of certaine silke and sellinge yt for 20 in 100 proffitt to Captaine Best, whereas he [Saris?] had directlie [given?] charge to have yt kept, knowinge that yt would yeild cent per cent; which when they were chargd withall, they could not awnsweare yt butt with teares.'

worste (pepper and simplest comodyties) for the Company; and of 17 peculls[1] of silke (which were for the 8th Voyage) hee pickt 8 of the best, at a lesse price then they stoode the Company in, and 133*li.* waight to a pecull, whereas the Companye have never above 125*li.* for a pecull. Hee denyed that he offended in any of those particulers; affirminge that whatt hee did was by consent of a councell: that Lorkin and Ball sould him those goods, the pepper at dearer rates then hee could have bought of the Chineses, by ½ a r[ial] of 8 in 10 sackes: that upon tryall hee found that a pecull houldeth out 133*li.*, and therefore the Company are wrongd if there factours doe not make good soe much, as hee is ready to justifie and approve: and [he] never urdgd the factours to either waight or price otherwise then for the Company. Yet it was delivered for a trueth by one, that, the factours at Bantam beeinge bad servannts, they feared least Captaine Best should have caryed them away; and therefore (to give him content) were willinge to lett him have what he would, and att whatt rates and prices hee listed.

Hee could not give any sufficient awnsweare wherefore hee neglected to proceed to the Molluccaes. Butt (as might upon good grounds bee conjectured) he hastned home with his private proffitt, haveinge made a good voyage for himselfe upon the ruynes of the 6th Voyage; and leaveinge the *Hosiander*, one of his shipps, in the countrye, contrary to the course of all other Generalls; yet [he] was one that had as greate wages as any other, and farre beyonnd Captaine Saris[2], whoe deserved farre beyonnd him, by the beneficiall retourn hee made of his voiage.

And, last of all, hee gloried in a letter sent him from Bantam by Captaine David Middleton, wherein hee gave him many thannkes for his care in disposinge of Sir Henry Middletons goods. Whereas yt was approved[3] that, he findinge sundrye packes of the Company (which hee supposed, as he saith nowe, were Sir Henryes, although without any marke of his), he neither brought them home nor any inventory of them.

And haveinge lefte 700 r[ial]s for his voiage in the countrye and brought home 700 doll[ars] more, besides 500 and od which he oweth upon his accompts (beinge found out erronious since his retourne), that money (within a very little) would have paid for the 8 peculls of silke hee bought and converted to his owne private accompt.

Soe that it appered that his service at Suratt was nothinge extra-

[1] As stated below, the *pikul* was equivalent to about 133 lb.

[2] The salaries allotted to Best and Saris are not recorded, but that the former had far the better terms appears from *The Voyage of John Saris*, p. lxxiii.

[3] Used in the now obsolete sense of 'proved' or 'demonstrated.'

ordinary: att Achen costlie and nothinge beneficiall: at Bantam much performed to the prejudice and wronng of the Company: his shipp lefte behinde: his voyage very poore, and one of the meanest that hath bene made for the Companye, and none greater for himselfe: his comission neglected, which directed him to the Moluccas: his bond forfeeted, and yet freelie delivered up unto him: noe fraight taken: butt all offences pardonned and a gratification given. And yet notwithstandinge he challengeth the Company of ingratitude. Butt Mr. Governor tould him that an ungratefull person is the worst of all others. Hee himselfe brought him to kisse the Kinges hannd; and, out of his good opinion of his desertes, gave him his bond. And afterwards, understandinge that hee expected some gratification (if it were but a suite of satten), and haveinge procured him 100 jacobus from the Companie, he putt them up and (as he understoode him) accepted them thankefullie, and shewed noe dislike at that time, as hee protested openlie before this courte; and therefore was the more condempned for taxinge the Company since at a publique table. Butt hee [Best] protestinge that he never intended any wronge towards them, and desiringe them to beleive thatt all such errors as he hath comitted proceeded, nott out of any dishonestie, butt out of ygnorance: the Company were contented to remytte all thatt is past, and to lett these things dye, which should nott nowe have bene ript up had not hee cald them in question himselfe.

And therefore it onlie rested to knowe at what rate those r[ial]s should be valued att which hee is to awnsweare backe unto the Companie, beinge found erronyous upon his accompt. He expected to have had them remytted, to awnswere his full desert of a further gratification; butt they, findinge noe such merrytt, demanded as much for a r[ial] as they doe allowe from one accompt unto annother, which is 10*s*. for ech r[ial][1], or else to give allowannce proportionallie for soe many r[ials] layd out by him in any comoditie which hee brought home, seeinge these proved to bee the Companies money which hee had soe disbursed for himselfe. And some time beeinge spent thereuppon, at last hee was contented to referre himselfe to Mr. Governor and Mr. Deputy, and submitte himselfe whollie to such a rate as they in their wisdomes should conceyve to bee reasonable....

7 *November* 1615 (vol. III, p. 545).

...Mr. Hanford acquainted this courte that Mr. Deputy and himselfe, haveing lookt into the accompts, doe finde that most of the

[1] The explanation of this apparent discrepancy is that the rial of eight carried to the Far East was held to have doubled its value, consideration being had to the cost and risk of its transportation and its increased value for the purchase of commodities.

Voyages doe growe neare to a period, and therefore that it were necessary to have the *Hosiander* praised [i.e. valued] and turnd over unto the Joinct Stocke for the 10th Voyage...houldinge it just to have good consideration had in praisinge the *Hosiander*, that it may bee at good rates, seeinge it is a shipp delivered there, and by the leaveinge of her in the countrye (to doe the Joinct Stocke service) the 10th Voyage is like to paye 6000*li.* for her fraight of such goods as were brought home for that accompt. Whereupon this courte entreated the Auditours (whoe have taken paines therein alreadye), and desired Mr. Deputy and Mr. Kirbie[1] to join with them, to undertake the care and paines to see the same effected.

Captaine Bests buysines haveinge formerly bene recomended to Mr. Governor and Mr. Deputye, to sett a rate upon the doller for payment of such moneys as hee oweth unto the Company, there is found annother debt of 30*li.* more, which he is to stand chargd with, as is observed out of Mr. Aldeworthes letters, by reason of certaine charges falne upon Captaine Bests particuler accompt. And therefore Mr. Deputy was entreated to putt Mr. Governor in mynd, that a rate may be sett, because his accompts cannot be ended untill that bee effected. They advised what rate might be thought indifferent [i.e. fair] for the riall; and consideringe that the Company doe paie 10*s.* a doller there themselves, they thought it unfitt to demannd lesse of him; but yet referd it to be concluded as before, and hastned soe soone as may bee.

10 *November* 1615 (vol. III, p. 546).

...This courte haveing considered at there last meetinge of the valewe of the doller, as it should be rated for Mr. Best to give satisfaction unto the Companie for his debt which he oweth unto them, were then of opinion that 10*s.* a riall was an indifferent rate, seeing themselves doe paye as much for goods in the country; yett left it to Mr. Governor and Mr. Deputie (accordinge to the former reference) to determine as they should conceive reasonable; whoe, haveinge duly weighed of some materyall circumstances, were of opinion that they could not thinke upon a more indifferent proportion then as the courte had forejudged; and ordered to have the rate sett at 10*s.* the doller, for him to awnswer unto the Company as before; which this courte confirmed and approved[2]....

[1] Jeffery Kirby, one of the 'Committees.'

[2] There is a gap in the Court Minutes from November 1615 to September 1617, and we are consequently ignorant of the relations between Best and the Company during that period.

3 *October* 1617 (vol. IV, p. 23).

...Mr. Best bringinge home a peece of plate[1] of 56 ounzes, the same beinge demanded, his awnswere was that hee had delyvered itt to somebodye, butt knoweth not to whome. It was therefore ordered to rest still upon his accompt....

7 *October* 1617 (vol. IV, p. 27).

...Mr. Hamersley acquaynted the courte thatt a ballance was delyvered upp of the 10th Voyage, which since hath bene found inperfect; for himselfe and Mr. Munne[2] have audyted the same and discovered some imperfections. For upon due examination (by some extraordinarye paines taken) they finde the Joincte Stocke indebted to the 10th Voyage 10,000*li*. since October last, for which they hould ytt juste to allowe interest, which will arise to 833*li*. They finde that there was 4000*li*. in chest, appertaineinge to the said Voyage, in June last; butt, because the Joinct Stocke made noe use thereof, they have therefore charged nothinge for interest. Butt Mr. Richard Burrell owinge good round somes, there is interest putt unto his accompt for the same untill this time. And [they] have abated from divers warrannts soe much as in conscyence they held fitt to be discharged, because they would hould an indifferent and conscionable course without partialytie. And therefore findinge Mr. Bell[3] indebted 900*li*. unto the said Voyage, whereby hee is falne into brokes[4], and other brokes from some other men, to the valewe of 60*li*., they cause the divident for the 10th Voyage to arise to 2½ more then was formerlie proportiond. Butt findinge withall somewhatt to bee layde out for warehouse roome for the *Hosianders* goods, with some other charges to bee defaulked, they will cutt of[f] the halfe and leave the divident to amounte to 48*li*. per cent to bee divided upon the said Voyadge[5]....

8 *October* 1617 (vol. IV, p. 30).

...Mr. Best[6] was approved for an excellent navigator and good commander, discreete and couragious in his fights. Butt itt is doubted

[1] Doubtless part of the equipment of the General's table, and as such to be returned or accounted for.

[2] Thomas Mun, the well-known economist, was one of the 'Committees' at this time; as was also Hugh Hammersley.

[3] Robert Bell, one of the 'Committees.'

[4] Penalties for non-fulfilment of a contract.

[5] This division was announced at a General Court held on 14 October, when it was stated to be due to those 'thatt have taken out two capitalls.'

[6] The subject of discussion was the choice of a commander for the Bantam fleet.

hee will nott bee rulde, beinge ungratefull, covetous, and prowde; whereby he will make the Companie paye for his service (as is thought) if they employe him; and nott to bee drawne from his private trade; supposinge thatt, if hee bee sought unto, he will bee insolent, and if he can bee brought to seeke, itt will bee the better. Butt some thatt have had conference with him have made him acknowledge thatt the Companie have had reason to be vyolent against private trade and thatt, if itt should bee sufferred, it would bee the overthrowe of the trade. And all houldinge him the fittest person, if hee maye be drawne within reasonable tearmes, it was thought that whosoever shall move for him must procure itt under his hand that he will bee conformable. And therefore they entreated Mr. Governor to proceede with him, as hee shall see cause, knowinge that, if hee bee thought upon, Mr. Governor is like to have the greatest trouble in the buysines. And desired Mr. Freeman to speake with Mr. Best, as of himselfe, and to bringe him to Mr. Governor....

10 *October* 1617 (vol. IV, p. 32).

...This courte beeinge nowe full, and the mayne buysines in question beinge for the choise of a cheife person to bee employed as cheife commander to Bantam, all were of opinion to have a knowne and sufficient man, and one that they hope well of. And haveinge had conference aboute many thatt were nomynated October 8°, as Sir Richard Hawkins, Sir Thomas Dale, Mr. Parker[1], and Mr. Best, and considered of whatsoever could bee delivered either for or against them, and fixinge their eyes more upon Mr. Best then the rest, it was demanded by Mr. Governor whether they will hould itt fitt to enterteyne him, if hee shall make offer of his service. And all concluded him the most sufficient, for his arte, experyence, and governement att sea, if he may bee conteyned within compasse and thatt he can free the doubt of private trade. Whereupon Mr. Governor acquaynted them with whatt had passed: howe he came and told him itt was to offer himselfe to bee employed where and howe Mr. Governor would; beinge nowe of opinion thatt private trade will overthrowe the Companyes trade if itt bee not prevented, and that the Companie have greate reason to hinder the same; promisinge confidentlye, if hee goe, nott to offend therein. Butt others advised to consider howe saufelye they maye employe him, whoe reguards nott his bond nor promise, haveinge bene ungratefull and opposite against the Companie since his retourne, prowde, and suspected to have had a hand in Keales

[1] Captain William Parker, who was afterwards appointed second-in-command of the fleet. He died on the outward voyage.

booke[1]. Butt, as all men have their imperfections, soe he hath his; yet, as the eyes of the State are upon this Companie, whereby it behoves them to bee espetiallye carefull to procure a very sufficyent man for to command soe greate a fleete, there is noe doubt butt, if his private trade can bee changed, hee is the most sufficyent man in the kingdome for this service; knowne an approved good marryner and souldyer, haveinge geven true tryall thereof by beatinge 4 gallionns 4 daies together with one shipp and a pinnace, to the greate honnor of this kingdome. And to satisfie thatt doubt of private trade, itt was awnswerd thatt, if he would bee dishonnest, he hath a good estate, which will bee a good meanes to satisfie, if he should offend. Butt Mr. Freeman offerred to undertake to make him honnest, and to enter bond in 500*li*. for him; as they shall have other sufficyent securytie given on his behalfe. Which beeinge heard, was thought as much, in the opinion of many, as can bee required; and do beleive that hee, understandinge his former errors and haveinge such freinds, will respect them in honestie. And therefore were contented to leave his errours, and hope of him as of an honnest man, and not to pull downe too much. Yet, haveinge manie competitours of good sufficyencie,

[1] The allusion is to the pamphlet entitled *The Trades Increase*, published in the spring of 1615. No name appears on the title-page; but the author was a certain Robert Kayll or Keale. The pamphlet contained an attack upon the East India Company, on the ground that it was largely responsible for the decay of the mercantile shipping of the country, owing to the number of ships lost or worn out in its service and the great mortality among the sailors employed. The Company, in its indignation, considered the question of prosecuting the writer, but in the end took no direct action; though it was probably at its instigation that Kayll was in April 1615 called before the Privy Council and committed to the Fleet Prison, until by his humble submission he obtained his release (*Acts of the Privy Council*, 1615–16, pp. 99, 107, 108).

The passage in the pamphlet that occasioned the Company's suspicions of Best's participation occurs on p. 29. This says: 'The third [voyage] that of Captaine Thomas Best, admirall of the fleete, a man whose former behaviour in sea-affaires drew [many?] into that journy with great expectation, and, which is very seldome and hard, his carriage in this employment went beyond the great expectation; of a reposed demeanour; indulgent to his men; vigilant in his charge; his courage like to his cariage; and his fortune above all. He checked the Indians; he mated the Portugals. Those honour our king; these feare his forces. He setled a trade in Cambaya, reduced things in order in Bantam, brought riches home for the merchants, and kept reputation for himselfe. Yet for all this he had *Nemesin in dorso*. The Indian vengeance hanted his ship even to our coasts; of some hundred and eighty men under him when he went forth depriving him of one hundred and odde men for ever. Some foure or five and twenty of the remainder are left on the desperate account of men for the countries facteridge. Only thirty are returned.'

Sir Dudley Digges, in his answer on behalf of the Company (*The Defence of Trade*, p. 36), declares that Best brought home sixty-five men. Apparently, however, this figure includes twenty-three who had belonged to the *Trade's Increase* (p. 34).

they would not tye themselves to any one in particuler, nor resolve nowe of him nor any other, butt lefte the matter whollie to Mr. Governor and Mr. Deputie to conferre with him upon whatt conditions he maye bee had; to satisfie themselves and then acquainte this courte, whoe wilbee contented with thatt which they shall doe some beleiveinge that he will goe for honnour, to shewe his sufficiencie and honestie....

23 *October* 1617 (vol. IV, p. 44).

...Accordinge to an agreement made with Captaine Best upon his enterteynement to have the freedome of the Companie to be bestowed upon one whome hee should nomynate, Mr. Nicholas Andrewes, citizen and grocer, was admitted and sworne a free brother of this socyetie gratis....

24 *October* 1617 (vol. IV, p. 47).

...This courte was made acquainted thatt Mr. Best hath spoken with Mr. Randall to procure him a preacher[1]. And the Companie, haveinge an intent to employe annother, entreated the assistannce of all, to enquire out a sufficyent person....

11 *November* 1617 (vol. IV, p. 58).

...Mr. Offley[2] acquaynted the courte that Captaine Best desireth to have 6 or 7 musitions (besides trumpetours), which cannott bee had but at deare rates, 40*s*. per mo[nth] the least; which Captaine Best peremptorilie saith hee must and will have. But because of the greate charge to provide such persons and small use of their service, Mr. Ofley desireth the opinion of this courte what they please to have done therein; who consideringe that formerlie he had some allowed, and therefore will nowe alsoe expect the like, they were contented to give him satisfaction in the same manner as formerlie, by allowinge the some of 33*s*. 4*d*. per mo[nth] to each of them, butt noe more[3]; which is as much as they can or will doe. And entreated Mr. Offley to lett him knowe soe much, when hee shall renewe the said motions....

Mr. Governor made knowne that Captaine Cristen[4] hath oftentimes solycited him for his favour and mediation to procure him employment with the Company, and hath bene earnest with him of late

[1] Best first nominated a schoolmaster named Wilson, who was rejected. Thereupon Best recommended the Rev. James Rynd, and he was appointed.

[2] Robert Offley, one of the 'Committees.'

[3] It was subsequently reported that none could be found willing to take less than 40*s*. a month.

[4] Edward Christian, who, after commanding the *Hosiander* for a time, had come home as captain of the *Globe*.

and prest him for awnsweare; whereupon he hath thought fitt to move his suite, and soe will leave him to their censures[1], to determyne as they shall see cause; himselfe beinge of opinion (wherein hee would bee as free, without taxation[2], as any other that shall bee of a contrarie mynde) that he may bee fitt to succeede in command, upon occasion of mortalitie; yet his opinion doth not binde, butt profest that it is the good of the Companie that hee reguardeth, and will not be disconted [discontented?] whatsoever shall bee resolvd upon. Captaine Best thereupon delyvered his knowledge of his skill, judgment, care, and resolution, as he had found him upon tryall; being driven to necessitie at Achein, where most of his men were sicke, Mr. Bonner undertakinge the boatswaines charge and Captaine Cristen the masters; which he performed with such greate dilligence, sufficiencie, and care (night and daie), and such discretion in his command as that he [i.e. Best] houldes him fitt to governe the best shipp the Companie have; professinge that, if the best shipp they have were his, he would make him master of her; and that, if himselfe did not goe, and the Companie would make him admirall, they should not wrong themselves; thinkinge that neither age nor youth ought soe much to bee respected as the sufficiency of the person; and if occasion were, he would as soone putt in adventure under his command as any man that hee knowes. Thereupon some tooke occasion to call to mynd his former carriage: his command amongst his men (which was somewhatt harshe, as is said): and his endevours more for his private gaine then for the good of the Companie, wherby, out of small meanes, he raised a greate estate; which hath made him carrie himselfe too proudlie ever since against many of the Comittees, and at last gave noe content in the matter of accompts. But it was awnswerd that he hath since discovered his owne follye, repentes what is past, and desireth employment as his mayne end to regaine his lost reputation; is willinge and readie to give content and amend what is amisse; will submitt himselfe to what orders the Company shall thinke fitt, and be bound to forbeare all private trade; aymeinge whollie to perfourme the like service that Captaine Middleton[3] did, who, havinge lost the Companies good opinion by his carriage towardes his men and Companie, undertooke his next voiage onelye to regaine the same; which, by his good endevours, he effected. And seeinge Mr. Governor hath a good

[1] In the now obsolete sense of 'opinion' or 'judgment' (favourable or otherwise).

[2] 'Reproof' or 'blame' (obsolete).

[3] The reference is to David Middleton (brother of Sir Henry). He commanded the *Consent* in the Third Voyage (1607–9), and afterwards the *Expedition* (Fifth Voyage, 1609–11). On p. 115 of *The First Letter Book* will be found an allusion to 'complaintes made on him by an audatious cooke,' which had led to his disgrace.

hande over him [i.e. Christian] and Captaine Best affects him, it is supposed that they may worke a deepe impression in him of amendment, not easilie to bee forgotten. And for a convenient place, Sir James Lancaster[1] propounded to make him Leiuetenant, a place that is propper and usuall in such fleets; but for succession, not to have it publisht, butt referre them in such a casualtie unto the Companies resolution, enclosed in a box and sealed up (as was with Captaine Josep[2]). And havinge fullie argued all thinges that might be found for or against him, they referd him to bee further considered of att the next courte, that in the meane time the Companie might advise and better satisfie themselves, upon some good deliberation, what to conclude and resolve upon[3].

This courte was enfourmed that Captaine Best hath disposed a sonne of his[4] as a masters mate with him in the *Sonne*; which some distasted, in reguard of the behaviour of the young man in tymes past. But because it was awnswerd that he is in the *Exchange* in the Straicts, which, [it] is supposed, cannott bee here tyme enough before the departure of the fleete, it was therefore lefte to be further considered of hereafter, if he shall retourne....

18 *November* 1617 (vol. IV, p. 67).

...Captaine Best haveinge solicyted Mr. Governor sundrye tymes for satisfaction and performance of some thinges resolvd on at his enterteinement (as hee pretendes), takinge it very yll to have them now questiond (as well the 2 suites of apparrell which he claymeth, as alsoe 40 jacobus to make his wife a chaine), Mr. Governor made knowne that, Captaine Best having motiond those thinges, they were sleighted by himselfe and Mr. Deputye and putt by as frivolous matters, not to bee insisted upon, neyther beseeminge their gravitie nor the reputation of the Companie to enterteyne tearmes of that nature (as making suits of apparrell and the lyke), nor the discretion of a person, held fitt to bee their cheife commannder, to propound or insiste upon; and therfore had racte[5] itt out of the note, and drawne conditions of substance betwixt the Companie and him, whereunto they enterchangablie had putt to their handes. And [they] demanded

[1] At this time one of the 'Committees.'

[2] Benjamin Joseph, commander of the fleet of 1616. For the practice of nominating a successor, whose name was placed in a sealed box, see *Letters Received*, vol. III, p. 321, and vol. V, p. 143.

[3] The matter was further considered a week later, when it was resolved not to employ Christian that year. He applied again in 1618 and 1622, but was refused on each occasion.

[4] Nathaniel (see the introduction).

[5] Raked (scratched out).

of Captaine Best whie he would urge those particulers that were not mentioned in the covenants. There was an agreement, as hee saith, parte whereof was sett downe in wrightinge and parte not, namelie, the 2 suits of apparrell and chaine; and he sometimes remembringe the same to Mr. Governor, was confirmd in his hopes and expectation by Mr. Governors silence; which he imputes as a faulte to have them nowe questiond, and himselfe discourteouslie dealt withall, to bee denyed them; which doth soe discourage him as that it doth alienate his affection from the voyage; and if they bee not perfourmd, he desireth that he maye parte with the Companie fairely (as hee beganne). It was remembred that, after conference had att Deptford with Captaine Best, and thatt Mr. Governor and Mr. Deputye could not conclude with him, Mr. Burrell came the next daie and acquaynted them, at a courte, that Mr. Best was contented to accept of the tearmes offered at Deptford, wherein noe speech was of apparrell or chaine; and therefore it was nowe much distasted by the Companie that hee should make demand of such triviall things, and urge them in such manner, which is more offensive then five tymes the value. Hee presentlie fell upon a newe matter: that he never made suite to goe, but Mr. Burrell and Mr. Salmon and some of the Comittees had importunde him beyond reason, usinge Mr. Governours name. Wherein it was approved [i.e. made clear] that the Comittees never had made suite unto him, but that Mr. Burrell had wrongd Mr. Governours name, if he used itt in that nature. Captaine Best further urgd that he will have it in comission that, havinge servd the Companie in the countrye 12 or 14 mo[nths], he will then bee free to retourne from thence, if hee will. But they conceyved it too prejudiciall to bee tyed to any such agreement; for, although their determynation bee not to binde him to staie in the countrye, yet they would not have their discretions cald in question, to bee bound to give him power to doe what hee will att his owne pleasure. Butt, to end the former buysines, Mr. Governour motiond to have a scarlett cloake given unto him, instead of the apparrell, if that will satisfie. But because of his unreasonable demandes and uncertainetyes, as alsoe the slender reguard he made of the Companie, houldinge them unworthie of thankes for any thinge which he saith is upon agreement, and which he conceyveth to bee his due, many were therefore of opinion to leave him and thinke upon annother. But others wisht not to fall of[f] too suddenlie, but to have a charter partie to binde him to whatt services he should perfourme in the countrye. That was distasted, as a buysines that will not end in any reasonable tyme. And seinge the Companie have to doe with him upon a greate disadvantage, as some conceive, havinge bene chosen, his goinge knowne and approved, they held itt unfitt to leave him for a small matter, butt to thinke of sufferringe rather then to seeke out for annother, and, for the good of the Companie, not to stand upon such a small matter, in reguard of the service which is expected—dryvinge a trade att the Mullaccaes and attempting a trade in China; but yet wisht not to leave thinges to his discretion, butt seeinge his disposition and uncertainetie when the Companie shall have an end with him, therefore to resolve what to trust unto, and to tye him to certaynetyes; which if he shall refuse, then to thinke upon some other worthie fitt person. And entreated Mr. Governour, Mr. Deputy, and Sir James Lancaster to conferre with him, to the end there may bee an awnswere at next courte, and lett him knowe howe distastfull his courses have bene unto the Companye, and to perswade him to reason (if they may), or els reporte their opinions, that they may determyne of some other course....

21 *November* 1617 (vol. IV, p. 72).

...This beeinge the daie appointed to Mr. Best for awnsweare to his demandes (concerninge the 2 suites of apparrell and the chaine for his wiefe and other thinges), in reguard that hee never came since nor used meanes to Mr. Governor, whereby it apperreth that the pride of his harte contynueth in contestation against the Companie, they considered more seryouslie of his former speeches, and proved by many circumstances that the Company never made meanes unto him to goe this voyage, nor sett any others to perswade him thereunto. Butt it was found that some private persons of the Comittees havinge motiond the voyage unto him for his good and to performe service for the commonwealth, he construed itt as the deed of the Companie and make [made ?] use of itt as their motyve[1]. Butt it was remembred by Mr. Bell that Mr. Best, in conference with him, had protest[ed] his readynes and willingnes to bee employed in the Companyes service, if Mr. Governor would send for him, to treate with him to thatt purpose; but Mr. Governor whollie refusde, knowinge his disposition. And afterwardes Mr. Governor tooke knowledge, by recordinge the tyme in his booke, thatt upon the tenth of October last Mr. Best came unto him, accompanyed with Mr. Burrell, and tould Mr. Governor that he was ready to bee disposed by him, where he would and to whatt place hee pleased. And therefore the Companie have justlie distasted his carriage since, by the tearmes hee hath used against them in generall to their disgrace, butt yet to the discoverye of his owne pride and uncyvell behaviour. Notwithstandinge all which, some were of opinion to have him sent for, and to lett the buysines bee ended suddenlye, and nott to suffer triviall thinges to bee any hindrance. It was utterlie dislikt to send for him; but if he shall come of

[1] In the obsolete sense of 'motion' or 'proposition.'

himselfe (as some conceive he would), then it was held fitt to offer him the articles thatt are drawne betwixt the Companie and him, and to cause him [to] enter into a bond of 5,000*li.* to performe them; which if he shall refuse, then the Companie may, with their reputation and his disgrace, leave him. And Mr. Burrell, beinge in courte, made knowne in what manner Mr. Best and he had treated upon the voyage; which he never motiond in the name of the Companie, butt as one freind might perswade annother; and findes him much offended with him for moveinge him to the voyage, sayinge that he had made him a foole. But he made him knowe howe much he had wrongd himselfe and the Companie by makinge other demandes and propositions then had bene att first concluded on; wishinge him nott to halt and falter with the Companie. Butt the manner of his proceedinges argue his inconstancye not to proceede; and therefore dishonestlie picks quarrells and seekes occasions, by these triviall thinges of apparrell and chaine, to fall of[f]. And when there was lyklihood of giveinge way to his humor therein, he then falls most unconscionablye upon the pointe of comission, to have free libertie to retourne att his pleasure, contrarie to his articles of agreement under his hand, which should tye him and all honest men to performe whatt they stand engaged for. And therefore [they] were of opinion it were better to leave him nowe then drive the time further on, to have newe tricks upon the Companie, which he is like dailie to offer. And [they] chargd Mr. Burrell nott to goe unto him, nor thatt any man should bee sent; but leave him to himselfe, to see whether he will come betwixt this and Tuesdaie next....

25 *November* 1617 (vol. IV, p. 74).

...This courte was enfourmed thatt Captaine Best hath dischargd his men and given it out that he will not goe upon the voyage, tould Mr. Mountney soe much, and wisht the Companie to [send?] Captaine Parker. Theis his proceedinges were very scornefullie taken att his handes, as alsoe his prowde and dishonest carriage; beinge of opinion that, if he doe not goe, some maisters will falle of[f], and by them some mates, whereby thinges doe followe by a kinde of conspiracie; and therefore held fitt to have him sent for, to knowe his resolution, and, if it shall prove negative (except he have the apparrell and chaine), then to lett him rest; not speakinge of any discharge, butt to tell him the Companie must then doe as they maye (because a discharge will cleare all further complainte). And in the opinion of some it will not be fitt to leave him soe, butt complaine of him to the Councell, that Their Lordships may see the wronge [that] is done in a matter of such importe, that concernes the State. It was alsoe movde to consider what to doe, if he shall awnsweare that, upon better advice, he is willinge to goe; whether it wilbe fitt to employe him, because of the hurtes hee may doe, havinge power in his handes. ...It was wisht to thinke upon annother sufficient person to supplie his place, if Mr. Best shall fall of[f]...but because nothinge can saufelie bee concluded, nor newe treatie enterteynd for annother, untill Captaine Bestes awnswere be receyved, it was therefore thought fitt to appointe a meetinge with him this afternoone betwixt 2 or 3 of the clocke, to urge his wronges unto him, and accordinge to his awnsweare soe to resolve what to doe; Mr. Governor giveinge in charge unto all present to conceale whatt hath bene delyvered, that noe speeches be made thereof, whereby Captaine Best should take any notice of the Companies intentes.

25 *November* (*afternoon*) 1617 (vol. IV, p. 75).

...This meetinge beinge intended for Captaine Best and hee presentinge himselfe, his resolution was required aboute his goinge. And he insisted upon performance of the writinges and all the covenantes, as well unwritten as written, or none, and soe houldes himselfe free. The contract was produced, and urgd as apparant; butt he insisted upon the apparrell and chaine, which beinge frivolous thinges thrust in by himselfe, the Companie scornd them as ridiculous. He pretended his unwillingnes to have falne of[f], untyll he found that they performed not with him accordinge to promise and his expectation (as he allegd). Butt they made it to appere, as well by the articles themselves as the testimonie of Mr. Governor and Mr. Deputy, that they still putt by those demandes as ydle, and that, makinge meanes for his employment, he had referd himselfe to Mr. Governor (in the hearinge of Mr. Burrell) to be disposed by him howe he would and whether [i.e. whither] he would, and upon what conditions he pleased. But Mr. Best labourd to prove that he sought not the Companie, but the Companie him, and that Mr. Burrell, with his sonne and Mr. Salmon, labourd him in Mr. Governors name. But those thinges were denyed and disproved by the parties themselves, and...the trueth thereby made to appeare that he had sought employment the last yeare and this. Howsoever, he still laboured to justifie himselfe, and said that he would not have come nowe, if he had not bene sent for. Butt they seeinge his vaineglorie and desiringe to drawe the buysines to a head, Mr. Governor caused the articles under his hand to bee red, and demanded whether he would seale a bond of 5,000*li.* to perfourme the same. Which he utterlie refused, pretendinge that there be some other thinges not incerted, which are to be done by the Companie (as the chaine and suites of apparrell), which beeinge denyed, he houldes himselfe freed. Butt those allegations haveinge bene formerlie disproved, theis exceptions were found to be meere cavylls; as by the yssue apperred, because hee excepted against the Companies love towardes him, beinge jelous that it was lesse towardes him then heretofore and therefore inconvenyent for the Companie to employe him or for him to goe. Mr. Governor made knowne that his insolent carriage and behaviour towardes the Companye had alienated their myndes and affections whollie from him; whereby their love was tenne tymes lesse towardes him then heretofore; and nowe refusinge the covenants which he hath formerlie signed, expostulatinge about the time of his staie in the Indies, and prescribinge rules unto them whoe are to direct him...and findinge his inconstancye, troublesome spiritt, newe propositions dailie invented, and every way his uncertainetye, they were of opinion that it were fitt to leave him now, whilest there may be time to consider of annother, rather then to lett it rest still neerer unto his departure, and then be enforced to give waye to his unreasonable demandes, or else be subject to his scornefull and prowde humor of leavinge their service att his will and pleasure. The question beinge therefore nowe propounded, upon due and serious consideration of the premisses it was resolvd by erection of handes to putt him of[f] as unfitt and unworthie for their service; with a purpose to thinke upon annother more worthie in his place....

INDEX